Three Way Fight

Revolutionary Politics
and Antifascism

Edited by Xtn Alexander and Matthew N. Lyons

Foreword by Janeen Porter

Afterword by Michael Staudenmaier

PM

KER
SPL
EBE
DEB

Three Way Fight: Revolutionary Politics and Antifascism
© 2024 selection and editorial matter, Xtn Alexander and Matthew Lyons; individual chapters, the contributors
This edition © 2024 PM Press

ISBN: 979-8-88744-041-5 (paperback)
ISBN: 979-8-88744-051-4 (ebook)
Library of Congress Control Number: 2023944313
Cover by John Yates / www.stealworks.com
Interior design by briandesign

10 9 8 7 6 5 4 3 2 1

PM Press
PO Box 23912
Oakland, CA 94623
www.pmpress.org

Kersplebedeb Publishing and Distribution
CP 63560
CCCP Van Horne
Montreal, Quebec
Canada H3W 3H8
www.kersplebedeb.com
www.leftwingbooks.net

Printed in the USA.

Contents

III COMPLEX POLITICS, MULTIPLE OPPONENTS

IV GLOBAL CAPITALISTS AND THE FAR RIGHT

V MAKING SENSE OF TRUMPISM IN REAL TIME

VI THE GEORGE FLOYD REBELLION

VII ORGANIZING AND STRATEGY

Foreword

Janeen Porter

"A breath of fresh fucking air." That was my reaction to learning of the young antiracist activists who were organizing to confront fascists in their communities in the early Eighties. And that is my reaction to this very compelling and comprehensive collection of current antifascist theory, positions, and activity. Those who are trying to figure out what it means to effectively combat fascism today will benefit from the thought-provoking, sometimes contentious, serious discussions in this book.

Let's back up a minute. When I joined Sojourner Truth Organization (STO) in the late Seventies, our focus was on production organizing and solidarity with national liberation struggles, not on antifascism. We had some confrontations with Klan forces in the South and with far-right settlerists in the Dakotas and the Northwest, but these were more reactionary local and regional state structures than radical autonomous threats.

We had noted the fascist resurgence in Italy and England and the right-wing populism that exploded in the Midwest in response to the economic restructuring of the late Seventies. However, the antifascist aspect of our practical work was generally confined to investigating and exposing far-right activity and the involvement of the state and police.

There were two important developments at the end of the Seventies that changed this approach. First, William Pierce's National Alliance and *The Turner Diaries* marked the emergence of a new strategy for US fascists based on a disciplined, clandestine armed organization, the Order, and a rejection of traditional racist conservatism.

Second was the murder of five Communist Workers Party members at an anti-Klan demonstration in Greensboro in late 1979. The CWP had organized an action around calls for "Death to the Klan." The Klan and its supporters took the slogan more seriously than the anti-Klan demonstrators.

I was part of the STO delegation to the Greensboro conference called to organize a response to the Klan attack. I had expected a high-energy, militant campaign that emphasized self-defense against armed Klan/nazi forces, but I could not have been more wrong.

Many left antifascists were frightened by the Greensboro outcome and were concluding that anti-Klan organizing was too risky. Rather than militant action, they were willing to cede responsibility for dealing with the Klan/fascists to the liberal sectors of the state. The insurgent momentum of the Sixties was replaced by increasingly legalistic and pacifist reform projects.

Greensboro was a reality check for the left, but radically different lessons were learned. STO reoriented our work to emphasize direct action, confrontation with authority, and mass illegality. We organized a number of direct action political initiatives that were explicitly illegal. While none of these focused on antifascism, these actions brought us into contact with antiracist crews in Chicago, the Twin Cities, and Portland who were fighting emerging fascist formations like Tom Metzger's WAR (White Aryan Resistance). We admired their tactics, courage, and commitment to defending popular cultural and political space.

In the mid-Eighties in Chicago's Uptown neighborhood, a white skinhead fascist street force broke away from the white gang structure. There was a sharp increase in Klan/nazi activity peppered with street confrontations.

A group of leftists began a public campaign against this upsurge. In early 1986 a shouting match between a small group of antifascists and the Uptown fascist crew escalated into a street fight. When the fascists they had been calling cowards and boneheads produced jack handles and bats and beat the hell out of them, they were unprepared and/or unwilling to defend themselves. Worse yet, the antifascists publicly blamed the police for not defending them.

We realized we had to develop a mass alternative that didn't look to the state for protection and fought back. We joined the antifascist coalition with a contingent of radicals and militant antiracist punks who were committed to taking responsibility for their own defense and directly confronting the Klan/fascists.

This produced two actions. The first broke through police lines and ran off a small group of dress-up nazis. However, this action was not located in the home base of the Klan/nazi threat. A second action did take place on their turf, but the coalition leadership covertly joined the local Democratic structure to preempt militant tactics under the guise of broadening the struggle to keep liberal and pacifist supporters out of danger.

This particular fascist upsurge succumbed to internal divisions, and the loss of a clear and immediate target drained the momentum of the antifascist coalition. However, we had developed close relationships with a small group of folks committed to mass militant antifascism.

We maintained ties with the antifascists in Portland and the Twin Cities who were battling the Klan/nazis and were neither liberal nor pacifist. They traveled, they fought, they were wounded, and then they traveled again and fought their asses off. A fucking heroic lot in my view.

What was left of STO knew it was important to maintain these relationships. In the political dead zone of the late Eighties, our numbers had dwindled and we were older and tired. But mostly we were unwilling to participate one more fucking time in normal demos and coalitions.

By the early Nineties, we were relating to the growing anarchist scene politically and culturally. This is where we met Chicago Anti-Racist Action (ARA) activists. These were fucking tough, committed, and smart comrades. Their willingness to think beyond the important militant street tactics and attempt to place antifascism within a clear and revolutionary framework set them apart. It was because of them that we were involved with ARA's work against Church of the Creator and various other fascist groups throughout the Midwest.

An eventual outcome of that joint work and dinners, drinks, and debates was the *Three Way Fight* project. I am proud to be part of this history and the ongoing arguments and positions that will shape the future of antifascist organizing.

I also want to express my gratitude to a few of these ARA members with whom I remain close. Their comradeship impacted my life in significant ways and allowed me experiences I will treasure for fucking ever.

Acknowledgments

We are grateful to everyone who helped make this book possible. Thanks to all of the contributors who agreed to make their work available here, and especially to Janeen Porter and Michael Staudenmaier, who wrote new essays for the book. Thanks to the PM Press staff for their enthusiasm and support in bringing the project to completion. Thanks to Kristian Williams for invaluable help with navigating book contracts and the publishing industry and for his ongoing contributions to *Three Way Fight* in general. Karl Kersplebedeb's thoughtful criticisms and suggestions strengthened the book in countless ways both large and small, and he drew on both his excellent editorial skills and his deep knowledge as someone who has himself actively contributed to the development of three way fight politics for more than a quarter century.

This book grows out of the *Three Way Fight* project and is intended as a contribution to it. From first discussions through completion of the manuscript, work on the book has benefited from periodic consultations with an informal network of *Three Way Fight* participants and supporters. We are grateful to everyone who has offered ideas, responses, or encouragement to this effort or to the *Three Way Fight* project as a whole, including Becca Sandor, Claire McGuire, Dan Berger, David Mitchell, Devin Zanc Shaw, Don Hamerquist, Janeen Porter, J.M. Wong, Joe Lowndes, John Garvey, Kieran, Kristian Williams, Luis Brennan, Michael Pugliese, Michael Staudenmaier, Mike Morgan, Paul Messersmith-Glavin, Rebecca Hill, rowan, Steve Swart, Xloi, and others unnamed. We also want to thank Nick Paretsky, Dave Ranney, Samantha Maynard, and Mike Mann for their help and support both in terms of ideas as well as the practical.

The interview with Zhandarka Kurti and Jarrod Shanahan titled "States of Incarceration: A Discussion" originally appeared in the *Brooklyn Rail* and is reprinted with permission.

Introduction

Matthew N. Lyons and Xtn Alexander

What's the relationship between fascism and capitalism? What's the relationship between combating far-right political forces and working to overthrow an exploitative and oppressive social order? Does antifascism mean radicals need to build alliances with liberals or even conservatives, and if so on what terms? How do we make sense of far-right calls to fight the state, oppose Western military power, or challenge economic elites—and how should we respond?

Antifascists, specifically militant and revolutionary antifascists, have been faced with these questions for over a century, but they haven't always grappled with them in the best ways, and the answers they came up with in the past don't necessarily provide good guidance today.

In 2004, a small group of revolutionary antifascists started the *Three Way Fight* blog and website as a project to share information and analysis about political movements and the context in which they operate. The project's name captured its emphasis on challenging binary models of antifascism. Its supporters rejected the conventional liberal model that portrayed authoritarian extremists threatening a democratic center, but they also challenged the standard leftist binary that saw fascism and liberalism as arrayed together in defense of capitalism against the working-class left. As editors of the website would later put it:

> Unlike liberal anti-fascists, we believe that "defending democracy" is an illusion, as long as that "democracy" is based on a socio-economic order that exploits and oppresses human beings.

Global capitalism and the related structures of patriarchy, heterosexism, racial and national oppression represent the main source of violence and human suffering in the world today. Far right supremacism and terrorism grow out of this system and cannot be eradicated as long as it remains in place.

At the same time, unlike many on the revolutionary left, we believe that fascists and other far rightists aren't simply tools of the ruling class. They can also form an autonomous political force that clashes with the established order in real ways, or even seeks to overthrow global capitalism and replace it with a radically different oppressive system.

This meant that "leftists need to confront both the established capitalist order and an insurgent or even revolutionary right, while recognizing that these opponents are also in conflict with each other." Hence the term "three way fight."[1]

The essays and interviews in this book offer an in-depth look at three way fight politics: where it comes from, what it has to say about recent political struggles and the systems that underlie them, and how it can inform sharper and more effective organizing strategies for human liberation in the time ahead. The voices we've brought together here don't always agree, but they're grappling with a shared set of questions largely using a shared set of tools. We offer them both to help clarify how we got to the present moment and as an intervention in ongoing debates among radicals and antifascists on how to move forward.

Origins

As a concept and a political project, three way fight (3WF) was shaped by earlier developments in the US left, in large part by two organizations: Anti-Racist Action (ARA) and, even earlier, the Sojourner Truth Organization (STO). Anti-Racist Action was a large, decentralized network of local groups focused on a physical, direct action approach to combating fascist and far-right organizing. ARA, which was founded around 1987 and reached its greatest extent and level of activity in the 1990s, emerged from skinhead and punk subcultures but grew beyond these scenes to become a broader, more diverse youth-led movement. While most ARA members were nonaligned ideologically and joined the movement simply to organize and fight the fascists and far right, a significant number of members were anarchist or antiau-thoritarian in orientation. However, Marxist, feminist, and other perspectives were also represented and showed ARA's organizational nonsectarianism. Unlike liberal "anti-hate" organizations such as the Southern Poverty Law Center, ARA explicitly rejected relying on the police or the courts, and some of its chapters organized against racist police violence and state repression as well as the far right. While ARA did not take a position on capitalism or the overall political system, it included a number of currents that advocated a more radical and at times comprehensive revolutionary anticapitalist and antisystem analysis and approach to struggle.[2]

Unlike ARA, STO was a relatively small Marxist organization, and it was active from 1969 to about 1985. It was an offshoot of the New Left based primarily in the Chicago area. STO developed a distinc-tive form of independent Marxism—influenced by W.E.B. Du Bois, Antonio Gramsci, and C.L.R. James, among others—that emphasized working-class agency and targeted racial oppression as a key contradic-tion within the US working class. STO practiced a rare combination of revolutionary politics and public openness about internal debates and disagreements. STO also developed a concept of fascism that sharply challenged both Stalinist and Trotskyist assumptions, arguing that while fascism has "intimate connections with the needs of the capitalist class," it also "contains an anti-capitalist 'revolutionary' side that is not reducible to simple demagogy."[3] Although it was always a small organization, STO influenced a number of later leftist organi-zations, and former STO members have been active in a wide variety of campaigns and projects.

Other currents have also contributed to the development of three way fight politics. A notable example was the loose network of independent revolutionaries that included J. Sakai (best known as the author of *Settlers: The Mythology of the White Proletariat*), Butch Lee (contributor to *Bottomfish Blues* and coauthor of *Night-Vision: Illuminating War & Class on the Neo-colonial Terrain*), and Bromma (author of *Exodus and Reconstruction: Working-Class Women at the Heart of Globalization*).[4] Influenced by Maoism but applying it in unorthodox ways that even many anarchists engaged with, these writers have, since the 1980s, put forward sharp and original critiques of modern capitalism's changing landscape with a strong emphasis on white supremacy and male supremacy both in the structure of society and within political movements.

Another early influence on three way fight politics was the Revolutionary Socialist League (RSL), which was active from about 1972 to 1989. The RSL's politics evolved from Trotskyism to anarchism, and several of its former members helped found the Love and Rage anarchist organization in 1989.[5] In parallel to STO, the RSL identified far-right and fascist forces as an organizing—and terrorizing—force within working-class communities, and it sought to build a diverse multiracial, militant, and working-class opposition to the Ku Klux Klan. The RSL promoted an early "them, them, and us" approach that saw antiracist forces as being in a struggle against the KKK and nazis on one side and the police and the state on the other. While the RSL's positions on fascism have received little attention in recent decades, and its writings on the issue are difficult to locate, its approach to antifascist organizing has had a lasting impact.

During this same period, some investigative journalists began to study the emerging rightist movements in ways that would directly inform three way fight analysis. Of particular note were Sara Diamond, who broke new ground in studying the Christian right as a well-organized, politically autonomous mass movement, and Chip Berlet, whose work included both anti-nazi organizing and investigation of police and FBI repression, and who helped found the antirightist think tank Political Research Associates in 1981. Berlet's 1994 report *Right Woos Left* warned against far-right infiltration of the antiwar movement and the spread of conspiracist ideology in sections of the left. Berlet and Matthew N. Lyons coauthored *Right-Wing Populism in America* (published in 2000), which traced the long history of US movements that have combined antielitism with efforts to intensify social oppression.[6]

The growth of ARA in the 1980s and 1990s was part of a broader upsurge of confrontational "antifa" organizing across much of Europe and North America. In 1997, Minneapolis ARA and the Toronto-based Anti-Fascist Forum helped found the International Militant Anti-Fascist Network. The new network was weakened by deep political disagreements at its founding conference and lasted only a few years, but its launch statement declared, in terms that helped further revolutionary currents within ARA,

We stand for the physical and ideological confrontation of fascism, and we are not fighting to maintain the status quo. We see the challenges facing us as a three cornered fight, between the militants, the fascists and the state. We recognize that the ultimate guarantee against the far right penetrating the mainstream, is a strong politically independent working class movement.[7]

Around this same time, increased focus on clinic defense and an ongoing internal debate led ARA in 1998 to add a commitment to "abortion rights and unrestricted reproductive freedom for all" to its Points of Unity. The new language reflected a struggle against sexism within ARA, but also many militant antifascists' developing understanding that the far right encompassed Christian rightists as well as neo-nazis and that the fight against patriarchy must be at the forefront together with the fight against white supremacy.

Two events around the turn of the millennium—the Battle of Seattle in 1999 and the 9/11 attacks in 2001—highlighted the need for fresh thinking on the relationships between far-right politics, the capitalist state, and the left. The Battle of Seattle was a series of militant mass protests against the World Trade Organization conference in Seattle in November and December 1999, and it marked the rise of the "antiglobalization" movement as a broad-based challenge to transnational corporate power. Politically, antiglobalization was all over the map, from the anarchist-oriented "black bloc" forces who targeted capitalist property and any symbols of power, through reformist NGOs and labor unions at the center, to hard-line nationalists and far rightists. Many ARA activists and other antifascists rallied to the movement's militant, anticapitalist wing, where they found themselves confronting not only global corporations and intergovernmental bodies but also both procapitalist liberals and fascists—as well as the wider spread of fascistic ideas such as antisemitic conspiracism—within the movement's own ranks. Part of this struggle is documented in the 2000 book *My Enemy's Enemy: Essays on Globalization, Fascism and the Struggle against Capitalism*, which was compiled by Anti-Fascist Forum and included an essay by Sakai.[8]

Less than two years after Seattle, the September 11 attacks showed even more dramatically that global capitalism's enemies could be found not only on the radical left but also on the far right. In destroying the Twin Towers and damaging the Pentagon, al-Qaeda struck at prominent symbols of Western imperialism and capitalism. But these attacks, which killed some three thousand people, were carried out in the service of a political vision that was profoundly authoritarian and reactionary. The United States responded with the decades-long "War on Terror," increased repression both at home and abroad, and a wave of racist attacks against people of color, particularly Arabs and Middle Easterners. US fascist groups both fueled these fears and looked for ways to take advantage of them. Radical antifascists found themselves forced back on the defensive, yet they began to analyze the attacks, the responses to them, and their wider implications.

Two 2001 essays from the *ARA Research Bulletin*, both reprinted in this book, show how some movement activists were beginning to stake out 3WF-type positions. "No Tears for the Nazis, No Support for the State" warned against antifascism being used to reinforce the repressive state apparatus (specifically the racist institution of the death penalty). Kdog's "Fifth Column Fascism," written shortly after 9/11, declared "All resistance [to US imperialism] ain't liberatory and all fascists ain't aryan," warned against fascistic tendencies within the radical left, and urged leftists to reject alliances with far rightists such as al-Qaeda or Third Position fascists.

A bigger and more rigorous effort along these lines was the 2003 book *Confronting Fascism: Discussion Documents for a Militant Movement*, which centers on an essay by former STO member Don Hamerquist and a response by Sakai. In these and other sections, *Confronting Fascism* put forward many positions that would become foundational for three way fight politics: that fascism is an active and dynamic current that doesn't necessarily look the same now as it did in the 1930s or 1940s, that it feeds on popular hostility to big business and the state and has the potential to gain mass support in the United States and beyond, and that it represents a revolutionary challenge to capitalist power—not revolutionary in any liberatory sense, but in that it aims to seize power and systematically transform society along repressive and often genocidal lines. In a period when many leftists saw antifascism as a distraction, *Confronting Fascism* argued that radical politics needs to be antifascist and antifascism needs a revolutionary outlook, warned against a potential convergence between fascism and sections of the radical left, and posed basic

#2 • fall 2001 • $3

ARA research bulletin

Anti-fascist research, analysis, and debate

the state,

the fascists,

and us...

It's on...

project of Chicago ARA

Issue number two of the *Anti-Racist Action Research Bulletin*, Fall 2001. The issue was published within weeks of 9/11 and both its cover graphic and its included content laid the conceptual basis of the three way fight—them, them, and us.

questions about organizing and strategy. Echoing struggles within
ARA, Xtn Alexander's introduction to the book also offered a friendly
critique of both Hamerquist and Sakai for "insufficiently address[ing]
the condition of women in relation to capitalism and fascism." Xtn
noted, "Women will play a subservient role in fascist, patriarchal politics, but they can also act as active agents in its realization." Instead
of offering settled answers, *Confronting Fascism* called for ongoing
discussion to rethink old assumptions and respond dynamically to an
uncertain and changing situation.[9]

To further that discussion, some of the contributors to *Confronting
Fascism* and other antifascists connected to ARA launched the *Three
Way Fight* website in 2004. Initially, the site's blog was one of only
a handful of public vehicles for antifascist writings, especially for
antifascists who advocated revolutionary anticapitalist politics. Like
Confronting Fascism, *Three Way Fight* took an inclusive approach to
radicalism, bringing together Marxist and anarchist contributors and
sometimes offering conflicting positions in dialog with each other.

Over the following several years, writers associated with *Three
Way Fight* began to develop a distinctive approach to radical antifascism.
Some core features of this approach can be summarized as follows:

- We need to look critically at standard leftist assumptions about
  fascism: that "the cops and the Klan go hand in hand," that
  fascism is always white and automatically white supremacist,
  that fascists and capitalists are basically working toward the
  same goals. Those assumptions are at best oversimplified and
  often out-and-out wrong.

- Antifascists need to take fascists seriously rather than dismiss
  them as liars, opportunists, cowards, or nutcases. We should try
  to understand fascist ideas and goals and what gives fascist politics the potential to appeal to masses of people. And we should
  pay particular attention to far-right militancy, hostility to elites
  and established institutions, and efforts to win working-class
  support, all of which pose a particular danger to liberatory
  anticapitalist movements.

- Political differences and disagreements between fascists and
  other forces on the right matter—notably differences over how
  to relate to the state—particularly because they may call for
  different strategic responses to combat them.

- Women's oppression and gender politics more broadly are central, foundational issues for the far right, and fascist movements have often been marked by a tension between efforts to intensify patriarchy and efforts to build a mass base among women. Yet many leftists and antifascists have treated these issues as secondary to race and class or have ignored them completely.
- Antifascism should involve efforts to understand developments in the global capitalist system and in ruling-class strategies, which shape the context in which both liberatory movements and insurgent far rightists operate.

Evolution of the Website, Interaction with Movements

In its first year and a half, *Three Way Fight* featured reports on a range of recent events: community resistance to nazi rallies in Ohio and Michigan, police repression in New Orleans following Hurricane Katrina, a US tour by Iraqi labor organizers, a protest against sex discrimination by women in Iran.[10] There were more analytic posts as well: a discussion of neoconservative strategy and international capitalist interests, the current state of fascist and antifascist organizing in the US and Britain, Venezuelan anarchist perspectives on the Hugo Chávez "Bolivarian socialist" government, the gender politics of far-right movements.[11] Over the following several years, the site's coverage largely focused on nazi and anti-nazi activism in the United States and Europe but also addressed other political struggles and other parts of the world, such as the 2005 North African youth riots in France; the 2006 uprising in Oaxaca, Mexico; the Hindu nationalist movement in India; the upsurge in racist attacks in the US following Barack Obama's 2008 election as president; and the assassination of an abortion provider in Kansas in 2009.[12] There was extensive discussion of Hezbollah and the Islamic right more broadly starting with Israel's 2006 invasion of Lebanon, as well as the political implications of the global capitalist crisis following the 2008 financial collapse.[13]

Three Way Fight's character evolved as the context changed. Its initial attempt to be a general forum for news and information related to antifascism became less useful as other leftist websites emerged that were able to fulfill this role more effectively, such as *Anti-Fascist News* and It's Going Down. In its early years, *Three Way Fight* often published brief posts and quick links to news articles, but after social media platforms such as Facebook and Twitter emerged that were better suited to sharing such content, *Three Way Fight* focused mainly on analytical essays. The site attempted to focus on topics that were underreported or often misrepresented elsewhere, such as tensions between fascists and the state, internal debates within the fascist movement, and complexities in far-right politics around race or gender. *Three Way Fight* also criticized liberal responses to the far right as well as far-right attempts to infiltrate or form alliances with radical political forces.[14]

To a limited extent, *Three Way Fight* also grappled with questions of revolutionary strategy. A 2005 essay by Xtn compared two movements that had moved away from revolutionary armed struggle. In Northern Ireland, the Provisional IRA/Sinn Fein had "opted to integrate themselves fully into transnational capitalism," disarm, and take part in elections under British rule, a shift that followed a longer process of political decay in which "thuggery and intimidation" of dissenters had replaced open rank-and-file debate. The Zapatistas of Chiapas, Mexico, by contrast, were inviting broad-based strategic discussion among their supporters and attempting to subordinate their military organization to popular governing structures while rejecting electoral politics as inherently untrustworthy.[15]

Participation in the *Three Way Fight* project evolved over time. The site's blog was always conceived as a collaborative project and featured contributions by multiple people from 2004 to 2011 and starting again in 2018, but during the middle years one contributor (Lyons) kept the website going on his own while attempting to maintain contacts with antifascist and radical networks. This middle period reflected a temporary decline in openly fascist organizing in the United States and decisions by many *Three Way Fight* participants to shift their focus to a range of other political initiatives. At the same time, they continued to articulate a three way fight perspective and to see the project as an important vehicle in developing a framework for analysis and organizing within larger emerging class and social struggles.

The first major example of this shift to other initiatives was the Occupy movement of 2011–12, which like the earlier antiglobalization movement was largely "left" but had vague and amorphous politics and allowed space for rightist and even fascist attempts at insertion. The three way fight framework helped some antifascists within Occupy articulate a position against the right.[16] A few years later, with the rise of the Black Lives Matter movement against racist police violence, militants influenced by three way fight politics continued to see the concept as essential to understanding the dynamics between social justice movements, the state, and far-right or fascist forces. The concept was put to the test even more acutely in 2020, when the police murders of George Floyd and other Black people sparked the largest antisystem rebellion the United States had seen in half a century, and this rebellion was met with everything from liberal co-optation to rightist vigilante violence to being wooed by anti-cop far rightists of the boogaloo bois movement.[17]

The resurgence of far-right organizing in the 2010s and Donald Trump's election as president in 2016 further highlighted the relevance of three way fight politics and helped strengthen the interplay between political organizing and the *Three Way Fight* project. During the presidential campaign and the Trump administration that followed, *Three Way Fight* argued for a nuanced analysis of Trump and the far right as distinct but interconnected forces and challenged simplistic claims that Trump was a fascist or that a broad rightist alliance from libertarian think tanks to neo-nazi gangs had come together behind the goal of "neoliberal fascism."[18]

Trump's presidential candidacy received pivotal support from the alt-right, a loose network of white nationalists, misogynists, and authoritarians that was the first significant fascist movement to be based mainly on internet activism rather than in-person organizing, and whose content and style broke sharply with previous fascist initiatives. Most leftists and liberals didn't become aware of the alt-right until 2016 or later, but *Three Way Fight* had been studying it for years. Starting in 2010, Hamerquist and others in *Three Way Fight*–related circles called attention to several important new voices and websites that helped shape the alt-right—including Richard Spencer's AlternativeRight.com, Keith Preston's "anarcho-pluralist" Attack the System, and "male tribalist" author Jack Donovan—and Lyons responded with a series of articles, culminating in a major report on the alt-right in 2017. Lyons's November 2016 essay "Calling Them 'Alt-Right' Helps Us Fight Them" challenged readers to study Trump's far-right supporters for their specific strengths and weaknesses.[19]

These writings were pivotal for antifascist organizing in 2017, as alt-rightists launched a major push to translate their online success into street-fighting formations and public rallies, most notoriously the murderous Unite the Right rally in Charlottesville in August 2017. Among the organizations to which former *Three Way Fight* participants had shifted their focus were the First of May Anarchist Alliance, the Industrial Workers of the World–affiliated General Defense Committee, and the largely Michigan-based Solidarity & Defense Network. All of these groups were part of a new emerging network of antifascist militants, and they played key roles in the struggle against the alt-right. As alt-rightists and antifascists squared off in confrontations around the country, alt-right and adjacent forces carried out a series of shootings and stabbings that resulted in hospitalizations and even deaths.[20] Against this backdrop of attacks, folks associated with three way fight politics helped popularize the concept of "community self-defense," which centered antifascism within a broader class struggle and social revolutionary program. When Richard Spencer launched a planned university speaking tour, organized opposition by antifascists around the country made it more and more impossible for him to hold his events. The tour came to an end when Spencer and an assortment of nazi groups sought to rally in East Lansing, Michigan. There, Solidarity & Defense helped organize a series of confrontations and a five-hundred-strong mass demonstration that shut him down and helped end the alt-right's ability to function openly or with popular influence.[21]

Beginning in 2018, in the context of this intensified antifascist struggle, there was a renewed effort to reconstitute *Three Way Fight* as a collective project, encompassing both returning participants from the early years and new people. By 2020, the number of writers and activists represented in blog posts had increased dramatically, and the website experimented with different ways to bring in more voices, such as interviews and solicited guest posts. Although no formal organization or membership developed, a loose network of people began to communicate about ways to strengthen the project and began to use the *Three Way Fight* moniker in other contexts, such as panels and workshops.

In recent years, *Three Way Fight* also increased its attention to questions of antifascist organizing, strategy, and tactics, for example posting a series of diverse responses to an August 22, 2021, physical confrontation between antifa and Proud Boys, as well as a review of militant "Strategies to Defend Abortion Access" after the US Supreme Court overturned *Roe v. Wade* in June 2022.[22] Without holding to a specific "line" on strategy, the website's approach was rooted in Anti-Racist Action's principles, such as nonsectarian defense of antifascists, not relying on the police or courts, and linking antifascism to struggles to overthrow systems of oppression and exploitation, while also recognizing that ARA's approach could not be applied mechanically to new circumstances and enemies who had learned from past battles.

Anti-imperialism and International Conflict

Although *Three Way Fight* has primarily focused on political struggles within the United States, throughout its history the project has also addressed other countries, ranging from Germany's antiauthoritarian left to misogynist violence in India, as well as US far rightists' positions on international issues, such as US-China relations.[23] In many of these discussions, *Three Way Fight* has highlighted challenges to US and global capitalism by right-wing movements and regimes around the world. Writers for the site have challenged the assumption that anti-imperialism is inherently progressive and have been critical of leftists defending authoritarian or even far-rightist governments in the name of anti-imperialism.[24] More broadly, *Three Way Fight* has attempted to promote greater recognition of nuance and complexity in looking at political struggles in different countries, including recognition of political tensions and conflict among far rightists themselves.

As an example, Venezuela's left-populist Hugo Chávez government (1999–2013) was celebrated by many US leftists for its social welfare programs, challenge to traditional elites, and opposition to neoliberalism, but its outreach to US opponents not only on the left (Cuba) but also on the right (Iran and Russia) highlighted the ambiguities of "anti-imperialism." *Three Way Fight* and its contributors published a range of perspectives on Venezuela and Chávez over the years. In a 2005 report on their recent visit to Venezuela, Michael Staudenmaier and Anne Carlson rejected one-sided portrayals of Chávez as either a "near dictator" or "the new Che Guevara of radicalism" and highlighted Venezuelan anarchists' widely divergent assessments of Chavismo. A response by Francis noted that "both Chavez and the opposition

represent wings of global capital," emphasized Venezuela's political fluidity, and outlined a range of possible outcomes with both
fascist and antifascist dimensions. A 2007 satirical essay by Bromma
condemned Chavismo much more sharply as a kind of fake socialism
that promoted authoritarianism, social conservatism, corruption, and
an unsustainable economic model. In 2013, Lyons surveyed assessments of the recently deceased Chávez by English-language fascists,
which centered on a debate between advocates of traditional white
supremacism and those who favored multicultural red-brown alliances
against the United States.[25]

Three Way Fight encountered much more controversy in 2006
when Lyons published a series of posts about Hezbollah and the question of how US leftists should respond to Hezbollah's resistance to
Israel's invasion of Lebanon. Grappling with the reality that the main
force opposing Israeli aggression on the ground advocated an Islamic
state modeled after Iran, Lyons criticized Hezbollah as right wing
while urging that leftists should nonetheless support it against the
Israeli military. These articles evoked strong criticisms from some leftists. Some argued that radicals should reject both Israel and Hezbollah
equally, but the main criticism came from those who declared it was
wrong to characterize Hezbollah as right wing, that Lyons and *Three
Way Fight* were imposing US categories on a situation we didn't
understand, and that this played into Islamophobia and rationales
for US imperialist aggression. In response, Lyons acknowledged that
Hezbollah had made a number of concessions to secular pluralism in
practice, but he noted that the organization was formally subordinate
to Iran's supreme leader and still declared theocratic rule to be the ideal.
Staudenmaier continued the debate about Hezbollah in an exchange
with Rami El-Amine (one of *Three Way Fight*'s leading critics on the
issue) in the journal *Upping the Anti* in 2007.[26]

A third example concerned the 2014 overthrow of Ukraine's
pro-Russian government following the three-month-long "Euromaidan"
protests. US portrayals of this event were largely split between
those who saw it as a popular, democratic revolution and those who
saw it as a Western-backed coup. In contrast, a series of *Three Way
Fight* articles by Lyons argued that the overthrow was propelled by
a politically diverse mass-based movement spanning from liberals
to far rightists, in a context where Ukraine's oligarchy was divided

between pro–European Union and pro-Russia factions. In this view, the overthrow was not an outside-orchestrated coup but did represent an important breakthrough by fascists, who gained popular support, validation, and important positions in the new government. But far from celebrating, Lyons argued, most US far rightists were either ambivalent or hostile to the revolution. Some of them distrusted the Ukrainian fascists for their involvement in a Western-oriented movement, and some supported Russia's expansionist goals toward Ukraine—goals that were being promoted by Russia's own far right. The growing conflict between Ukraine and Russia, far from being a simple conflict between democracy and authoritarianism or between fascists and antifascists, was a messy struggle in which fascists were active on both sides and against each other.[27]

Three Way Fight returned to discussion of Ukraine after Russia launched its full-scale invasion of the country in 2022, with an annotated list of useful articles and a favorable in-depth review of writings by British independent Marxist Simon Pirani, titled "No Longer a Gendarme for the West: Simon Pirani on Russia's Invasion of Ukraine." Pirani argued that Russia was a subordinate imperialist power using military aggression to compensate for its economic weakness within the global capitalist system, and called for solidarity with the Ukrainian resistance while warning against romanticizing either Ukraine's capitalist state or the motives of the NATO governments supplying it with arms.[28] Yet *Three Way Fight* proponents were in fact divided between some who advocated support for Ukraine's popular resistance forces against Russian imperialism, others who rejected such support as implicit endorsement for Ukraine's capitalist state, and still others who were conflicted or unsure about how to respond.[29] This division pointed to an underlying lack of theoretical clarity: beyond rejecting simplistic claims that any opposition to US or Western imperialism is progressive, supporters of three way fight politics have not developed a general framework for navigating geopolitics, particularly for situations where forces supported by the United States face imperialist aggression by rival powers.

Hamerquist's Influence

From the days of STO to the Trump era and after, Don Hamerquist's work has been a vital connecting thread in the development of three way fight politics. After coauthoring the 2003 book *Confronting Fascism*, Hamerquist wrote the very first blog post on *Three Way Fight* in December 2004 and, directly or indirectly, has contributed significantly to that project and broader debates around radical antifascism ever since. The primary vehicle for Hamerquist's thinking has been a series of long articles—posted on *Three Way Fight*, other websites, or private listservs—that look at fascism and antifascism in the context of global capitalism's political dynamics and ruling-class efforts to maintain control. These articles have repeatedly challenged radicals to rethink common assumptions and to look beyond a national context, and they have brought a macro-level perspective to three way fight politics that might otherwise be missing. Although Hamerquist's analysis has evolved over time, some central, common themes stand out.

Elaborating on points from his *Confronting Fascism* essay, Hamerquist has continued to criticize widespread leftist claims that fascism is essentially a ruling-class tool or expression of capitalism's own authoritarian tendencies, arguing instead that it represents "an array of emerging reactionary anti-capitalisms" whose totalitarian antiegalitarianism poses an "existential threat" to the capitalist world order. Hamerquist also delineates fascist currents from right-wing populist movements as a distinction between revolutionary and reformist branches of the political right.[30]

At the same time, over the past decade or more Hamerquist has become increasingly concerned with dangers connected with ruling-class *anti*fascism, which he sees as a cornerstone of efforts to rebuild mass support for global capitalism. A starting point for this line of thinking is the Marxist recognition that global capitalism is experiencing a deep, long-term structural crisis. This crisis has multiple dimensions, but in Hamerquist's view it includes a crisis of legitimacy—a large-scale erosion of mass support for (or acceptance of) the existing order. Global recession and widening economic inequality have helped fuel the rise of both left-wing and right-wing populist movements in many countries. Capitalists are looking for ways to restore the system's popular legitimacy, and they're doing it, Hamerquist argues, not just at the national level but as a transnational class. (While many Marxists emphasize growing interimperialist rivalry as a driving force in geopolitics, Hamerquist has instead argued that "the global ruling elites increasingly subordinate inter-imperialist rivalries to an appreciation of common enemies and common risks," citing as evidence the support by nearly all national governments for the so-called War on Terror and the collaborative efforts to resolve the 2008 financial crisis.)[31]

Hamerquist argues that the most likely ruling-class strategy for rebuilding mass support, at least in industrialized countries, is global social democracy, a term he borrows from Walden Bello. In Hamerquist's usage, this is not so much a renewed welfare capitalism as a "quasi-wartime social democracy, premised on obedience to authority and accommodation to austerity and explained and rationalized by fears of a fascist possibility" that is partly real and partly fabricated (mainly by misrepresenting right-wing populist forces as fascist).[32] He argues that in the early 2000s the Global War on Terror's characterization of the enemy as "Islamofascism" represented an early example of this, but that more recent versions shift the focus away from the Islamic right.[33]

Hamerquist has elsewhere pointed out that during World War II, the US government used antifascism both to co-opt the Communist left and as a rationale for strikebreaking, the racist mass imprisonment of Japanese Americans, and other repressive measures.[34] With global social democracy, he sees official antifascism again being used both to corral leftists and to legitimize state repression, which won't necessarily expand but will become more focused and more sophisticated. He has warned against a "resurrected popular front against fascism," in which leftists set aside radical goals and demands in order to "defend democracy," because this not only helps to restabilize transnational capitalism but also fails to offer a liberatory alternative to fascism for those who are angry at the established order.[35]

Contributing to a Larger Conversation

As a political approach, three way fight has always been broader than a specific project, and people associated with the *Three Way Fight* website have had opportunities to exchange ideas with a number of writers and organizations we appreciate and respect. For example, the radical organization Bring the Ruckus (BTR), which operated from 2001 to 2012, embraced the basic 3WF concept that the revolutionary left was in conflict with both "the state/ruling class" and a "reactionary right" with anticapitalist tendencies, although its members were divided about the relative importance of antifascist work for building a radical movement.[36] BTR members undertook an extended dialog with Don Hamerquist about fascism, the organization's documents periodically referenced the *Three Way Fight* blog, and in later years several former BTR members participated in the project more directly. More recently, *Three Way Fight* developed a relationship with It's Going Down, one of the most influential anarchist media organs, which has cohosted panel discussions with *Three Way Fight* on fascism and antifascism and has conducted interviews with people associated with the project.[37]

Other radicals and antifascists have taken up the three way fight concept in various ways.[38] The anarchist collective CrimethInc. has argued that we are now in "an era of nonbinary conflict" and "increasingly finding ourselves in three-way fights that pit us against both the reigning authorities and far-right nationalists." Political Research Associates (which describes itself as "progressive" rather than radical) has referenced *Three Way Fight* in outlining a "three-sided struggle" between the far right, dominant political institutions, and advocates of social justice.[39]

Three Way Fight has also collaborated with the projects Kersplebedeb Publishing, *Insurgent Notes*, and *Hard Crackers*. Kersplebedeb, copublisher of this book, has supported and helped to develop three way fight politics for over twenty years. It has promoted the *Three Way Fight* project while also putting forward critical feedback and analysis that has helped to sharpen up our perspectives and content. *Insurgent Notes*, an independent Marxist journal, has included a number of *Three Way Fight* participants in political forums on various topics. *Hard Crackers*, a project that grew out of the Race Traitor tendency,[40] publishes works that focus on what is important and transformative in everyday people's lives and experiences. *Hard Crackers* and *Three Way Fight* share contributors and editors as well as a growing engagement of ideas and concepts around liberatory visions and antifascism.

How This Book Is Organized

The writings in this book are organized around a few key themes. "Origins," the first section, looks at the roots of three way fight politics in the Sojourner Truth Organization and Anti-Racist Action and some of its early articulations, which in places feel a bit dated but help to show how ideas and analyses evolve over time. The BRICK Collective's "Above and Below: Them, Them, and Us" was one of the very first statements to use the term "three way fight." It did so in a controversial and challenging way by grouping "Authoritarian movements" of the right and the left together as both being barriers to liberatory and autonomous movements from below.

The second section, "Basic Principles," offers four distinct perspectives on the core idea that fascist politics is rooted in, but also autonomous from and at odds with, the established liberal capitalist order. Rowland Keshena Robinson examines fascism's relationship with settler colonialism in North America from an Indigenous perspective, while Tammy Kovich (Petronella Lee) focuses on the central role of gender politics in fascism and the need to ground antifascism in feminist principles. Devin Zane Shaw's "Seven Theses" is one attempt to summarize the three way fight, addressing fascism's relationship with a broader far right, the societal changes that fuel both, and militant antifascism's strategic and tactical implications and challenges. In contrast to this analytic approach, the interview with rowan emphasizes the three way fight's ethical commitment to revolutionary honesty in recognizing our enemies' complexity and calling on radicals to be willing to examine ourselves and be self-critical.

The book's third section, "Complex Politics, Multiple Opponents," includes essays with a range of political targets, from white nationalists and Christian theocrats to liberal "anti-hate" analysts. In keeping with rowan's point noted above, these writings emphasize political complexities that have often been misrepresented or ignored, from Christian Zionism's inherent antisemitism to US fascists' internal debates about China. To varying degrees, most of these essays also highlight radical leftists' vulnerability to overtures from far rightists or representatives of the state.

Section four, "Global Capitalists and the Far Right," probes ruling-class responses to the rise of right-wing populist politics in the United States and internationally. Using different approaches, both Don Hamerquist and Matthew N. Lyons counter the widespread leftist claim that capitalists support a drive toward fascism, arguing instead that the predominant ruling-class response has been to oppose or at most manage and contain far-right and right-wing populist upsurges.

The fifth section, "Making Sense of Trumpism in Real Time," traces the shifting reality of Donald Trump's presidential administration, from its early symbiotic relationship with the alt-right to the January 6 attack on the US Capitol four years later, in which Trump supporters tried to overturn the result of the 2020 presidential election by force. In these three essays and one interview, three way fight proponents offer in-the-moment efforts to understand the meaning of Trump's rise, assess the shifts in Trumpism's political content and direction, and look beyond defensive responses to maintain what Devin Shaw calls the "revolutionary horizon."

The George Floyd Rebellion of 2020 affirmed that revolutionary possibility was very much alive during the Trump administration, and in the process it highlighted the tensions between the far right's repressive and insurgent tendencies. Section six focuses on the rebellion and includes four articles that explore its meaning and implications for revolutionary politics. Two articles from the Twin Cities Workers Defense Alliance uphold abolition of the police as a revolutionary demand and offer radical guidelines for community self-defense groups. Shemon Salam and Arturo Castillon published their "Seven Theses" four weeks after the mass wave of protests, riots, and strikes began, while Zhandarka Kurti and Jarrod Shanahan's 2022 interview drew on two years of postrebellion reflection and analysis. These texts speak to a number of issues integral to a three way fight approach, including an emphasis on addressing complexity and contradictions both in movements for social change and in the contexts in which they operate, the tension between struggling for meaningful reforms and getting co-opted into dead-end reformism, and a need for new forms of radical organizing that address people's actual struggles in the real world.

"Organizing and Strategy," the last section, includes reflections on a number of different mobilizations against far-right movements, from defense of reproductive health clinics in the 1990s to confrontations with alt-rightists and Proud Boys in the past few years. Several recurring themes stand out: the importance of a nonsectarian approach to antifascist organizing, in which there is room for people to express different politics and use different tactics; the need for autonomy from liberal nonprofits and the Democratic Party, which repeatedly try to corral resistance into "respectable" channels that don't threaten those in power; and a measured support for physical confrontation as a tactic that is sometimes useful or necessary but in itself can't substitute for building community-based mass movements. Significant discussion of organizing and strategy along related lines can also be found in both Devin Shaw and Tammy Kovich's essays in the "Basic Principles" section. The latest essay in this section (and in the book as a whole) is "Gaming's Three Way Fight: Why Antifascists Should Organize in and around Video Games." The three authors of this work take 3WF analysis into important new terrain and posit the world of online gaming as both a key arena of struggle and a space to develop skills, build community, and imagine liberatory futures.

In putting this book together, we've made it a priority to include articles and interviews that are accessible (even if they contain complex ideas and concepts) and that represent a range of experiences and perspectives. We've been forced to leave out many valuable writings. In order to keep the scope manageable, we've concentrated on political developments in the United States (although several contributions are from north of the US-Canada border), and aside from the "Origins" section almost all of the pieces selected date from 2017 or later. We've also left out some topics because they are well covered elsewhere. For example, Matthew Lyons's 2018 book *Insurgent Supremacists: The U.S. Far Right's Challenge to State and Empire* (Kersplebedeb Publishing and PM Press) includes detailed discussion of the far right's complex and fractured racial politics, with tensions between white nationalists (who literally want to create an all-white nation), advocates of "color-blind" ideology (who protect racial oppression by denying that it exists), and proponents of multiracial organizing. As a result, that topic doesn't get in-depth discussion in any of the essays included here. In addition, we have limited our selection of Don Hamerquist's contributions in recognition that Kersplebedeb Publishing put out the collection *A Brilliant Red Thread: Revolutionary Writings from Don Hamerquist* in 2023.

To the extent that three way fight politics is an active, living political current, no single book can represent it fully. In this period of dramatic and in some ways unprecedented political struggle, we see a need for radicals and antifascists to engage in thoughtful, open-minded discussion and debate about our changing situation and the challenges ahead. We hope that the writings collected here will show what's valuable about three way fight politics, as a tool to help us both understand the opponents we face and develop smarter and more effective strategies to defeat them.

A Note on the Cover

The cover design for this book incorporates the Three Arrows motif, which is widely recognized as a symbol of militant antifascism and antiauthoritarian, antisystem politics. Its meaning has evolved from the 1930s, when it was introduced by the German Social Democrats, to the 1980s and 1990s, when it was used by anarchist antifascist punks in Europe and people in Anti-Racist Action and Red and Anarchist Skinheads (RASH) in North America. The Three Arrows motif does *not* stand for three way fight politics specifically, but we see ourselves as part of the current it represents.

ORIGINS

Theses on Fascism

Sojourner Truth Organization

Urgent Tasks no. 13 (Spring 1982)

1. Central to STO's approach to the question of fascism has always been its understanding of the historic operation of the white-skin privilege system as a means of social control over white workers as well as people of color, and the view that so long as that system continued to function through the traditional institutions, the bourgeoisie as a class would have no reason to turn to fascism to maintain its rule. We affirm the above insight as having been valid and useful in steering STO on a course opposed to all forms of popular front reformism. However, we failed to appreciate fully the complexities of white supremacy, and in particular the fact that, once established, it developed a life of its own not entirely under the control of the bourgeoisie. This aspect, coupled with a new situation in which white supremacist ideology has become an important weapon in the revival of the Ku Klux Klan and the nazis, demonstrates the inadequacy of our previous writings.

2. Among the features that define the new situation are: (a) the loss of US capitalism's overriding dominance within the world capitalist system; (b) an economic crisis that is leading to the decay of certain areas of industrial activity traditionally the center of capitalist strength; (c) a social crisis that has led to a rapid decline in popular loyalty to traditional institutions—without the development of a popular vision of the revolutionary way out of the crisis. If the communist movement does succeed in gaining a following among the workers, sectors of the bourgeoisie will probably strengthen their backing of fascist movements.

3. Fascism is a totalitarian dictatorship coming to power through
    a mass movement of sectors of the dispossessed that breaks up
    the traditional institutions of bourgeois control and brings about
    important structural changes both within the ruling class and in
    the mode of exploitation while leaving intact the relations char-
    acteristic of a class society in the modern epoch.

4. To understand fascism as growing out of the crises endemic to
    capitalism is not to say that it is a simple tool of the capitalist class.
    One important element in fascism is its autonomous character,
    expressed in a mass movement among sectors of the population
    who have been dislocated by the capitalist crisis and alienated
    from the traditional institutions of conciliation and repression.
    Fascism contains an anticapitalist "revolutionary" side that is not
    reducible to simple demagogy.

5. To point out the autonomous aspect of fascism is not to deny its
    intimate connections with the needs of the capitalist class. The
    growth of state repression and extralegal right-wing organiza-
    tions, tolerated and often covertly assisted by the state, while not
    fascist in itself, is necessary for the implementation of bourgeois
    policy and serves to ease the way for fascism. Certain sectors of
    the bourgeoisie may find a fascist movement useful in enhanc-
    ing their own power within the ruling class (to discover, too late,
    that their ox, too, will be gored). And opportunism within the
    working class, which depends on the bourgeoisie for its authority
    and whose main form here is not European-style social democ-
    racy or revisionism but white labor reformism, while not fascist
    itself and indeed slated to be among the first victims of trium-
    phant fascism, nevertheless prepares the way for fascism both
    by providing legitimacy to bourgeois policy and by offering the
    people only more of the same reformist politics which they have
    already found wanting.

6. Although no single, hegemonic fascist movement can yet be
    said to have emerged, there exist a number of groupings which
    contain some of the elements of such a movement. The traditional
    conservatives, who have increasingly adopted "populist" rhetoric,
    the far-right paramilitary patriotic organizations, the anti-busing
    and anti-abortion activists, the various Klan organizations, some
    of whom have always contained a "pro-labor" ingredient, the US

Janeen Porter being arrested in Chicago in 1986 during a confrontation with nazis. Porter, a militant in the revolutionary Marxist group Sojourner Truth Organization (STO), had participated in a broad coalition of antifascists which included STO, John Brown Anti-Klan Committee, antiracist punk rockers, and independent anti-imperialists.

Labor Party, the nazis—all of these are undergoing a process of differentiation, evolution, and regroupment that may lead to the emergence of a single fascist center. The Klan and nazi movements have achieved a higher degree of ideological unity and practical military collaboration than their organizational fragmentation would indicate. The most immediately dangerous among the above-named groupings is the Ku Klux Klan, owing to its paramilitary character and its deep roots in American tradition.

7. In addition to the primary anti-Black and other racist manifestations, virulent anti-Jewish policies, sometimes masquerading as anti-Zionism, are important unifying ideological features of the new fascists, as in the past. The denial of the Nazi Holocaust (propagated by the very organizations that propose exterminating Jews and people of color) is an important propaganda front, and needs to be countered. This propaganda offensive has been accompanied by a wave of antisemitic terror unequaled in recent years. The virulence of this antisemitic campaign often gets boosted demagogically with a bogus expression of sympathy for the plight of the Palestinian people. Despite the obvious difficulties, the antifascist movement will need to expose and vigorously fight the new wave of antisemitism, while never wavering on Palestine.

8. To the extent that fascism becomes a mass movement, and to the extent that revolution is not an immediate possibility, the revolutionary organizations must adopt the stance of the united front, which is a defensive posture aimed at achieving an alliance for the sole purpose of stopping the fascist advance. Within that alliance, however, it is necessary to criticize certain incorrect approaches which currently hold sway. Foremost among these are: first, the view that it is possible to defeat fascism through reliance on liberal, constitutional sectors of the bourgeoisie and their representatives in the popular movement; second, the view that holds fascism and the bourgeois state to be identical, therefore overlooking the autonomous character of the fascist movement which is an important source of its dangerous potential.

9. Key to a successful struggle against fascism is the forging of a left pole within the broad united front, distinguished by the following features: (a) it recognizes the organic connection between fascism and "ordinary" bourgeois rule and carries out struggles in a way

that reveals the connection, particularly challenging the ways in which white supremacy is reflected in the general repression—cutbacks in social services, inner-city plant shutdowns, etc.; (b) while defending parliamentary institutions, trade unions, etc., against fascist attacks, it poses a total revolutionary alternative to both the vision of the fascists and the present hegemonic view of bourgeois society; (c) it is able to fight the fascists militarily, through mass, armed confrontations and disruptions of fascist military activity.

Adopted by the general membership meeting, April 1981

No Tears for the Nazis, No Support for the State

ARA Research Bulletin no. 1 (May 2001)

After a period of disarray and demoralization, the Anti-Racist Action Network is back in the thick of things. ARA militants actively participated in the Black rebellion in Cincinnati against police brutality, the protests and street fighting in Quebec countering the capitalist FTAA [Free Trade Area of the Americas] summit, and an aggressive campaign against the white supremacist World Church of the Creator in central Illinois, among other struggles and projects.

The reemergence of the radical antiracist/antifascist movement is a welcome development, but we can expect serious challenges as the struggle intensifies—there are many questions that will have to be discussed, debated, and dealt with.

One issue that we face immediately is the use of capital punishment against nazis. First we have Timothy McVeigh, convicted for the 1995 Oklahoma City bombing and scheduled for federal execution. Second, we have the death sentence imposed on John "Polar Bear" Butler for the torture and murder of two ARA members, Lyn "Spit" Newborn and Dan Shersty, outside Las Vegas almost three years ago.

The media hype surrounding McVeigh's execution has predictably focused on side issues such as whether or not it should be televised. For our movement—militant antifascists and revolutionaries—the important question is: Where do we stand when the racist state eliminates a fascist killer? Our attitude and the stance of the movement will influence our ability to remain a radical, independent force in the future.

We believe the antifascist movement has to oppose the government executions of McVeigh and Butler. We do not call for this out of any solidarity with the fascists or the movements and organizations they are associated with.

McVeigh was briefly in the KKK and later rubbed shoulders with a number of different tendencies in the white nationalist movement. He traveled the gun show circuit selling copies of *The Turner Diaries*, the racist novel describing a white-power revolution—including an evidently inspiring section that details the bombing of a federal building. McVeigh's target may have been a government facility, but the Oklahoma City bombing, which killed 168 people, was primarily a massacre of civilians—including children from a day care center.

With a smaller "body count," the Las Vegas murders still hit us harder. Spit and Dan were our comrades, members of both ARA and the Las Vegas Unity Skins, an antiracist skinhead crew. They were tortured and assassinated because of the significant influence and respect for antiracist politics they had established in the Las Vegas youth scene. Butler, the only one of several assassins to be arrested, is a pathetic piece of shit and a traitor to his class. A drug dealer and police informant, Butler was also a leader of the Independent Nazi Skins, a bonehead gang that had clashed with ARA and the Unity Skins.

It is not out of sympathy that we oppose these executions (maybe Odin can do something for them cuz we see no hope of saving their souls on planet earth)—our position is strategic. In the short term, these death sentences reinforce the state's power and authority as the sole legitimate practitioner of violence in society. This violence is used again and again to maintain the rule of a racist, sexist, exploitive system and to repress those that challenge it—as seen in Cincinnati and Quebec City.

The death penalty is a racist institution rooted in legal lynchings. It is increasingly under attack because of its blatantly racist disproportional application to Blacks and the exposure of numerous death row frame-ups directed mainly at Black people. The use of the death penalty against McVeigh and Butler will serve as token examples. McVeigh's execution date has been moved up in order to restore public support for the death penalty and whitewash the faces of the executed.

In the long term, these death sentences will not weaken the fascist movement, but build it. A couple of aryan soldiers may be lost but their movement as a whole is credentialized as the revolutionary opposition with the martyrs to prove it. This will mean something serious if the economy takes a dive or some other crisis erupts that leads working-class whites to look for solutions outside the status quo.

The murders of Spit and Dan were devastating to those who knew them and to the network as a whole. By raising the ante higher than we were prepared to go, the Independent Nazi Skins exposed a major shortcoming—we lacked the ability to fully defend ourselves. After the shock, our collective reflex was to fall back on the leftist trap of calling on the state to "do its job." This is understandable, but only confirmed our weakness.

The responsibility for the failure to adequately confront the murders rests with the entire antifascist movement: US and Canadian, anarchist and socialist, skinhead and student. Despite some tough talk late in the game, no alternative approach was ever attempted. It is no accident that the Las Vegas murders, along with splits in several important chapters, marked the beginning of a decline for ARA in size and activity.

What could have been done instead? Right after the first mobilization in Las Vegas, a crew from the ARA Network could have stayed behind. They could have set up shop as a publicly and legally armed group and begun a campaign of outings against the nazis. This would have sent a strong message that we would not be intimidated, but it would have been risky, controversial, and hard to sustain. It also leaves aside the question of retaliation. But this kind of discussion would have at least been consistent with our refusal to rely on the cops and courts and our vision of a radical egalitarian movement.

Now, ARA has wind in its sails again, and in some ways is involved in more important work than ever before, and it is essential that we try to learn from Las Vegas. A first step is to get our heads screwed on right about these executions.

Fifth Column Fascism: Fascism within the Antiwar Movement

Kdog

ARA Research Bulletin no. 2 (Fall 2001)

The events of September 11. An anti-imperialist attack that is also a fascist attack. A body count that makes McVeigh look like just an angry postal worker. Neo-nazis debating whether to embrace the Jew-hating al-Qaeda or the wave of anti-Arab and anti-immigrant violence sweeping the US. George W. denouncing the Taliban as nazi-like, followed by missiles, bombs, and special forces. Arafat's cops shooting down anti-US youth in Gaza. Red, white, and blue ribbons and pins at work unless you're one of the tens of thousands patriotically downsized.

For radical antifascists it is time to reset our compass. As the smoke clears a few things become clear:

- The chickens have surely come home to roost; there is a cost after all to continued US domination of the planet's people and resources.
- All resistance ain't liberatory and all fascists ain't aryan. The September 11 actions apparently carried out by the al-Qaeda network were a major blow to the US. But al-Qaeda's program is to put as much territory under Taliban-style rule as possible. In typical fascist fashion civilian casualties were sought out, not avoided.
- The emergence of al-Qaeda and the Taliban's armed fundamentalist/fascist movement has for now eclipsed the antiglobalization movement—including the growing libertarian, militant, anticapitalist tendency—as "the main threat to capital." This also underlines the ultimate failure of revolutionary nationalism or Marxism/Leninism to resist integration into or

reproduction of the worse horrors of capitalism—leaving the fundamentalists to redefine the resistance and recruit the rebels.
- The war, the recession, and the new levels of state repression necessarily provide opportunities for us, but also for the fascists, to organize.

The Antiwar Movement

The antiwar movement is one such arena where there will likely be competition between fascists and antifascists to define the resistance. This sounds funny to say, since we're used to any and all antiwar movements being the property of the left. But like George Bush-Laden keeps reminding us, after September 11 "everything has changed."

The Neo-nazis

It is a fact that the first response of the major US hard-core nazi groups to the September 11 attacks was a "chickens come home to roost" attitude, with a heavy emphasis on the US backing of Israel as the main source of the attack. In the wake of all the anti-Arab violence, many of the nazis have tried to connect with that vibe by emphasizing anti-Arab, anti-immigrant demands. But if a significant antiwar movement develops, look for the National Alliance, World Church of the Creator, WAR, etc., to make appearances at antiwar events. ARA and other antifascists should develop intelligence on their intentions and prepare to confront and physically expel the neo-nazis from any and all antiwar events.

Third Position/Red-Brown

Slightly more complicated is the fascist Third Position tendency (represented in North America by the American Front and some Canadian-based website). This tendency has a more developed anti-imperialist line and will frown on mob violence against Arabs. Much of their politics so closely resemble third world nationalist/state-socialist forms and rhetoric that confronting them only physically will be inadequate. We'll have to be prepared to take on their arguments as well. It is guaranteed that they will try to enter the movement in Europe (especially Russia, Greece, Italy, Germany, Spain, Britain), where this tendency is most developed, strongest, and already has some links with a few Arab nationalists.

Fascism on the Left

While the fascist Third Position tendency makes open appeals to the radical left for united fronts, there are no equivalent (in North America anyway) groups on the left making appeals to the fascist right.

Still there are some disturbing trends in this direction.

The International Action Center, a front for Workers World Party (WWP), is a major organizer of the antiwar movement, especially mass mobilizations in DC. WWP has thoroughly authoritarian politics supporting the Tiananmen massacre, Saddam Hussein, the Mugabe regime in Zimbabwe, etc. This unfortunately does not make them unique on the left. WWP, however, formed a de facto red-brown alliance during the US war on Yugoslavia. WWP supported Milosevic, denied the genocide against Bosnians and Albanians, and held joint rallies with the Serbian National Front (a US-based fascist pro-genocide grouping). A large WWP forum in NYC broke into fascist-led chants of "long live Serbia."

WWP has developed a bizarre relationship with Ramsey Clark, a former US attorney general during the Vietnam War. Clark fronts their International Action Center, making missions to Iraq and Yugoslavia. Interestingly, before hooking up with WWP, Clark had a legal/political relationship with the LaRouche organization—a notorious fascistic cult that gathers information on the left for sale to corporate and government agencies when not spouting conspiracy theories involving the queen of England.

The dynamics of this war are different than the Yugoslav war; still, the WWP will play ball with nearly anyone and should be watched carefully, and exposed to the rest of the movement by antifascists.

Within the rest of the left, including Black and Latin nationalist movements, there is always a tendency to uncritically support whoever is fighting the US (or whoever the US is fighting). In the past this often meant support for various Stalinist movements and regimes; now it could mean supporting the fascists of al-Qaeda or the Taliban. Combating this tendency means clearly opposing, through direct action and counterinformation, all of the US imperial moves while also exposing the fascistic anti-woman politics of al-Qaeda/Taliban, organizing direct aid to autonomous forces in the region such as RAWA (the Revolutionary Association of the Women of Afghanistan), and developing a liberatory political/philosophical framework for resistance and revolution that is a clear alternative to capitalism, Stalinism, and fascism. I believe this framework will have to be an anarchist/antiauthoritarian one.

Even the Anarchists

But even within the anarchist movement there are tendencies which could potentially embrace fascist forms. Some in the green anarchist or "primitivist" tendency have greeted past terrorist atrocities as welcome blows to the industrial machine. Separately, the founders of the Anarchist Black Cross Federation have generally supported anyone with a gun (including Peru's Shining Path) while at the same time refusing to defend or privately disagreeing with women's reproductive freedom. This combination makes me fearful of where they might fall on al-Qaeda.

Anti-Racist Action

ARA's first point of unity says: "We go where they go, never let the fascists have the streets." In the past we've interpreted this narrowly in terms of taking them on in isolated demonstrations in scattered communities. Now we have to realize that this pledge has a broad and deep interpretation as well. The fascists want to "go" into a major social struggle against the new world order; we have to be ready to "go" there as well. Against the dominant system, and also against the many shades of fascism: aryan, red, brown, black, green, Islamic, Christian, Jewish, red, white, and blue.

The youth music scene was the first real turf battle between ARA and the fascists, then the organized KKK rallies and counterrallies. Next maybe the coming antiwar movement.

"… and never let them have the streets!"

Above and Below: Them, Them, and Us

BRICK Anarchist Collective

Chicago, April 2003

This is one of three tasks and perspectives discussion documents drafted to help stimulate debate with the Federation of Revolutionary Anarchist Collectives.

George Bush and his war hawks swarm down on the world from the heights of power and authority. The massive US war and occupation of Iraq has several aims: to aggressively establish US military and political dominance in the Middle East; to prove total US power to capitalist rivals around the globe; to ensure direct control over the Middle East's resources; and to favorably position itself for the ongoing struggle against a startling insurgency from below: Islamic fundamentalism/ fascism.

This is a bold and radical course for the capitalists, full of risks and challenges. It already has caused injury, possibly fatal, to major ruling-class institutions like NATO, the European Union, and the United Nations. It has provoked a massive outpouring of antiwar sentiment, protest, and direct action, all across the globe. The chill that fell on the US protest movement after 9/11 has thawed.

Less spectacular but equally a part of this drive is the offensive directed at the working classes internationally, including within the US. Trade pacts, like Plan Puebla Panama, open up countries' labor and resources; IMF austerity and privatization measures drive down wages and living standards and put education, healthcare, water, land, and infrastructure directly in the hands of the corporations. Antiterrorism is used to justify extensive new police powers, the erosion of civil liberties, carrying out advanced population mapping, and opening up public discussion of internment, assassinations, and torture.

The Bush government, in alliance with the Christian right, is working to roll back the victories women have won at home, on the job, and in wider society. There is no doubt that this will also be true for GLBT communities. War has always increased racism here in the Homeland. Arabs and Muslims continue to face both official and vigilante attacks. Mexicans and other Latinos have had to deal with increased repression at the border, deportations, and sweatshop conditions. In the Black community, systemic police brutality and incarceration, economic marginalization, and an imposed drug epidemic have not let up. The white sections of the working classes are now too feeling the effects of downsizing and cutbacks. This presents opportunities for class unity, but also for white supremacist and fascist backlash and balkanization.

The official opposition (Democratic Party, AFL-CIO bureaucracy, major civil rights groups, the Greens) are either totally complicit in this offensive or serve as a means to co-opt and dilute any autonomous struggle against these attacks.

Below

The world system of capitalism, patriarchy, white supremacy, and the state is going through a monumental reorganization which involves a great deal of inner-ruling class competition. This has temporarily weakened it at points, providing openings for resistance from below. Roughly speaking we would divide the resistance into two camps: (1) authoritarian, and (2) autonomous and anarchist. The differences between the two general approaches and visions are significant, and cannot be bridged by a shared militancy. In fact, as anarchist revolutionaries, antifascists, and radical feminists we understand our situation as a three way fight. Them, Them, and Us.

Authoritarian Movements

9/11 and the war in Afghanistan have brought home the fact that there is a serious force committed to fighting and overturning the US government and other Western governments and radically remaking society. But they are our enemies also. Al-Qaeda and movements like it include tens of thousands of fighters with sophisticated weapons and communications, a major bankroll, and the ability and the audacity to pull off spectacular acts of sabotage and terror. The Taliban regime in Afghanistan gave us a glimpse of what this kind of force looks like in power. Women were removed from public life, stripped of all rights. A large paramilitary force physically policed public morality. War, conquest, and criminal enterprise were central to the economy. No activity outside of the ruling structures was allowed.

In North America and Europe, but also in parts of the Global South, right-wing nationalism, white supremacy, and fascism have reemerged. In Europe, populist-fascist parties have made serious runs at state power. In India, Hindu fascists in political power have sanctioned mass pogroms and rape of Muslims. In the US, a relatively small (but large by left standards) fascist cadre organization, the National Alliance, is carrying out professional mass outreach, carving out a music and cultural underground, and has started to test the streets. The fascists in the US have actually felt more repression from Ashcroft's feds than any section of the left outside of the Arab communities.

Beyond fundamentalism and fascism there remain other authoritarian currents of opposition from below. Authoritarian communists and nationalists continue as guerrilla groups in several Third World countries and as opposition parties in the West. Their goals, which once may have seemed radical, are now clearly about control by a party elite (usually middle-class intellectuals) of a revolutionary state, that in turn controls all of society. While instituting certain reforms from above, their obsession with centralization, production, and total ideological control have devastating effects on the land, working people, and any autonomous movements or impulses.

Autonomous Movements

So who is the Us? Who do we stand with on this planet? The Zapatistas uprising, the Battle in Seattle, and Argentina's revolt. The anarchist and alternative unions in Europe, the land seizures in Brazil, and the heroism of RAWA (the Revolutionary Association of the Women of Afghanistan). The antiprivatization movement in South Africa, the Belfast-based free-speech forum the Blanket, and the bonfires in Quebec City. Peoples' Global Action, the IndyMedia Center, and the International Libertarian Solidarity network.

This sample of movements, organizations, actions, and projects may seem unwieldy, but it has a logic. As a movement, its main characteristics include: conscious anticapitalism, a rejection of vanguardism and statecraft, a broad repertoire of militant direct action, a directly democratic process, an egalitarian vision, a commitment to autonomy, political and physical hostility to the fascists and fundamentalists, an ecological understanding, and deep reservations about the effects and effectiveness of an armed-struggle strategy—among others.

Anarchism is a significant minority within these movements, better known and with more momentum than at any time in the last sixty years. Marxists and ex-Marxists also exert significant influence, and Indigenism and different religious beliefs are also important guides or references for many.

Anarchists cannot be passive participants in these movements. We have a responsibility to argue for explicitly anarchist methods and goals. There is nothing guaranteed about these struggles. Many first launch themselves with a strong autonomous character, only to come under the domination of an authoritarian group or be co-opted back into the system. The Solidarity movement in Poland and the first Palestinian Intifada are examples. The anarchist role is not seizing leadership, but encouraging and defending the most far-reaching self-organization against all authority.

Culture has played an increasingly important role in our movement. It gives life to the resistance. We also know that any culture becomes a target for capitalism to be sold back to us as a commercialized empty shell. Within hip-hop, punk, queer, and other subcultures, battles are being waged between a committed underground and corporate colonization.

The autonomous movements are not without significant weaknesses and flaws. In general there is not a clear orientation toward insurrection—an immediate abolition of the state and collective appropriation of wealth and resources. The wariness toward armed struggle, often learned from direct experience, sometimes verges on pacifism. This gives the movement a distinct reformist side, though not as visible partly because of a general disinterest in electoralism. The enthusiasm this current has inspired among radical youth, Indigenous communities, and campesinos has not yet found a strong base in the urban working classes around the world, and this has to change.

In the North American Great Lakes region, two small but important groups are examples of the autonomous movement. The Ontario

Coalition Against Poverty (OCAP) has come the closest to merging the antiglobalization movement with the poorest sections of the working classes through direct-action case work and mass mobilization, and the Anti-Racist Action Network (ARA), which has doggedly struggled both physically and ideologically against the fascists, is forming a core of young militant organizers.

The balance of forces in Mexico is also extremely important to us here. The EZLN in Chiapas are in many ways the prototype of what we mean by autonomous movement, because of their rebellion, their refusal to seek state power or to disarm, their liberated municipalities, and sharp exchanges with authoritarian groups like the Basque ETA. Also in Mexico, we are starting to learn more about the struggles of the Consejo Indígena Popular de Oaxaca–Ricardo Flores Magón (CIPO-RFM), a similar group with more explicitly anarchist sympathies. We are committed to building a relationship with this group and other autonomous movements south of the border.

FRAC

In trying to sum up this paper, we feel it is important for our federation to: be able to analyze the moves of the ruling class and what problems and possibilities these present, in particular this war against Iraq; understand and be able to differentiate between authoritarian and autonomous resistance; build and participate in the autonomous movements, especially among the working classes; fight for revolutionary anarchist methods and goals within these movements, and struggle against repression, reformism, and rising elites; contest the authoritarian movements both physically and politically; and link up with other struggles and movements around the world for discussion and mutual aid. We are a new grouping on a new world stage. Most of what we try to do will necessarily be experimental. We must be bold as we advance while encouraging a thorough dialog around all our activities.

Some Specific Tasks

1. We need to develop our politics and vision. We need both a historical understanding of revolutionary anarchism, including the debates around the platform, and a clear analysis of our current situation, the moves of the ruling class and the resulting problems

and possibilities. We need to understand and be able to differentiate between authoritarian and autonomous methods and goals.
We need to write short position papers on a whole range of questions facing us, for debate and discussion. We should hold at least
one educational day school annually, maybe jointly with NEFAC
(Northeastern Federation of Anarcho-Communists) and others,
that concentrates on internal education, debate, and discussion.
Not just by and for experts and intellectuals, but recognizing we
all have things to teach and learn. This also involves paying attention to, learning from, and building ties with the international
anarchist movement.

2. We need to strengthen the organization. FRAC needs more of
    a public face with publications, position papers, a web page.
    The antiwar poster was an excellent start. We need to better
    collectively sum up our experiences, in local organizing, demos
    and actions, etc., with regular reports and discussion from the
    members, collectives, and secretaries. We also need to stimulate
    and help bring out more collectives in our region. We need a
    strong sense of security culture, an understanding of different
    methods of repression including sophisticated counterinsurgency.
    We need to be able to organize a fighting movement that can
    successfully organize direct action, on both mass and small-group
    levels. We should also systematically build ties with the new wave
    of anarchist organizing in North America—NEFAC and the other
    regional federations and networks.

3. We need to experiment more with trying to build organization
    and action in the workplaces and communities outside of the left
    and anarchist scenes. In Chicago, the small Uprise! initiative at
    UPS has proven that we can get a favorable hearing and engage in
    some struggle in these areas. Our effort to organize in the Pilsen/
    Little Village neighborhoods holds even more promise. We need
    to experiment, and try to draw lessons from the experience. This
    will take collectives and individuals committing to get these types
    of projects off the ground.

4. Developing revolutionary culture is equally important. A number
    of comrades are artists, musicians, and DJs, and almost all of us
    have connections to the subcultures. We need to analyze what's
    going on in popular and rebel culture and figure out how to

participate and impact cultural consciousness and movements. We need to make sure all of our activity has flava. We are not the rigid, boring left and we don't want to look like it.

About Us

Three Way Fight

Three Way Fight, June 12, 2005

This site is directed toward the revolutionary anticapitalist movements that have emerged over the last several years. The rise of these
movements shows the potential for radical struggle that breaks with
parliamentary reformism and the remnants of the various state social-
isms. However, much of this potential remains untapped. Our side is
small, undeveloped, and, in the recent past, mainly on the defensive.
Our inability to consolidate a substantial political alternative out of
the very real potentials points to the difficulty of the tasks.

The contributors to this site consider the fracturing of the global
capitalist system to be a real possibility. However, there is no guarantee that political opposition to global capital will coalesce around a
radical liberatory alternative. There is another opposition emerging—a
reactionary neofascism that aims to overthrow the current capitalist
hegemony and institute a radically different oppressive social order.
This leads us to conclude that we are in a three way contest where the
fault lines don't conform to a simple "Us" and "Them."

We have set up this site to contribute to the development of ideas
for action. We need to clarify the actual political processes, not manu-
facture some new slogans, and work out some political strategies that
aren't just chewed-over reruns of past debates and failures.

What you will find here is opinions, analysis, debate, and news
covering the politics and culture of our current world and the new
movement(s) we are attempting to create. Some posts may be long, in
depth, and part of ongoing discussions, while others may be short and
to the point. What we are aiming for is the transmission of engaging
and informative commentary.

II
BASIC PRINCIPLES

A Demand That Radicals Tell the Truth: On Three Way Fight Politics and Why It Matters

Interview with rowan

Three Way Fight, May 30, 2021

Editors' note: This interview with a friend of the *Three Way Fight* project was conducted during the run-up to the November 2020 election.

Three Way Fight: Please tell us something about your political background and how you came to be interested in three way fight politics.

rowan: I got politicized as a teenager through the anarchist punk rock scene in the 1990s. In 2000, I moved to Portland, Oregon, where I was active in the local post-Seattle antiauthoritarian radical scene. Following September 11, 2001, I was involved in trying to build a radical anti-imperialist pole in the antiwar movement. From 2003 until its dissolution in 2012, I was a member of Bring the Ruckus, a national political organization that sought to develop and implement revolutionary politics and that saw fighting white supremacy as central to the fight against capitalism and oppression. From 2004 until 2012, I was a member of a local copwatch organization that engaged in training folks about their rights, cop-watching, participating in protests, and developing a police abolitionist politics.

I think I first encountered the three way fight political perspective when Don Hamerquist and J. Sakai's book *Confronting Fascism* came out in 2002. Some folks from Chicago Anti-Racist Action actually ended up doing an event out here where they talked to local activists about the book. That was probably how I was introduced to this political framework.

Several of my political mentors were radical men who had participated in driving neo-nazi skinhead gangs out of Portland in the early 1990s. As a result, antifascism has been a central part of my political landscape throughout my adult life. I've been involved in various mobilizations against the far right throughout the 2000s and early 2010s.

Bring the Ruckus, the national "revolutionary cadre" group I participated in, was one of the proponents of a kind of three way fight politics. We applied this framework to international questions in the context of the "War on Terror" and increasingly also to US politics as the Portland local prioritized antifascist work. Veterans of the Sojourner Truth Organization were a significant influence on our thinking and debates, and while there were real differences around the priority of antifascist organizing, we generally agreed with the perspective that fascism was an autonomous political threat and not merely a strategy of the ruling class. Since that time of my membership in Bring the Ruckus and my high level of political activity, I've become a parent and stepped back some from political engagement, but the importance of three way fight politics and the struggle against right-wing violence have only become more urgent.

Three Way Fight: What does a three way fight approach mean to you? What do you find most significant or helpful about it?

rowan: In many ways, what feels important about the three way fight perspective is as much about how we do politics as it is about the particular content of those political positions. As much as the three way fight is an intellectual orientation, it feels like in some ways an ethical stance toward political struggle. Amílcar Cabral, in the anticolonial struggle in Guinea-Bissau, urged his comrades to "Hide nothing from the masses of our people. Tell no lies. Expose lies whenever they are told. Mask no difficulties, mistakes, failures. Claim no easy victories." Similarly, the three way fight asks us to forsake triumphalist sloganeering and to instead engage in sober analysis and face difficult and uncomfortable truths about the world.

Too often "radical left" politics in the US consists of platitudes and posturing. Fascism has functioned as a nasty word we call folks we don't like, and "strategic analysis" is whatever set of slogans makes us feel righteous. Too often in the interests of simplicity we argue that "cops and Klan" are always "hand in hand," that all of our enemies are the same enemy. It is incredibly attractive to believe that the world is neatly divided with bad guys on one side representing oppression and exploitation, racism, patriarchy, bigotry, empire, and fascism, and good guys on the other representing liberation, feminism, decolonization, and a free society.

Perhaps the most important thing to me about the three way fight approach was that it was a demand that radicals tell the truth.

This orientation toward truth and humility also asks us to take our enemies seriously in ways that we often fail to do. We must not only pay attention to our enemies' (both state and fascist) strength, but also listen to and learn from what they say about themselves and the world. A lot of the time it feels like radical analyses of the far right just start from the assumption that they're lying. Thus, when folks on the right oppose economic exploitation of the working class, prioritize ecology and defending the earth, or even oppose white supremacy, leftists often dismiss these as lies or attempts to trick people. The three way fight perspective helps us to listen, to be open to the possibility that they speak the truth about their visions, and to recognize that our enemies are complex, which makes them all the more dangerous as we struggle to defeat them.

The three way fight perspective also helps radical leftists to critique ourselves and sharpen our political perspectives. I certainly think that any kind of horseshoe theory that equates "extremism" on the left and right should be rejected. That said, I do think that three way fight politics can help us see the potential ways that radicals can betray our own political commitments to liberation.

In recognizing that the right often is critical of the neoliberal global order of inequality and exploitation (for its own reasons), we can see the overlaps that do exist between the politics of the far left and right. This recognition can help us clarify how our own (liberatory anarchist/communist/etc.) critiques of capitalist civilization contrast with those of our rebellious enemies. From anti-Zionism that singles out Israel for its Jewishness, to eco-radicalism that is disdainful of the survival of vulnerable people, to Stalinist anti-imperialisms that fetishize militarism and nationalism, to populisms that celebrate the forgotten "common people" in opposition to parasitic metropolitan elites, leftist talking points can—if we're not careful—echo those of the right. By recognizing and combating this danger, we can strengthen our movements and develop perspectives and visions that point more clearly to a free world.

On the other hand, three way fight politics stands in uncompromising opposition to official society and the dominant order. We must reject and distance ourselves from any kind of official "antifascism" that serves to defend this murderous system from its enemies on the right. Antifascist politics that fail to break with and oppose capitalist civilization too often serve as the foot soldiers or private investigators on behalf of power. This not only fails to fight against exploitation and for a better world, but actually serves the fascists by proving their narrative that they are the true rebels against this wretched order.

Three Way Fight: What do you think three way fight politics offers that the US left needs? Are there particular issues or struggles where you see this approach as particularly important?

rowan: When the three way fight perspective emerged out of the experiences of the antiglobalization and antiwar movements of the early 2000s, few on the radical left saw antifascism as being at the center of their perspective.

It's my sense that the current historical moment is a terrifying validation of this perspective. Leaving aside semantic battles over whether Trumpism is fascist, it does seem clear that we are seeing the emergence of right-wing movements that speak to the crisis of capitalist civilization.

What feels important right now is to understand that the escalating conflicts that we are witnessing and participating in are not static or permanent, but instead are evolving aspects of an unfolding historical process. We can debate all day about whether Trump is a fascist or just a particularly unpleasant Republican, whether he's system loyal, system oppositional, or just self-loyal. These attempts to understand the current terrain and array of forces are of course incredibly important. However, it's also important to recognize that the current terrain and forces are not permanent, but shifting. What if we are in fact in the early stages of a period of instability, polarization, and escalating violence and upheaval. Trump, rather than being our period's Mussolini, may be one of the conditions that shapes the horrors to come.

It seems likely to me that the right that is today storming capitols, street fighting with antifascists, and plotting to kidnap governors may well look tame and sweet in comparison to the right-wing movements to come. The obvious possibility is that the right (or sections of it) may coalesce around leaders who are master strategists and cunning political thinkers, as opposed to Donald Trump's clownish narcissism. Also of concern is the possibility that participants and leaders of the right-to-come may be drawn not only from their traditional bases, but also from folks who are currently on the left but become disillusioned, or that even entire sections of the current "left" may be won over to alliances with and participation in right-wing social movements. Thinking through the potential convergences between left and right is for us not a liberal opposition to extremism, but rather an attempt to sharpen the liberatory content of our own extremism in opposition to both official society and its supremacist enemies.

Three Way Fight: Have you witnessed or experienced examples of people applying three way fight politics in concrete political situations?

rowan: I certainly feel like Portland right now is a place where we are absolutely watching a three way fight play out. Portland has a dynamic and inspiring radical left that has been confronting Patriot Prayer and the Proud Boys in the streets for years. Over the summer, radicals took to the streets to engage in mass and militant action in defense of Black lives and in opposition to police violence, gentrification, and heavy-handed federal interventions by the Trump regime. While I wasn't able to be very involved in the uprising in the streets, from where I stand, it definitely looks like radical leftists in Portland have been fighting a three way fight against multiple enemies. On the one hand, the movement has targeted, and faced repression from, Mayor Ted Wheeler, a neoliberal who serves the interests of developers and real estate interests and oversees the brutal and racist Portland Police Bureau. On the other hand, right-wing groups like Patriot Prayer and the Proud Boys have engaged in street violence against the left, often motivated by loyalty to Trump and opposition to liberal elites like Wheeler. Wheeler's (and the police's) hostility toward the left is understood by some as him siding with the far right. Three way fight politics allows us to understand the possibility that instead we face multiple enemies contending for power and influence with competing visions. It may not be a pretty or comforting reality, but only by facing reality can we organize to win.

On a larger scale, I think that US politics in general right now is taking the form of a three way fight between an emerging radical left (consisting of rebels for Black lives, "antifa," folks engaged in mutual aid efforts, and some electorally oriented socialists), the defenders of the collapsing neoliberal status quo (Biden and the Democrats), and a diverse far right, which in recent years has often but certainly not always been oriented around loyalty to Trump. The contending visions of these forces are expressed in many ways, including through their approaches to the COVID-19 pandemic. The right is engaged in straight-up denialism, whether suggesting the virus is a hoax or conspiracy or violently opposing public health interventions like masks or shutting down some businesses. Meanwhile, the centrists and liberals have largely settled for some minimal economic shutdowns, but mostly a campaign of public shaming and blaming of individuals who don't properly engage in social distancing in their personal lives. They demand we go to work and face immense risks in workplaces (and prisons), but blame us if we go out after work. Finally, we on the left need to develop a response to this apocalypse (and those to come) rooted in mutual aid, radical solidarity, and a recognition of our interdependence. This response includes mutual aid to help those thrown into crisis, organizing by nurses, teachers, and other "essential workers," and perhaps even some demands on the state backed by militant action and organizing rooted among the communities most vulnerable to this genocidal pandemic and their allies.

Three Way Fight: Do you see problems or limitations with three way fight politics? Issues it could do a better job with?

rowan: Three way fight politics is essential for developing a revolutionary left that can both fight and think to win. But this framework is, of course, useful as a tool, not as a dogma. There is always a danger of applying any categorization in vulgar and mechanical ways that can actually undermine our critical thinking. In the case of the three way fight politics, this might potentially mean assuming that any political struggle must have only three sides that fit with the predetermined theory. Trumpist right-wing militant patriots, right-wing Islamist guerrillas, and authoritarian anti-imperialist governments may all be both our enemies and the enemies of the neoliberal imperialist order, but that doesn't necessarily mean that they are all part of the same political pole. Our politics is one that seeks to grapple with complexity and nuance in order to tell the truth to understand the world to win liberation. Any theory or framework can end up being an obstacle to that.

Fascism and Antifascism: A Decolonial Perspective

Rowland Keshena Robinson

Maehkōn Ahpēhtesewen, February 11, 2017 (revised 2023)

In the wake of the 2016 election of Donald J. Trump in the United States, a quickly blossoming discussion on fascism, its nature, and what to do about it rapidly emerged and took hold of the left in North America.[1] While antifascist discourse has long been a part of the left, dating back to the emergence of European fascism as a significant political force in the 1920s, the period of Trump signaled a quantitative shift in the level of such discussion. More so, one often found that it spilled out from the bounds of the traditional anticapitalist left to encompass sectors of mainstream liberalism as well. Fascism was on the tips of everyone's tongues, something which ran through Trump's chaotic four years in office, culminating in the events that occurred in Washington, DC, in early January 2021, and their subsequent fallout. And so, I want to begin this discussion of fascism with a brief sojourn through the current terrain of right-wing electoralism in North America.

While fascists and others who we might term parafascists have seized power through the weapon of the coup d'état and other military means (as in Spain under the Francisco Franco regime or the government of Augusto Pinochet in Chile), others have strategically deployed electoralism as an essential element of their political arsenal. Both the Fascists of Benito Mussolini as well as the German National Socialists used elections, combined with paramilitary violence and other extra-electoral pressure tactics, to seize power.

In more recent time, far-right electoralists have once again been on the march across Europe. One can look to the perennial French presidential candidate Marine Le Pen, as well as Hungary's Fidesz party, Poland's Law and Justice party, and, most recently, the Brothers of Italy party.

However, one may be quick to point out that on this side of the Atlantic open fascists have not become an electoral force, or at least not one of serious political effect. But what the Trump movement—before, during, and after his presidency—has signaled in a quite notable way is that this has begun to change. While certainly preceding Trump in important ways, the Trump candidacy and presidency has been an important signpost for a new era of fascist entry into the mainstream of North American politics. Trump was quite content to mobilize fascist and other far right elements as well as to provide unprecedented contemporary political space for them.

Thus, here in North America the current debate on fascism and the far right is now ineluctably tied to the presidency of a failed billionaire real-estate mogul and former reality television host turned champion of white nationalist populism. His presidency, arguably a failure due to its inability to sustain itself beyond a single term, was brought about in no small way by the political mobilization by the formerly outré political forces. This included many open white supremacists, the alt-right, and, by the time of his second electoral effort in 2020, an additional complex of right-wing conspiracy theorists best represented by the 8chan-born QAnon phenomenon.

His presidency saw the Unite the Right rally in Charlottesville, Virginia, an event in which clean-shaven young white men paraded through the streets to the light of tiki torches and moved to the chants of "Jews will not replace us" and for "blood and soil." In its aftermath, Trump pleaded to the American public to recognize "good people" on both sides. Even more nakedly, during Trump's disastrous 2020 presidential debates, upon being asked about the Proud Boys, he instructed the organization to "stand down and stand by," all the while claiming that the real blame for political violence in the US should be directed toward "antifa" and "the left."

Beyond the formally organized far right, Trump was also able to tap into something broader: long-simmering feelings of resentment and ressentiment within a certain sector of the white American population. Long before Trump was ever even a candidate, the backlash against the presidency of Barack Obama, indicted by movements such as the Tea Party and the Birther conspiracy, was a canary in the coal mine. For many white Americans, liberals, represented by the Democratic Party, were the force of systematic fine-tuning in the interests of big capital, finance capital, and a process of neoliberal globalization that sent their jobs overseas. Liberals are also often perceived as those who allowed, or even facilitated, the takeover of the United States by creeping political correctness, feminists, queer people, and nonwhites.

The perception then was one of an "American" way of life under attack, of the crumbling of privileges long felt to be deserved, and thus the end of *a* world. In tapping into this undercurrent of white American ressentiment, Trump's 2016 candidacy crumbled the traditional Democratic strongholds of the Rust Belt and Upper Midwest, carrying him into office. This was arguably more significant than Trump's flirtations with the organized far right.

All this culminated in the events of January 6, 2021. Facing a humiliating defeat in his bid for reelection, Trump stoked the conspiratorial flames of his most ardent supporters even further with claims that the election had been a sham. Rudy Giuliani, former mayor of New York City cum personal legal counsel for Trump, called for a "trial by combat" to decide the true outcome of the election. And Trump's far right and conspiracist followers—the Proud Boys, QAnon, the Oath Keepers, and others—answered the call, storming the US Capitol building in Washington, DC, and attempting to put a violent stop to the election certification process.

The events of that January of course failed to secure Trump's power. Biden, a moderate liberal, was officially declared the winner of the 2020 election. Following this, many believers left, or even fled, the cause, under the weight of the state's retaliation. Some organizations such as the Proud Boys experienced fractures. Others, particularly of the more conspiracist-tinged wing, began to leave the movement when faced with the failure of Trump.

However, Trump's influence is far from gone. In the same election as Trump's defeat, Marjorie Taylor Greene, an ardent Trump supporter and promoter of a range of far-right conspiracy theories, took office as the congressperson for Georgia's Fourteenth District. Ted Cruz, the junior Texas senator and onetime opponent of Trump, also reoriented his political career to become a staunch peddler of the election theft theory.

Whether or not Trump himself is a fascist is up for debate. Undeniable though is that Trump and his closest advisers are right-wing national populists, which in the context of the North American settler colonialism is invariably inseparable from white nationalism. What is also undeniable is what I have already noted: a number of *explicitly* white nationalist organizations, theorists, and influencers have been highly motivated and emboldened by Trump.

Additionally, as I write this from Canada, it would be foolish to believe that this country is somehow sealed from these events. Figures in the federal Conservative Party have sought to emulate Trump's rhetoric and even openly call for bringing his message here. We should not forget that before Trump's executive orders barring immigration from seven Muslim majority countries and authorizing the building of a wall on the Mexican border, the previous Tory administration passed the nakedly Islamophobic Zero Tolerance for Barbaric Cultural Practices Act, as well as the Anti-terrorism Act, 2015, and the Strengthening Canadian Citizenship Act.

Additionally, other conservative dissidents, dissatisfied with their ability to seize the reins of the mainstream right-wing parties, have formed their own fractious formations. These have included the People's Party at the federal level, which, while not obtaining a single seat in Parliament, leapfrogged over the Canadian Green Party in terms of the popular vote in the 2021 election. In Ontario, the New Blue Party has been launched in opposition to the Progressive Conservatives. Declaring the decidedly conservative PC government to be filled with "left-wing ideologues," the New Blues have sworn to oppose all mandates relating to the COVID-19 pandemic and to oppose what they see as "woke" activism in Ontario schools, including the banning of "critical race" and "gender identity" theories.

One also cannot speak of this movement here in Canada without taking into consideration the so-called Freedom Convoy which descended on Ottawa in January 2022 in opposition to ongoing COVID-19 regulations, but which certainly built on other longstanding feelings of resentment and ressentiment among a section of the Canadian population.

Thinking through all of this, what I want to do here is ask a basic question: What is fascism? And, more specific to our context, what does fascism mean considering the conditions of settler colonialism?

Is it even a useful analytic category given existent social conditions, technologies of governance, and patterns of power? And, finally, what does antifascism mean, or how should it be rethought?

Defining Fascism

So, what is fascism then? Open most texts or follow most online discussions and one is likely to encounter one of two definitions. The first, more common, views fascism as some form of particularly virulent authoritarian nationalism. Generally, it attaches the label of fascism to manifestations of aggressive racism, reactionary and conservative traditionalism, antiliberalism, and anticommunism, as well as expansionist and revanchist approaches to foreign policy as part of a general movement toward the seizure of absolute political power, the elimination of opposition, and the creation of a regulated economic structure that will transform social relations within a modern, self-determined culture. Other essential features include a political aesthetic of romantic symbolism, mass mobilization, a positive view of violence, and promotion of masculinity, youth, and charismatic leadership.[2]

The general historical examples of fascism are the Fascist Party of Italy and the National Socialist movement that seized political control of Germany in the early 1930s. Additionally, such definitions may look to Franco's Spain, the clerical fascism of Romania under the Iron Guard and Ion Antonescu, or the various governments of Hungary in the 1930s and during the Second World War.

To the left of this historical-descriptive, though still helpful, definition is the one taken up by the majority of anticapitalists, especially Marxists. The major form of this definition traces itself back to the Bulgarian communist and general secretary of the Communist International Georgi Dimitrov. Dimitrov's description of fascism was that it is "the open terrorist dictatorship of the most reactionary, most chauvinistic and most imperialist elements of finance capital."[3] While there is more that can be said about this formulation, its pithy nature has an easy appeal to it. However, it lacks the degree of specificity that is necessary to make it more than a little helpful.

Reflecting on this lack of specificity within Dimitrov's formulation, the Irish political economist Zak Cope, in his book *Divided World, Divided Class: Global Political Economy and the Stratification of Labour under Capitalism*, says:

Fascism is the attempt by the imperialist bourgeoisie to solidify its rule on the basis of popular middle-class support for counter-revolutionary dictatorship. Ideologically fascism is the relative admixture of authoritarianism, racism, militarism and pseudo-socialism necessary to make this bid successful. In the first place, authoritarianism justifies right-wing dictatorship aimed at robbing and repressing any and all actual or potential opponents of imperialist rule. Secondly, racism or extreme national chauvinism provides fascist rule with a pseudo-democratic facade, promising to level all distinctions of rank and class via national aggrandisement. Thirdly, militarism allows the fascist movement both to recruit déclassé ex-military and paramilitary elements to its cause and to prepare the popular conscience for the inevitable aggressive war. Finally, social-fascism offers higher wages and living standards to the national workforce at the expense of foreign and colonised workers. As such, denunciations of "unproductive" and "usurers" capital, of "bourgeois" nations (that is, the dominant imperialist nations) and of the workers' betrayal by reformist "socialism" are part and parcel of the fascist appeal.[4]

As Cope further notes, this summation is not out of line with the pre-Dimitrov (and, also, pre-Hitlerian) discussion of fascism in the *Programme of the Communist International*, which noted that "the combination of Social Democracy, corruption and active white terror, in conjunction with extreme imperialist aggression in the sphere of foreign politics, are the characteristic features of Fascism."[5] Cope, though, essentially remains within the general contours of Dimitrov's thought, holding fascism to be an "exceptional form of the bourgeois state."[6]

Dimitrov's definition of fascism, or one that cleaves closely to its general contours,[7] is in many ways still the *definitive* explanation among the left. Yet, as already noted, while it may in some ways be necessary, it is far from sufficient.

Notably, the traditional Comintern definition of fascism, while placing it in a relationship with the rule of capital, understates the way fascist movements are often ideologically, if not praxiologically, in antagonism with it, or at least certain manifestations or elements of it, namely finance capital. Considering this, several recent attempts to think through the question of fascism have attempted to develop this line of inquiry more fully.

Important work here begins with the autonomist Marxist Don Hamerquist's article "Fascism & Anti-fascism." In this text, Hamerquist rejects the traditional view of fascism as simply a tool for big business, stating, "In opposition to this position, I think that fascism has the potential to become a mass movement with a substantial and genuine element of revolutionary anti-capitalism. Nothing but mistakes will result from treating it as 'bad' capitalism."[8]

Centrally, Hamerquist sees the danger in a *new fascism* that is both more independent than classical "euro-fascism" and more oppositional to capitalism. Here, fascism is not merely a blunt instrument used to prop up industrial capitalism but is, rather, a whole new form of barbarism, one that quite disconcertingly comes with mass support. Importantly, Hamerquist emphasizes the degree to which fascism has its own independent political life, and as such, while the bourgeoisie can influence it, it is ultimately independent of it. For him, fascism is a form of populist right-wing revolution.[9]

Agreeing with Hamerquist in broad strokes, while also putting forth criticisms and contributions, the American activist J. Sakai calls "disastrous" the old "1920s European belief that fascism was just 'a tool of the ruling class.'"[10] Sakai also emphasizes both the revolutionary nature of fascism as well as the class composition of such movements, using as his primary case study the German National Socialist movement, noting them as primarily formed by men of lower middle class and declassed backgrounds "that are abandoned on the sidelines of history."[11]

Matthew Lyons in his article "Two Ways of Looking at Fascism" attempts to synthesize this tendency and gives the following provisional definition of fascism as "a revolutionary form of right-wing populism, inspired by a totalitarian vision of collective rebirth, that challenges capitalist political and cultural power while promoting economic and social hierarchy."[12]

In his more recent book *Insurgent Supremacists: The U.S. Far Right's Challenge to State and Empire*, Lyons builds on this definition further. In this work, he moves away from the label of fascist to broaden the scope of the discussion and to think of the far right as a disparate array of forces, which can sometimes find themselves in coalition with one another but which do not necessarily share the same constellation of goals. What is essential is the question of *supremacy*. On this he says:

> As an imprecise working definition (not for all times and places but for the United States today), "far right" is used here to mean political forces that (a) regard human inequality as natural, inevitable, or desirable and (b) reject the legitimacy of the established political system. This definition cuts across standard ideological divisions. It includes insurgent factions among both white supremacists (whose supremacist vision centers on race) and Christian rightists (who advocate social and political hierarchy based on gender and religion, among other factors). It also includes many Patriot movement activists, who may or may not advocate racial or religious oppression but who champion unregulated capitalism and the economic inequality it produces.[13]

What also becomes key is the distinction between what Lyons refers to as rightists who are *system loyal* and those who are *insurgent*. Again, he notes:

> The definition excludes system-loyal white supremacists, Christian rightists, and Patriot activists, as well as other rightists who want to roll back liberal reforms but leave the basic state apparatus in place.[14]

By shifting of the resolution with which we see the phenomenon of the far right to include those forces that might not be recognized as traditionally fascist, we can begin to see the core of fascism's relationship to capitalism. Central here is fascism as an *insurgent* politics committed to the overturning of the current social order.

Hearkening back to my initial comments in the introduction to this article, this line of thinking from Lyons also allows us to bring into clearer focus the politics of the Trump regime and its Canadian interlocutors. In this, despite his commitment to a form of right-wing national populism, Trump does not represent an insurgent politics. Quite to the contrary, Trump is the definition of a bombastic but still *system-loyal* rightist. His electoral promise to "drain the swamp" was a plan to deal with perceptions of institutional corruption, *not* to smash it into sand and configure something new. Even the Capitol riot, while it mobilized insurgent supremacists and conspiracy theorists, was less of an effort to institute a whole new social order and more of the fading gasps of a dying term in office.

Hamerquist, Sakai, and Lyons's writings on the question of fascism provide an incredibly important line of thought for us to consider as part of the broad effort to combat the growth of fascist movements. Further, their work to retheorize the question of fascism and the far right should encourage us to consider yet more deficiencies within the traditional antifascist perspective.

Colonial Violence Turned Inward

Moving beyond Hamerquist, Sakai, and Lyons then, the traditional definitions of fascism are insufficient for a host of other, equally important reasons. In this regard, despite his own insufficiencies, Cope's work points us toward what I believe the heart of fascism is, at least as it is constituted in the developed countries of the Global North. He says: "Geographically speaking, on its own soil fascism is imperialist repression turned inward."[15] This is an aspect of fascism which I believe is missing from all other attempts to give definition to the phenomenon and whose vital importance cannot be overstated. To begin to follow this line of reasoning, we can say that fascism is when the violence that the colonialist nations have visited upon the world over the course of the development of the modern/colonial/capitalist world-system comes back home to visit.

This direct lineal connection from colonial violence to fascism was beautifully, if disturbingly, described by Aimé Césaire in his *Discourse on Colonialism* (1972), saying:

> We must show that each time a head is cut off or an eye put out in Vietnam and in France they accept the fact ... each time a Madagascan is tortured and in France they accept the fact, civilization acquires another dead weight, a universal regression takes place, a gangrene sets in, a center of infection begins to spread; and that at the end of all these treaties that have been violated, all these lies that have been propagated, all these punitive expeditions that have been tolerated, all these

prisoners who have been tied up and "interrogated," all these patriots who have been tortured, at the end of all the racial pride that has been encouraged, all the boastfulness that has been displayed, a poison has been instilled into the veins of Europe and, slowly but surely, the continent proceeds toward savagery.[16]

Regarding the shock of fascism's recapitulation of colonial violence arriving on the shores of the homeland, Césaire adds:

People are surprised, they become indignant. They say: "How strange! But never mind—it's Nazism, it will pass!" And they wait, and they hope; and they hide the truth from themselves, that it is barbarism, but the supreme barbarism, the crowning barbarism that sums up all the daily barbarisms; that it is Nazism, yes, but that before they were its victims, they were its accomplices; that they tolerated that Nazism before it was inflicted on them, that they absolved it, shut their eyes to it, legitimized it, because, until then, it had been applied only to non-European peoples; that they have cultivated that Nazism, that they are responsible for it, and that before engulfing the whole of Western, Christian civilization in its reddened waters, it oozes, seeps, and trickles from every crack.[17]

However, if we are to work through these issues in North America, we must consider a second specificity: settler colonialism. Given this, how can we read even Cope's discussion of fascism "whilst on foreign soil" as "imperialist repression employed by comprador autocracies" or Hamerquist and Sakai's considerations of the *globalization of fascism*?[18] To ask the question more precisely, what does it mean for an analysis of fascism when the binary between "foreign soil" and "own soil" is disintegrated by settler colonialism's geographical overlaying of the metropole and those it colonizes?

My argument here then is that for any theory of fascism, much less antifascism, to carry any kind of meaningful weight in North America, it must contend with the *fact* of settler colonialism and its ongoing, central structuring of the entire symbolic, social, and political order of North America. Anything else threatens to become a repetitive loop, unable to break through to the actual core of fascism.

The Terrain below Fascism

Building on this recognition of fascism as colonial violence turned inward, we are immediately confronted with how the spaces of possibility for the development of a North American fascist movement is a terrain—in terms of both the literal material meaning of the land, as well as less direct meanings of the psychic, political, social, cultural, ideological, and economic fields—is already overcoded by blood and death. It is a terrain that is already socially coded by the violences, both historic and very much so contemporary, against Native, Black, and other nonwhite peoples.

In the case of North America, the sense of exteriority inherent in Césaire's description of the perfection of fascist oppression within colonial violence overseas becomes interior. While for Césaire and Cope the violence of fascism is brought home from the distant colonies to the metropolitan center, in the settler-colonial context this violence is one that was perfected within the exceptional state of the expansion of the frontier, the clearing of Indigenous people to make the land ripe for settlement, and the carceral continuum that has marked the Black experience on this land from chattel slavery to the modern hyperghetto.

Thus, before one can even begin a discussion of fascism and the possibility of its emergence here, it is important to recognize that fascism in North America can only occur in a context always-already defined by two fundamental axes: Native elimination and anti-Black violence. Broadly we can say, though, that both the psychic and material life of white settler-colonial society is sutured together by anti-Native and anti-Black solidarity and violence. Further, these two axes also overlap and intersect with the economic hyperexploitation of the Global South by the North.

Settler Colonialism and Indigenous Elimination

As a configuration of settler-colonial power, one of the principal features of North American political society is the fundamental drive toward the elimination of Native peoples.[19] This is what the late theorist of settler colonialism Patrick Wolfe referred to as the *logic of elimination* when he described settler colonialism as an inclusive land-centered project that mobilizes a diverse assemblage of agencies with a program of destroying Native nations in order that they may be replaced.[20] Indeed, for there to even be a Canada or a United

States, Native people must disappear in order for the emergent settler order to claim rightful title over the continent. Further, the logic of elimination exists in a dialectic with an extensive project of settler self-Indigenization. While this process is most stark in regions such as Appalachia and Quebec,[21] it is pervasive across the continent.

Additionally, while much of these processes have taken place juridically, and are daily reinforced within the symbolic coding of the civil society of the settler nation, these processes are, and always have been, drenched in literal blood. To define Native life under the existence of settler colonialism is to see it defined through the multiple, converging "vectors of death" arrayed against us.[22] All of these processes can be summed up in what Nicolás Juárez refers to as the grammars of suffering of Native life: clearing and civilization.[23] The former are those processes which not only destroy Native bodies and lives in the meat grinder of settlement, but also evacuate Native sovereignty, not only from the spatial coordinates of the continent, but also from notions of linear, settler temporality as well. The Native is made into feral, savage flesh who not only is made nonsovereign at the moment of contact, but who, within the ontological ordering of the settler world, was never sovereign, and who has no possibility of ever being sovereign. The latter is what Juárez describes as the processes designed to "the process of extracting the savageness from the Savage," which, in tripartite fashion,

> transposes indigeneity from the Red body onto the Settler, commodifies the ontological resistance to whiteness found in indigenous lifeways to the point of no longer having any resistance to the ravishing of capitalist valuation and deracinates the Savage to the point of social death. A tri-operative process, the grammar of civilization hollows out the Indian, mines any cultural accouchements and values, and places them within the prerogative and definitions of value of the Settler.[24]

Further, while the violence of settler colonialism possesses structural and ontological qualities, it is also enacted in a quotidian fashion by the settler population itself. This point should be emphasized. There is an ongoing general tendency on the left in North America to evacuate what we might call "the everyday settler" of an agential role in both the historic expansion and the current enforcement of settler hegemony and its logics of elimination and dispossession. However, the individual settler and the collectives that they have formed and continue to form have a wide degree of agency in forwarding the settler-colonial project. As Wolfe puts it, the settler-colonial project's

> primary dynamic arose permissively in the absence of official regulation. This highly productive absence should caution us against viewing settler colonialism as a narrowly governmental project. Rather … settler invasion typically combines a shifting balance of official and unofficial strategies, initially to seize Native territory and subsequently to consolidate its expropriation. Rather than something separate from or running counter to the colonial state, the irregular activities of the frontier rabble constitute its principal means of expansion.[25]

Put even more succinctly by the Mohawk anthropologist Audra Simpson, "States do not always have to kill; its citizens can do that for it."[26]

Anti-Black Violence and the Continued Legacy of Slavery

Along with the clearing of the continent of Native peoples, many associated with fields as diverse as critical race theory, Black feminism, Black existentialism, racial capitalism, and Afro-pessimism have long noted how Blackness is equated with an inherent (and inheritable) status of enslavability and criminality and is marked for permanent exclusion from the social fold.[27] While, as sociologist Loïc Wacquant has pointed out, the particular manifestations of this process have evolved over time—from chattel slavery, to Jim Crow, to the ghetto, to the modern hyperghetto with its accompanying carceral continuum (the ghetto-to-prison-to-ghetto circuit)—the underlying logic has remained the same for the past several centuries.[28]

Under this regime, the Black body itself becomes a site of accumulation, nothing more than fungible property, which can then be subjected to gratuitous violence; that is, violence without the requirement of any previous transgression or reason within the social order. This is what Frank B. Wilderson III means when they note that the grammars of suffering for Black life are accumulation and fungibility.[29] The enduring legacy of the project to build an anti-Black world[30] is the direct line from enslavability through lynching, extrajudicial

executions of Black people, modern hyperincarceration, and the criminalization of Blackness. All of this is enforced and made allowable by
continuous, gratuitous anti-Black violence.

Taken together with the elimination of Native people, the nature
of Black oppression in North America, while long a topic of discussion, has been a lacuna within the analysis of the North American
anticapitalist and antifascist left. This is not to say that analysis of
the oppression of Black people has been absent from the left; to claim
that would be rather simply to lie. Rather, the point may be made
that, in light of ongoing critical Black thought over the past several
decades, large sectors of the left miss what is crucial. In large part
this is because the anticapitalist left, both Marxist and anarchist, and
setting aside for this discussion certain outliers, has focused on the
centrality of the wage and relations of economic exploitation. While
Marx, of course, made his remarks regarding the "rosy dawn" of capitalist accumulation and the role within that process of enslavement,
elimination, and colonization, his theory of "so-called primitive accumulation,"[31] it is something that remained undertheorized by those
who have come since.

On the one hand, as the Dene theorist Glen Sean Coulthard points
out, as have others such as Rosa Luxemburg and Peter Kropotkin, in
part this is because for Marx the process of so-called primitive accumulation quite literally *was* rather than *is*.[32] Thus, Marxists have, for
the most part, failed to consider how such direct processes of extra-
economic violence *continue* to structure the world that we live in. It
is apt to consider here then also Wolfe's statement that "invasion is a
structure, not an event."[33]

On the other hand, as noted by Chris Chen, drawing on the insights
of Frank Wilderson, the focus on the wage relation also obfuscates the
way in which these relations are ones of direct violence and terror.[34]
The point here, contrary to common left-wing objections, is not to
argue that class is unimportant or ceases to be central to any analysis
of the rule of capital, but rather to point out that these violences
form the position of an underthought within left-wing discourse. This
should be particularly important for us as not only are such violences
inseparable from the origins of capitalism, but on the terrain of settler
colonialism they fundamentally code society in toto, including the
possibility of fascist emergence.

What Is Fascism Then to Native and Black People?

So, what then does fascism mean to those colonized by and within a settler-colonial project? What does it mean if power is seized by fascists? What does it mean if Trump and others of a similar ilk are system-loyal right-wing nationalist populists who, while not themselves representative of the insurgent supremacist politics of a genuine fascist, still facilitate the rise of movements, theorists, organizers, and influences who do espouse that commitment?

More specifically, what does the potential rise of fascism in North America mean to those who have suffered, and who continue to suffer, the hells of genocide, slavery, land theft, convict leasing, forced marches, Jim Crow, popular lynchings, public police murders, corralling and containment in reservations and ghettos, mass incarceration numbering in the millions, residential schools, economic quarantine, and military occupation of their communities? What does fascist violence mean to those who already face structural processes that seek to drive them to alcoholism, drug abuse, suicide, mental illness, and abject poverty, and which, in collusion with the more blatant aspects of our colonial oppression, seek to remove them from the sphere of life? What does fascist violence mean to those who already live under such states identified by Jodi Byrd as "unlivable, ungrievable conditions within the state-sponsored economies of slow death and letting die."[35]

Put simply, from such a standpoint, for such people with whom we are concerned, it may seem that to equate the predicament with which we are currently faced with fascism is erroneous, if not outright outrageous, given that those colonized by a society such as this have already experienced—and what we continue to experience on a daily basis—the worst kinds of dehumanizing, eliminative, and gratuitous violence, seemingly without end. However, with that said, it would also be folly to ignore the potential within insurgent far-right movements for violence in excess of settler-colonial everyday techniques of governance.

This is seen most starkly in events such as the Quebec City mosque shootings. While the suspect, Alexandre Bissonnette, appeared to have acted alone, his attack occurred in a city where the local Soldiers of Odin chapter stated previously that it wished to launch patrols of Islamic neighborhoods. As noted by Stephen Pearson,[36] in excess of the right-wing nationalist populism of Trump, these forces, whether they explicitly engage in the kind of German Nazi fetishism associated with such individuals and organizations as Andrew Anglin of the *Daily Stormer* or the National Socialist Movement, something which many people continue to stereotype as the most publicly visible mark of fascism, they all desire for a *new frontier*, for *recolonization*, for territories, for a *white homeland*. In other words, they desire the fulfilment of the settler dream—which is a project, it is important to note, they think has failed—to be dreamt anew.

And in this we also return to distinction between a genuine fascist movement, which is a movement of insurgents, and the system-loyal right-wing nationalist populism of the Trump presidency. While Trump drove home the slogan "Make America Great Again," it was not fundamentally premised on the idea that the American project has failed. The modern fascist movement, however, embraces a politic that embodies a love for what the settler nation "might have been, if only." In this sense, it is a rhetoric and politic different from that of Trump, not only in form, but also in essence. Indeed, we must recognize that it exceeds the standard settler-colonial project of settler self-Indigenization (though, of course, they engage in this as well) by way of a complete embrace of the settler self, including all its horrors. It is a proclamation of reassertion: white power naked and with no smiling lies. It is white power that is not only unashamed, but proud.[37]

This issue folds back in on itself, though, because of the fact of the foundational anti-Native and anti-Black violence which always-already codes the settler-colonial political project. Such violence is ever omnipresent. The base liberalism of settler-colonial political life and civil society has always articulated a war over life and death with two fundamental aims: the elimination and dispossession of Native peoples and the subjugation and violent exclusion of Black peoples. In this regard, liberalism and fascism within the territories of North America can only be properly placed on the same ethical-political continuum of a much larger settler colonialism.

In considering this, the final inadequacies of the Dimitrovian formulation of fascism are exposed. And so, we return again to the question of colonial violence in the politic of fascism, because, in a faint echo of Bordiga, from the perspective of colonized life, whether the governing political logic of the colonial state is liberal or fascist, the fundamental warfare remains in place.[38] The principal threat then of fascism to colonized peoples is not that they would face movement *from* a state of having *not* been subjected to violence from every possible angle to one *where they would*, but rather that the pacing of the eliminative and accumulative logics of settler colonialism would be accelerated.

This means that finally the question being posed to colonized peoples by left-wing allies sounding the antifascist alarm is a choice between nonfascist, nominally "democratic" colonialism and fascist colonialism. Not only is this an impossible choice, but it is also a false one, because what is fascism in the face of grueling colonial violence without end? At best the choice lies between a slow ("democratic") and a fast (fascist) colonialism, in which the latter would most certainly accelerate underlying anti-Native and anti-Black logics.

Even placing antifascist theory and praxis within an explicitly Marxist or anarchist perspective is unable to offer a solution. This is because Native and Black ghosts, both living and dead, haunt the possibilities of socialism well. A socialism that does not, at the deepest possible level, engage with and seek to combat the fact of settler colonialism can only result in a reconfiguration of the arrangements of settler power into a new form, nominally in the hands of the working class. It would be yet another colonialism, a socialist colonialism. As such, the possibility of a newly socialized dispensation of settler colonialism could only be described as *national socialism* pure and simple.

Simply, one cannot choose between "democratic" colonialism, even a socialist one, and fascist colonialism, because the ultimate problem is the same: colonialism.

What Is Left to Be Done?

Where does this leave us? How do we tackle the question that remains: How do we fight fascism? I want to be clear on this, because while I have sought to excavate deep, systemic problems within general left-wing theory and praxis around the question of fascism, I do not want to understate the importance of continuing the struggle against fascism, whether political, social, cultural, or in simple everyday life.

So, what then? The answer is quite simple: antifascism without decolonization is meaningless. This is a basic truth that I believe should, and indeed must, be grasped by all who wish to resist the fascist wave. But what does decolonization look like? A program of decolonization was broken down into three succinct aspects by Eve Tuck and K. Wayne Yang,[39] to which I have made a few extensions and expansions of my own. Though not comprehensive, it gives us a point of opening. Rooted in a drive toward breaking what they refer to as the "settler-colonial Triad," it is as follows:

1. The rematriation of land and recognition of different ways of relating to land and the abolition of land as property; all the land, and not just symbolically.

2. The abolition of slavery in its contemporary forms, including the carceral continuum of anti-Blackness.

3. The dismantling of the imperialist metropole and an end to the parasitism of the Global North upon the Global South.

To put it another way, and to echo the revolutionary anticolonial leader of Guinea-Bissau and Cape Verde, Amílcar Cabral,[40] while we cannot be sure that the defeat of fascism (or capitalism) alone will be enough to bring about the decolonization of Turtle Island, we can be sure that the defeat of colonialism on this land will be the final defeat of even the possibility of fascism, much less fascism itself.

A better world awaits us all.

Antifascism against Machismo: Gender, Politics, and the Struggle against Fascism

Tammy Kovich (originally using the pseudonym Petronella Lee)

North Shore Counter-Info, 2019

Introduction—The Rising Tide of Fascism

> It's a naturalized, state-sanctioned, normalized and deepening fascism, whose waves of violence seem to measure the strides of a giant.... So here this question is key: What do we mean when we speak of feminism? Feminism cannot be defined at the surface level.... It's a struggle that is only renewed by restoring the historical memory of our women fighters, those who have been forgotten in the dustbins of revolutions.... We cannot think of a feminism, an anti-patriarchy, without anti-capitalism, without anti-fascism, without anti-racism and without class struggle.[1]

In spring 2017, a video of an antifascist being beaten at a counterdemonstration in Berkeley went viral. The video depicted counterprotester Louise Rosealma being punched in the face and knocked to the ground by white supremacist and founder of Identity Evropa Nathan Damigo. On social media, in major news articles, and within movement circles, the video was the subject of extensive commentary. This incident and the various reactions to it tell us much about our current moment. It reveals that we are living through a time where alt-right, white nationalist, and neo-nazi forces are gaining momentum and becoming emboldened. As the video circulated, the response of the far right laid bare the depth of their misogyny and vividly illustrated the extent to which patriarchal ideology is a key component of their politics. Louise was doxed and viciously denigrated online—her personal information including home address and phone number was widely distributed, and her career as a sex worker was publicized. She was called disgusting and a whore and was inundated with both rape and death threats. Photos of her being punched, as well as photos taken from her work in porn, became the backdrop for a plethora of memes appearing on both the internet and the streets. For example, on the streets of Berkeley, oversized posters appeared showing Louise's naked body beside Damigo's smiling face with the text "I'd hit that" written across.[2] Her attack and violence against women in general were promoted and celebrated. Others chimed in on the video, and their responses were equally revealing.

The reaction of liberal feminists was predictably disappointing and highlighted the many shortcomings of their political project. Some speculated about whether or not the attack would have happened under Hillary. Others framed Louise as a victim and in many cases as nonviolent. Narratives circulated claiming she was attacked while attempting to deescalate and prevent the violence of others, or was attacked unprovoked while peacefully protesting. A gendered pacifism was implied, and violence was presented as something done to Louise (as a woman), but not something that Louise (as a woman) could or would do. Hand in hand with these claims were calls for police involvement and the arrest of Damigo. In the style typical of carceral feminism, increased policing, criminalization, and incarceration were proposed as the appropriate response to the incident. Reactions coming from the left weren't much better and exposed the sexism ingrained in antifascist politics. Posts, photos, and memes covering the incident were highly patronizing and critiqued Damigo on the basis that he was a coward for hitting a woman (assumed to be weaker and less of a threat). Despite a long history of women putting their bodies on the line to fight fascism, physical confrontation was implicitly presented as the realm of men.

Even in supposedly progressive circles, the popular image of the antifascist is a male body, often a white male body that borrows heavily from the aesthetics of antifa movements in Europe. Based in a tacit denial of women's agency, conversations about Louise became a matter of identity (of her being a woman), rather than a matter of politics or activity. Last and certainly not least, this incident and the fact that it got so much attention speaks to the deep-seated racism that undergirds both the left and the right. Women get attacked all the time, white supremacists beat women all the time, and women of color disproportionately face the brunt of it. Louise's experience went viral and garnered such broad interest undoubtedly because she is a white, conventionally attractive cis woman.

The far right has been on the rise, and over the course of the last several years their ideas have been gaining traction. First at the level of grassroots politics, and now more and more at the level of institutional politics, far-right ideology has a notable foothold. It isn't only that far-right movements have grown, but further, that far-right ideas from the margins have seeped into the mainstream. The situation is bleak, but not hopeless. We have to know our enemy and we have a lot of work to do; however, many of the options presented to us can be found lacking. We're given the choice between a pacifying liberal feminism of "pussy hats" and "protective policing" or a reductive antifascism defined by machismo and sexism.

Against such a backdrop, this article seeks to examine the gendered dimensions of fascist movements and antifascist struggle, as well as to consider the possibilities for an antifascism rooted in revolutionary feminism. For the purpose of this article, I use the term *fascism/fascist* broadly to refer to a complicated and diverse phenomenon that includes a plethora of far-right groups, ideologies, and movements, including white nationalists, neo-nazis, ultra-patriots, the alternative right, identitarians, and traditionalists, among others.[3] The article is divided into three distinct yet interrelated parts, intended to cover the politics, practices, and histories of fascism, gender, and militant resistance. Part 1 explores the gender politics of fascism today, part 2 examines the history of women's participation in antifascist resistance, and part 3 concludes with a consideration of the challenges and prospects for developing an explicitly feminist antifascism.

Part 1—The Gender Politics of Fascism: Across the Spectrum of Fascist Sexisms

Fascism, then, is an exacerbation, a more militant extension, of the patriarchal relationships between men and women that have persisted for centuries. It is a worsening of the fantasies, the violence, the misshapen desires of the whole system of gender relationships that have long prevailed in European societies and those in the new world that are descended from them. Rather than a thing, which is categorically distinct from other social and political systems, fascism is a process, which can easily recur, and wherein we can see men, and groups of men, who have commenced the journey.[4]

Following the death of Heather Heyer in Charlottesville, an organizer of the Unite the Right event commented that Heather was a "fat, disgusting communist" and her death was "payback."[5] In a similar vein, comments were posted online celebrating her murder and calling her a "useless slut" on the grounds that "a 32-year-old woman without children is a burden on society and has no value."[6] Beyond being attacked for her antifascist politics, Heather was attacked for being a woman. At the 2018 Women's March in Seattle, posters exclaiming "Make Women Property Again" made an appearance. During this same time at a similar march in Providence, members of the white nationalist group Vanguard America showed up with a banner reading "Feminists Deserve the Rope."[7] On International Women's Day, an article on a popular neo-nazi website proposed that an "International Burn a Witch Day" and an "International Shame a THOT Day" be celebrated as "it's only fair that we reward AND punish."[8] Only a few years earlier at an International Women's Day celebration in Sweden, neo-nazis attacked the crowd and seriously injured five women.[9] More recently, in Santiago this past July [2018] a feminist march in support of free and legal abortion in Chile was attacked by the Social Patriotic Movement, a fascist group. Several hundred members of the group—infamous for describing feminists as animals and arguing for their sterilization—attempted to block the march and in the process covered the streets in animal blood, physically attacked the demonstrators, and stabbed three women.[10] Such examples are seemingly endless.

Incidents such as these are taking place with growing frequency, as those on the far right increasingly decry the role of feminism in propagating "Cultural Marxism" and destroying "Western Civilization."[11] Echoing the idea promoted in Nazi Germany that women's emancipation "would destroy the German race and lead to the introduction of Bolshevism," feminism (and women) are still the enemy.[12] Then as now, patriarchy is fundamental to fascism. Taking this assertion as a starting point, this section focuses on where and how the question of gender fits into fascism. To do so, I explore the rise of the alt-right, examine the differing perspectives on gender and sexuality found on the contemporary far right, and, finally, consider the role of the "white woman victim" trope in propping up white supremacy.

MRAs, "the Manosphere," and the Rise of the Alt-Right

The current resurgence and proliferation of far-right movements in North America has frequently been linked to the rise of the alt-right. Short for the alternative right, the alt-right can be understood as a loosely organized collection of ideological tendencies, groups, podcasts, websites, think tanks, and figureheads that have created a new breed of white supremacy. It takes inspiration from the identitarian ideas of the European New Right and is tied together by "a contempt for both liberal multiculturalism and mainstream conservatism"[13] and a "trenchant opposition to all socio-economic, cultural, and political propositions based on egalitarianism and collectivity."[14] While it is best known for its politics of white nationalism and antisemitism, politics of misogyny are also formative. Patriarchal ideology fundamentally shapes the alt-right, and misogyny is undoubtedly one of its central pillars.[15] The alt-right advocates not only for white supremacy, but more specifically for white male supremacy.[16] Sexism, rather than racism, is the gateway drug that has led many to join the alt-right. Romano explains: "The basic idea that 'women are getting too out of hand' is the patriarchal common denominator. And it aligns perfectly with male rage against 'social justice' activism, which in turn paves the way for white nationalism and white supremacy to gain a foothold."[17] To understand this dynamic, it is useful to look at some of the precursors to the alt-right movement.

Countless observers have linked the alt-right to the so-called "manosphere," arguing that the alt-right arose in part from and continues to be closely intertwined with it.[18] Emerging in and around the 2010s, the manosphere is most simply defined as "an online antifeminist male subculture that has grown rapidly in recent years, largely outside of traditional right-wing" circles.[19] It entails a disparate network of websites, internet forums, blogs, and videos that focus on men's issues, share a chauvinistic orientation, and are united by an emphasis on male victimhood. Those involved speak out against the tyranny of SJWs (social justice warriors) and PC (politically correct) culture and condemn feminism, along with other equity-seeking movements, as instigators of societal decline.

The manosphere first entered the public limelight in 2014 with the "Gamergate" controversy, in which a large online campaign was undertaken against a number of women who worked in the video game industry and had spoken out against sexism. Supporters of Gamergate claimed that the campaign was about defending free speech and fighting for journalistic ethics; however, in practice the campaign marked a blatant attack against women in the industry. In the words of one researcher: "This campaign took the diffuse online harassment of women and sharpened it into coordinated attacks against specific women, who faced streams of misogynistic invective, rape and death threats, and doxxing."[20] This event was a harbinger of things to come, foreshadowing the rise of the alt-right and offering a glimpse into the future.[21] Indeed, the tactics forged by Gamergaters, such as online harassment, targeted abuse, and doxing, were picked up by the alt-right and have become a common tool of the far right.[22]

The manosphere universe is composed of a variety of different and overlapping circles, including MRAs, PUAs, MGTOWs, and incels. The first of which, men's rights activists (MRAs), assert that the legal system, media, and society at large unfairly discriminate against men. They talk of misandry, argue that men (and not women) are oppressed and otherwise disadvantaged, and advocate on a number of different issues such as suicide, domestic abuse, and child custody. The metaphor of the "red pill" is central; it is evoked to describe one's awakening to the dark truths of our world, such as "feminism is toxic, sexism is fake, men have it harder than women, and everything the media teaches about relationships is a lie."[23] Paul Elam, founder of the influential MRA website A Voice for Men, has promoted beating women[24] and infamously commented, "There are a lot of women who get pummeled and pumped because they are stupid (and often arrogant) enough to walk through life with the equivalent of a I'M A STUPID, CONNIVING BITCH—PLEASE RAPE ME neon sign glowing above their empty little narcissistic heads."[25] Their vitriolic hatred of women is undeniable.

Moving to the next category, pickup artists (PUAs) focus on helping men learn how to pick up women and manipulate them into having sex. They talk about "the game," are obsessed with the notion of an alpha/beta male hierarchy, and advocate a predatory sexuality based on asserting dominance.[26] One of their best-known figures, Daryush Valizadeh, who writes under the name Roosh V on the PUA website Return of Kings, has argued for the legalization of rape on private property.[27] In May 2014, Elliot Rodger injured fourteen and killed six at the University of California, where he hoped to "slaughter every single spoiled, stuck-up blond slut." His manifesto stated among other things that PUA forums had confirmed his theories "about how wicked and degenerate women really are."[28] The garbage continues, and next we have men going their own way (MGTOWs). MGTOWs are basically male separatists—they choose to avoid relationships with women altogether as a "protest against a culture destroyed by feminism."[29] Websites like MGTOW.com advocate men's independence from women, argue for the importance of male preservation, and discuss the fight of modern man to protect his sovereignty. Their writings are "peppered with references to a 'bitch' who will cheat, leave, use you for your money" and discussions of how "women will either trick them into raising children that aren't theirs, get pregnant intentionally in order to trap them, or falsely accuse them of rape."[30] Essentially, women are viewed as degenerate and untrustworthy sluts programmed to ruin men's lives.

Finally, involuntary celibates (incels) are a subculture of primarily young men who identify as involuntarily celibate. Influenced by a sense of unfulfilled sexual entitlement, they speak of swallowing the "black pill" (basically a more nihilistic version of the "red pill") and conceive of their condition—defined by the absence of romantic or sexual relationships—as immutable. They have learned the dark truths of the world, but unlike other groups belonging to the manosphere who set out to challenge and change that reality, incels see their situation as fundamentally unchangeable. Their situation, and more broadly their life, is hopeless. Sparrow explains: "Incels understand biology as destiny. They regard themselves as losers in life's genetic lottery. They're self-described betas, condemned by their faces and physiques to perpetual isolation while women (whom they deride as 'Stacys') seek out the muscular, handsome males (known in the incel lexicon as 'Chads')."[31] While some amount of blame is placed on other men, incels primarily hold women responsible for their misery. As a result, they denigrate women online, discuss the best ways to punish them, and in some cases advocate mass rape, maiming, and murder.[32] In spring 2018, Alek Minassian drove a van into a crowd of pedestrians in Toronto, killing ten people, eight of whom were women.[33] Hours before the attack, he made a post on Facebook celebrating the "Incel Rebellion." In the aftermath of the incident, Jordan Peterson (psychology professor and darling of the right) insisted that such acts of violence are what happens when men do not have partners. To address this issue, Peterson and his followers suggest enforced monogamy as the rational solution to redistribute sex and prevent single men from committing mass violence.[34]

These various online communities and the different patriarchal orientations they represent have led many insecure, marginalized, and otherwise struggling men to broader fascistic politics. They function to create a culture united in the belief that white male masculinity is under attack and the status of men must be protected at all costs. In the context of changes in capitalism and the organization of labor, coupled with various cultural-political changes said to favor women and "minorities," more and more men are embracing the far right. Reflecting on this reality, Bromma attests:

> Millions of men are losing "their" women, and "their" jobs, and it's driving them crazy.... The anger of male dispossession fuels reactionary populist, fundamentalist and fascist trends in every part of the world. These right-wing movements are typically led by men of the middle classes, furious at losing the privileges they held under the previous male capitalist order. But millions of poor and de-classed men are joining in, forming a kind of united front of misogyny.[35]

In what has been referred to as the "MRA-to-white-nationalist pipeline," men concerned with the demise of patriarchal culture and their declining material conditions in general are seduced by white supremacist thought and xenophobic ideas. As a result, they come to embrace white nationalism and advocate the vision of "an ethnically cleansed future" that is "hostile to female power."[36] Misogyny plants the seeds of fascism and operates as a stepping stone to the larger movement.

Across the Spectrum of Fascist Sexisms

White supremacist movements have always been entangled with misogyny. As Spencer notes, their understanding of "racial hierarchy is intimately tied up with other social hierarchies."[37] That said, although virtually all fascists are antifeminist, their views on gender and sexuality are not monolithic. In the words of one researcher: "All far rightists promote male dominance, but the kinds of male dominance they promote differ enormously."[38] There is much disagreement and frequent debate on the topic within the far right. Speaking to the place of women, some argue for the complete banishment of women from the public sphere, while others argue that (white) women have a role to play in the white nationalist movement. On the topic of homosexuality, some argue for the extermination of all queers, while others argue for (and even celebrate) the inclusion of openly gay men. There is no consensus, and substantial tensions exist. Before mapping out some of these tensions, it is useful to note the points of agreement that unite the far right in regard to the question of gender.

Despite extensive disagreement, there are a number of general ideas on which almost all agree. Some of the most common include: (1) gender essentialism; (2) gender difference; and (3) gender hierarchy. First and foremost is the idea of essentialism, understood as "the view that anything, creature, or person has an essential nature that categorically defines it, materially and/or spiritually."[39] Gender, like race, is essential—it is a biologically determined fact that defines the essence of a person and shapes everything from ability to intelligence to motivations to vices to human worth. It is a universal category that is not socially constructed but is the unchangeable product of nature.[40] Based on this understanding, the second shared idea is that of binary gender and specific gender roles. Gender is conceptualized as binary and rigid. One is born either a man or a woman, and this inescapably dictates one's place in the world. Each gender comes with a unique set of innate traits and predetermined characteristics, and as such, men are suited to specific roles and women to others.

It is worth highlighting that this position translates to agreement on opposing the notion of gender as nonbinary, and thus agreement on opposing (and frequently enacting violence against) genderqueer and trans people. In general, the far right shares a revulsion for trans people, and a particular hostility for transwomen, who "are seen as men who reject their natural roles and privileges and 'voluntarily' become the hated other."[41] Lastly, the third shared idea concerns gender hierarchy and inequality. Gender is necessarily viewed as a hierarchy. It is not only that men and women are fundamentally different, but that men are fundamentally superior to women. Inequality between men and women is the product of biology and is a fact of nature—some genders, some races, some abilities, and some sexualities are simply inferior. In sum, gender is determined by nature, gender differences are immutable, and a clear gender hierarchy, where men dominate and rule, exists (and is desirable). These ideas are the basis on which the gender ideology of the far right is built.

Drawing on these guiding threads, a number of different orientations emerge. In his study of misogyny and right-wing movements, Lyons suggests that all far-right positions on gender draw on four ideological themes—patriarchal traditionalism, demographic nationalism, male bonding through warfare, and quasi feminism. As part of this framework, patriarchal traditionalism is most frequently formulated in religious terms, promotes rigid traditional gender roles, and emphasizes the nuclear family as the mechanism for male control over women. Demographic nationalism is primarily concerned with reproduction. It is often connected to the fear that a nation or race isn't reproducing fast enough and/or that the stock is declining in quality (e.g., through racial mixing) and declares that women's main duty to the nation or race "is to have lots of babies." Male bonding through warfare is also referred to as the cult of male comradeship, and it "emphasizes warfare (hardship, risk of death, shared acts of violence and killing) as the basis for deep emotional and spiritual ties between men."[42] Historically associated with war in the trenches, it is today more commonly associated with street fighting and militias. It sees physical confrontation as the most important aspect of life—the foundation on which everything is built. Activities related to physicality are thus prioritized and celebrated above all others. Since women are and will always be noncombatants, they have little to no value. Lastly, quasi feminism advocates specific rights for women, although not equality, and promotes "an expanded political role for women while accepting men's overall dominance."[43] Movements may draw heavily on a single theme or a mixture of several, and this may or may not change over time.

Along with these "warring visions of patriarchy,"[44] the approaches taken by far-right groups can be conceptualized as falling into one of two distinct categories—what I am going to refer to as patriarchal fascism and misogynistic fascism. In the category of patriarchal fascism, women are considered inferior, but useful, and they have a role or particular roles to play in the white supremacist movement.

This approach is exemplified by the infamous "Fourteen Words." Described as the most popular white supremacist slogan in the world, "Fourteen Words" is typically written in one of two variations: "We must secure the existence of our people and a future for white children" or "Because the beauty of the White Aryan woman must not perish from the earth."[45] In both versions women are valued—as mothers, as symbols of beauty, and as protectors of the future.

This orientation has a long legacy. Throughout the 1920s, the Ku Klux Klan actively recruited women and combined white supremacy with a "specific, gendered notion of the preservation of family life and women's rights." They criticized inequality among whites and promoted the "special mission of Klanswomen" to protect "pure womanhood" and the home.[46] In Germany, the Nazi Party had a women's wing—the National Socialist Women's League. According to Nazi ideology, women belonged to three areas of activity: "Kinder, Küche, Kirche" (children, kitchen, and church). Women's roles were highly restricted; however, they were also highly regarded. Mothers were seen as fighting a battle for the nation and were "accorded with the same honourable status as the soldier."[47]

Turning to our contemporary moment, this legacy continues. Coming to prominence in the 1980s, the neo-nazi group White Aryan Resistance created the affiliate group Aryan Women's League. It denounced the feminist movement as a Jewish conspiracy while arguing that women had subordinate but complementary roles to play in the race war.[48] The largest neo-nazi organization in the United States, the National Socialist Movement, has a specific Women's Division.[49] Another example, Women for Aryan Unity, was founded in the 1990s and has chapters on several continents. They call for the reinvention of feminism "within the parameters of Race and Revolution" and urge women to develop both domestic and survivalist skills in order to take care of home life and be ready to take up arms if their men require it.[50] Self-proclaimed Western chauvinists, the Proud Boys have as one of their central tenets "venerate the housewife." They argue that "women are equal but different," interpreted to mean men go to work and women stay at home.[51] Women cannot join the Proud Boys; however, they can join the Proud Boys' Girls—a supporting group composed of "the wives, girlfriends, and cheerleaders" of the Proud Boys.[52]

While the above examples are far from progressive, they are also far from being the worst. Over the course of the last decade, the far right's engagement with "the woman question" has taken an even darker turn. Well-known commentator on the manosphere David Futrelle elaborates:

> Like many traditionalists, Hitler and his fellow Nazis tempered their misogyny—or at least tried to make it seem more palatable—with praise for the supposed purity and womanly honor of Aryan women who fit themselves neatly into their restricted roles. Today's neo-Nazis, or at least those who've come to Nazism through 4chan and the meme wars of the alt-right, have a much darker view of women, one influenced more by bitter misogyny of "Red Pill" pickup artists and Men Going Their Own Way than by sentimental fantasies of "Kinder, Küche, Kirche."[53]

Going beyond traditional claims about the sanctity of the family and natural gender roles, many contemporary groups influenced by the alt-right promote an intensely misogynistic ideology that straight-up hates women. They have largely abandoned the idea that "women have important, dignified roles to play as mothers and homemakers," to instead promote the message that "women as a group are contemptible, pathetic creatures not worthy of respect."[54] For instance, men's rights activist and white nationalist F. Roger Devlin refers to women as the new "white man's burden," arguing that traditional visions of marriage and the family "did not oppress women enough" and should be replaced with "a vision of absolute servility."[55] This is the realm of misogynistic fascism—women are not only inferior, but useless, and they have little to no role to play in the white nationalist movement. Examples of this orientation are terrifyingly ample.

Renowned white supremacist website the *Daily Stormer* has banned women from contributing to the site, virulently argues against their inclusion in anything, and has come into conflict with women associated with the older white supremacist website Stormfront.[56] At several rallies in the last year, crowds of white nationalists could be found chanting "white sharia now."[57] Promoted by some on the far right, the idea of "white sharia" proposes that in a future white ethnostate "the sexuality, reproduction, daily life, and right to consent of White women should be controlled by White men."[58] In a video promoting the idea, one proponent asserts: "Under 'white sharia' our women will no longer be permitted to live their lives as sluts.... And you won't have any career women invading your workplace either. Nope. Under 'white sharia' our women won't even be able to leave the home without being escorted by a male family member."[59] Many defenders of the concept also advocate making abortions forbidden for white women and mandatory for women of color.[60] Equally vile, members of the (now-defunct) militant Atomwaffen Division encouraged the rape of white women as a tool to force the birth of more white babies[61] and promoted the rape of nonwhite women as a tool to terrorize by forcing "them to carry around the spawn of their master and enemy."[62] Beyond such obvious suspects, this particular orientation to women in far-right politics takes some less expected turns.

Under the umbrella of misogynist fascism, there exists a strain specifically defined by a queer misogyny. This subsection, referred to by Kirchick as "homofascism," is composed of aggressively sexist and generally hypermasculine gay men who literally have no use for women.[63] As mentioned earlier, the far right's position on sexuality is somewhat complicated. On the one hand, LGBTQ rights are seen as a sign of social degeneration, Jewish influence, and an attack on white society. In response, it is not uncommon to see "open calls for the expulsion or violent eradication of LGBT+ people."[64] On the other hand, when speaking specifically of the "homosexual question," things are much less clear cut. Nazi Germany rounded up and slaughtered homosexuals by the tens of thousands, yet it is also common knowledge that there were gay Nazis, the most famous being Ernst Röhm, a high-ranking official and head of the Nazi Party's paramilitary force (the SA). Along with Hitler, Röhm was a "founding father of Nazism,"[65] and his particular brand of fascism "was identical to the Nazi Party's ideology in almost all respects, save on questions of male-male eroticism." Under Röhm, homosexuality was highly regarded in the SA, where "they promoted an aggressive, hypermasculine form of homosexuality, condemning 'hysterical women of both sexes' in reference to feminine gay men." They celebrated ancient warrior cults and frequently referenced the Greek tradition of sending gay soldiers, who were believed to be the most fierce fighters, into battle.[66] In the 1980s, an explicitly gay neo-nazi skinhead movement emerged in the UK.[67] In the late 1990s, the American Resistance Corps (ARC) was founded in North America with the goal of uniting gay and straight skinheads to create "a new era of tolerance and compassion between racist heterosexuals and homosexuals in their war against non-whites."[68]

Looking to our current period, some on the far right simply do not care about male sexuality one way or another. For instance, Greg Johnson, editor-in-chief of the influential Counter-Currents Publishing, argues: "White Nationalism is for the interests of whites and against the interests of our racial enemies. Period. Anything else is beside the point." Similarly, the infamous alt-right figurehead Richard Spencer insists that homosexuality is a nonissue—something that has been part of European societies for millennia and isn't "something to get worked up about."[69] Against this backdrop, several openly gay figures and the ideas they promote have gained some traction on the far right. A featured writer on several alt-right websites and author of a number of books, James J. O'Meara is best known for his book *The Homo and the Negro*,[70] where he makes the argument "that gay white men represent the best of what Western culture has to offer because of their 'intelligence' and 'beauty,' and that 'Negroes' represent the worst, being incapable of achievement."[71] He insists that homosexuality is essential to Western civilization and promotes gay participation in fascist movements.[72] O'Meara and others like him advocate a future in line with the classic Aryan fantasy of the Männerbund. Associated with male warrior tribes and homoeroticism, the concept celebrates the unique bonds between men and speaks to a social order where elite bands of men rule.[73] Male dominance is central, and the fundamental building block of society isn't the church or family, but close-knit groups of organized men.

Arguably the most infamous of this camp, self-described "anarcho-fascist" Jack Donovan promotes a blend of white nationalism, gang masculinity, and androphilia (love or sex between masculine men). He calls for the establishment of a tribal order called "The Brotherhood"—an order that is composed of men who swear an oath to each other and is based on "the way of the gang," understood as a life centered "on fighting, hierarchy, and drawing the perimeter against outsiders."[74] Utilizing violence, gangs of men are to create decentralized "homelands/autonomous zones" marked by the exclusion of women from public life.[75] Donovan is a prominent member of the neofascist cadre organization the Wolves of Vinland. Inspired by the theories of the late Italian philosopher Julius Evola, the group promotes a particularly antipopulist and antiwoman take on fascism. They prioritize physical fitness and combat training and argue that the solution to Western decline is "a return of heroic masculine warrior-kings."[76] All of these groups and figures advocate a politics defined by extreme hypermasculinity based in an almost pathological veneration of "manliness" and a disdain for femininity. They reject gay culture for its association with decadence and hate effeminate men as much as they hate women.

White Supremacy, Complicity, and the Legacy of Savior Politics

Beyond understanding the contemporary far right's varying positions on women, it is furthermore valuable to consider the ways in which women, and white women in particular, are used as a generic symbol to promote and further white supremacy. Hand in hand with the far right's condemnation of feminism comes the condemnation of immigration and a particular disdain for Black and Indigenous women. Combined, these represent the core dangers threatening Western civilization and white nationhood. In a somewhat contradictory dynamic, as groups advocate "putting women in their place," they simultaneously express concern for women's safety from supposedly dangerous Black and Brown men. For example, it is common for anti-immigrant arguments to be framed in terms of the threat migrant men—who are discussed as violent and/or as rapists—pose to "their women." Founded in Finland and now with chapters across Europe and North America, the far-right vigilante group Soldiers of Odin exists for the avowed purpose of conducting street patrols to keep women safe from refugees with a propensity to rape.[77] Since taking over the White House, Donald Trump has frequently invoked the threat of "Mexico sending rapists" to justify increased border security and stricter immigration policy.[78] Such claims are not unique to discussions of migrant men alone, but pop up frequently in discussions of homegrown nonwhite men as well. In 2015, when white supremacist Dylann Roof opened fire and massacred nine Black churchgoers at a prayer service in Charleston, he reportedly exclaimed: "You rape our women, and you're taking over our country, and you have to go."[79] Calls to defend (white) women from the threat of the barbaric "other" play a critical role in upholding the white supremacist project.

The image of the "white woman victim" who must be protected is frequently employed by reactionary forces to whip up hysteria and justify vehemently racist actions. This classic image "implicitly calls out to white men to defend 'their women' and their nation, indeed, whiteness itself."[80] White women's bodies—understood as central to the reproduction of race and nation—become symbols to be fought for, and these symbols become powerful tools of propaganda.

Discourses of safety and appeals to patriarchal ideals of womanhood are invoked to construct the figure of the vulnerable (white) woman under attack from the dangerous (racialized) other. This dynamic functions to produce and reproduce particular race and gender formations, as well as to establish and enforce a particular vision of white nationhood. As Keskinen notes: "Gender and sexuality have not only been by-products of colonial and racial encounters, but essential for their (re)structuring."[81] The trope of the "barbaric dark-skinned rapist"—of Black and Brown men as sexual predators who target white women—has been a key tool in upholding racial hierarchies and carrying out white supremacist politics. From the colonization of North America to lynchings in the United States to xenophobic attacks in Europe and much else, calls to defend women have been used to incite racialized violence and establish incredibly racist policy. A brief look into this history is telling.

The stereotype of "the Black brute" and the threat of "the Black rapist" are fundamental to the history of white supremacy in America. The idea of the Black brute was drawn on to contribute to justifications for slavery, while the myth of the Black rapist was "a political invention" cultivated to promote a "strategy of racist terror" to keep "the Negro" in check following emancipation. The myth of the Black rapist, complemented by the continued rape of Black women, helped to assure the ongoing domination and exploitation of Black people. In the aftermath of the Civil War, the claim that Black men were sexual predators was used as pretext for murder and mob violence. Lynching came to be rationalized "as a method to avenge Black men's assaults on white Southern womanhood."[82] According to Angela Davis, the myth functioned to both demonize Black men and thus legitimize contempt for them, as well as to exalt white men and excuse their brutality. She explains: "In a society where male supremacy was all-pervasive, men who were motivated by their duty to defend their women could be excused of any excesses they might commit. That their motive was sublime was able justification for the resulting barbarities." It is worth noting that as the myth gained traction, "former proponents of Black equality became increasingly afraid to associate themselves with Black people's struggle for liberation," and by the end of the nineteenth century many white women, including leading suffragists, "publicly vilified Black men for their alleged attacks on white women."[83] There is a long legacy of white women's complicity in propping up racist narratives that have very real consequences, and this is not just a matter of the distant past.

At first glance, calls for safety—things like calls for safe spaces or safe neighborhoods—sound harmless enough. Almost everyone desires to feel safe. However, within the context of a society defined by racial domination (institutional and interpersonal racism), calls for safety often draw on and act to perpetuate racist tropes (e.g., "the Black thug," "the dangerous Black man," etc.) and frequently go hand in hand with actions and/or policies that enact racialized violence. Wang elaborates:

> When considering safety, we fail to ask the critical questions about the co-constitutive relationship between safety and violence. We need to consider the extent to which racial violence is the unspoken and necessary underside of security, particularly white security. Safety requires the removal and containment of people deemed to be threats. White civil society has a psychic investment in the erasure and abjection of bodies that they project hostile feelings onto, which allows them peace of mind amidst the state of perpetual violence.[84]

Looking at the history of the feminist movement against sexual violence, Wang observes that calls for the safety of women were answered with the expansion of a racialized penal state. Drawing on the age-old trope of the Black male rapist, appeals to ensure women's safety acted to sanction the expansion of the police and the prison system as the state came to be presented and positioned as the protector of women (almost always conceptualized as white women).

Through the process of raising awareness about violence and fighting for aggressive prosecution of sex crimes, feminists inadvertently aided in the creation of a tough-on-crime model of policing and punishment that reflects the racism of the society from which it came—a society in which the Black male is almost always conceived of as a threat.

Similar to the function of the anti-Black myths in North American history, anti-Indigenous tropes have played an equally influential role. The convergence of racialized rape narratives and white nation-building is also integral to the history of colonization and Indigenous genocide in North America. Ideas of "the savage Indian" and "Native sexual perversion" were essential to the colonial imagination.[85] These myths, combined with notions of European superiority and the righteousness of "civilizing missions," were used to justify war against Indigenous nations, the theft of Native land and resources, and the decimation of Native communities. Popular captivity narratives spread stories about the abduction and barbaric treatment of white women by violent, lust-driven Native men. These stories, along with other writings, helped to solidify the image of Native men as wanton savages and promote the idea that "both Native and white women have to be protected from Indian men."[86] In addition to providing a rationale for appropriation and assimilation, Nagel notes that stories of "Indian depredations and savagery also became a means of justifying white misbehavior and atrocities and provided opportunities for white self-aggrandizement."[87]

More recently, the trope of "the immigrant rapist," "the barbaric refugee," and "the Muslim extremist" have been central to cries to close the borders and save the (white) nation. Examining the refugee crisis in Europe, Caitlin Carroll observes that those on the right have drawn on the myth of the immigrant rapist "to call for the closing of the borders as a way to protect white, European women against the dangerous, brown men who are coming to Europe seeking asylum."[88] In addition to impacting state policy, such myths produce grassroots backlash. Last year, Italian and Polish neo-nazi groups announced that they were joining forces to launch patrols of European beaches in order to "protect women and children from migrants" in the face of a "muslim invasion."[89] The Quebec-based Islamophobic group La Meute claimed it "was founded for the protection of our women from religious fundamentalism," and before it imploded in 2019, it repeatedly held rallies at the US-Canada border and elsewhere, protesting against "illegal refugees."[90] Calls to protect white women are used to justify everything from border policy to vigilante violence to the formation of white-nationalist paramilitary organizations.

Following a related logic, in their fight against migrants (particularly Muslims) some on the right have begun to publicly advocate for the safety of LGBTQ people. Calls to protect queers from the threat of Islamic extremists/gay-hating Muslims have been employed in an attempt to spread anti-immigrant sentiment and appeal to a different demographic. Shortly after the Pulse nightclub shooting in Orlando, white nationalist and explicit homophobe Butch Leghorn proposed taking advantage of the event. Writing on the alt-right website the Right Stuff, Leghorn argued: "This shooting is a very valuable wedge issue.... We simply need to hammer this issue.... Drive this wedge. Smash their coalition. Make it cool to be anti-Muslim because Liberalism."[91] Over the past year, "gay pride" marches that go almost exclusively through Muslim neighborhoods have been organized by fascists in France, Sweden, and the UK.[92] Their calls to protect women, just like their calls to protect LGBTQ people, are of course disingenuous. They hate women and queers, but calls for their protection are a politically useful mechanism. Under these circumstances, Faye aptly notes that the task of feminist and queer liberation "cannot be merely sexual or gendered, but it must also be sharply critical of its alignment with whiteness as a system of persecution."[93] This is not just a matter of being aware of opportunistic white nationalists duplicitously using calls for LGBTQ safety to further their vile agenda, but also of critically evaluating the ways in which queer movements themselves buttress and reinforce white supremacy.

In regard to this responsibility, it is worth keeping in mind that the LGBTQ movement, like the feminist movement, has a history of pushing for safety in a manner that has had violent consequences for others. Examining the history of the LGBTQ movement in the United States, Hanhardt observes that appeals to safety have had racialized consequences. Since the 1970s, activist responses to anti-LGBTQ violence have taken one of two forms: the establishment of protected gay territories and the identification of anti-LGBTQ violence as a criminal category. Rooted in the implicit assumption that white gays need to be protected from violent (often read as Black) criminals, these two approaches have led to gentrification and mass incarceration—both of which disproportionally impact and devastate Black communities. Hanhardt explains:

> Messy distinctions between crime and violence, safety and justice, underscore the flexibility of concepts such as risk and their centrality to the politics of development. Here risk is simultaneously the value of speculative capital (real estate) and the justification for crime control (bad neighborhoods), the ever-present threat to gay autonomy (violence), and the symptom of irresponsibility (the designation "at risk").[94]

Calls for the creation of safe spaces came to be interpreted as calls for state violence in the form of criminalization and privatization, and through this process, became inextricably linked to spatial development and crime control strategies that play out along race and class lines.

There's a lot that needs to be challenged and much organizing to be done, and knowing the nuanced ins and outs of the forces we face is advantageous. Given that misogyny is a foundational element of contemporary far-right politics, it is valuable to know its specific role and function. This, however, is only one piece of the puzzle, and it is useful to consider other things. As we strive to challenge the rise of fascism, it is worth looking back to the antifascist resistance that came before us.

Part 2—Against Heroes: An Incomplete History of Women's Antifascist Resistance

> The past does not pass; the dead are not dead, for they continue to move us today.... These ghosts have not risen simply to be put to rest, but to speak in the manner for which they were killed; some of them must be battled anew in our hearts.[95]

For as long as there has been fascism, there has been antifascist resistance, and from its origins onward to our present moment, women and queers have been active participants. However, these histories are routinely glossed over, and while there has been much talk of our "grandfather's antifascism" there is much less said about the antifascism of our grandmothers. Speaking to the politics of antifascist history, Richet notes: "Most of the sources of the history of antifascism deal with the political space occupied by men. This is the case of the fascist sources built on the assumption that women could not be autonomous political subjects. It is also the case of the sources collected by the antifascist groups whose male leadership shared similar assumptions."[96] This has an impact on antifascism in our present moment. When people think about or hear the term *antifascist*, the image most likely to pop into their head is not CeCe McDonald or an armed partisan woman, but a generic antiracist skinhead dude or perhaps the antifascist man as depicted in classic propaganda posters with rifle, sickle, and hammer in hand.[97] Against such trends, this section considers the gendering of history and explores women's participation in antifascist resistance during the first half of the twentieth century. The intention is not to provide an exhaustive account, but to provide a snapshot of a history too frequently forgotten and, in the process, to challenge the dominant image of the antifascist hero. To the extent to which such an image holds a certain pervasiveness, it acts only to hinder actions and limit possibilities.

Gender, Memory, and the Stories We Tell

The stories and, more importantly, the histories we tell matter—they frame events, contextualize theory, and situate agential subjects. Antifascism and antifascist history are not gender neutral, or race or class neutral for that matter. Gender plays a huge role in how we think about antifascism and how its history is commonly told. The history of antifascist struggle is depicted as the history of great moments and even greater men. It is a history of the heroic and necessarily male subjects who dared to fight back against the behemoth of fascism. If women or queers do appear in these histories, they are predominantly presented as secondary characters—as minor participants, romantic partners, or bystanders. In the realm of revolutionary history, there is a long legacy of women's activities being dismissed as: (a) personal/private/home matters (e.g., bread riots; various feminist campaigns, and even the march that sparked the Russian Revolution, etc., are framed as home issues, not disciplined politics) or (b) an irrational/emotional matter (e.g., they act from eruptions of emotions, and thus are inclined to spontaneity but not organized politics). Women's involvement in explicitly political movements in the public sphere, as well as the day-to-day support, reproductive, and behind-the-scenes work they perform in the private sphere, is simply disregarded.[98]

Specific figures and activities are glorified and romanticized, while others are neglected and downplayed.

This common approach to history leads to the erasure of particular experiences, the loss of whole histories, and, beyond that, a skewed and inaccurate picture. The creation and dissemination of accounts of radical history shape our collective political imagination and influence the events and actions thought to be desirable (and even possible). They convey specific ideas about who counts as history, what counts as history, and by default, what counts as political work and who can be a political actor. In sum, histories frequently present a hierarchy of who and what matters, and when the accounts are particularly gendered (and thus exclusionary) they stand in the way of challenging a fascist threat steeped in misogyny. As a result, it is important to look to the margins of history and seek out alternative accounts.

Women against Fascism
As already mentioned, women, femmes, and queers have been active participants in antifascist struggles for as long as there has been fascism. Their involvement is as diverse as it is extensive, and any attempt at a comprehensive telling is beyond the scope of this piece of writing. With this in mind, I take a narrow and inevitably limited approach to presenting antifascist history. While the histories of antifascist women and queers frequently dovetail, they are also different things, and it would be impossible to cover both in this text. The vibrant legacy of queers against fascism is a history in its own right.[99] Thus, this section focuses exclusively on women. It draws on a small sampling of case studies from Europe, Africa, and North America to examine women's resistance to the rise of fascism following the First World War. Contrary to popular notions, women were involved in all aspects of the historical fight against fascism. Ingrid Strobl, feminist historian and former political prisoner associated with the women's guerrilla group Rote Zora, elaborates: "They were activists in urban brigades, the ghetto underground, and partisan units.... They organized underground movements and ghetto uprisings; they were political cadres and military commanders of groups."[100] To explore this further, it is instructive to look at resistance in Ethiopia, Spain, and Yugoslavia.

As of 1934, Ethiopia was one of just two African countries that had not been colonized by Europe.[101] Unfortunately, this was not to last, and in October 1935 Mussolini's forces invaded Ethiopia. After capturing the capital the following year, Mussolini declared Ethiopia part of the Italian Empire, ushering in a period of fascist occupation. Resistance to the occupation, to fascism and to colonialism, commenced immediately and lasted until Italy was expelled in 1941. From the beginning, women participated in the struggle in large numbers and fulfilled many critical roles. Reflecting on this period, historian Aregawi Berhe contends that women's participation was crucial, arguing that while it is difficult to assess their military contribution, "their supplementary support activities, spying and sabotage actions in some instances were decisive." During the occupation, the Ethiopian Women's Volunteer Service Association (EWVSA) was turned into "a clandestine movement of resistance." Women who were part of the association engaged in a diversity of activities, ranging from supplying those fighting in the field with clothes, food, bandages, and ammunition to providing shelter, forging important documents, producing propaganda, and gathering intelligence.[102] Some women became camp-followers, women who traveled to the front and took care of maintaining weapons, as well as feeding and providing medical care to those engaged in fighting.[103]

Other women fraternized with Italian soldiers and artfully engaged in deception to further the struggle. Women took Italian soldiers, including high-ranking officers, as lovers to build a false sense of trust and gain access to information and materials. With a relationship established, women took the opportunity to steal arms, and it was not uncommon for these women to kill their lovers in order to do so.[104] Such relationships were used as a tool of sabotage as well: after pretending to be a defector and declaring their allegiance to fascism, women would supply their lover with false information and point the Italians in the wrong direction. Women took Italian lovers, found employment as domestic servants, or ran drinking houses to gather intelligence and collect sensitive information, such as the location of arms and ammunition depots or plans for upcoming offensives.[105]

In addition to these roles, women were also actively involved in the military aspect of the struggle. Some women became guerrilla fighters and fought on the battlefield, and some even led fighters and planned military operations. Although wars in Ethiopia were predominantly fought by men, women were not entirely excluded from warfare.[106] For instance, in circumstances where a wife or daughter—in the absence of a male successor—inherited a family's land and weapons, "they were expected to perform the duties attached to the land and weapons, whether or not the duty was military or administrative."[107] Thus, it was not unheard of for women to play leading military roles. In this context, a handful of women from prominent families led their own armies, and many more from all rungs of society took up arms and joined the guerrilla war.[108]

The antifascist/anticolonial struggle in Ethiopia caused ripples far beyond its borders. In the United States, Mussolini's invasion sparked protests, riots, and solidarity campaigns throughout the country. Massive demonstrations took place in New York and Chicago, street fights broke out between Black antifascists and Italian profascists, pickets were held outside of the Italian consulate, leaflets were distributed, dockworkers refused to load Italian ships, and fundraising drives were organized. Black Communists set up the Joint Committee for the Defense of Ethiopia and along with other Pan-African groups spearheaded these activities. Crabapple notes, "black Americans recognized the dangers of Fascism abroad early.... They saw Mussolini's Blackshirts reflected in the white hoods of the Klan, and Hitler's Jew-baiting mirrored by the systemic violence of Jim Crow."[109]

Women in the American Communist Party spoke out against the threat fascism posed to women's rights and with the invasion of Ethiopia sought to develop a cross-racial alliance to build class solidarity against fascism, and with varying degrees of success, they worked with Black organizations to build support for Ethiopia.[110] In Britain, Black rights and anticolonial activists formed the International African Friends of Abyssinia (IAFA) to promote resistance to fascism in Ethiopia.[111] Black radicals in America, Britain, and elsewhere drew connections between the fight for Ethiopia and their own experiences, as well as putting forth analyses of antifascism rooted in Black internationalism, anticolonialism, and anti-imperialism.[112] Several members of the Abraham Lincoln Brigade came to Spain as a result of their activism in support of Ethiopia. For example, Salaria Kea—the only Black woman in the brigade—fundraised for Ethiopian hospitals, and when her application to join the Ethiopian army was rejected she sailed for Spain.[113]

In July 1936, General Francisco Franco initiated a military rebellion against Spain's Republican government. The instigators anticipated a swift victory. However, the coup d'état was met with a spontaneous uprising, and Spain was thrown into civil war. In many of the besieged cities, everyday civilians raided local armories, requisitioned weapons, and took up arms to fight against the fascists. During these early days of popular resistance, women took part in the storming of barracks to obtain weapons, built barricades, and participated in armed street fighting.[114] Beyond a fight against fascism, the Spanish Civil War was also a highly contested fight for revolution. Anarchists and dissident Marxists sought to combine the antifascist fight with the fight for broader revolutionary change, while Communists and Socialists rejected such positions, arguing for the necessity of engaging in the war exclusively in terms of antifascism. This conflict led to what Nash refers to as a "civil war within the civil war."[115] In this context, women essentially found themselves in a struggle on three fronts—fighting against fascism, fighting to push antifascist forces toward a revolutionary orientation, and then, finally, fighting to make revolutionary forces take gender liberation seriously. In response, women's organizations were founded to aid the antifascist cause while promoting ideas of revolutionary change that included women's emancipation.

Founded a few short months before the official outbreak of the Civil War, Mujeres Libres (Free Women) was an anarchist organization that sought to contest women's subordination and mobilize women to take part in the struggle against fascism. Beginning with just a few hundred members, its numbers soared during the war, eventually reaching a membership ranging from twenty thousand to sixty thousand women.[116] Members of the organization were active in all aspects of the Civil War, from fighting on the front lines, as well as aiding the wounded, to maintaining collective kitchens and organizing schools for refugees and engaging in political debate.

Central to Mujeres Libres, and what made them unique, was an emphasis on organizational autonomy. The founding members of Mujeres Libres were all militants in the broader anarcho-syndicalist movement who "found the existing organizations of that movement inadequate to address the specific problems confronting them as women, whether in the movement itself or in the larger society."[117]

The organization was built on the belief that women needed separate organizations to address their specific needs and, ultimately, to build their capacities to intervene and shape the political landscape. To this end, the organization took on a variety of initiatives, including: the publication of a regular newspaper aimed at political consciousness-raising; the running of classes to overcome illiteracy; the facilitation of discussion groups to challenge ignorance; the opening of women's health clinics; and the offering of industrial and commercial apprenticeships.[118] Political instruction and basic education sought to help in addressing women's cultural and sexual subordination, and professional training aimed to aid women in their economic subordination by increasing employment opportunities.

In addition to challenging women's subordination, the organization's initiatives were aimed at recruiting women into the antifascist movement and creating a conscious force of women who were prepared for the "social revolution." To build this force, the organization emphasized two interrelated goals and corresponding programs: *capacitación* and *captación*. The first, capacitación, was concerned with "preparing women for revolutionary engagement." Related to the educational and consciousness-raising activities outlined above, capacitación focused on the empowerment of women such that they would feel confident in their abilities, recognize their potential, and ultimately conceptualize "themselves as competent historical actors." This emphasis on personal development, individual growth, and building capacity was the result of conceptualizing struggle not only in quantitative terms, but also in qualitative ones. Moving to the second program, captación was concerned with "actively incorporating them [women] into the libertarian movement."[119] In practice, this entailed working to increase women's participation in other, larger revolutionary organizations. As Mujeres Libres worked with women to address their everyday material needs, they created the conditions necessary to bring more of them into the fold of revolutionary politics.

By spring 1941, the Kingdom of Yugoslavia was occupied and partitioned off by Axis forces. A portion of the country was occupied by German troops, other areas were occupied by Bulgarian, Hungarian, and Italian troops, and Croatia was established as a Nazi puppet state ruled by a local fascist militia. In response, a Communist-led resistance movement emerged and the National Liberation Army (NLA) was formed.[120] From the outset and continuing for the duration of the conflict, women played a huge part in the partisan resistance movement. In the words of one scholar: "The mass participation of women in the communist-led Yugoslav Partisan resistance is one of the most remarkable phenomena of the Second World War."[121] Similarly, Bonfiglioli describes women's contribution as "unprecedented in Europe," explaining that "out of a population of sixteen million ... [official records] report one hundred thousand women fighting as partisans, and two million participating in various ways to support the National Liberation Movement. It has been calculated that approximately twenty-five thousand women died in battle, and some two thousand women attained officer's rank."[122]

While noteworthy, women's contribution as fighters is only one part of a much bigger picture. Women participated in the antifascist struggle in a variety of different ways. Acting autonomously, women led food riots in the face of the widespread hunger caused by the country's food stock being exported to the Third Reich.[123] Otherwise disconnected, peasant women passed information to partisans on enemy troop movements and spies, as well as harvesting crops for neighbors who were at the front or in prison. In addition to taking care of important agricultural work, many of these women also tended to wounded partisan soldiers, took care of orphans, and housed those on the run.[124] As part of organizations and collectives officially connected to the resistance movement, women took on many more roles still.

Shortly after the formation of the National Liberation Army, the Antifascist Front of Women (AFZ) was established. A specifically women's organization, the AFZ was founded as an organ of the Yugoslav Communist Party and was charged with the twofold mission of mobilizing "large masses of women in the struggle against the German occupation and in support of the combat and noncombat activities of the Liberation Movement."[125] Antifascist women's committees were formed in towns, villages, and cities across the country, and members canvassed both liberated and nonliberated territories to recruit new women into the organization.[126] Once members, the work taken on by the women was all-encompassing and ranged from typical gendered tasks, such as sewing and laundry, to espionage and sabotage. The women knitted socks and sweaters, sewed uniforms, and made shoes for the troops, as well as mended and laundered their clothes. They collected food, clothing, medical supplies, money, arms, and ammunition.[127] They prepared hideouts for partisans on the run, "looked after the families of the arrested and organized prison escapes." Women acted as couriers, transporting important messages, outlawed literature, attack orders, weapons, and explosives throughout the country. They printed underground newspapers, published and distributed clandestine antifascist publications, and ran illegal radio stations. They dug up streets to inhibit the movement of fascist tanks and served as guards in liberated villages.[128] Women destroyed roads and rail lines, cut telephone lines, blew up power stations and other strategic targets, and burned enemy crops. They were also engaged directly at the front as nurses, cooks, and armed fighters.[129]

Local AFZ councils ran hospitals and orphanages, set up public kitchens, and organized accommodations for refugees.[130] They engaged in constructive, socially useful projects to provide much-needed services and care. In addition to building women's involvement in the resistance movement, the organization agitated for women's rights and to facilitate political education.[131] The AFZ had the mission to help transform women into equal and deserving citizens of the future socialist state.[132] Specifically, this meant working to "eliminate illiteracy among women, 'raise' their political consciousness, and train them professionally" so that they could effectively participate in the process of building socialism.[133] To this end, the organization carried out a comprehensive literacy campaign offering courses that taught reading and writing in urban as well as rural areas. Along with literacy courses, the AFZ held general education classes on topics such as hygiene and health, first aid, and other practical skills.[134] Special political courses were offered for more "advanced" members and covered discussions of politics, economics, history, and culture. Working in tandem with the courses, the AFZ released publications that "besides being tools for the dissemination of propaganda, featured educational pieces and political texts in a simple, accessible language."[135] This is a limited account—a small handful of examples from a much larger history. Nonetheless, these examples are powerful and offer lessons, inspiration, and other takeaways for antifascist resistance in our present moment. To explore this further, the next section considers some of the key insights that can be garnered from these histories.

Part 3—Learning from Our Predecessors: Toward a Feminist Antifa

> We conspire; we breathe together. We share what we have been gifted to us by those who came before us. We attempt to walk beside each other. But what will we carry over with us past the emancipatory horizons we'll approach together? What histories will inform our collective actions? What energies of solidarity and creativity will animate these movements?[136]

Invoking the history of women's participation in antifascism, a number of lessons can be drawn and carried into our current moment. While the uncritical introduction of organizing models and ideas from other places and times is problematic, it can be useful to draw inspiration and take insights from elsewhere. History certainly does not hold all of the answers, but it can be a place (one among many) to start. Akemi and Busk, discussing anarchism, insist that building "an anarchist feminist historical tradition will give us a platform to advance our own politics, understand our work in the context of what has already been done, and then forge ahead.... We have always existed, but we have not always been seen."[137] The same can be said for an antifascist feminist historical tradition. With this in mind, I propose seven general insights that can be teased out from the history of women's antifascist resistance and applied to contemporary antifascist struggles. These are not intended to be universal or prescriptive, but merely contextual and suggestive.

First, conceptualize antifascist resistance broadly and engage in multilayered struggle. Embrace a variety of organizing strategies and tactics, and move away from the tendency to look at antifascist struggle in terms of a hierarchical ranking in which certain forms of activity (e.g., combat/fighting, involvement in formal political organizations, etc.) are placed at the top and all other forms of activity are seen as secondary and less important. Antifascist resistance isn't just one thing. It involves a lot of different types of activities and requires a diversity of things. Describing the range of activities that antifascists historically engaged in, Anna Bravo notes that while armed resistance and the ideal of a "young, healthy, tough, and preferably male" body were disproportionality glorified, there was also space for unarmed resistance where "the human frame was far less strictly defined" and "one could be old, weak, physically inept, sickly, and still useful and not excluded."[138] Resistance was lived every day by many different bodies, from those who took up arms and fought Nazis to those who engaged in sabotage, to those who aided clandestine activities, to those who fed and clothed those resisting. It encompassed both formal and informal involvement, as well as individual and collective actions. It took place in both the public and the private spheres, included physical confrontation, public education, labor and community organizing, surveillance and information gathering, the building of infrastructure, and so much more.

Building on the first, the second insight is related to the task of building an antifascist political culture. Calls to develop a "physical culture of class combat" or to form "ultras" football supporter clubs are fine, but limited.[139] If we want to develop a strong resistance movement, we cannot focus almost exclusively on physical activities and/or traditionally male-dominated spaces.[140] It's important to have spaces, roles, and activities that account for the variety and diversity of social life—for example, considering things like ability and age. Historically, there existed a wide range of antifascist cultural spaces. These included things like reading groups, social clubs, collective kitchens, daycare centers, workplace organizations, and sports associations.

Thirdly, the next insight concerns the propensity to associate particular types of activity with particular types of bodies. Against the tendency to associate women with passivity and nonviolence, it is crucial to recognize that combative politics is not exclusively the domain of men. Throughout the history of antifascist resistance and continuing today, women, queers, and trans folks have been involved in armed uprisings, self-defense initiatives, physical confrontations, coordinated attacks, and various other forms of violent activity. Critiquing such actions as inherently male and exclusionary to all others marginalizes the diverse voices of those engaged in confrontational tactics and, furthermore, perpetuates restrictive gender stereotypes.

That said, it is also true that antifascism has issues with sexism and patriarchal behavior, and "that whenever confrontation is part of the repertoire, it is an extra concern."[141] Which leads to the fourth insight: couple antifascist politics with feminism and conceptualize gender liberation as a nonnegotiable component of antifascism. This means centering gender considerations and taking trans politics and queer struggle seriously, not treating them as peripheral concerns.

Relatedly, the fifth insight concerns the value of autonomy and autonomous organizing. Creating autonomous spaces and/or pushing for organizational autonomy were crucial to many historical antifascist groups. Many women found themselves in a situation where they were fighting against fascism and fighting for revolutionary change, all the while pushing their movements to take gender oppression seriously. To address this layered struggle, women founded separate organizations to undertake the work that was otherwise brushed off.

Sixth, look to and draw on other antiracist and anticolonial resistance traditions and not just those most commonly associated with antifascism. Popular accounts of antifascist history privilege Europe and disproportionately focus on white actors. The prototypical antifascist hero is presented not only as male but also as white, ignoring all other histories. There is an incredibly long legacy of Black and Indigenous struggle; however, these are often overlooked and go unrecognized. Ashoka Jegroo notes: "While many people think of white anarchists ... punching Nazis when they talk about antifa, Black folks in the Western hemisphere have essentially been doing antifascist work for centuries. It just hasn't been recognized as such."[142] Particularly in North America—a continent defined by settler colonialism, Indigenous genocide, and anti-Blackness—Black liberation and decolonial movements have either explicitly or implicitly been engaged in fighting against fascism for hundreds of years.[143] Even though much of this work wasn't done under the label of antifascist, that doesn't make it any less relevant. These histories and their continuation today are crucial to conceptualizing and engaging in antifascist struggle.

Moving to the final point, the last insight is to connect antifascism with more ambitious revolutionary goals. Antifascism in and of itself is a necessarily limited struggle. It is a reactive and defensive movement that, while incredibly important, is much more of a jumping-off point than a desired final destination. In the past, many groups rooted their antifascist work in a commitment to revolution and pushed for a broader vision of collective liberation and societal transformation. Antifascism wasn't a single struggle, but an overlapping set of struggles taking place simultaneously. It was an antifascist war, but also a civil war and a class war fighting for sweeping social, political, and economic change.

Conclusion—Against Machismo, for Militancy

> Part of making anti-fascist politics stronger means contending
> with the hyper-masculinity and predominant whiteness of antifa
> spaces.... Rather than be dismissed as secondary issues that
> fall behind the primary goal of confronting fascists, disability
> justice, anti-racism, and feminism should be at the forefront of
> any revolutionary analysis.... This also means recognizing that
> anti-fascism is a necessary but insufficient political solution to
> the problems of our time.[144]

Misogyny is a fundamental pillar of contemporary far-right politics;
it is not just an aside. With the proliferation of far-right movements
over the last few years, and more recently with the recuperation of
those movements and their abhorrent ideas by political parties and
ruling institutions, it is crucial to understand all that we are up against.
Part of what we face is the growth of political forces shaped by variations of intensely patriarchal ideology, and as such, forces that aspire
to establish (or rather further establish, more accurately) not just
white supremacy, but white male supremacy. This reality desperately
calls for a response—it is a growing nightmare that is all too quickly
becoming normalized—and the only appropriate response is struggle.
Unfortunately, the ready-made options presented to us leave much to
be desired. On the one hand, liberal feminism fundamentally lacks the
teeth to address our current political climate, leading to a dead end
of permitted marches, electoral campaigns, and "pussy hat" politics.
On the other hand, antifascism is plagued by machismo, leading to
a highly reductive understanding of struggle and the glorification of
hypermasculine activities above all else. Antifascism doesn't have to
be that way—we can do better.

Looking to histories of women's participation in antifascist movements, we can catch glimpses of a different antifascism. Contrary to
the common conception, women were involved in all forms and formations of the historical fight against fascism. Ingrid Strobl paints a
vibrant picture; referencing women's involvement in antifascist activities, she explains:

> They printed and distributed the illegal press; they forged
> papers; they transported weapons and themselves participated

in armed actions.... [They engaged in sabotage.] They found hiding places for Jewish children and youth, brought them to these hiding places, provided them with clothing, money, food, and with forged documents and encouragement over months and sometimes years.[145]

There is a lot of inspiration and many lessons that can be taken from this history. This is not to say that all aspects of these histories are applicable to our current situation—we are struggling in a vastly different context. However, there are valuable takeaways, as were explored above, and these takeaways offer solid ground on which to build an antifascism rooted in revolutionary feminism. Against an antifascism shaped by machismo, a revolutionary feminist antifascism is shaped by the concept of militancy. Before discussing the latter, it is useful to look at the former.

There is a thread that flows through antifascist movements, and while it does not exclusively define contemporary antifascism, it is influential and worth noting. The thread is an orientation/attitude that tends toward machismo. This inclination is one of bravado and dogmatic combativity, and it leads to a political position that prioritizes confrontation while it more or less ignores (or at least downplays) other aspects of struggle. It reproduces some of the worst characteristics of hegemonic masculinity with a self-righteous zeal and considers discussion of things like sexism to be needlessly divisive and a distraction from the "important things." This strain is almost exclusively concerned with physical conflict with fascists, where if you aren't willing or able to "throw down," you aren't an antifascist. It is individualistic and leans toward an orientation of doing what one wants, regardless of the consequences. It is concerned more with the act of the fight itself than it is with the outcome. There is no room for nuance or any consideration of context, and strategy largely falls by the wayside.[146] These characteristics can be described as machismo, and an antifascism rooted in machismo is the political equivalent of a bar fight—as haphazard and chaotic as it is incoherent and often sloppy.[147]

In contrast, an antifascism oriented toward militancy instead of machismo is concerned with commitment, collectivity, and effectiveness. It isn't about image or ego; rather, it is about doing what needs to be done, choosing the methods/tactics best suited for a situation, and looking at the bigger liberatory picture. This approach couples anti-fascist politics with feminism and conceptualizes gender liberation as a nonnegotiable component of antifascism. Such politics starts from the understanding that antifascist resistance isn't just one thing—it involves a lot of different types of activities and a large diversity of roles. A vibrant movement would have a place for a two-year-old child up to their eighty-two-year-old grandparent. This does not mean a move away from street politics, confrontational tactics, or the use of violence; it acknowledges that antagonism and conflict are inherent to antifascist politics and that confrontation/violence is both necessary and justifiable in certain circumstances. It also acknowledges that women, queers, and trans folks do often "throw down" and are involved in physical altercations and other confrontational activities. Thus, there is an emphasis on dispelling the gendered myth that only men engage in such activities.

Beyond recognizing the role of combative politics, there is also an emphasis on expanding the number of people who participate in confrontational moments, and thus in putting effort into building the comfort and capacity for more women and queers to take part in those activities that are usually coded as hypermasculine. While it values these activities, an antifascism that is rooted in militancy rather than machismo knows that violence is not appropriate in all situations and that the habit of narrowly focusing on physical confrontations is detrimental to our movements. Fighting isn't winning—there's a lot more to it than that. Even in the example of street violence, there's more to it than just fighting. There's a lot of background work involved, including intelligence gathering, neighborhood organizing, logistical planning, and legal/prison support.

This work, which is usually feminized, is as valuable as the confrontational activities it supports. It's just that the one type of work isn't particularly sexy and is perpetually undervalued, while the other is exciting and easily glorified. A feminist antifascism does it all and values it all; it knows that the unglamorous and boring work plays an essential part in struggle. Of related importance, an antifascism rooted in militancy considers both the qualitative and quantitative sides of struggle. This means it isn't just concerned with how many fascist rallies it shuts down, but also with the subjective experience and the personal development of those involved. Ideally, people are learning skills, developing confidence, and becoming more capable revolutionaries. Beyond the immediate benefits, these developments will be helpful for other struggles moving forward. The infrastructure and abilities we build, and the resources we develop, should be part of and put to use by broader struggles. Our antifascist organizing should be grounded in revolutionary politics, in pushing for a vision of collective liberation, meaningful autonomy, and endless possibility. The problems we face are so much bigger than the question of fascism, and our aspirations should be so much more than this limited struggle.

Seven Theses on the Three Way Fight

Devin Zane Shaw

Three Way Fight, August 1, 2021

The seven theses I propose here were first published as part of a preface to T. Derbent's *The German Communist Resistance, 1933–1945*, published by Foreign Languages Press (2020). I have reworked parts of that preface here as a stand-alone essay that aims to summarize the praxis of the three way fight and forecast problems and prospects going forward.

In leftist—that is, socialist, anarchist, and communist—circles, it is still common to hear discussions of fascism couched in terms similar to Dimitrov's formulation of the Comintern's popular-front line as established in 1935. He asserts that "fascism in power is the open terrorist dictatorship of the most reactionary, most chauvinistic and most imperialist elements of finance capital."[1] The prolonged afterlife of this definition is likely due in part to the fact that it was later adopted, with slight modification, by the Black Panther Party in its call for a united front against fascism in 1969: "Fascism is the open terroristic dictatorship of the most reactionary, most chauvinistic (racist) and the most imperialist elements of finance capital."[2] Though I readily accept that fascism must be understood as a movement that is enabled by and a reaction to capitalist crises, and I maintain that fascism cannot take power without some factions of capital collaborating with far-right movements, there are numerous problems with identifying its overriding class character with the most extreme factions of capital. If we reexamine Dimitrov's two major essays from 1935—"The Fascist Offensive" and "Unity of the Working Class"—we find that his analysis hints at a more complicated picture of the class character of fascism but that it is largely explained away as a product of demagoguery.[3] In any case, from this overarching perspective, the nonbourgeois elements of fascist movements are treated as mere instruments or lackeys of the fascist bourgeoisie.

Some critics reject the orthodox Marxist line represented by Dimitrov, but nonetheless preserve part of its form: where Dimitrov focuses on the specific *class character* of fascism, that is, locating its leadership within the most reactionary and extreme factions within the bourgeoisie, this nonorthodox interpretation treats fascism as an extreme version of some aspects of capitalist *social relations*. In other words, while Dimitrov focuses on fascism as a particularly extreme and terroristic form of one particular faction of bourgeois class rule, these critics treat fascism as a new particular application of the state's repressive apparatuses. These critics also overstate how contemporary fascism breaks from patterns of classical fascism: Enzo Traverso's "postfascism," Samir Gandesha's "posthuman fascism," or Alberto Toscano's "racial fascism" (which evokes a parallel to the concept of racial capitalism, but adding "racial" to fascism is redundant) or "late fascism."[4] Fascism, though, is not merely a new phase of capitalism or state repression.

These variations on the thesis that fascism represents an extreme faction or policy of capitalism fall short for the same reason: they do not reflect the reality on the ground, in the concrete struggle between militant antifascism and far-right and fascist movements. It's clearly not the bourgeoisie who were holding the tiki torches in Charlottesville. And while there are connections and ideological similarities between the far right and certain apparatuses of state power (such as the police), their organizational interests do not necessarily align. In sum, the received concept of fascism as an extreme faction or policy of capitalism does not explain the presence of system-oppositional currents in the far right that fight against bourgeois political and cultural power. (Which is different than saying bourgeois class rule; as I argue in theses two and five, far-right movements seek to reorganize capital accumulation on advantageous terms, not to overthrow capitalism.) Indeed, these Dimitrov variations, as it were, could each lend themselves to a supposed leftist argument against using direct action: if fascism is the product of the most reactionary elements of the class rule of capital or an extreme implementation of repressive state power, the argument goes, then using direct action against the far-right malcontents in the streets siphons resources from broader anticapitalist organizing. In other words, from this perspective, militant antifascism combats symptoms rather than causes.

Hence there is a need, from a militant perspective, for a different approach. Unsurprisingly, there has been a growing interest in the history and practice of nonorthodox approaches to antifascist organizing: for example, the 43 Group, the John Brown Anti-Klan Committee, Anti-Racist Action (ARA), and, as evidenced by the re-edition of the anthology *Confronting Fascism* in 2017, the three way fight.[5] These groups sometimes had similar approaches, but we must also highlight their differences. The three way fight differs from the other groups because, despite the organizational, extralegal, and militant aspects of these groupings and movements, they did not develop the necessary revolutionary outlook to orient their activity. Even with ARA, the revolutionary concepts which formed the basis for three way fight were a minority tendency. What is needed now are the revolutionary, liberatory visions and living forms of praxis of the three way fight. I will tentatively define the three way fight, which I will outline in more detail below, as an approach to antifascist struggle that situates militant action against both system-oppositional far-right groups and bourgeois democracy (as it is embodied, in North America, in both bourgeois democratic institutions and what I call settler-state hegemony, liberalism as ideology, and the repressive state apparatus). Reality on the ground is more complicated and rife with contradictions than a one-sentence definition can encapsulate, so while this tentative definition cannot replace the seven theses I propose below, it does serve as a starting point for the discussion.

The Present Conjuncture

Before presenting the seven theses on the three way fight, I want to underline that, compared to the last five years, the coordinates of antifascist struggle have changed. While militant antifascism is best known for its embrace of the diversity of tactics, over the past several years many militants have worked to create a broader social atmosphere of everyday antifascism, which brought those who I would call "liberal antifascists" into the broader struggle against far-right groups. Fostering everyday antifascism makes it possible to organize a broader movement in opposition to far-right groups when they mobilize in our cities. Everyday antifascism could, under the right conditions, bring larger crowds to counterprotests; it also provides political education on how the seemingly small things, like seating far-right groups at restaurants or providing lodging, enables the far-right threat to communities. With Trump in office, there was no chance that antifascism could be funneled back toward state-sponsored American civic participation, although as election day approached, intellectuals such as Cornel West described their support for Biden as an "antifascist vote." A united front of militant antifascists—largely drawn from socialist, communist, and anarchist backgrounds—was formed within a broader milieu that included sympathetic liberal antifascists who, if they were not drawn toward militant action, at least provided room to maneuver.

With Trump deposed from power, the situation has changed. The differences between liberal antifascists and militants are more starkly illuminated as the immediate threat—or, frankly, what is perceived by some to be the immediate threat—of fascism has abated. Thus we should reiterate the differences between these two currents of antifascism:

- *Militant antifascism* upholds the diversity of tactics to combat far-right and fascist organizing; it organizes as a form of community self-defense which (at least ideally) builds reciprocal relationships with marginalized and oppressed communities. In addition, it ought to recognize and uphold the "revolutionary horizon" of antifascist struggle: fascism cannot be permanently defeated until the conditions which give rise to fascism are overthrown.

- *Liberal antifascism*, in Mark Bray's concise definition, entails "a faith in the inherent power of the public sphere to filter out fascist ideas, and in the institutions of government to forestall the advancement of fascist politics."[6] Liberal antifascists appeal to the democratic norms of these institutions, but they also assume that law enforcement will apply force to repress fascism when it constitutes a legitimate threat; furthermore, they also tend to accept the converse of the foregoing proposition: if law enforcement doesn't intervene, then no legitimate threat is present.

In the wake of the far-right attempted *putsch* on Capitol Hill on January 6, 2021, when I was working on the first version of this essay,

I suggested that the Biden administration was poised to marshal the popular outrage toward that event to siphon parts of the broader atmosphere of everyday antifascism—which previously made it possible to organize militant antifascist actions relatively openly—to fortify Democratic blocs. Biden had, for example, in August 2017, only a few weeks after the Unite the Right rally in Charlottesville, published an editorial in the *Atlantic* denouncing Trump's equivocations about the far right; he had also referenced Charlottesville several times during his campaign. However, as it turns out, mainstream liberal antifascists were content to encapsulate and isolate fascism around so-called "Trumpism," which was defeated with the victory and inauguration of the Biden administration, though, they sternly warned, a more effective demagogue could wreak more havoc than Trump in the future.

We must, by contrast, disentangle an array of far-right phenomena: Trump's particular propaganda campaign against the legitimacy of his electoral defeat; the drift, or push, of the Republican Party toward far-right ideology; Trump's attempt to suppress the anti-police uprising; and the temporary alignment of ideologically system-oppositional groups as system-loyal vigilantism against antifascist and antiracist organizing. What differentiates our perspective from the critique of "Trumpism," which we must emphasize, is that we cannot lose sight of the far right as a relatively autonomous social movement. Trump's ascendency was based in part on the emergence and growth of far-right organizing, and he certainly didn't conjure them out of the blue. Likewise, his electoral defeat does not signal their defeat and dissolution.

In order to examine the present conjuncture, we must admit that coalitions which have formed over the last five years between militant and liberal antifascists were, from the beginning, fraught. The two groups adhere to incompatible ideological commitments and organizational strategies. As I have already noted, militant antifascists struggle against both the far right *and* bourgeois democracy. This dual struggle necessitates criticism of liberal antifascism as well. First, militant antifascists, as I argue in thesis six, must maintain a revolutionary horizon, in which their practices are directed toward not only fighting the far right but forging organizational capacity and skills for broader social—though in its various manifestations, also class—struggle against capitalist rule. This struggle brings antifascist action into direct conflict with both the far right and the repressive state apparatus, and hence militants must carry out investigations into the relationship between law enforcement and far-right organizing. Liberal perspectives and militant perspectives will never align on law enforcement.

But as militant and liberal antifascist coalitions fragment, we must also pay close attention to the vicissitudes of liberal antifascism. In the interregnum between January 6, 2021, and the inauguration, some liberal antifascists framed American civic participation and protection of democratic institutions as antifascist, and on this basis, I had previously examined the potential for Biden to appropriate this discourse. As it turns out, Biden's administration pivoted—not unlike numerous liberal antifascist intellectuals—from formulating an opposition of antifascism and fascism to an opposition between liberal norms and extremism. We must interpret this pivot.

Given that liberal antifascists rely on democratic norms and rational persuasion to criticize fascist positions, under normal circumstances they carry out criticism within the parameters of liberal institutions, especially through the medium of intellectual exchange and debate. And under normal conditions, liberal ideology writ large—and liberal antifascists as a whole are typically no exception—condemns insurgent organizing, whether it is the militant left or the far right, as political "extremism" (patterned on the discourse of so-called totalitarianism, which equivocates between communism and fascism). Hence liberal horseshoe theory, which empties fascism and militant antifascism of their explicit (and incompatible) political content in order to present them as two iterations of purportedly irrational violence, although, of course, the only thing the two share is a rejection of the state's asserted monopoly on violence.

But when the far right mounts a significant challenge to bourgeois political and cultural power, threatening liberal institutions, and (unsurprisingly) intellectual exchange and debate prove ineffective, some liberal antifascists enter into coalitions with or within militant groups. We saw numerous instances of this over the last few years. Though there are pronounced theoretical and practical differences between them, these two currents of antifascism converge around a shared sense of egalitarianism, which opens for militants a broader horizon for organizing around the practices of everyday antifascism. As a consequence of this practical readjustment, as we have seen, liberal antifascists set aside the framework of "extremism" in order to enter the struggle between militant antifascism and the far right.

However, when the threat of fascism seems to have passed—that is, at least from the liberal perspective, when it appears that the far right has been unable to seize political, cultural, or institutional control—we should expect, and must prepare for, liberal antifascism to revert to its normal institutional habits. Thus, as liberalism shores up political hegemony, liberal antifascism returns to the paradigm of "extremism" for categorizing militant and revolutionary leftist movements and the far right as two sides of the same extremist coin. I believe we are witnessing these shifts at the present moment, and hence it is all the more important that antifascist intellectuals both critique and refuse to collaborate with those think tanks and university institutions that push the "extremist studies" approach to fascism and antifascism. An academic pedigree for parts of the state security apparatus does not remove their ultimately repressive function.

When liberal antifascists categorize militant antifascism as extremist, they not only work to delegitimize militant currents, they also provide the ideological justification for the political use of force by repressive state apparatuses. If liberal antifascism succeeds in pulling everyday antifascism back toward bourgeois forms of institutional and cultural power, it will effectively empty everyday antifascism of any concrete political and organizational content while setting the stage for state repression of militant antifascists.[7] The extension of law enforcement powers that followed in the wake of far-right actions related to the Capitol riot will redound against left-wing militants, because the repressive state apparatus specifically frames its work in this domain as a fight against extremism.

In my view, the political success of liberal antifascism will always be a Pyrrhic victory. Militant antifascism draws its strength from its organizational capacity—that is, its ability to undermine far-right organizing. When words no longer match deeds, when theory no longer matches practical results, then militant antifascism enters into crisis. The principal contradiction of militant antifascism is that these forms of organizing often only last as long as the threat of far-right groups effectively persists.

But repressive state violence, under the auspices of fighting political extremism, can apply force to accelerate the decomposition of militant organizing capacity. Liberal antifascists do not recognize, or do not adequately challenge, how their typical political framework legitimizes state power. They do not recognize how dismantling militant antifascist organizing capacity undermines community self-defense, and hence how it enables conditions for far-right forces to regroup. The danger remains that conditions arise in the future that are even more conducive to far-right movements than they have been over the last five years.

Seven Theses on Militant Antifascism

The foregoing scenario is far from a fait accompli. It can be forestalled by renewed efforts at militant political education and organizing around a united front policy. The electoral defeat of the Trump administration has untethered far-right organizing from its momentary system-loyal pretensions, though without necessarily undermining alliances that were forged by the mutual opposition of some far-right groups and police departments to the anti-police uprising of 2020. I will conclude by proposing a series of theses concerning a united front policy for militant antifascists in North America, though I believe some points also hold in other situations. I defend them in more detail elsewhere.[8] We will begin with defining two terms: *fascism* and *the far right*.

1. Fascism is a social movement involving a relatively autonomous and insurgent (potentially) mass base, driven by an authoritarian vision of collective rebirth, that challenges bourgeois institutional and cultural power while reentrenching economic and social hierarchies.

This definition of fascism—adapted from the work of Matthew N. Lyons and drawing from the discussion between Don Hamerquist and J. Sakai in *Confronting Fascism* (2002)—is a marked departure from the most common Marxist definition, which holds that fascism is "the open terrorist dictatorship of the most reactionary, most chauvinistic and most imperialist elements of finance capital."[9] Whereas Dimitrov's formulation, as it is typically applied, treats fascists in the streets as instruments of the most reactionary faction of capital, the definition I offer asserts that fascist social movements are relatively autonomous formations that challenge bourgeois institutional and cultural power. This autonomy does not preclude hegemonic forma- tions between fascists and the bourgeoisie. As Hamerquist argues, the Nazis' seizure of power united factions of the ruling class interested in imposing fascism "from above" with nonsocialist factions (and I'm using the term "socialist" as loosely as possible here) of the fascist movement, and "nazi political structure had a clear and substantial autonomy from the capitalist class and the strength to impose certain positions on that class."[10]

As to the class composition of fascism, T. Derbent comments that "workers were the only social group whose percentage of Nazi party members was lower than its percentage in the total population."[11] Closer to the present, an examination of 49 of 107 persons arrested for participation in the Capitol riot indicates the generally petty bour- geois character of participants.[12] Both observations affirm that the class composition of the far right and fascism is more complex than the most reactionary faction(s) of the bourgeoisie. In North America, the far right draws from elements of the white petty bourgeoisie who are seeking to protect their social status—purchased, as W.E.B. Du Bois argues, through the wages of whiteness—and/or their class position. Fascism is, in my view, relatively autonomous because it is antibourgeois, but it is anticapitalist only to the degree that it seeks to reorganize capital accumulation on terms conducive to its base. To illustrate: Hamerquist has adduced examples where fascist policies have interrupted the normal functioning of capitalism, but as Lyons notes, "no fascist movement has substantively attacked core capitalist structures such as private property and the market economy."[13]

2. Fascist ideology and organizing develops within a broader far-right ecological niche.

Lyons defines the far right as inclusive of "political forces that (a) regard human inequality as natural, inevitable, or desirable and (b) reject the legitimacy of the established political system."[14] Lyons's definition focuses our attention on two key features of the far-right milieu within which fascists organize. First, far-right groups seek to reentrench social and economic inequalities, but the social hierarchies they advocate aren't necessarily drawn along racial lines. Lyons gives the example of the Christian far right, which advocates for a theo- cratic state that centers heterosexual male dominance. In general, this movement has embraced Islamophobia and "promotes policies that implicitly bolster racial oppression," but some groups have conducted outreach to conservative Christians of color while others have formed alliances with white supremacist groups.[15] Fascist movements emerge within a broader milieu of right-wing social movements, and these various groups sometimes establish alliances and sometimes conflict. In fact, one purpose of antifascist counterprotesting when these groups rally is to put pressure on their organizing; when these rallies are disrupted or dispersed through antifascist action, far-right alliances often rapidly splinter as prominent figures and groups within the far right trade accusations and recriminations.

Second, far-right groups reject the legitimacy of, as I would phrase it, bourgeois-democratic institutions of political and cultural power. Though mainstream conservatism has been pulled toward the far right in ideological terms, organizational differences between "oppositional and system-loyal rightists [are] more significant than ideological differences about race, religion, economics, or other factors."[16]

3. Militant antifascism is involved in a three way fight against insurgent far-right movements and bourgeois democracy (or, in ideological terms, liberalism).

More precisely, each "corner" of the three way fight struggles against the other two while at the same time this struggle offers lines of adjacency against a common enemy. The first and most fundamental lesson of the three way fight is that while both revolutionary movements and far-right movements are insurgent forms of opposition against bourgeois democracy, "my enemy's enemy is not my friend." Given that far-right groups also aim to recruit or ally with some leftist groups, it is all the more important to root out all forms of chauvinism within our practices and organizations. Second, we must recognize the line of adjacency between militant antifascism and the egalitarian aspirations of bourgeois democracy. It is the shared appeal to egalitarianism that makes fostering a broader sense of everyday antifascism possible. But it also means, as I will argue in thesis six, that militants must uphold a revolutionary horizon to keep the limitations of liberal antifascism in focus.

We will deal with the line of adjacency between the far right and bourgeois democracy (or liberalism) in the next two theses. But before moving on, we must examine the relationship between far-right groups and law enforcement. The slogan that "cops and Klan go hand in hand" expresses two fundamental aspects of this relationship. First, it acknowledges the systemic role of law enforcement: that is, law enforcement protects the systemic white supremacy of North American settler-colonial states. Second, it also emphasizes not only shared membership between the two groups (when police, for example, are also members of the KKK), but also the ideological bases through which police and system-loyal vigilante groups find common cause in opposition to leftist movements.

However, it would be incorrect to assume that there are no antagonisms between law enforcement and far-right groups. In my view, it is more accurate to differentiate between what I would call system-loyal vigilantism and system-oppositional armed organization. On the terms established by Lyons, all far-right groups are ideologically system oppositional, *but not all of them are organized in system-oppositional forms.* Over the last few years, many framed their actions as system-loyal vigilantism, which I would define as the use of violent tactics to harass, intimidate, or physically harm individuals or groups participating in transformative egalitarian movements. While some levels of law enforcement tend to be permissive or deferential toward system-loyal right-wing vigilantism, there are recent examples of law enforcement at the federal level moving to repress system-oppositional groups organized around armed insurgency. In 2020, law enforcement moved to incapacitate numerous far-right armed accelerationist groups, including members or groups affiliated with the Base, Atomwaffen, and the more loosely affiliated boogaloo movement. Nevertheless, we must not mistakenly take law enforcement repression to signal an unequivocal antagonism between police and the far right or any degree of common cause between these targeted far-right groups and militant and revolutionary leftist movements.

4. The particularity of the three way fight is dependent on concrete social relations.

Far-right and fascist groups draw on and respond differently to different social contexts. For example, during the interwar period, fascist movements drew from the imperialist aspirations of European nationalisms. In North America, far-right movements emerge in relation to broader ideological and material forms of settler colonialism (which includes—meaning that capital accumulation is imbricated in—elements of white supremacy, heteropatriarchy, ableism, and Indigenous dispossession).[17]

In North America, the historical development of liberal political and cultural institutions is inseparable from the development of settler colonialism. Nonetheless, it would be undialectical to treat them uncritically as the same thing. Instead, in my view, it is more precise to contend that settler-state hegemony is formed by the mediation of bourgeois liberalism and white supremacist settlerism. I would define white supremacist settlerism as an ideological framework which privileges both white entitlement to land (possession or dominion) over the colonized's right to sovereignty and autonomy, and entitlements encapsulated in what Du Bois calls the "public and psychological wage of whiteness." Examining the end of the Reconstruction period in the southern United States after the Civil War, Du Bois argues that the potential for the formation of abolition democracy, built on solidarity between the Black and white proletariat, was defeated by the hegemonic reorganization of settler-state hegemony which ensured forms of deference and the institutionalization of racial control, as well as opening institutional access to education and social mobility to poor whites, drawing them, even if only aspirationally, into the petty bourgeoisie and labor aristocracy.[18]

Du Bois's analysis remains the prototype—though it must be theoretically corrected by incorporating the role that the settlement of the western frontier played in this dynamic—for conceptualizing settler-state hegemony and the role that whiteness plays within it. The presidential campaigns of 2020, in the midst of the COVID-19 pandemic and then the widespread antipolice uprising, offered two competing visions of reorganizing American settler-state hegemony—one which attempted to pull some system-oppositional far-right movements toward system-loyal organizing (embodied in fall 2020 as vigilantism) and the other, which took on a form of superficial antifascism—but they also demonstrated that a common interest in defending settler-state hegemony against challenges from the revolutionary left and the liberation struggles of oppressed peoples forms the basis of the line of adjacency between bourgeois liberalism and white supremacist settlerism.

5. Far-right movements are system loyal when they perceive that the entitlements of white supremacy can be advanced within bourgeois or democratic institutions, and they become insurgent when they perceive that these entitlements cannot.

In the first thesis, I stated that fascist groups appeal to an authoritarian vision of collective rebirth. In North American settler-colonial societies, far-right and fascist groups demand the reentrenchment of the social and economic hierarchies which enabled white social and economic mobility; they perceive that their social standing is in jeopardy and demand that settler-state hegemony be tilted "back" toward their advantage. In sum, far-right movements assert supposed "rights" of white settlerism which supersede the formal guarantees and protections granted through the liberal institutions of settler-state hegemony.

This thesis seemingly contradicts Lyons's definition of the contemporary far right offered in thesis two. Though contemporary far-right movements are system oppositional now, that has not unequivocally been the case historically. Ken Lawrence, in "The Ku Klux Klan and Fascism" (1982), outlines how the KKK shifted between system-loyal and system-oppositional forms: in its earliest form, the KKK was a "restorationist movement of the Confederacy"; in the 1920s, it was a mainstream bourgeois nativist movement; in the 1960s, it was a reactionary movement fighting to preserve segregation; then finally, around the time Lawrence was writing, it shifted toward its present system-oppositional, insurgent position.[19]

I would suggest—as a provisional hypothesis which remains to be developed in more detail elsewhere—that liberalism and white settlerism were historically able to coexist in North America because the latter's interests did not substantially interfere with the former's. Fascism failed to emerge as a profound challenge to American political hegemony in the 1930s and 1940s because, as Sakai notes, "white settler colonialism and fascism occupy the same ecological niche. Having one, capitalist society didn't yet need the other."[20] From the 1950s to the 1970s, a variety of civil rights and liberation movements leveled a profound challenge to settler-state hegemony. Liberalism accommodated challenges from social-justice movements by extending formal legal protections to marginalized groups and by introducing new patterns of economic redistribution (social welfare). This did not overturn the expectations and entitlements of the wages of whiteness.

As Cheryl Harris contends, "after legalized segregation was overturned, whiteness as property evolved into a more modern form through the law's ratification of the settled expectations of relative white privilege as a legitimate and natural baseline."[21] In other words, white entitlements could be codified into law as long as they could be framed in supposedly color-blind terms—but these color-blind terms would also contribute to the (incorrect) perception that systemic white supremacy had been pushed to the margins of American society.

As recent events reveal, settler-state hegemony is not immune to crisis. As Marx and Engels argue in *The Communist Manifesto*, the social position of the petty bourgeoisie is always tenuous because "their diminutive capital does not suffice for the scale on which Modern Industry is carried on." While the white petty bourgeoisie has repeatedly been "bought off" by social mobility or access to land (available due to Indigenous dispossession), even during the period of neoliberal policy, that does not mean that settler-state hegemony will continue to reorganize future hegemonic blocs successfully. The threat remains that an insurgent fascist movement, organized around the rebirth of the settler-colonial project, will fill that hegemonic vacuum.

6. A revolutionary horizon is a necessary component to antifascist organizing; that is, there is no meaningful way in which fascism can be permanently defeated without overthrowing the conditions which give rise to it: capitalism and white supremacy and, in North America, settler colonialism.

Militant antifascism is organized in order to meet the imminent threat of fascist organizing; it is an instantiation of community self-defense. A united front is necessary in situations where the revolutionary left is present but lacks a mass base, but it is always caught in a contradiction: the major leftist ideological currents—socialism, anarchism, and communism—converge in a united front but diverge around the particulars of the revolutionary horizon. While combating fascism is the immediate task of militant antifascism, antifascists must maintain a revolutionary horizon, even if only in broad outline, in order to avoid being absorbed within the ideological parameters of liberal antifascism. At the same time, militants must also recognize that antifascist work cannot merely be absorbed into revolutionary work; antifascism is community self-defense.

7. Militant antifascism must uphold the diversity of tactics.

From a practical perspective, militant antifascism is distinguished from liberal antifascism by a willingness to use the diversity of tactics, up to and including physical confrontation, to disrupt far-right organizing. Effective militant organizing, though, must not transform the diversity of tactics into *merely* physical confrontation.[22] Antifascism seeks to raise the cost of fascist organizing, and that is the most obvious reason why the diversity of tactics plays an important role in organizing. As Robert F. Williams observed in 1962, racists "are most vicious and violent when they can practice violence with impunity."[23] Physical confrontation raises the stakes for fascist attempts to harass and intimidate communities as they organize. But it is important to emphasize that physical confrontation still tends to come late in practice: antifascists conduct research and publicize the fascist threat and dox fascists, we put pressure on supposedly community-accountable institutions to de-platform or no-platform far-right groups, and when fascists rally we meet them in the streets to disrupt their actions. Militants uphold the importance of the diversity of tactics but that doesn't mean, against popular conceptions, that violence is necessary. The critical question is always: Which tactic can cause the greatest disruption to far-right movements at each stage of organizing?

●

Events of the last year especially have revealed the weaknesses of liberal mechanisms to stem far-right organizing. For years, liberal antifascists interpreted the lack of law enforcement pressure against the far right as a lack of urgent threat, and when the potential scope of far-right violence erupted into popular consciousness on January 6, 2021, it was years too late. The failure of far-right and fascist groups to undermine the transition of government power was due not to police repression (in fact, there was a distinct absence of police repression on that particular day), but primarily to internal organizational weaknesses, which I would attribute in part to pressure brought to bear on these groups over the last five years of antifascist organizing.

When confronted with emerging far-right movements, and unlike liberal antifascists, militant antifascists act sooner so that we don't have to take greater risks later. Antifascists must maintain a revolutionary horizon, but at the same time remain focused on the immediate threat of fascist organizing. A world where fascists can openly organize is worse than one where they cannot. Though German fascism and Italian fascism were historically defeated in 1945, it will take a greater effort to defeat fascism once and for all. Part of that work must be done now by a united front of militant antifascists.

III
COMPLEX POLITICS, MULTIPLE OPPONENTS

American Strasser

Kdog

Three Way Fight, December 9, 2020

Tom Metzger is dead. Fuck that muthafucker.

For those of us who came of age in the 1980s antifascist wars against white power boneheads—Tom Metzger was an archenemy. The California TV repairman and ex-Klansman was the founder and leader of White Aryan Resistance (WAR), a radical and innovative fascist group that was among the first to embrace the alienated young proles in the white power music scene.

Metzger played a crucial role in the 1970s–1990s American fascist movement—one that left him with bloody hands that he never fully paid for. Back in the late Eighties I was told by multiple sources that Metzger had put out a hit on me and a couple of Black antifascist skinheads—one from Chicago and one, like me, in Minneapolis. In the early Nineties my now partner, traveling from Chicago, was thrown up against the wall with dozens of other antiracist skinheads by Portland cops while protesting outside Metzger's famous trial. We thought about that fucker—and he was more than aware of us.

Metzger could read the playing field better than any other American fascist of his time—and he was committed to making an impact. This made him incredibly dangerous to people of color, to the Jewish community, to queer folks, to antiracists and leftists. But Metzger was also regarded as dangerous by the System, which while still as structurally racist as ever, was anxious to modernize the face and methods of its rule in the post–Civil Rights era. In fact, in contradiction to widespread leftist assumptions of constant police-fascist collusion, Metzger's organizing was repeatedly infiltrated and spied on by agents and informants.

WAR

When the British white supremacist band Skrewdriver first started catching on at the margins of the North American punk scene, most fascist leaders only saw their fans as trouble: lumpen, violent, disorganized, drug users, etc. Metzger, though, probably grinning and rubbing his hands together, saw only (to borrow a quote) "good trouble, necessary trouble."

Metzger reoriented his entire operation toward this emerging generation of radical racists. His new organization adopted the militant name White Aryan Resistance, and his newspaper combined crude racist cartoons with revolutionary calls to smash the system. Metzger didn't have time for a right-wing version of "respectability politics"—he embraced confrontation. WAR's shocking appearances on Oprah Winfrey's and Geraldo Rivera's TV shows spread the word in the pre-internet era that there was a new racist in town—one who wouldn't back down. This was underlined in red when WAR kicked Geraldo's ass on TV, leaving him with a busted nose.

But propaganda stunts weren't their only game. Metzger was a committed organizer who would take personal phone calls from outcast racist youth from all over the country. (An Anti-Racist Action militant recently recalled phoning the WAR hotline to leave a nasty antifa message, only to be left speechless when the devil himself answered.) WAR promoted the white power music scene—like the "Aryan Woodstock" music concerts—a decade before the National Alliance was convinced to fund Resistance Records. And crucially, Metzger sought to recruit them into an organization. Alongside WAR, Metzger promoted the White Student Union, WARSkins, and the Aryan Women's League as different avenues leading to the same place.

It was not just Metzger's nose for opportunity that made him so influential—it was also his politics. Metzger was the most serious proponent of "Third Position" politics ("neither capitalism nor communism") among American fascists of this era. Metzger saw himself as a revolutionary, not a conservative; an anticapitalist, not an elitist. For antifascists, understanding the politics and approach of Metzger and WAR will give us a better understanding of the spectrum of nazi politics and the specific threats and potentials posed by the Third Positionist wing of the fascist movement.

When a mass white power gang culture emerged on the streets of Portland, Oregon, in the late 1980s (law enforcement estimated there were three hundred nazi skins in the city of three hundred thousand), Metzger was the only nazi organizer to respond. A young WAR organizer, Dave Mazzella, was sent up to Portland to try to cohere and organize the several white power skinhead gangs, like East Side White Pride (ESWP), into a more political and disciplined force. This was an Aryan version of the Fred Hampton approach. Mazzella partied with and agitated the gang members; three weeks into the mission, a crew of ESWP skins attacked and beat to death an Ethiopian student named Mulugeta Seraw with baseball bats.

The conflagration that followed included years of organizing and street fighting by militant antifascists for the streets of Portland and the soul of its youth subcultures, a special statewide gang unit aimed at containing this breach of social peace, and a lawsuit by the Southern Poverty Law Center (SPLC) to try to take Metzger off the field.

The Dragons

Tracing Tom Metzger's path is useful in understanding fascist politics and organization in North America. Metzger had been the California chief of David Duke's revitalized and "nazified" Knights of the Ku Klux Klan. He was part of an important generation of state Klan leaders—"Grand Dragons"—including Louis Beam in Texas (went on to author the influential "Leaderless Resistance" strategy), Don Black in Alabama (later founded the Stormfront discussion board), and Glenn Miller of the Carolina Knights of the KKK (pioneered adopting camouflage and armed marches and was a participant in the Greensboro Massacre death squad, and subsequently murdered three people at the Overland Park Jewish Community Center and Village Shalom retirement home in 2014).

Like most of this crew, Metzger was a veteran—enlisting in the US Army in the early Sixties. After getting out of the military, Metzger moved from Indiana to work in California, and it was there his affiliation to the radical right began. Metzger attended anticommunist luncheons sponsored by the Douglas Aircraft Company (a predecessor to the McDonnell Douglas aerospace giant) and joined the far-right John Birch Society. Metzger worked on the presidential campaigns of Barry Goldwater and George Wallace and on Ronald Reagan's gubernatorial run—but soon found that framework too tame. Even the virulently anticommunist Minutemen militia, which he was briefly involved in, was not radical enough. He also found himself disagreeing with the right on a key issue—Metzger opposed the US war in Vietnam.

Metzger was still deeply racist and antisemitic—he preached that people of color were subhuman "mud people" and that Jews were a sinister race of manipulators holding white workers in check. These themes remained continually embedded within his political outlook.

In Duke's Knights of the KKK, Metzger began to hit his stride. He successfully combined provocative action with mainstream media engagement. Metzger and his California Klan ran armed "Border Watch" patrols against Mexican immigrants that received wide attention and created a blueprint still used by racist vigilantes today.

In 1980, Metzger led his California Klan into a militant confrontation against the police and left-wing antifascists at Oceanside, California. Metzger's KKK eschewed the white robes for motorcycle helmets, battle shields, and dogs—antifascist protesters that day at first assumed that the assembling white supremacists were sheriff's deputies in riot gear. The rally and counterprotest turned into a melee with fists and clubs swinging on all sides. Bruce Kala (who later became a well-known anarchist activist in the East Bay) was taken down by several Klansmen and viciously beaten with baseball bats, leaving him with permanent injuries. Metzger's crew also fought the police that day, and a Klan member's Doberman pinscher was shot and killed after attacking a cop.

Metzger's explicitly revolutionary (as opposed to conservative) approach and his consistent attempts to wrap his vile racism and antisemitism in class struggle colors represented a break with much of the US white supremacist scene. Metzger fits more in the tradition of the Strasser brothers than typical nazis or fascists.

Strasserism

Gregor and Otto Strasser were German national socialist activists whose careers and activity ran parallel with Adolf Hitler's. After serving in Germany's military in the First World War, both the Strasser brothers joined the proto-nazi street militia Freikorps. While Gregor became a well-known figure and led the Lower Bavarian "Storm Battalion," Otto actually defected to join the mass German Social

Democratic Party for a time. Both brothers reunited in Hitler's NSDAP, after it had gained hegemony over the mass, disparate milieu of right-wing World War I vets. But inside the Nazi Party the Strassers maintained their clearly "revolutionary" brand of national socialism that called for the Nazis to liquidate the German ruling class through mass mobilization of the working class, to establish a rabidly racist and antisemitic dictatorship. This position found an echo in the ideas of the even more influential Ernst Röhm, leader of the Nazi SA ("Brownshirts"), who advocated a "second revolution" of Aryan workers against the bankers and monopoly capitalists.

Hitler, however, was interested in sealing a deal with the German elite—and was willing to calm their nerves by suppressing the "socialist" aspect of the National Socialists. Gregor Strasser was removed as editor of one of the Nazis' daily newspapers and was then kicked out of the party. Both Gregor Strasser and Ernst Röhm were killed during the "Night of the Long Knives," an organized purge that eliminated a number of Hitler's rivals and served to show the German ruling class that the Brownshirts could be reined in. Otto Strasser had already left the Nazis, forming his own separate fascist party, "the Black Front," advocating for the overthrow of Hitler from exile. Since then, "Strasserism" has become the label for nazis who seek to emphasize the "socialist" aspect of their politics alongside the national and racial. "Third Position" is another, broader name for a similar set of politics.

All this is to point out that Metzger's revolutionary and anticapitalist rhetoric is not novel. And the historical precedent suggests that there will continue to be a "left-wing" trend within fascism. We can't be caught off guard by this and must be prepared to combat this trend's particularities as well as its familiar white supremacist, patriarchal, and antisemitic pillars.

Third Position

It's unclear to me when and how Metzger moved fully to Third Position politics. I haven't built up the stomach to wade through the many episodes of his *Race and Reason* TV talk show or issues of the *WAR* newspaper to discover if there are clues there. We do know that Metzger had a falling-out with David Duke—at first over what Duke was doing with the dues paid by state KKK chapters, then over Duke's suit-and-tie strategy of mainstreaming the fascist message and eventually joining the Republican Party. Metzger regarded Duke as becoming just another bourgeois politician, unwilling to be bluntly honest or take needed militant action.

Metzger was also a student of political history and of the left. Metzger was a big fan of Jack London, the famous author of *The Call of the Wild* and *The Iron Heel*, who was an ardent socialist *and* racist. Metzger bragged of recruiting leftists to WAR—much of this was probably hype, but he did enlist and promote an ex-member of the Socialist Workers Party and a former member of the Industrial Workers of the World.

In 1985, Metzger attended a Louis Farrakhan speech and made a donation to the Nation of Islam (a path already walked by American Nazi Party leader George Lincoln Rockwell in 1961). Metzger's daughter organized the Aryan Women's League—promoting the image of women as "brave racial warriors" in contrast, they said, to the passive image of women that Judeo-Christianity encouraged. And Metzger heaped praise on the soon-to-be-expelled anti-immigration "Deep Ecologists" of Earth First.

Metzger loved to troll the left. When the John Brown Anti-Klan Committee (JBAKC) started targeting Metzger, he responded with an article in his newspaper praising the Weathermen as "young white street-fighters" (Metzger being well aware that JBAKC traced its political roots to the Weather Underground).

But beyond the trolling and PR stunts, there was another aspect of Metzger's politics that seems to have been influenced by the left: the question of organization. Metzger aimed to make White Aryan Resistance into a popular, insurrectionary organization of political combat. An organization based in the (white) working class, lumpen-proletariat, and petite bourgeoisie and hostile to and contemptuous of the elite and their law and order.

Metzger hoped his media efforts would spark organic racial "resistance" among lower-class whites and wanted WAR to be an organization that straddled the line between legalistic and armed struggle.

Metzger's consistent solidarity with neo-nazi prisoners—or "POWs," as he called them—like the captured terrorists of the Order, was clearly modeled on similar efforts by the left on behalf of Puerto Rican, Black liberation, and anti-imperialist prisoners. And similar to much of the left, WAR argued for solidarity with these prisoners despite advocating a different strategic approach than underground armed struggle.

It was only after the SPLC bankrupted Metzger and crippled WAR in their civil lawsuit on behalf of the family of Mulugeta Seraw that Metzger jettisoned his mass public approach in favor of advocating clandestine "lone wolf" tactics. Instead of seeing "lone wolf" tactics as cutting edge, we should understand them as the establishment apparently sees them: a marginalizing and losing strategy—and one they believe can be imposed on formerly dangerous groups.

Third Position versus the Three Way Fight

We need to sum up the aspects of Metzger's legacy that are distinct and represent a Third Positionist/Strasserite tendency posing unique problems for antifascists—but also understand why Metzger and his brand of fascism are an enemy of all of the alienated, exploited, and oppressed—including so-called "whites."

Third Positionism is dangerous even if it remains marginal among organized fascists. It can serve to sharpen up the overall fascist movement—make it more aware of class grievances within the white working class and provide cover against accusations of class collaboration with the white elite.

It can also be used by the state and the media to try to muddy the differences between revolutionary antiauthoritarians and the fascists, to present struggles against capitalism, patriarchy, and the state as racist and antisemitic.

Metzger showed that fascists can and will advocate revolution against the system, clash with police and mainstream institutions, and embrace a strategy that looks to organic popular militancy and that aims to spark (white) working class–based action. Metzger was open to alliances with nationalists of other ethnicities (except Jews) and to allowing independent organizations of white women.

While all of this conflicts with common left understandings of fascists, none of it is actually liberatory, and it just represents a different kind of threat to the multiracial working class. Third Positionism does not break with the colonialist conceptions of "race" brought about by emperors, plantation owners, and slave catchers—it positions it as the central struggle of humanity. Capitalism isn't opposed by these fascists for its exploitation of human labor and destruction of the earth—but for its tendency to favor profit over any racial loyalty to white workers. These nazis may want to eliminate the present ruling class, but they want a new, sharper social hierarchy—one they delude themselves into believing is built on the firmer foundation of Nature and/or God.

For all of Metzger's noise about fighting the system, a look at the pages of the *WAR* newspaper will show that he was most committed to one kind of war—a race war against Black people, the Jewish community, and Mexican immigrants. In Portland it was not a banker or a CEO or an elitist politician—and not an antifa enemy combatant—whom Metzger's contacts in the field murdered, but an unarmed college student from one of the poorest countries on the planet.

However "radical" Metzger's strategy, it would only mean massive violence and bloodshed among the multinational working classes of the United States Empire and the abdication of any moral, human grounding for its white participants. These fascists might fire up a base on hatred for the rich—but their fire is not directed upward. And ironically, this makes this kind of politics potentially interesting to the rich and their security services. When the chips are down and forces are needed that can speak the language of "socialism," the Third Position could become useful.

To oppose these horrors, we must take to heart the slogan of the CNT labor union in the Spanish Civil War: "The War [against fascism] and the Revolution Are Inseparable." We must understand that fascism is capable of donning a "revolutionary" face—and must never cede our opposition to the system. Left support for the status quo concedes to the fascists the mantle of righteous opposition. And our opposition is not only to this present arrangement of the pyramid—because unlike the fascists we oppose *all* forms of exploitation, oppression, and rank.

The alternative we champion cannot just live in slogans and theses, but must be perceivable on the ground, in the culture of our campaigns and organizations. The three way fight is for freedom.

Further Reading

Flores, Celina, Mic Crenshaw, Erin Yanke, et al. *It Did Happen Here*. Independently produced podcast, 2020. See also the book edition: Moe Bowstern, Mic Crenshaw, Alec Dunn, Celina Flores, Julie Perini, and Erin Yanke, *It Did Happen Here: An Antifascist People's History* (Oakland: PM Press, 2023).

Hamerquist, Don, et al. *Confronting Fascism: Discussion Documents for a Militant Movement.* 2nd ed. Montreal: Kersplebedeb Publishing, 2017. First published 2002.

Langer, Elinor. *A Hundred Little Hitlers: The Death of a Black Man, the Trial of a White Racist, and the Rise of the Neo-Nazi Movement in America.* New York: Macmillan, 2003.

Moore, Hilary, and James Tracy. *No Fascist USA! The John Brown Anti-Klan Committee and Lessons for Today's Movements.* San Francisco: City Lights/Open Media, 2020.

Ridgeway, James. *Blood in the Face: White Nationalism from the Birth of a Nation to the Age of Trump.* Chicago: Haymarket Books, 2021. First published 1990 by Thunder's Mouth Press (New York).

Zeskind, Leonard. *Blood and Politics: The History of the White Nationalist Movement from the Margins to the Mainstream.* New York: Farrar, Straus and Giroux, 2009.

Principal Enemy: Demystifying Far-Right Antisemitism

Matthew N. Lyons

Three Way Fight, November 15, 2018

I can think of at least four reasons why leftists and antifascists need a good analysis of antisemitism:

1. *Antisemitism kills Jews.* There should be no question about this after the Pittsburgh synagogue massacre. In the United States, Gentiles are not killing Jews on anywhere near the scale of cops killing Black people, or husbands and boyfriends killing women, or cisgender folks killing trans people, but anti-Jewish violence is real. And if the current political climate means anything, it is likely to get worse.[1]

2. *Antisemitism drives far-right politics.* From the neo-nazis who call Jews the main enemy of the white race, to Patriot groups that stockpile weapons to confront "globalist elites," to Christian theocrats who look forward to mass killings of Jews and mass conversion of the survivors, US far rightists put antisemitic themes at the center of their belief systems. These forces have been closely bound up with Donald Trump's political rise, and over the past two years they have helped blast away the taboo against antisemitism in US political discourse.

3. *Antisemitism is a problem within the left.* Conservatives have long portrayed the left—falsely—as the main source of Jew-hatred, but that doesn't mean leftists have done a good job of combating it. Antisemites such as Gilad Atzmon and Kevin Barrett have been welcomed into respected radical venues such as *CounterPunch* and Left Forum, and efforts to correct this have had mixed success, often meeting fierce opposition and denial. Many radical Jews have encountered antisemitic attitudes in leftist circles, such as

"Jews control the media" or "the Zionist lobby controls Congress." Excusing antisemitism, let alone promoting it, hurts the left's credibility and integrity and weakens all our efforts.[2]

4.   *The charge of antisemitism has been widely misused.* Zionist groups often label criticisms of Israel or calls for Palestinian self-determination as inherently "antisemitic." Such claims falsely equate Jews' safety with Israel's repressive and murderous policies, discredit principled efforts to combat antisemitism (whether by opponents or supporters of the Israeli state), and mask Zionism's own long history of collusion with Jews' oppression. Misuse of the antisemitism charge doesn't cause or excuse anti-Jewish scapegoating, but it highlights the need for clear radical analysis.

My aim here is to help strengthen radical antifascist analysis of antisemitism by pulling together some of the best insights I've found in other people's writings. I'm primarily concerned with far-right antisemitism, because far rightists are spearheading the resurgence of scapegoating and violence against Jews in the United States and elsewhere. At the same time, it's important to look at how far-right antisemitism is rooted in US political culture as a whole, and in the structural dynamics of Jews' roles in US society. In addition, it's important to recognize that far-right antisemitism can take sharply different ideological forms, resulting in different policies and with different implications for antifascist strategy.

There are a lot of good writings about antisemitism. In this post I will highlight four works that explore the topic in different ways and, in combination, address many of the key issues involved. All four are freely available online. Three of them were published in 2017, against the backdrop of Trump's election and the far-right upsurge that contributed to it; the fourth was published in 2009, about a year after Barack Obama took office, at a time when US far rightists of various kinds were mustering their forces. Here are the four:

- Eric K. Ward, "Skin in the Game: How Antisemitism Animates White Nationalism"
- Jews for Racial & Economic Justice, *Understanding Antisemitism: An Offering to Our Movement*
- Ben Lorber, "Understanding Alt-Right Antisemitism"
- Rachel Tabachnick, "The New Christian Zionism and the Jews: A Love/Hate Relationship"[3]

"The Driving Force of White Dispossession"

I want to start with Eric K. Ward's "Skin in the Game: How Antisemitism Animates White Nationalism," because it lays out a case for why understanding and combating antisemitism should be a strategic priority. As Ward argues, the modern white nationalist movement sees Jews not just as one of its enemies, but as the *main* enemy—the group that's chiefly responsible for most of what's wrong with US society today:

> The successes of the civil rights movement created a terrible problem for White supremacist ideology. White supremacism—inscribed de jure by the Jim Crow regime and upheld de facto outside the South—had been the law of the land, and a Black-led social movement had toppled the political regime that supported it. How could a race of inferiors have unseated this power structure through organizing alone? For that matter, how could feminists and LGBTQ people have upended traditional gender relations, leftists mounted a challenge to global capitalism, Muslims won billions of converts to Islam? How do you explain the boundary-crossing allure of hip hop? The election of a Black president? Some secret cabal, some mythological power, must be manipulating the social order behind the scenes. This diabolical evil must control television, banking, entertainment, education, and even Washington, D.C. It must be brainwashing White people, rendering them racially unconscious....
>
> White supremacism through the collapse of Jim Crow was a conservative movement centered on a state-sanctioned anti-Blackness that sought to maintain a racist status quo. The White nationalist movement that evolved from it in the 1970s was a revolutionary movement that saw itself as the vanguard of a new, Whites-only state. This latter movement, then and now, positions Jews as the absolute other, the driving force of White dispossession—which means the other channels of its hatred cannot be intercepted without directly taking on antisemitism.[4]

The Pittsburgh synagogue massacre offers an example of how antisemitism is bound up with other white nationalist themes. Shortly before taking his guns to Tree of Life synagogue in Pittsburgh, neo-nazi Robert Bowers denounced the Jewish refugee aid organization HIAS for bringing "invaders in that kill our people."[5] Here and elsewhere, white nationalists see Jews as the wire-pullers directing other groups that threaten the white race.

Ward notes that white nationalism is a "fractious" movement that "does not take a single unified position on the Jewish question."[6] To elaborate on Ward's point, some white nationalists think all Jews should be killed, while others think we wouldn't be a threat if we all moved to Israel. And a few, such as Jared Taylor of *American Renaissance*, have even reached out to a few right-wing Jews to join them. Nevertheless, scapegoating Jews and Jewish power has been a "throughline" from David Duke's remake of the Ku Klux Klan in the 1970s to the alt-right of today.

Much of "Skin in the Game" traces Ward's political development as a "Black male punk" who grew up in Southern California and moved to Oregon, and who "began to fight White nationalism because my world, my scene, my friends, and my music were under neonazi attack." It was in this context that he came to identify antisemitism as "a particular and potent form of racism so central to White supremacy that Black people would not win our freedom without tearing it down." Yet he also encountered resistance to addressing antisemitism from "the most established progressive antiracist leaders, organizations, coalitions, and foundations around the country." These groups were committed to a simple model of racial oppression, in which Jews (or at least Ashkenazi Jews) were white and therefore talking about antisemitism would "deny the workings of White privilege."[7]

Ward's solution to this dilemma is to call European American Jews' white privilege into question. The argument here is ambiguous: at some points he refers to this privilege as a "myth" or a "fantasy," which I think is at best oversimplified (because clearly we European American Jews do have access to white privilege, at least most of the time), but elsewhere he refers to it as "provisional," which hints at a more complex analysis.

The Most Accessible Targets for Popular Anger

Some of that analysis can be found in my second recommended work: the pamphlet *Understanding Antisemitism: An Offering to Our Movement*, produced by Jews for Racial & Economic Justice. JFREJ argues that Jews

suffer from "definitional instability" when it comes to race....
Like the Irish and Italians, light-skinned Jews of European
descent once faced pervasive, racialized bigotry. Today they
primarily identify as white and are read as white, benefit from
white privilege, and participate in upholding the system of white
supremacy. However, this whiteness is contextual and conditional.... Antisemitic beliefs predate modern white supremacy
ideology. But white supremacy has since been incorporated into
antisemitism, creating a shifting, slippery mixture of religious
intolerance, mythology and racism. This means that Jews can
sometimes be racialized as white, but antisemitism persists, and
white Jews can still be considered "other" because of religious
difference and cultural stereotypes.[8]

I've argued elsewhere that American Jews' racial "instability" falls
into distinct historical periods: through most of US history, Jews of
European descent have been defined as white, but this was not the case
from the 1880s to the 1940s, when millions of southern and eastern
Europeans (including most Jews) "temporarily formed an intermediate group in the racial hierarchy, above people of color but below
native-born whites. During this time, and none other, Jews in the US
faced a wave of systematic discrimination in jobs, schools, and housing,
and anti-Jewish propaganda, organizing, and violence reached record
levels." During other periods, white privilege has mitigated the impact
of antisemitism, but it has never offered Jews full protection from
scapegoating and violence.[9]

JFREJ's *Understanding Antisemitism* is notable in particular
because it presents a structural model of antisemitism, in which Jews
(a) become concentrated in highly visible positions of relative privilege, (b) are used as scapegoats to divert popular anger away from the
real centers of power and oppression, and (c) experience alternating
periods of relative acceptance and intense, violent persecution:

> Many oppressions, such as anti-Black racism in the United
> States, could be said to require a fixed hierarchy or binary values
> system.... By contrast, antisemitism is often described as "cycli-
> cal." The Jewish experience in Europe has been characterized
> as cycling between periods of Jewish stability and even success,

only to be followed by periods of intense anti-Jewish sentiment and violence.... In order for [myths of Jewish power] to be plausible and gain purchase, Jews must accumulate at least some wealth and standing in society.... When the workers in these countries got angry about their exploitation, the most accessible targets were often Jews, rather than the elite political and economic actors who actually had power over the system and were almost exclusively Christian.[10]

This same dynamic, JFREJ argues, has been replicated in the modern United States, in a context of "racialized capitalist exploitation":

As they became classified as white, a large sector of assimilable Jews in the United States acquired real privileges such as a path into professional roles like teachers, social workers, doctors, or lawyers. They took on roles as intermediaries—middle agents— between large institutions and the people that they service. In big cities, these professionals are often the face of systemic racism and class oppression, delivered through schools, hospitals, government agencies, and financial institutions and service provision non-profits. Neither the professionals in middle-agent roles, or their poor, working class and POC clients are actually empowered to change the system. However, the professionals do have more positional power relative to their clients. For those clients, these doctors, lawyers, social workers and teachers— often Jewish—are the most immediately accessible face of those systems. They are the "middlemen" between the oppressed and the systems oppressing them. This focuses anger about racism on Jews, and because of antisemitic stereotypes about Jews, that anger spreads and persists even in places where there are few, or no, Jews.[11]

This structural model of antisemitism has been around for decades and is partly based on Belgian Trotskyist Abram Leon's theory of Jews as a "people-class,"[12] yet it is widely ignored by today's US left. *Understanding Antisemitism* presents it effectively while wisely cautioning against treating the cyclical dynamic as universal or permanent. As JFREJ notes, it doesn't necessarily describe the history of Jewish-Gentile relations in North Africa or the Middle East, for example. I would extend the caveats further. In particular, I disagree with JFREJ's claim that the Nazi genocide was a "clear example" of scapegoating Jews to redirect working-class rage away from the ruling class. If, as JFREJ quotes Aurora Levins Morales, "the goal [of antisemitism] is not to crush us, it's to have us available for crushing,"[13] then Nazism went completely off script, by making the systematic extermination of Jews a goal that overrode all other political and military priorities. However, as a first approximation for understanding what generates and sustains antisemitism today, JFREJ's approach is miles ahead of the conventional—and tautological—claim that antisemitism is simply an expression of "hate."

Understanding Antisemitism has a lot more to offer, such as a good overview of Jews' ethnic and economic diversity in the United States, a thoughtful discussion of how anti-Jewish and anti-Muslim oppressions are related, and a good argument for the strategic value of supporting the leadership of Jews of color. The pamphlet also offers a useful starting discussion of Israel and Zionism, arguing on the one hand that it is legitimate to criticize Israel and Zionism as oppressive to Palestinians, and on the other hand that Israel's oppressive policies are comparable to what many states practice around the world, and thus singling out Israel for special condemnation tends to play into antisemitism.

But the pamphlet has other shortcomings as well. *Understanding Antisemitism* includes no discussion of gender or the ways that antisemitism and male supremacy have interacted and reinforced each other. The pamphlet says nothing about Zionism's long history of promoting antisemitic stereotypes and allying with antisemites in the name of building the Jewish state. And aside from a brief note in the glossary, there is no discussion of the Christian right, although the United States has far more Christian rightists than white nationalists. This is consistent with the silence about Zionism's support for antisemitism, since most Christian rightists are both pro-Zionist and antisemitic.

"Embedding Themselves Like a Virus"
To begin to address these limitations, I turn to my third recommended work on the topic: Ben Lorber's essay, "Understanding Alt-Right Antisemitism." Lorber's aim here is to examine "the ideology of

antisemitism on the alt-right, and its intersection with alt-right Zionism, in comparison with anti-Jewish ideologies of the 20th century." In the process, he elucidates some themes whose significance goes far beyond Richard Spencer and his comrades.

Lorber's analysis of alt-right antisemitism focuses largely on the work of Kevin MacDonald, a retired academic and one of white nationalism's most influential theoreticians. MacDonald edits the *Occidental Quarterly* and its online counterpart, the *Occidental Observer*, and has published a series of books on Jews and Judaism. The basic premises found here and in the works of other alt-rightists are standard antisemitic fare going back to *The Protocols of the Elders of Zion* and earlier. As summarized by Lorber, "a tight-knit Jewish 'ingroup' embeds itself, like a virus, within the pores of [Western societies], siphoning off resources, rising to the elite and disarming all defenses against their invasion." This in-group has worked stealthily to gain control of all the major power centers from Hollywood to the IMF and has promoted civil rights, multiculturalism, feminism, and open immigration policies within the United States—while using neoliberal austerity policies to subjugate nation-states in Europe and elsewhere. In all these spheres, Jews function as the master puppeteers. "While other hated ethnic and religious groups, such as blacks, Latinos, Arabs and Muslims, represent external threats, Jews, [alt-rightists] claim, destabilize White European-American society from within, through the gradual, imperceptible institutionalization of creeping white genocide."[14]

In drawing parallels between the antisemitism of today's alt-right and twentieth-century fascist movements, Lorber draws on Moishe Postone's brilliant essay "Anti-Semitism and National Socialism," which elucidated modern antisemitism's concept of Jewish power:

> What characterizes the power imputed to the Jews in modern anti-Semitism is that it is mysteriously intangible, abstract, and universal. It is considered to be a form of power that does not manifest itself directly, but must find another mode of expression. It seeks a concrete carrier, whether political, social, or cultural, through which it can work.... It is considered to stand behind phenomena, but not to be identical with them. Its source is therefore deemed hidden—conspiratorial. The Jews represent an immensely powerful, intangible, international conspiracy.[15]

Modern antisemitism, Postone explained further, set up a phony dichotomy between the "abstract" (rootless, cosmopolitan) power of "unproductive" finance capital and the "concrete" (rooted, patriotic) power of "productive" industrial capital (ignoring the reality that industrial and financial capital are integrally connected). Thus, anger at capitalism could be channeled into hatred of Jews—the socialism of fools. At the same time, Jews' abstract power was identified not only with the ruthless financier but also the dangerous leftist—two faces of the modern world, both of which threatened the traditional social order. Both Nazism in the 1930s and the alt-right today follow this same basic schema.[16]

Along with these parallels, Lorber's essay also points to certain distinctive features of alt-right antisemitism. One, which Lorber mentions only in passing, is the emphasis on evolutionary psychology. Although earlier generations of antisemites made use of social Darwinism and the image of a ruthless struggle between races, alt-rightists have updated this approach for the twenty-first century. MacDonald, an evolutionary psychologist by profession, has labeled Judaism a "group evolutionary strategy," providing scapegoating and demonization with a modern-sounding, pseudo-scientific veneer. Looking beyond the scope of Lorber's essay, evolutionary psychology has also strongly influenced alt-right gender theory, via the writings of various manosphere figures and male tribalist Jack Donovan (who was active in the alt-right for years before repudiating its white nationalism in the wake of the August 2017 Unite the Right rally).[17]

Lorber devotes more attention to another distinctive feature of the alt-right: its admiration for Zionism. As he notes, "old-school" white nationalists such as David Duke have tended to demonize Israel and treat "Zionism" as a code word for the international Jewish conspiracy. In contrast, many alt-right figures have endorsed the Zionist project as a positive step toward racial separation. "I do not oppose the existence of Israel," Lorber quotes Counter-Currents editor Greg Johnson, "I oppose the Jewish diaspora in the United States and other white societies. I would like to see the white peoples of the world break the power of the Jewish diaspora and send the Jews to Israel, where they will have to learn how to be a normal nation." Other alt-rightists, such as Richard Spencer, have written admiringly about Zionism as an example of ethnonationalism that white Americans and Europeans should emulate.[18]

Lorber points out that there is a long history of antisemites supporting Zionism—such as Henry Ford in the 1920s—and that political Zionism's founder Theodor Herzl proposed that his movement work with "respectable anti-Semites" who would support the removal of Jews from Western societies. In the process, Herzl believed, "the anti-Semites will become our most dependable friends, the anti-Semitic countries our allies." (The State of Israel later implemented Herzl's vision when it cultivated friendly relations, for example, with antisemitic governments in South Africa and Argentina.)[19]

By highlighting the compatibility of antisemitism and Zionism, Lorber's essay fills one of the important gaps in JFREJ's *Understanding Antisemitism* pamphlet. It also helps us understand the politics of Donald Trump, who offers aggressive support for Israel's apartheid and settler colonialism while also echoing and amplifying antisemitic conspiracy theories.

Fish to Be Caught

My fourth recommended text follows a related thread. Rachel Tabachnick's essay "The New Christian Zionism and the Jews: A Love/Hate Relationship," first published in late 2009, examines a form of right-wing antisemitism that often gets left out of the discussion. The Christian right, a mass movement that aims to impose a repressive, reactionary version of Christianity on US society, is anti-Jewish by definition, but it's rarely viewed that way because most Christian rightists are staunchly pro-Zionist.

Tabachnick's essay identifies both similarities and differences between Christian right antisemitism and its white nationalist counterpart. Christian rightists, and specifically Christian Zionists, promote standard antisemitic tropes, such as portraying Jews as preoccupied with money and claiming that Jewish bankers engage in sinister plots to weaken the US economy. Christian Zionists also look forward to future mass killings of Jews as a key part of a divine plan. On a more basic level, Christian Zionists, like white nationalists, see Jews as exercising an influence over human affairs that is vastly out of proportion to our numbers or actual roles in society.[20]

But there are also important contrasts between the Christian right's *religious* antisemitism and white nationalists' *racial* antisemitism. White nationalists believe that Jews are a race apart, intrinsically threaten whites, and must be either physically separated from whites or exterminated. But most Christian rightists claim, insidiously, to love Jews. They believe that Jewishness is a redeemable flaw, which can be overcome by accepting Jesus as humanity's divine savior. Most of them believe, further, that as God's original chosen people Jews have an important role to play in the End Times, and that Israel's founding and growth are important steps toward Jesus's return. "Christian Zionists," Tabachnick notes, "talk about themselves as 'fishers' who entice Jews to move to Israel, while 'hunters' are those who violently force the Jews who are unresponsive to the fishers." John Hagee, a prominent Christian Zionist leader, notoriously referred to Hitler as a hunter who was sent by God.[21]

Tabachnick also describes a trend within Christian Zionism that is intensifying its anti-Jewish momentum:

> The traditional fundamentalist leaders of the movement preach that Jews returning to the Holy Land are a necessary part of the end times in which born-again Christians will escape death as they are raptured into heaven. Jews and other nonbelievers will remain on earth to suffer under the seven-year reign of the anti-Christ. Then, as the story goes, Jesus will come back with his armies, be accepted by the surviving Jews, and reign for a thousand years. This belief motivates adherents to send funds for West Bank settlements, to lobby for preemptive wars seen as precursors to the end times, and support Jews in the diaspora to make "aliyah" and move to Israel.
>
> Now Christian Zionism—along with much of evangelicalism— is being swept by a charismatic movement which has rewritten the role of Jews in their end times narrative.... In their increasingly popular narrative, it is not unconverted but only converted or so-called Messianic Jews who will serve as the trigger for the return of Jesus and the advent of the millennial (thousand year) kingdom on earth. This growing belief is driving the movement to aggressively proselytize Jews and to support "Messianic" ministries in both Israel and Jewish communities worldwide. One splinter group has even taken this story to an extreme, saying they themselves are the "true Israelites" who will play the prophetic role of establishing heaven on earth by moving to Israel.[22]

This Christian right focus on "Messianic" Jews (those who have converted to Christianity but still retain Jewish identity and elements of Jewish ritual) is part of the context in which Mike Pence invited a "Messianic rabbi" to offer a public prayer for those killed in the Pittsburgh synagogue massacre.[23]

The charismatic movement that Tabachnick refers to is called New Apostolic Reformation (NAR). Founded in 1996, NAR has over three million followers in the United States and many more worldwide, as well as an extensive network of ministries and media organs. It is one of the leading forces on the far-right end of the Christian right spectrum, calling on Christians not just to ban abortion and same-sex marriage, but to "take dominion" over all spheres of society. As I wrote in *Insurgent Supremacists,*

> NAR combines a theocratic vision with an organizational struc-
> ture that is far more centralized and authoritarian than most on
> the Christian right.... NAR leaders use "strategic-level" spiritual
> warfare to cast out evil spirits that are supposedly ruling over
> whole cities, regions, or countries—or over whole groups of
> people, such as homosexuals or Muslims.... NAR leaders teach
> that their adherents will develop vast supernatural powers, such
> as defying gravity or healing every person inside a hospital just
> by laying hands on the building. Eventually, these people will
> become "manifest sons of God," who essentially have God-like
> powers over life and death. In the End Times, too, some one or
> two billion people will convert to Christianity, and God will
> transfer control of all wealth to the NAR apostles.[24]

NAR's leaders have also enthusiastically supported Donald Trump's presidential candidacy and administration.

Because of their political support for Israel, Christian Zionists have been warmly received by Israeli prime minister Netanyahu and other members of his Likud Party, as well as leading American Jewish figures such as Anti-Defamation League head Abraham Foxman and the American Israel Public Affairs Committee. Yet as Tabachnick writes,

> Christian Zionists openly teach narratives that parallel the story
> lines of overt anti-Semitism in which Jews are portrayed not as
> ordinary people, but as superhuman or subhuman. With almost

no challenge (and often endorsement) from Jewish leadership, Christian Zionists are stripping away the hard-won humanity of Jews with a broadcast capacity and international reach that overtly antisemitic organizations could never match.[25]

•

Each of the four essays I've profiled here offers important insights about far-right antisemitism, and in combination they enable us to begin piecing together a fuller and more powerful analysis. Some of the themes I would emphasize in summary are:

- Antisemitism centers on a myth of Jewish power—a power that is superhuman, hidden, and dangerous. This mythical power often stands in for actual systems of oppression and exploitation.
- Antisemitism demonizes Jews and often seeks to expel or annihilate us, but it can also involve twisted forms of respect or admiration.
- Antisemitism plays a strategically pivotal role in the politics of multiple far-right movements. White nationalists regard Jews as their principal enemy, while Christian Zionists regard Jews as a special community whose elimination is essential to God's plan for the world.
- Far-right antisemitism takes dramatically different forms, as embodied in the contrast between racial and religious ideologies, and in varying positions with regard to Zionism.
- Antisemitic scapegoating is historically rooted in structural dynamics that tend to concentrate Jews in prominent positions of relative privilege.
- Antisemitism in the United States is interwoven in complex ways with the system of white supremacy, and Jews are targeted in ways that differ from but are interconnected with the targeting of people of color.

The texts discussed here are just a few of many useful writings about antisemitism and its relationship with far-right politics. Strengthening our understanding of these issues is a vital part of building a strong antifascist movement.

Threat or Model? US Rightists Look at China

Matthew N. Lyons

Three Way Fight, April 20, 2020

The coronavirus crisis has spurred a sharp increase in scapegoating, harassment, and physical attacks against Chinese and other Asian people in the United States.[1] This racist upsurge has been fomented not only by white nationalists, but even more dramatically by President Trump, other government officials, and right-wing media organs such as Fox News.[2]

But there's more going on here than knee-jerk racist scapegoating and dog-whistle rhetoric. The US right has been heavily concerned with China for years, and its views on the subject are complex, involving a shifting mix of political themes and a range of positions that relate to the current pandemic but have implications far beyond it. This article explores some of these broader rightist positions on China. Specifically, I compare the geopolitical focus of America Firsters such as Donald Trump and Steve Bannon with white nationalists' racial focus, but I also look at divisions among white nationalists themselves, with some vilifying China and others praising it.

Three Themes of Anti-Chinese Politics

Historically, anti-Chinese politics in the US has centered on three major themes: racist demonization, anticommunism, and geopolitical fear. While these themes are interconnected and often presented in combination, each is rooted in a distinct historical period and set of developments.

Chinese people first came to the US in large numbers in the mid-nineteenth century. By the 1870s, they formed an important and heavily exploited part of the labor force in California and other parts of the West. White workers spearheaded campaigns to drive Chinese out of jobs, called for a ban on Chinese immigration, and carried out a series of pogroms and expulsions, such as an 1885 massacre of at least twenty-eight Chinese miners in Rock Springs, Wyoming. The 1882 Chinese Exclusion Act barred Chinese laborers from immigrating, and the ban was extended to all Chinese in 1884 and to immigrants from many other Asian countries in 1917. Chinese immigration was completely forbidden until 1943 and not permitted in substantial numbers until 1965.

Racist demonization of Chinese people in the nineteenth century sometimes equated them with Blacks or Native Americans, but sometimes portrayed them in ways that resembled anti-Jewish stereotypes—as crafty schemers with mysterious powers, or as blood-sucking parasites or vampires. Like Jews, Chinese men were alternately portrayed as effeminate or as sexual predators who lured or forced white women into prostitution. Sometimes Chinese people were linked with disease. During a 1900 bubonic plague scare in San Francisco's Chinatown, one newspaper warned that "The almond-eyed Mongolian is watching for his opportunity, waiting to assassinate you and your children with one of his many maladies."[3] All of these motifs have persisted in US racist discourse.

China and people of Chinese descent became targets of anticommunism following the 1949 Chinese Revolution and especially after the People's Liberation Army intervened in the Korean War in 1950 on the side of North Korea. During the McCarthy era in the 1950s, Chinese Americans were widely suspected of political disloyalty, and conservative and liberal politicians alike regarded China as an expansionist threat second only to the Soviet Union.[4] Anticommunist fears of China intensified in the 1960s, with the Cultural Revolution and the Chinese government's expressions of support for anti-imperialist and revolutionary movements across the Global South.

The specter of a Chinese Red Menace declined in the 1970s and '80s with improved US-China relations, Mao's death, and China's shift toward a market economy, yet many US rightists have continued to see Communist Party rule in China as inherently threatening. Since the Chinese government has effectively abandoned all pretentions to represent a force for anticapitalist revolution, American denunciations of Chinese communism have tended to focus on human rights issues. There's no question that the Chinese government is profoundly authoritarian and has engaged in mass-scale repression against dissidents and ethnoreligious minorities, but anticommunism demonizes Chinese repression selectively, as if it were qualitatively different from similar or worse practices carried out by overtly capitalist regimes.

The newest thread of US anti-Chinese politics is fear of China as a geopolitical threat to the United States. This fear has emerged over the past few decades, as China has pursued dramatic and relatively uninterrupted economic growth, and particularly since it became the world's second-biggest economy about ten years ago. As its economic power has grown, China has sponsored high-profile development projects in other countries of Asia, Africa, and Europe and has expanded its military forces and geographic military presence. While the US ruling class and political elites as a whole view these developments with concern, many right-wingers view an increasingly powerful China not as one part of a global capitalist system operating according to the same basic interests as other powers, but rather in Manichean terms as a fundamentally different and malevolent force uniquely bent on world conquest.

In the years leading up to the coronavirus pandemic, US rightists have tapped into all of these traditions, but they've done so in different ways. In broad terms, Donald Trump and many of his America Firster allies and supporters have been driven primarily by geopolitical fears in relation to China while making use of anti-Chinese racism to mobilize support. By contrast, race is the critical concern for alt-rightists and other white nationalists (who helped President Trump get elected but have become increasingly disenchanted with his administration), and their views of China center on promoting the interests of the white race before anything else. However, white nationalists are themselves sharply divided on whether China is an ethnostate to be admired and emulated or a racial threat second only to Jews.

Trump and America Firsters

Trump's nationalist rhetoric has been targeting China for years, with an emphasis on claims that the Beijing government uses unfair trade practices (such as stealing US firms' intellectual property) and currency manipulation. Defying neoliberal orthodoxy, in 2018 the Trump administration launched a tariff war with China, promoting it as a way to bring manufacturing jobs back to the United States. Although the policy measures are economic, Trump has often framed the conflict in broader existential terms. At a 2015 campaign rally he referred to China as "our enemy," and at another rally the following year he denounced China's trade practices as "rap[ing] our country."[5] Trump adviser Peter Navarro, one of the strongest advocates of economic nationalism within the administration, has published a series of books that the *New York Times* describes as "anti-China screeds." Going far beyond economic concerns, he has warned against "the growing dangers of a heavily armed, totalitarian regime intent on regional hegemony and bent on global domination."[6]

America Firsters warning about China often sound like liberals and centrists warning about Vladimir Putin's Russia. This past December, Fox News commentator and informal Trump adviser Tucker Carlson got in a heated on-air debate with a former Clinton adviser over whether the United States' biggest threat was China or Russia.[7]

Another leading America Firster preoccupied with China has been Steve Bannon, who served as chief strategist at the beginning of the Trump administration and remains influential with the president. Bannon's anti-Chinese ideology combines geopolitical and anticommunist themes. Bannon has praised Trump for defining China as the greatest threat facing the United States and has predicted a US–China war within five to ten years. He has referred to COVID-19 as a "CCP [Chinese Communist Party] virus" and has argued that China's government is in league with globalist economic elites against the United States.[8]

Both Bannon and Trump have also evoked racist fears of Chinese people as a hidden malevolent force. The "Committee on the Present Danger: China," a group Bannon cofounded in 2019, warns that Beijing is "undermining and subverting Western democracies from within" through its supposed control of Chinese students and professors in the United States. Trump, as early as 2012, declared that to "Lie, Cheat & Steal in all international dealings" was "the Chinese M.O."[9]

But in Trump's politics with regard to China, racism is a useful tool—not the driving force. As evidence, Trump only started using the racist dog-whistle phrase "China virus" in mid-March, after referring to it inoffensively as the coronavirus for months. As Lili Loofbourow noted in *Slate*, "the turn to racism is a sign of Trumpian distress. It means that Trump—who hasn't been able to hold rallies amid his adoring fans—is feeling not just insecure but trapped. He thought the coronavirus was one more narrative he could control. He couldn't."[10]

Anti-China White Nationalists

White nationalists (who, unlike Trump and his Republican supporters, want to dismantle the United States and establish a white ethnostate) draw on many of the same themes with regard to China, but configure and prioritize them differently. In their view, any geopolitical challenges to the United States, or ideological challenges to capitalism, are only of concern if they threaten the perceived interests of the white race. And white nationalists are themselves divided on this question when it comes to China.

Sometimes white nationalists sound a lot like America Firsters. Brenda Walker at VDare warns that "Unlike Russia, Red China actually represents a long term threat to America" and "hasn't really changed that much from the bad old Mao days." Michelle Malkin at American Renaissance declares that "Chinese Communist Party agents are using our suicidal pathologies—blind worship of 'diversity,' naive exaltation of 'cultural exchange' programs, and reckless surrender of our education system—against us for economic espionage, intellectual property theft and world dominance."[11] But Robert Hampton at Counter-Currents, a leading alt-right "intellectual" forum, makes a more explicitly racial appeal to white nationalists:

> China doesn't care about our cause, and the Han will never be our allies. China is developing biological weapons to specifically target whites. The Han treat all of their ethnic minorities like dirt, and they can't wait to treat us the same way. Chinese global domination will mean the eclipse of white civilization. It will probably be worse for white people under GloboHan than globohomo. At least globohomo doesn't put us in concentration camps.[12]

Over the past four years, Counter-Currents has featured one of the most virulent and comprehensive compendiums of anti-Chinese racism available: a series of at least eight articles by "F.C. Comtaose," who in 2016 described himself as "a man of East Asian extraction currently living and working in the neo-imperialist China."[13] Comtaose, who also writes under the name "Riki Rei" and appears to be Japanese, denounces China and the Chinese people in hard-line national socialist terms, claiming that "if the Jews ... are the worst enemies white people face from within, the most dangerous external enemy ... is China: the single most ruthless, ambitious, far-sighted, astute, disingenuous, and aggressive adversarial power in the world today."[14]

Unlike Trump or Bannon, Comtaose doesn't just bolster his warnings about China with the occasional racist swipe, but rather puts racial demonization front and center. "In terms of acting as a fifth column for their homeland," he declares, "the Chinese in diaspora certainly rival, and perhaps exceed, the diaspora Jews and their relationship with Israel." In addition, "the Chinese and the Jews, both being races of shrewd and unscrupulous merchants, have long admired and felt affection for each other," and have been working "hand-in-glove for decades in order to further their joint objective of compromising, taking down, and eventually finishing off the white race and Western civilization."[15]

Pro-China White Nationalists

For white nationalist websites such as Counter-Currents to demonize China and Chinese people in racial terms shouldn't surprise anybody. What may be a surprise is that there are other equally staunch white nationalists who take an almost diametrically opposite view of China—seeing it as a successful example of racial nationalism to be emulated rather than feared.

Countering claims that China is a dangerous expansionist dictatorship with a worrisome belief in its own cultural superiority, Thomas Jackson at American Renaissance argues that China is simply "behaving like a healthy, 19th-century world power" that is "not yet shorn of the vigorous racial nationalism that characterized Western nations until only a few generations ago." Jonathan Peter Wilkinson at Amerika writes admiringly that China has "a profound unifying force"—racism—"that allows them to even survive their own Drano-drink of Full-blown, idiotic Marxism" and that represents "an awesome force multiplier" in strategic terms. *Daily Stormer* editor Andrew Anglin sees China as a threat to "ZOG" (Zionist Occupation Government) rather than to the white race and warns that the coronavirus pandemic is actually a desperate ploy to stir up a war quickly between the US and China: "The Jews have realized that the jig is up and they won't be able to act how they act now in a world that is controlled by the Chinese. So they're staging one last hurrah."[16] Anglin of all people, whose supremacist rhetoric has been criticized as too harsh even by other white nationalists, even warns that the media is stirring up "aggressive race hate" against Chinese people.[17]

One of the strongest pro-China voices among US white nationalists is Brad Griffin, who runs the alt-right and neo-Confederate blog *Occidental Dissent* under the name "Hunter Wallace." It's not just that Griffin as a rule writes favorably about China; he directly reverses the polarity on all three traditional anti-Chinese themes of the US political right. His writings on China exemplify far rightists' knack for incorporating leftist ideas and insights into a fundamentally oppressive and antiegalitarian framework:

- On geopolitics, Griffin draws heavily on right-wing anti-interventionist themes to argue that China's conflict is with liberalism and US expansionism, both of which white nationalists reject: "We have no desire to 'police the world' as the US Empire has done in the Western Pacific for generations now. We certainly don't support encircling China with military bases and hostile alliances. We don't support interfering in China's internal affairs." In addition, "We don't believe in 'American exceptionalism' or forcing the American culture on China. We admire and respect China which is one of the world's ancient civilizations. We think China has been smart to shield itself from the degenerating effects of Western culture."[18] And unlike the United States, he writes, "China's foreign policy isn't controlled by Israel."[19]

- On race, Griffin applauds the Chinese people as "ranked high among the world's top races" and hopes whites can create "an ethnostate for our people not unlike China." Further, "we don't mind at all if the Chinese decide to colonize and civilize the negroes [*sic*] of Africa."[20]

- On anticommunism, Griffin argues that China's state-directed economy is just plain better than US neoliberalism: "The life expectancy of White people in the United States is dropping" and "what used to be the American middle class is now descending into poverty thanks to our current economic model!" In contrast, "the Chinese have lifted half a billion people out of poverty" and are "building high speed rail and investing in deep learning to beat the United States in the race to a 21st century economy." Unlike the US, "the Chinese aren't being overrun by Third World immigrants." Explicitly rejecting claims by Steve Bannon that China's unfair trade practices have gutted US manufacturing, Griffin counters that "China is a convenient scapegoat and a way to distract attention from the fact that it is automation that is devastating the working class."[21]

Some of Brad Griffin's views on China dovetail with those of the Lyndon LaRouche network, which espouses a multicultural version of fascist ideology. The LaRouchites have for years celebrated Xi Jinping's combination of political authoritarianism and massive, centralized infrastructure projects such as the Belt and Road Initiative. This month, for example, Helga Zepp-LaRouche (Lyndon's widow and successor as head of the network) denounced "the vicious anti-China campaign being promulgated in the West" as an attempt to deflect blame for Western governments' own shortcomings in responding to the coronavirus pandemic. She also declared "China is not an aggressive force. But naturally, it does threaten the idea of a unipolar world order, which some neo-con and British elements had tried to impose in the period after the collapse of the Soviet Union, through interventionist wars."[22]

•

The range of positions on China outlined above shows us once again that the US right—and even the white nationalist right—is not monolithic in its views. This is significant for several reasons. Racist portrayals of Chinese people—like anti-Jewish stereotyping—can sometimes take an ostensibly positive form while still carrying a dehumanizing message. Rightists can also avoid racist portrayals altogether while still promoting other anti-Chinese themes. And as we've seen, not all rightists vilify China, and even direct criticisms of anti-Chinese racism may come from far-right sources.

The fact that a significant subset of white nationalists take a friendly view of China raises the possibility that some of them may seek to forge ties with the Chinese government, much as some far rightists in the US and other Western countries have received support from Putin's government in Russia. And as different factions of the US ruling class debate how to respond to China geopolitically, rightists won't necessarily all line up on the same side of the debate.

Moscow Conference Draws Fascists, Neo-Confederates, US Leftists

Matthew N. Lyons

Three Way Fight, February 2, 2015

For decades, some far-right opponents of the US empire have been trying to make common cause with leftists. They got another opportunity in December 2014 at an international conference in Moscow on the "Right of Peoples to Self-Determination and Building a Multi-Polar World." The conference was organized by the Anti-Globalization Movement of Russia (AGMR). Participants included US leftists from the United National Antiwar Coalition (UNAC) and the International Action Center (IAC)—both of which are closely associated with the Workers World Party—alongside Russian and Italian fascists and US white nationalists from the neo-Confederate group League of the South. It's worth looking at this convergence in some detail, as it speaks to an important pitfall confronting leftists involved in anti-imperialist coalitions.[1]

UNAC and IAC articles about the Multi-Polar World conference portrayed it as a progressive event against war, racist violence, and repression. The IAC reported, "Major themes of the discussion were the US-backed war against the people of Donetsk and Lugansk in eastern Ukraine, the expansion of NATO into the former Soviet Union and economic war against Russia, Venezuela and Iran, and the ongoing uprising against racism and police brutality in the United States." Neither IAC nor UNAC mentioned that a number of far-right groups were represented. UNAC did note that attendees included Israel Shamir, "a leading anti-Zionist writer from Israel," but didn't mention that Shamir is also a notorious antisemite.[2]

The conference declaration was in keeping with the UNAC/IAC portrayal. It called for an international "united front against discrimination, violation of human rights, religious and racial intolerance" and condemned the "predatory foreign policy of the US and its NATO allies." The declaration also denounced the oppression of people of color in the US and demanded the release of US political prisoners such as Palestinian activist Rasmia Oda, Leonard Peltier, and Mumia Abu Jamal. The declaration urged "the consolidation of the progressive part of mankind" and promised that "we will make every effort to build a multi-polar world!"[3]

Maybe it's a coincidence, but the phrase "multi-polar world" is a major theme in the work of Aleksandr Dugin, Russia's leading fascist theoretician, as in his 2012 book, *The Theory of a Multi-Polar World*.[4] Dugin is leader of the Eurasia Party and the international Eurasianist movement; he envisions a renewed Eurasian "empire" based on authoritarianism, patriarchy, and traditional religion, in which Russians will play a "messianic" role. Dugin disavows biological racism but has called for "the rebirth of the primordial Aryan conscience."[5]

It's unclear to me how close the relationship is between the Anti-Globalization Movement and Dugin, but members of the Duginist Eurasian Youth Union took part in the AGMR's December 2014 conference and have worked with AGMR at other events.[6]

Like Dugin, the AGMR envisions a broad alliance of political forces against US imperialism, ranging from grassroots social movements to Communist Party states to right-wing dictators. The lynchpin of this alliance is Russia. The AGMR website features a list of seven "Faces of Antiglobalization," almost all of whom are or were friendly with Putin's government: Belarusian president Alexander Lukashenko, Syrian dictator Bashar al-Assad, Iran's ex-president Mahmoud Ahmadinejad, the late Muammar Gaddafi of Libya, Venezuela's deceased left populist president Hugo Chávez, and Cuba's Fidel Castro. The one outlier on the list—and only nonstate figure—is Subcomandante Marcos of the Zapatista Army of National Liberation, whose 1994 uprising was a pivotal event in the global justice movement's development.[7]

The overall position statement on the AGMR website opposes "the emerging unipolar world"—i.e., the international dominance of the United States and its allies—and "supports the full sovereignty of nation-states including the sovereignty of Russia as an independent player on the political, economic and cultural world stage."[8]

The AGMR position statement seems carefully designed to appeal to both leftists and rightists. For the leftish side, it criticizes "the global dominance of transnational corporations and supranational trade and financial institutions." For the other end of the spectrum, it warns against "the attempts to impose a 'new world order'" and the threat of "a single mega-totalitarian world state," both of which are standard targets of right-wing conspiracy theories. AGMR also "aims to promote all aspects of the national security and traditional moral values."[9] (According to Interfax news service, the AGMR joined with several rightist groups in 2013 to plan a public protest against same-sex marriage outside the French embassy.)[10]

The AGMR position statement also includes a lot of language about tolerance and self-determination, for example, "respect for other peoples and their sovereignty, value systems and lifestyles." Such phrases appeal to both leftists and liberals, but are also favored by the neofascists of the European New Right (ENR), who have replaced traditional fascist talk of national or racial supremacy with slick appeals to "ethno-pluralism" and "biocultural diversity." Aleksandr Dugin is the ENR's leading representative in Russia.[11]

On one of its web pages, AGMR also gives a hat tip to the Lyndon LaRouche network as some of the "like-minded people" from around the world who took part in conferences that laid the groundwork for the AGMR's founding. The LaRouchites promote a quirky crypto-fascist ideology and in recent years have become increasingly aligned with the Russian government on geostrategic issues, for example echoing a pro-Russian line on the civil wars in Syria and Ukraine.[12]

In addition to the Duginists from the Eurasian Youth Union, the December 2014 Multi-Polar World conference also included representatives of the right-wing Rodina Party (which in 2005 was barred from participating in Moscow Duma elections for inciting racial hatred against immigrants) and the Italian neofascist group Millennium, which has had a close relationship with Dugin's organization for several years. In December 2013, AGMR head Alexander Ionov spoke at a Millennium-sponsored far-right conference in Milan.[13]

The Multi-Polar World conference also drew representatives from Novorossiya, or New Russia, the entity in eastern Ukraine that, with Russian backing, has declared its independence from Kiev. The UNAC/IAC folks portray the Ukrainian conflict as aggression by neo-nazis and US imperialists against the people of eastern Ukraine—utterly ignoring the Russian far rightists who are heavily involved in the eastern separatist movement, as well as the Russian government's own expansionist aims in the region.[14]

US participants in the Multi-Polar World conference included representatives of two Southern secessionist groups, the League of the South and the Texas Nationalist Movement, who promoted their own version of "self-determination." League of the South president Michael Hill spoke at the Multi-Polar World conference and offered a report on the LS website:

> Hill discussed The League of the South and its goal of the survival, well-being, and independence of the Southern people and how the South's identity as an historic "blood and soil" nation conflicts with the current globalist agenda of the USA regime. He emphasized the importance of The League's work not only in preserving a particular people living on a particular land, but also its direct Southern nationalist challenge to the political, economic, and financial engine of globalism—the Washington, DC/European Union alliance.[15]

While the Texas Nationalist Movement seems to avoid taking positions on other political issues besides Texas independence, the League of the South is well known for its advocacy of white nationalism and Christian theocracy.[16] Still, it's a bit surprising to see them openly invoking the Nazi-identified phrase "blood and soil."

The Multi-Polar World conference has drawn some criticism. In a mid-January email to the UFPJ-Activist listserv (UFPJ = United for Peace and Justice), Andrew Pollack criticized UNAC leaders' participation in the conference. Pollack denounced the presence of US white supremacists at the event and the AGMR's involvement in homophobic activism and support for dictators Gaddafi and Assad. He also highlighted the UNAC representatives' praise for the Putin regime, as in the following passage from the UNAC's official report on the conference:

> While in Moscow, we also watched the TV coverage of Russian president Putin giving his annual press conference.... During the press conference, Putin gave figures to show that their economy

has been growing in the past year. He then addressed the question of the falling ruble. He explained that they will be able to weather the crisis but it has pushed them into a position where they need to create more diversity in their economy. This, he projects to happen within a two-year time period.

Moscow is a modern city much like any large US city. The people were dressed well and looked healthy and cared for. We learned that many of the social benefits that existed under the Soviet Union still exist. These include free universal healthcare. For most people, college was free, and students received a stipend for their living expenses. Putin is very popular with a high approval rating among the Russian people. The people see him as a kind of populist leader.[17]

Pollack commented, "If only someone would tell the Russian working class how well off they are!" He concluded: "[Joe] Lombardo [UNAC co-chair] announced that 'The leaders of the Anti-Globalization Movement of Russia have expressed an interest in attending UNAC's conference in May.' Let's make sure the racist scum who UNAC is playing footsie with don't come!"[18]

In an email reply to Pollack, Lombardo wrote that the AGMR supported gay rights and its leaders denied having joined any anti-gay demonstration. Lombardo also stated that the Multi-Polar World conference organizers strongly repudiated the views of the Texas secessionists who attended, and that the organizers' participation in a Black Lives Matter solidarity protest at the US embassy proved they oppose racism.[19]

Maybe the Anti-Globalization Movement of Russia's extensive contacts with fascists and right-wing nationalists result from bad judgment rather than ideological affinity. Either way, their Multi-Polar World conference provided a useful service for far rightists who want to sanitize their image among liberal and leftist audiences.

Unfortunately, UNAC and IAC aren't the only leftists willing to play along with this. Marxist academician Efe Can Gürcan, for example, recently discussed Eurasianism (specifically including Duginism) as an ideological challenge to NATO and US imperialism but didn't mention that Aleksandr Dugin is a fascist. When I objected, Gürcan replied, "One should not avoid potentially transformative dialogue with such movements [as Dugin's] merely because they are not leftist or because their practices are in some areas objectionable." As a self-deluding rationale for red-brown coalition building, this is hard to beat.[20]

Postscript: In the years since this article was first published, the AGMR and its founder Alexander Ionov have received significant international attention. Following on the 2014 Multi-Polar World conference, the AGMR, with Russian government funding, hosted larger, similarly themed international gatherings in 2015 and 2016. In July 2022, US federal prosecutors charged Ionov with acting as an unregistered agent of the Russian government and claimed that he funded and "exercised direction or control" over several US political groups on behalf of the Russian security service to spread propaganda and "cause dissension" in the United States. One of the groups he allegedly funded and controlled was the African People's Socialist Party, whose leader attended the AGMR's 2015 Dialogue of Nations conference. These events highlight both that some leftists continue to collaborate with authoritarian rightists and that the US government and centrist politicians tend to frame such collaboration as a conspiracy by evil outsiders and use it to promote repression against the left (with Black leftists especially targeted).[21]

Network Contagion Research Institute: Helping the State Fight Political Infection Left and Right

Matthew N. Lyons

Three Way Fight, May 9, 2021

In the opening scene of Costa-Gavras's classic film *Z*, about the lead-up to the 1967 military coup in Greece, the chief of police (referred to as the General) addresses a gathering of senior government officials on the "ideological disease" he sees threatening their nation. "It is caused by harmful germs and various parasites," such as socialism, anarchism, beatniks, and pacifist tendencies. "Infection from ideological mildew" must be "fought preventively" by "the spraying of humans with appropriate mixtures"—indoctrination via schooling, military service, and leafleting the peasantry. In addition, the General declares, opponents of the left—who represent "the healthy parts of our society" or "antibodies"—must be used to "combat and eradicate all diseases." As the film unfolds, we learn that the disease eradication he has in mind consists of physically breaking up leftist gatherings, beating up antiwar protesters, and murdering their leaders.[1]

I'm repeatedly reminded of this scene when reading the work of the Network Contagion Research Institute, whose very name depicts harmful politics as ideological disease. The NCRI aims to "track and expose the epidemic of virtual deception, manipulation, and hate, as it spreads between social media communities and into the real world."[2] One of the institute's "Contagion and Ideology Reports" characterizes disinformation and distrust as "a virus that knows no race, that consumes the poor and rich, that infects and kills people of any political persuasion."[3] Another report warns that "viral ideologies infect mainstream communities" and urges the use of "information vaccines" as protection.[4] Costa-Gavras's slightly fictionalized police chief would have been right at home with this discourse.

To be sure, the NCRI has given Costa-Gavras's General a twenty-first-century upgrade: the think tank doesn't endorse nonstate violence, and the "unhealthy" ideas it aims to stamp out emanate from the right as well as the left. But in other ways, the two are strikingly similar. Like the General, the NCRI is a mouthpiece for the state security apparatus and its commitment to defend the established order. Like the General, the NCRI uses the language of epidemiology to strip threatening ideas of both political content and historical context, reduce people who embrace these ideas to passive vessels, and give its own political project a false veneer of scientific objectivity.

Anti-Hate Politics Meets Big Data

The Network Contagion Research Institute was founded in 2018 and is based at Rutgers University under the directorship of Princeton psychologist and neuroscientist Joel Finkelstein. The institute studies how so-called political extremism spreads and develops via social media. The NCRI hosts webinars, offers a college-level training program in "cyber social network threat detection and strategy," and has published a series of reports on topics such as COVID-19 disinformation, anti-Asian and anti-Jewish conspiracy theories, the Militia and boogaloo movements, QAnon, and "militant anarcho-socialist networks."

The NCRI uses a variety of research techniques, but its special sauce is large-scale quantitative analysis of slurs, memes, and code words. With data sets that consist in some cases of tens of millions of social media posts, institute staff and fellows track the frequency with which specific terms appear on various platforms over time. They correlate these patterns with real-world events, measure the spread of hateful ideas from fringe platforms such as 4chan to mainstream ones such as Twitter, and map associations between different frequently used terms to highlight changes in rhetoric and perhaps ideology. For example, the NCRI's report on COVID disinformation used such data analysis to argue that in early 2021 conspiracist opposition to vaccines and public health restrictions was being subsumed into a larger overarching conspiracy theory about a tyrannical New World Order government— and also that antivaccine protests tended to occur in counties where intimidation was used against Black Lives Matter protesters.[5]

I'm not a data scientist, and I'm not going to comment on the NCRI's quantitative methodologies. Yet despite the institute's seeming technical sophistication, its underlying analytic framework is quite crude and weak. The NCRI uses the "hate" framework that has been promoted by the Anti-Defamation League, Southern Poverty Law Center, and others. Kay Whitlock offers an incisive critique:

> In U.S. progressive politics the hate frame has four main assumptions: First, that hate is rooted purely in irrational, personal prejudice and fear and loathing of difference. In fact, it's also rooted in ideologies and supremacy, in a historical and cultural context. Second, that hate is hate, and the specificities don't matter. Third, that the politics of hate is about that crazy irrational feeling, which is caused by personal prejudice gone amok. In this view, hate is not about structures, not about power hierarchies, not about institutional practice. Finally, that hate is perpetrated by extremists, misfits, and loners who are violating agreed-upon standards of fairness, and that hate violence is unacceptable and abhorrent to respectable society.
>
> In fact, what is called "hate violence"—violence directed at vulnerable and marginalized groups—is not abhorrent to respectable society. On the contrary, respectable society has provided the models, policies, and practices that marginalize people of color, queers, disabled people, and in many respects, women. The hate frame disappears considerations of structural violence and substitutes in their place the idea that there are these crazed extremists, and that's who we have to go after.[6]

Hate frame assumptions are integral to the NCRI approach. NCRI draws a neat division between hateful and nonhateful speech, with no concern for the variety of ideologies underlying such speech or the historical context in which it arises. In NCRI reports, for example, you'll find lots of references to racist expression, but no discussion of the differences and relationships between genocidal white supremacism, Proud Boys style "Western chauvinism," and Oath Keepers–style color-blind ideology—and certainly no discussion of how all of these are rooted in a system of racial oppression that has always been central to US society.

As Whitlock argues elsewhere, the hate frame also treats violence against oppressed groups as a problem to be solved with more policing and longer prison terms—without addressing the ways that police and prisons are themselves active perpetrators of systemic violence against oppressed groups on a massive scale.[7] This too, is reflected in the NCRI approach, which is largely geared toward bolstering law enforcement. The institute's report on the boogaloo meme, for example, urges law enforcement agencies to "develop large scale and data-driven approaches and central information-sharing capacity" to track and analyze boogaloo-type threats—in other words, embrace the NCRI methodology as their own.[8]

The NCRI's use of the hate framework is particularly egregious because the institute applies it to the radical left as well as the far right. The NCRI's report on "militant anarcho-socialist networks" repeatedly uses language that links and equates leftists with far rightists. For example, the report refers to antipolice slogans such as ACAB (All Cops Are Bastards) and FTP (Fuck the Police) as "hateful codewords and memes"—putting them in the same category as calls to gas the Jews. The report claims that leftists—like far rightists—demonize and dehumanize political opponents, promote "classic authoritarian narratives," and advocate "violent insurgency." A table summarizing their findings asserts that "Anarcho-Socialist extremists" have displayed all or nearly all the same characteristics as Jihadis and boogaloo: expressing "apocalyptic beliefs," "utopian legends/narratives," and "martyr narratives"; using online propaganda and private or fringe internet forums; organizing armed militias; and carrying out "lone-wolf terror attacks." The only one they're unsure about is whether leftists have carried out "cell-like terror attacks."[9]

The equation of right-wing and left-wing violence is fundamentally dishonest for two reasons, as Kristian Williams has argued. First, rightists in the US have carried out far more terrorist attacks than leftists, as the eminently nonleftist Center for Strategic and International Studies has documented. Second, in Williams's words, whatever tactical or ethical disagreements we may have with leftist attacks, "there can be no equivalency between the violence of a slave revolt and the violence of a slave master, between the violence of antifascists and that of the Atomwaffen Division."[10] The NCRI report on anarcho-socialists doesn't acknowledge any of that, but its authors do maintain a fig leaf of deniability with a footnote cautioning, "This analysis does not suggest that violence from anarcho-socialist militants has yet become as widespread as an organized Jihadi group nor does it have the death toll or historical reach that right-leaning extremism has in the US. However, anarcho-socialist bloodshed has been historically substantial on other continents and Western countries."[11]

The same report also promotes the bogus claim, which has been made by both conservatives and some liberals, that the mass-based riots and violent antipolice activism that followed George Floyd's murder in 2020 were instigated by a few leftist agitators. The report asserts that small groups of activists such as the Portland Youth Liberation Front were able to "mobilize lawlessness and violence" through sophisticated use of online communication to call up a "network-enabled mob" in numerous cities simultaneously. In other words, a think tank that claims to be combating the spread of harmful conspiracy theories is itself replicating a classic conspiracist myth that has been used to demonize leftists for generations.

Toward a Centrist Anti-Hate Coalition

Although the NCRI is a relative newcomer to the extremist-monitoring field, its institutional credentials and impressive-sounding methodology have given it a prominent "expert" status for major media organs such as the *New York Times* and *Los Angeles Times*. The NCRI describes itself as "a neutral and independent third party whose mission it is to track, expose, and combat misinformation, deception, manipulation, and hate across social media channels," assuring us further that it has "no political agenda, profit motive, or university reporting obligations." A more honest description—based on its list of staff and advisers— would be that NCRI represents a convergence of academia (mainly psychologists and artificial intelligence experts), big tech (notably Google's director of research), and security agencies (with current or former members of the US military, Department of Homeland Security, National Security Agency, New York City Police Department, and private firms).[12]

In addition to Rutgers, the NCRI lists "affiliations" with three entities: the Anti-Defamation League, Open Society Foundations, and Charles Koch Foundation. The ADL is one of the most prominent watchdog groups monitoring the US far right, but it's no friend of the left. The organization has long misused the charge of antisemitism to attack Palestinians, Palestine solidarity activists, antiracist activists, and others. In the 1990s, it was revealed that the ADL had spied on a wide range of progressive organizations for decades; as recently as 2017 it publicly urged the FBI to spy on antifa groups, a call it later retracted.[13]

The combination of Open Society and Koch foundations is pivotal to the NCRI brand. Open Society (George Soros's grant-giving network) figures in countless right-wing conspiracy theories while Koch is one of the most hated capitalist names on the left, so by listing the two together the NCRI declares that it transcends political divisions by bringing together staunch liberals and conservatives. Put slightly differently, the combination of Soros and Koch support evokes an attempt to foster a broad—but anti-Trump—coalition within the ruling class. (Contrary to what some leftists have claimed, the Koch network never supported Trump and rejected his positions on both immigration and trade.)[14]

The NCRI's approach dovetails with centrist efforts to woo hardline conservatives away from Trumpism, as witness the institute's recruitment of former Republican congressmember Denver Riggleman to its advisory team. In Congress Riggleman was a member of the arch-conservative Freedom Caucus, but he lost his 2020 reelection bid after officiating at a same-sex wedding. Last month the *New York Times* profiled Riggleman as a courageous opponent of conspiracy-mongering under the title "One Republican's Lonely Fight against a Flood of Disinformation."[15]

Complementing its recruitment of Riggleman, the NCRI has recruited former leftist Alexander Reid Ross as a senior research fellow. He is the lead author on the NCRI's COVID disinformation report and a contributing author on at least one other of the institute's studies.[16] Ross, who teaches geography at Portland State University and used to moderate the *Earth First! Newswire*, has had significant influence on many liberal and leftist antifascists with his 2017 book *Against the Fascist Creep* and numerous articles on related topics. Although he has raised important issues, such as collusion between sections of the left and fascists, his past work is a mixed bag; one 2017 review of *Against the Fascist Creep* rightly faulted Ross for using guilt by association, name-dropping, and just plain bad writing.[17] In any case, by signing on with NCRI he has repudiated the left, yet his background helps burnish the NCRI's image as an inclusive home for anti-"hate" scholars of every persuasion.

Larger Trends

The Network Contagion Research Institute's rise reflects larger trends. One of these is the drive to apply big data analysis to the study of political propaganda and social media. There's a growing body of academic articles based on such studies, most of which have been published in the past five years,[18] and there are other outfits besides NCRI supporting comparable work, such as the Atlantic Council's Digital Forensic Research Lab. In principle this approach could yield valuable insights, but its potential is radically compromised when it is based on an analytic framework that shields established systems of power and oppression from critique. Such political bias seems unlikely to change, given the technical and institutional infrastructure required to support big data analysis.

Another trend, in the wake of Trump's downfall, is the drive by a resurgent centrist establishment to harness antibigotry and antifascism to its own ends. As Faramarz Farbod recently outlined, the resulting top-down "liberal/centrist antifascist discourse" poses a number of dangers: blaming Trump without explaining the conditions that made him popular, reproducing the myth that the United States is a democracy, ignoring the far right's roots in US society and the establishment's own complicity in the rise of violent reactionary forces at home and abroad, and expanding the powers of the national security state.[19] The NCRI is rooted firmly in this discourse.

The NCRI's efforts to lump together far rightist and radical leftist politics into the same "hate" category embodies an important theme of centrist antifascism. We see a similar approach in a recent threat assessment report on "domestic violent extremism" by the US director of national intelligence, which President Biden requested shortly after taking office. The DNI's report divides "domestic violent extremists" into five categories: "Racially or Ethnically Motivated Violent Extremists," "Animal Rights/Environmental Violent Extremists," "Abortion-Related Violent Extremists," "Anti-Government/Anti-Authority Violent Extremists," and all others.[20] Kristian Williams comments:

> The most striking thing about this classification system ... is its perverse refusal to divide between left and right, instead grouping opposing sides together under other categories. Right-wing

militias, sovereign citizens and anarchists, for example, are all listed under "Anti-Government/Anti-Authority Violent Extremists." Racist and anti-racist violence is compressed into "Racially or Ethnically Motivated Violent Extremists."

"Abortion-Related Violent Extremists" includes both those "in support of pro-life and pro-choice beliefs"—despite the fact that the FBI cannot point to any pro-choice violence that escalated above the level of online threats, while antiabortion fanatics have murdered eleven people and attempted to kill twenty-six more since 1993.[21]

These categories don't reflect intellectual sloppiness, but rather a deliberate distortion of reality to demonize leftists and protect the established order. It's an analytic approach we need to expose and critique, along with the Network Contagion Research Institute's pseudo-objective ideology and the state repression agenda it serves.

IV
GLOBAL CAPITALISTS AND THE FAR RIGHT

Distinguishing the Possible from the Probable: Contending Strategic Approaches within and against Transnational Capitalism

Don Hamerquist

Kersplebedeb, June 14, 2020

This paper attempts to estimate some features of ruling-class power and hegemony that are likely to play significant roles in the emergence of another systemic crisis of transnational capitalism in the relatively near future.[1]

The past few years have not been a period of calm for global capitalism and its US component. Major changes in working and social life in transnational capitalism were accelerated by the 2008 crisis and the halting and partial economic recovery that followed it. While the profits of finance capital have rebounded from the bottom of the 2008 crisis, the capitalist social order has not confronted the deeper systemic weaknesses that were revealed and, consequently, it has not recovered popular legitimacy anywhere. The problems of legitimacy are particularly notable in the "Lockean Heartland"[2] of capitalist societies where the collapse of "actually existing socialism" had led to widespread proclamations of the universal and final triumph of capital and the "end of history."

The current situation includes large reservoirs of popular discontent and sporadic episodes of rebelliousness and resistance that further weaken capitalist hegemony. Although these popular upsurges are increasingly frequent, widespread, and disruptive, their capacity to cxpand working-class power and autonomy is undermined by an atomized hopelessness and cynicism that also reflects the increased precarity of working-class life.

As the problems facing transnational capital grow in magnitude and urgency, the obstacles to forming and implementing a relatively unified transnational ruling class perspective are also growing. Toxic schisms within the ruling elites, based on diverging economic interests and substantive ideological differences, reduce their incentives and capacities to act coherently by either incorporating significant sectors of the popular classes or by utilizing repression efficiently.

These factors, affecting both the ruled and the rulers, produce a good deal of "flailing and churning"[3] as transnational capital deals with lingering effects of its last crisis while preparing for new and potentially more dangerous problems that are visible on the horizon— including inevitable "black swans" that by their nature are not that visible. It might seem that this situation, where increasingly dysfunctional structures of class oppression and exploitation have led to widespread questioning of the legitimacy of the social order, meets two of Lenin's well-known three conditions for a revolutionary situation. Does it follow that the only remaining strategic issue is to meet Lenin's third condition: a sufficiently organized and properly oriented working-class vanguard, a revolutionary party? Unfortunately—or perhaps fortunately, depending on one's perspective—experiences with left strategies based on such "party-building" presumptions point most of us in other directions.

A Worldwide Drive toward Fascism?

I'd like to begin from Basav Sen's recent argument for the emergence of a "worldwide wave of authoritarian ethnonationalist governments":

> What this points to is the disturbing reality that resistance to the dangerous BJP agenda in India and worldwide will have to contend with a similarly widespread coalition of fascists and capitalists, including from parts of the "liberal" end of the political spectrum. Indeed, the Modi government in India is part of an emerging worldwide wave of authoritarian ethnonationalist governments ... in the U.S., Brazil, the Philippines, Hungary, and elsewhere.[4]

Sen advances a "common sense" view of global capitalist reality that is shared by many US radicals. It posits a purposeful and universal drive of contemporary capitalism toward "authoritarian" and "ethnonationalist" regimes. While I agree that the future of modern capitalism will necessarily be increasingly authoritarian, Sen's addition of the term "ethnonationalist" makes it clear that he sees little space between his reactionary "worldwide wave" and an explicitly fascist trajectory.[5] The implication is that this "worldwide wave" is the chosen policy of hegemonic sectors of capital, and that the ruling-class option for fascism is not an outcome forced on them by strategic weakness in the face of radical mass challenges, but a preference. That this is Sen's actual view is further indicated by his endorsement of the familiar counterstrategies of the classic antifascist resistances: the hopeful "popular" and "united" fronts and the symbolic armed challenges. On these points as well, I would be in disagreement.

The argument for "an emerging worldwide wave" (of fascism?) assumes an essential commonality between different segments of the transnational capitalist system: the US, Brazil, India, the Philippines, Hungary, etc. I'm wary of arguments that claim to apply to both the capitalist metropolis and its periphery. In fact, when the question of actual fascist potential is considered within the capitalist core, the ruling-class support for fascist ideology and its related organizing projects, even recognizing that they are frequently covert, is far more limited and conditional than Sen thinks. And while there may be more tangible evidence for his "wave" elsewhere in the global capitalist system—perhaps, as he states, in places like Brazil and the Philippines—I'm skeptical about his claims there as well.[6]

There are good capitalist reasons for a lack of ruling-class support for fascism in societies where capitalist hegemony is deeply entrenched and broad based. In the political, economic, and cultural centers of the "Lockean Heartland," the blanket suppression and eradication of actual and potential regime enemies is not capital's objective. To the contrary, it avoids those policy options that would helpfully validate the popular left theme: "first they came for (?) ... then they came for everyone else."

The ruling-class opposition to fascism in these societies is no expression of democratic or egalitarian sentiment or principle. It is not a rejection of fascist divisions between "uber-" and "unter-." It is the residue of capitalism's historic experience with German Nazism that produced a broadly distributed ruling-class understanding that the not-so-ultimate potential of fascist politics in the capitalist core is the "common ruin of the contending classes"[7]—with their own class, the party of capital, being a likely casualty.

This common ruin might follow E.P. Thompson's notion of the "extermination of multitudes" through war, disease, and ecological collapse:

Exterminism designates those characteristics of a society—
expressed, in differing degrees, within its economy, its polity
and its ideology—which thrust it in a direction whose outcome
must be the extermination of multitudes. The outcome will be
extermination, but this will not happen accidentally (even if
the final trigger is "accidental") but as the direct consequence
of prior acts of policy, of the accumulation and perfection of
the means of extermination, and of the structuring of whole
societies so that these are directed towards that end.[8]

While a version of "exterminism" was integral to the German Nazi
program, the notion is not uniquely fascist. As Thompson indicates, it
can also be an unintended dystopian consequence of confused ruling-
class responses to complex social crises, particularly if working-class
and popular resistance is strategically weak and incapable of presenting a viable systemic alternative. (We might consider the possibilities
of the current pandemic in that context.)

Sectors of the metropolitan ruling class are increasingly aware
of the apocalyptic potentials of capitalism's long-deferred social and
ecological costs and other noxious byproducts of its development.
They will do everything possible to avoid and delay any transformation
of such potentials into actual crises. At least, and this is an extremely
important condition that I certainly don't intend to minimize, they will
take all the necessary steps that remain compatible with maximizing
the returns on their capital over the *medium and longer* term.

The contrast between the predominance of such precautionary
ruling-class stances in the metropolitan centers of capital and their
relative rarity on its periphery is not particularly mysterious. Capital's
hegemony, as contrasted with its military and police power, is particularly useful where it has enjoyed the most extensive popular buy-in
from the classes and strata that it oppresses and exploits. Its continuing
dominance in these areas requires fetishized structures and supportive
ideologies to sustain a plausible facade of popular participation that
can camouflage a social order based on oppression, exploitation, and
appropriation as a state of "freedom" based on "equal exchange" and
"equality before the law."[9] So long as this facade can be maintained
in the capitalist core, the entire global system is provided a sufficient
base of dreams and illusions to nourish and mobilize a range of reform

alternatives (color revolutions?) to the authoritarianism, bureaucrati-zation, warlordism, and quasi-fascism that feature prominently on the capitalist periphery. (Whether these reform alternatives have much long-term viability is quite another matter.)

This provides classical fascism with little appeal for the ruling elites in this country and other similar metropolitan capitalist nation-states. The most careful search will find few supporters of *The Turner Diaries* among the leading figures in transnational or US capitalist circles.[10] The radical reactionaries who developed and still advocate this variant of fascism are very aware of the fundamental hostility of the capitalist power structure to their program and their very existence. It is a welcomed and reciprocated hostility. Nevertheless, a substantial sector of the US left, most likely a majority of it, bases much of its poli-tics on the assumption that capital embraces a "drive toward fascism."

Rather than speculate about an impending "neoliberal fascism," the left should look at ruling-class political initiatives that are more clearly operational. I don't intend to minimize, much less dismiss, the danger of fascism and the importance of confronting its political and military expressions. Indeed, when fascism is seen as something beyond a manipulated capitalist policy option, a collateral benefit is a better insight into its actual nature and the particular dangers it presents; not to mention the need for a more concrete and effective, and more radical, antifascist response to it. Beyond the obvious reasons for this approach, it provides a much better framework for developing a comprehensive anticapitalist vision of society that goes beyond a critical compilation of some of capitalism's excesses.

An Alternative Possible Perspective for Capitalist Power

To understand the basis for transnational capital's strategic perspectives, we should begin with some central political and economic realities in the capitalist core. In the first place, this requires a clear acknowl-edgment that the leading sectors of the transnational ruling class, including important elements of the US ruling elites, are committed to relatively sophisticated strategies to keep populist mass movements away from the levers of government power.

The same transnational ruling-class elements that fret about populism are also aware that for millions of people in the capital-ist core the new global order is defined by its "failure ... to sustain cultures and communities that provide identity, meaning and purpose in life."[11] A widely circulated *Financial Times* interview with Ray Dalio, of Bridgewater Associates, offers a more detailed description of the "broken" nature of contemporary capitalism (I've highlighted Dalio's actual words):

> "*I'm a capitalist and even I think capitalism is broken,*" Mr Dalio said as he tweeted out his essay. Expanding on the theme to a mass audience on *60 Minutes*, the CBS current affairs television show, he said capitalism was "*at a juncture.*" Americans could reform it together, "*or we will do it in conflict.*"

Few other capitalists have acknowledged publicly that they share the immediacy of Mr. Dalio's fear of "some form of revolution," but more and more of his peers echo his concerns about inequality and the populist backlash it has fed. Globalization and technological change have "led to increased stress and declining living standards for many and created enormous wealth for a few."[12]

The transnational capitalist elites are quite aware of the instability of the structures and processes they manage and the volatility of the populations they subordinate.[13] They realize that their pursuit of profit also produces their populist oppositions and ensures that these will be generated and regenerated. Various key players in the ruling class also recognize any number of potential social disruptions that might reverse the economic and political "good times" and rapidly transform current populist challenges to their already-shaky political equilibrium into much larger and more destabilizing threats.[14]

Transnational capital's hostility to (right-wing) populism is not a simple uniform class stance. There is no clear consensus on the best way to implement it—or, in some situations, whether even to implement it at all. However, in the capitalist core the main tendency of this ruling-class segment is to weaponize its semiofficial hostility to the two main pillars of contemporary "right" populism: anti-immigrant nativism and economic nationalism. If the issues of economic inequality eventually emerge further, we should expect this hostility to intensify, since any challenge to growing inequality will raise more fundamental difficulties for transnational capital than anti-immigrant sentiment or economic nationalism. However, the complex politics that would be involved in any such process makes it likely that this ruling-class sector will avoid direct confrontations to the extent possible.

Any emergence of genuine left populist tendencies will greatly complicate the situation; the approaches of various capitalist fractions will become even more confused and the confusions will become more politically relevant. All of these complicated potentials and problems are part of the birth pangs of a transnational capitalist class and the halting process of cobbling together the elements of a transnational culture, ideology, and regulatory apparatus out of an array of different capitalist nation-states and antagonistic capitalist political and economic blocs of very unequal power—all of which are beset by different elements and degrees of institutional "failure"—a failure that is not limited to the nation-state level but is evident in many aspects of governmental and administrative structure and authority.

Important movements toward the development of a transnational state form for capital are unevenly constricted by the strongest nation-state institutional structures—such as the police, military, and other repressive bodies—despite their increasingly hollow character and general drift toward failure. In this country, for example, significant parts of the military-industrial complex and some extractive industries face specific competitive and ecological challenges that give them a compelling interest in economic nationalism. This sector's extreme centralization, combined with its financial precarity and its susceptibility to political corruption, provide it an exaggerated political influence in the current (impending crisis) conditions. The supportive attitude of this bloc of capital for Trump's regime has been obvious, as are its defining impacts on Trump's MAGA variant of nationalism. So long as these contradictions and similar ones elsewhere in the transnational structure work themselves out, the effective political power of transnational capital will continue to have definite limits, and its capacity for ultimate hegemony will remain in question.

Consider some more specific possibilities. The recent "energy independence" of the US rests on technological advances in shale oil/gas fracking that support major increases in US fossil fuel production. The entire structure is economically fragile, dependent on a sixty-dollar-per-barrel price that is well above the cost of production in many international oil-producing areas. This provides a significant social-economic bloc in this country with a vested interest in reduced oil production and higher production costs elsewhere in the world, and with some direct economic benefits from a continuing state of chaos in major oil-producing areas, particularly the Middle East. While this increased production entails a further ignoring of the longer-term environmental impacts of fossil-fuel dependence, the immediately relevant point is the distinctive set of state actions and interventions, both domestically and internationally, that it entails. These call for a nation-state that can maintain an aggressive military posture and sustain a large and expensive military force. However, neither transnational capital, nor the integrated international oil cartel, nor what there is of a domestic US oil industry will benefit if these conditions lead to a major war. While they need a supportive state, it must be one that, in the final analysis, lacks sufficient autonomy to be unduly burdensome and that can be trusted to not be so aggressive that it impacts global supply chains and distribution networks negatively.

If the unwanted happens, culminating in a profusion of crisis phenomena—serious trade wars, currency collapses, liquidity and solvency issues, not to mention actual serious military conflict—the elements of US capital that currently support a strong and aggressive nationalist posture will quickly find themselves in a greatly weakened position relative to other capitalist interests, priorities, and programs. Faced with such circumstances, these nationalist-oriented segments of capital will be put on a downward trajectory. They may continue to have some importance in this country, economically and politically, but in my opinion, their global and national importance will decline rapidly in relation to the FIRE (finance, insurance, and real estate) sectors of capital.[15]

When we consider the transnational capitalist system, the US included, the changing balance between transnational and national segments of capital in political and economic strength is quite evident. Even the most nationalist elements of what is termed "US capitalism" are increasingly dependent on transnational financial capital for funding and investment opportunities and "just in time" global supply and distribution chains for production and distribution of commodities. The global interdependence of all sectors of capital, including "energy," erodes the independent capacities of any elements of capital that might be inclined toward nationalism and limits the possibilities that they will develop and sustain a mass base for such goals. The arguments that are involved are less straightforward, but I think that these same transnational linkages will also restrict ruling-class support for the authoritarian structural changes and "mass politics" required by any type of "fascist" option.

Impact on Class and Social Struggle

As the current "normalcy" ends (which, thanks to COVID-19, it apparently has), its distinctive alignments, interests, and relationships are very likely to be upended and transformed. The specific characteristics of this process may not be predictable, but I'm confident that one feature of the process will be a further net shift in capitalist power toward the transnational level and away from the national. This will be the eventual situation, even if for some time there will be various historical accidents and other contingencies that sharpen the contradictions between different nation-states and different sectors of capital, producing outcomes that appear to support an opposed trajectory featuring a militarized autarchy. It might take some time to work out the different functional relationships between competitive blocs of capital, existing national state structures, and emerging transnational institutions and processes, particularly since these processes can be impacted by a sustained revolutionary upsurge anywhere in the transnational structure. The left must remain alert to these contradictory possibilities without fixating on features that may well be ephemeral.

While the global system currently remains profitable (at least according to some metrics), it still lacks the stability provided by a hegemonic equilibrium. However, the period ending with the emergence of the COVID-19 pandemic had provided transnational capital with some limited time and space to develop and implement a range of tactics within the framework of its general antipopulist orientation.

Tactical Options for Capital

In this situation, transnational capital has a variety of incentives and opportunities to provide tactical latitude to either right or left populist movements (and governments), in order to saddle them with the responsibility for dealing with emerging crises in circumstances where even partial success is quite unlikely. Of course, this approach presents capital with sufficient risks to guarantee that it will typically be contested within the ruling class. The very real confusions that develop from these internal struggles will make it difficult to determine the extent to which such preemptive tactical approaches are in play. However, in the current circumstances, the possibility that the ruling class is giving populist movements and regimes the rope with which to hang themselves shouldn't be too heavily discounted.

This is only one possible tactical response of transnational capital to the flexibility that recent economic and political developments provide for defeating or containing populist challenges through active and organized interventions in the class struggle. Additional possibilities range from frontal efforts to crush populist insurgencies (think of poor Syriza and perhaps fascist Golden Dawn as well), to the relatively subtle campaigns to impact movements with a populist potential and gradually diffuse and reincorporate their social base (e.g., Sanders and Corbyn). While metropolitan radicals are usually somewhat alert to the dangers of increased repression in these circumstances, this is usually combined with a blindness to the potentials for co-optation—particularly co-optation in the parliamentary arena. This produces a recurring triumphalist focus on questionable accumulations of popular "victories" that are more accurately seen as steps toward the defanging of organized resistance—particularly resistance with significant anti-systemic implications. Only hopelessly Panglossian attitudes toward the struggle make this incrementalism plausible, but such attitudes always seem to flourish in our movement.

Whatever tactical priority it chooses, a major social tipping point that involves a serious global economic reversal will certainly push the transnational ruling class toward better defined and more aggressive postures that aim to reassert effective political control while exposing populism's inability to govern under crisis conditions. Despite some shifting in the ruling class's tactical mix of repression and co-optation, a combination of both will continue to be used against any mass opposition movements that emerge. It will be prudent to plan on ruling-class tactics becoming both tactically more competent and better planned strategically. This doesn't necessarily imply a relative expansion of repression, but it does make it likely that there will be clearer distinctions between incorporative and repressive tactics and that ruling-class approaches to repression will focus on more carefully chosen and more serious enemies.

The most likely outcome of this period (assuming the COVID-19 episode is somewhat contained) is a regime characterized by enforced austerity and enhanced repression. However, as implied above, if the problems for capital become more severe, a quite different response may result, one which includes more significant incorporative tactics and ambitious structural reform schemes—perhaps the "Green" and "New" New Deals that we have noticed, possibly even some semiviable third parties. Since I believe that serious problems are likely for capital, I will emphasize these more radical potentials for its response.

Capitalist Strategies

At this point, I'd like to return to some earlier themes to make my argument more specific to this country, and specifically to the Trump phenomenon. Eventually I hope to demonstrate the importance of some organized ruling-class political initiatives that are emerging in this country, initiatives that I believe are motivated by strategic intentions that diverge significantly from their public relations packaging.

The more ideological (fascist-tending?) sectors of Trump's initial political/electoral base realize that his overtly procapital stances on social costs, regulations, and taxation have turned the "drain the swamp" element of his populism into a cynical joke, and that his reactionary mass appeals on issues of immigration and economic nationalism are rhetorical facades without real substance. At the same time, Trump has effectively implemented a good number of procapitalist policies, including many that run counter to fairly explicit campaign pledges made to the more militant sectors of his reactionary populist base. These actual policies have featured the expansion and militarization of economic production and the abandonment of various pledges about taxes, social security, and medical care—all making the rich relatively richer, which his campaign claimed he wouldn't do. And this is not to forget Trump's effective abandonment of the anti-interventionism that was an important feature of his 2016 campaign.

These changes, shifts that look like run-of-the-mill political opportunism to important sections of his base, may have gained Trump some additional ruling-class support and neutralized some opposition from that quarter—at least for the moment. However, all such increases in ruling-class support are accompanied by losses of politically effective support among the potentially insurgent right populist elements of his electoral coalition. Given the combination of these contradictory pressures, it's not likely that Trump's 2016 political base will survive another election cycle without industrial-scale complicity by Trump's official capitalist opposition to keep him in office on the basis of an increasingly transparently fraudulent pseudo-populist basis. This is unlikely to happen, although I'm not willing to rule it out given the oddities of our current politics. To be clear, though, this doesn't exclude the possibility that Trump might prevail electorally in 2020 with a significantly different platform and electoral base. However, that would be a result caused either by the cosmic incompetence of his opponents or by some unexpected impact from a major externality—a "black swan" event, or perhaps one a bit paler, like COVID-19.

As his original nativist and protectionist policies are forced to become more concrete, at penalty of losing plausibility, both ruling-class and popular attitudes toward Trump's administration will undergo further changes. The most predictable outcome is the erosion of support from the overtly reactionary and fascist-tending populist components of his initial base. Logically, this should end left efforts to define Trumpism as an emergent quasi-fascist social movement, but it almost certainly will not. Many left commentators will probably continue to promote the same Trump/Bannon "fascist-creep" perspective without much introspection about the fact that this is also the central plank of the platform of those "liberal" sectors of transnational capital that oppose Trump and his alleged populism.

While Trump's trade policy, tax policy, and his abandonment of what there was of regulatory control over capital will eventually damage his popular support, without a significant left opposition or an actually plausible establishment alternative, the time required for this to coalesce into a significant mass reactionary alternative will be "trumped" by the given parliamentary/electoral schedules. The ruling-class segments that were initially inclined toward Trump's neoliberal policies on climate change, taxes, and government regulations, but that were hostile to other elements of his economic stance—e.g., his trade and immigration policies—can mobilize much more rapidly and effectively than any of the disaffected in his popular base. The Koch brothers enterprises, the Business Roundtable, and the Chamber of Commerce, etc., are already categorical opponents of Trumpism on many central issues, and this ruling-class opposition is growing. Hopefully, these two anti-Trump factors, one semi-"popular" and one oligarchic, will cripple each other before either develop a significant social base for red-brown politics. However, that may be too sanguine since this also depends on the emergence of a competent left opposition.

It can't be repeated too often that when the global socioeconomic situation deteriorates through recession, war, perhaps a pandemic, or some combination of these factors—and it will—a substantial and rapid fragmentation of the current "Trumpism" is inevitable. What might replace it is a difficult question. The conflicts between Trump and his surrounding clique with the more manic elements of the anti-Trump resistance have produced a rash of nitwitted displays of power that exhibit an essential indeterminacy infused with the aspects of irrationality that the Greeks termed *akrasia*. As this mixes with the volatile nihilist potentials of the fascist-tending pro-Trump mass strata, I incline toward the possibility that the most likely developments are those that will make bad situations still worse. But as Trump would say, "We will just see."

The Party of Davos

The leading grouping of the transnational ruling class has been characterized as the "Party of Davos." As I have said above, this grouping's basic attitude toward the shifting policies and unpredictable tactics of the "Trump" phenomenon and the "populism" it represents is conscious, organized, and, for the most part, overtly hostile. The broad campaigns to hamstring Trump or remove him from office, to reverse Brexit, to limit the successes of anti-EU campaigns, as well as the successful strangulation of the feeble Greek social democracy are all related parts of this hostile response of transnational capitalist elites to potentially disruptive populisms. However, as I indicated above, this response also includes some significant contradictory aspects. The shape of these can be seen in a recent *New York Times* opinion piece that characterizes Trump as follows: "He ... is the face, however duplicitous, of a revolution against the Party of Davos."[16]

The ambiguity behind calling Trump a "duplicitous" representative of a populist challenge to global capital is apparent in the Davos opposition's alternatives to his politics. These alternatives wobble between a strange mixture of halting and tentative partial criticisms and efforts to eliminate him via the tactics of coup and putsch. While we can be sure that the underlying contradictions of capital will persist, post-Trump, there is very little that is inevitable about how they will develop in the interim. We should pay close attention to this confused and confusing asymmetric conflict between transnational capital and its populist challengers, recognizing the multitudes of potentials for diverse and even contradictory outcomes. Trump's fate might ultimately produce an outcome as successful for transnational capital as the defenestration of Syriza, but it's very likely that the process will be substantially more difficult. While Trump continues to survive situations that appeared to threaten disaster, we should keep in mind that it would not take much— possibly a serious misstep on China trade or another ecological disaster (perhaps COVID-19 or some even more dire "black swan"?)—to put a quick end to the specifically Trumpian features of this historic episode.

Despite Trump's evident willingness to compromise on any and all of the significant challenges to the international and domestic capitalist status quo that his 2016 campaign intimated—and despite his slide toward orthodox Ameri-centric conservatism—for the anti-Trump so-called "resistance" he remains a dangerous rebel and disrupter. Their resistance expands erratically, at moments creating potentially far more serious and longer-term problems for transnational capital than any of Trump's policies. In this way, both sides of the conflict take on characteristics that are difficult to explain by any rational calculus, since the conflict could result in the collapse of both sides of the US two-party parliamentary framework and the reformist illusions that are a part of it. In this historical context, that would be a major step toward chaos and, ultimately, "exterminism."

The strange polarization between a dubious personalized populism and the bizarrely exaggerated opposition to it is only one potential interpretation of our current circumstances. Despite its disruptive potentials, and to some degree because of them, the phenomenon of Trump "populism" might actually be of use to transnational capital and the "Party of Davos," gifting it with an unintended assist from a sector of the purported "left" opposition to capital. The transnational ruling class stands to gain significant benefits by presenting populism as a proximate threat—a foreshadowing of global fascism. This allows the resistance to the Trump variant of populism to present itself as a defense of parliamentary democracy and "good" capitalism, where an accurate understanding of the nature and dilemmas of the transnational capitalist system and the actual relationship between contemporary capitalism and the potentials for fascism and "exterminism" is replaced by fever dreams of a reformed (and reform-worthy) capitalism. In the process, sectors of the transnational ruling class might open some paths toward a renewed social consensus and a resuscitated hegemony, at least for some time and in some significant areas of the transnational system. It is likely, I think, that strategically placed sectors of transnational capital understand such potentials and are organizing to take advantage of them. However, it is very unlikely that there will be anything approaching a ruling-class consensus on the specific approach, and any attempts at implementation are certain to be a source of significant ruling-class division.

The CAP/AEI of John Podesta and Neera Tanden is a major official propagator of such politics. They announce as much in this crude marketing of the thesis: "Today, the Center for American Progress and the American Enterprise Institute released the results of a unique collaboration focused on defending liberal democracy and the transatlantic partnership in an era of rising authoritarian populism."[17] I've criticized this approach in other writings.[18]

The Left Version

Henry Giroux offers a very extended "left" version of the same thesis. Here are two citations from one of his recent essays, the first showcasing Giroux's propensity to exaggerate crucial points, the second illustrating more extended elements of his political confusion (my emphasis):

> The dark times that haunt the current age are epitomized by the barbarians who echo the politics of a fascist past and have come to rule the United States, Hungary, Turkey, Poland, Brazil, the Philippines, and elsewhere. The designers of a new breed of fascism increasingly *dominate major political formations and other commanding political and economic institutions across the globe.* Their nightmarish reign of misery, violence, and disposability is legitimated, in part, in their control of a diverse number of cultural apparatuses that produce a vast machinery of manufactured consent.[19]

Giroux asserts that neofascists "dominate major political formations and other commanding political and economic institutions across the globe." While the rulers and regimes in the countries he mentions certainly make up a mixed lot of reactionaries and demagogues with a range of reactionary politics, it is debatable which, if any, of them are fascist. There is no evidence that they command "political and economic institutions across the globe" and little evidence that they have any such authority within any specific nation-states. The existential musings of Ray Dalio about capitalism's future that I cited earlier are nearer to political reality than Giroux's assertion that "barbarians who echo the politics of a fascist past ... have come to rule the United States." None of Giroux's "barbarians" actually command very much, but a good case can be made that Dalio, Klaus Schwab of Davos, Jamie Dimon of the Business Roundtable, and other luminaries of the "shareholders to stakeholders" cohort of capitalist reformers actually do have the resources to command "political and economic institutions across the globe."

In those cases where Giroux's argument is most plausible (perhaps Brazil?), the circumstances appear to be reversible, although genuinely fascist movements and governments are not likely to be intimidated out of power through "legal" parliamentary means. In fact, the reactionary movements and regimes that Giroux cites all appear short on the ideological stability and the organized mass base that are essential for any fascist insurgency with a real potential to supplant bourgeois parliamentarianism. An argument might be made that Modi and the RSS in India would be possible exceptions. However, this particular pairing doesn't make Giroux's list—at least not this version of it.

Giroux argues further:

> Two worlds are colliding: First, as a number of scholars have observed, there is the harsh and crumbling world of neoliberal globalization and its mobilizing passions that fuel different strands of fascism across the globe, including the United States. Power is now enamored with amassing profits and capital ... and is increasingly addicted to a politics of white nationalism and racial cleansing. Second, there is the world of counter movements, which is growing especially among young people, with their search for a new politics that can rethink, reclaim and invent a new understanding of democratic socialism, untainted by capitalism.[20]

Laying aside the implication that capitalism has not always been "enamored with amassing profits," Giroux's central confusion is the political alternative to "neoliberal fascism" that he advances. This alternative is described as a "counter movement," a "new politics that can rethink, reclaim and invent a new understanding of democratic socialism, untainted by capitalism." Unfortunately, the actual "resistance" falls well short of this hopeful description. Along with Giroux, it includes the Ray Dalios as well as the Neera Tandens. Some might argue that the Hillarys and Baracks, all of whom are well removed from "democratic socialism, untainted by capitalism," should be included as well. Then there are the other important components of the anti-Trump resistance from the liberal intelligentsia and the NGO ecosystem that constitute the "nonprofit industrial complex." These make the capitalist taint more evident. Finally, even the various socialists and antifascists who also see themselves as part of the anti-Trump "resistance" tend to be fixated on a "revitalized" Democratic Party, a policy goal that is distinctly tainted by capitalism.

The actual exercise of power within the existing transnational and national capitalist state structures is complicated and confused, not only by this range of fragmentary and conflicting economic and social interests, but by major political figures and significant sectors of the ruling elites that frequently appear to act on transactional impulse—in opposition to anyone's better judgments of longer-term self and class interests. This produces incoherent, even contradictory, policies, including some that are only explicable as akrasia, a clear feature of Trumpism and various other autocratic capitalist political tendencies. The regimes that emerge are dominated by multitudes of Gramsci's "morbid symptoms" and frequently can only be labeled as kakistocracies[21]—constituent parts of capital's response to its flowering secular crisis that Dave Ranney aptly describes as "flailing and churning."[22]

These largely contingent and accidental factors are important aspects of current reality, but they shouldn't obscure some quite rational and organized ruling-class efforts to maintain and extend class power that may be hidden within the confusion and chaos of the moment. I would argue that some substantial and coherent ruling-class projects have recognized the need for a revamped global institutional and ideological framework that is capable of transcending transnational capital's inclination to essentially ignore its longer-term economic costs along with the problems presented by increasingly hollow state and governmental structures while becoming increasingly lost in the search for maximized short-term returns on investment. These are attempts to buttress the limitations of current approaches to class rule with better techniques and more efficient tools to manage oppressed and exploited populations, notably those populations that are increasingly marginalized and "redundant" to modern capitalist production.

Two Strategies ("Manufactured Consent")

I'd like to separate out two such ruling-class approaches that I believe are in play in the capitalist core. At times in practice these are complementary, but they imply different strategies of rule with very different ultimate potentials for success. The first approach aims toward a capitalism where potentials for revolutionary subjectivity are crippled and smothered by elaborate systems of mass surveillance and information control. Its trajectory is toward Bernaysian "manufactured consent" (Lippman and Chomsky), where a technologically based authoritarianism suppresses potential mass oppositions through variants of "repressive tolerance." The Valdai Club, a Russian Atlanticist source, presents a version of this approach.[23]

Earlier I cited Basav Sen's piece on the implications of Modi's recent victory in India. Modi heads one of the "authoritarian ethnonationalist governments" that play a central role in Sen's argument. Although Sen doesn't make this point and most likely wouldn't agree with it, there are good reasons to include Russia and China in his "authoritarian ethnonationalist" category. They are certainly authoritarian, and there is certainly no doubt that both, but particularly China, are well advanced in social control technology. If Russia, China, and other remnants of the "Second World" are included as I suggest they should be, some of Sen's examples—not only India, but Brazil, Argentina, and perhaps the Philippines and some Eastern European states—might be counted as at least partial successes for the Bernaysian approach. However, such a conclusion would have to confront many issues related to the differences in type and trajectory of each of Sen's "authoritarian ethnonationalist" examples. For the most part, these issues are outside of the limited scope of my arguments here. However, I question whether any of Sen's "ethnonationalist" formations present plausible solutions to the current legitimacy and profitability dilemmas of transnational capitalism. None of them provide either a model for a stable authoritarian capitalist regime or a model for a transitional state with a plausible potential to become a fully fascist society. Again, I would note that India remains as a possible exception and outlier to this not-fully-informed generalization.

Despite the substantial ruling-class buy-in and the fact that important elements are already well along the process of implementation,[24] I would argue that, over time, the "carceral state" approach to power in the capitalist core is unlikely to prevail. Ultimately, the viability of "manufactured consent" and comprehensive surveillance in these societies depends on already having attained the stable mass passivity that they are intended to generate, and this is an outcome that I believe is beyond political possibility. Let me attempt a general argument in support of this proposition.

Any effort to fully implement the political and social changes that define this approach, either as part of an overall plan for the entire transnational capitalist system or as a plan that is limited to a substantial portion of its metropolitan component, will include a series of incremental steps within existing ethnonationalist nation-states or blocs of such states. For its success in any sector of the global system, the competition between and within blocs of capital and an array of nation-state political formations would have to be sufficiently controlled to allow these steps toward a surveillance state to proceed without disrupting crucial elements of social cohesion in the targeted society (which almost necessarily must be a nation-state). However, the search for profit throughout the transnational capitalist system involves globalized production and financial networks with capital and population flows across current borders that the existing "hollowed" state structures are increasingly incapable of resisting. The operation of capitalist competition will elevate the contradiction between the social and economic costs of maintaining and extending a stable authoritarian domination and the drive to reduce production costs in order to successfully compete with other sectors of transnational capitalism (that will not be automatically subordinated to autarkic nationalist strictures elsewhere in the system so long as they can "out-compete" them in transnational markets).

Many of the participants in this intracapitalist competition have already been hollowed out by their integration into the transnational system, making it virtually inevitable that there will be breakdowns and tipping points in the near future. Some of these will develop in the normal run of the business cycle, and some will develop in combination with increasingly inevitable ecological disasters and pandemics and will contain contradictions that threaten to explode into war. And we should not forget the potential impacts of the "white" and "black swans" that are possible anywhere. The fallout from these tipping points ensures that the only "manufactured consent" social equilibrium with any shot at stability is one that is universal from the outset. However, that is a utopian perspective. It is far more likely that the current reality of global capitalist competition will undermine the potentials for carceral regimes over any considerable length of time in any significant portion of the capitalist core.

The actual outcome of attempts to implement such structural changes anywhere in the transnational capitalist system will be an accelerating general austerity and a destabilizing "race to the bottom," elements of which are already evident. This will put the viability of any version of the "carceral state" in question and will make it inevitable that attempts to implement it on a strategic level will find that Mao's central adages "it is right to resist" and "oppression … breeds resistance" remain important countervailing factors. Although the specific content of this "resistance" is not predictable and there are absolutely no guarantees it will meet with success, either in the medium or long term, it does have a clear potential to disrupt any attempts at establishing an authoritarian stability in a portion of the capitalist core.

Two Strategies (A Different Capitalist Hegemony)

My next argument is a minority view in the US left. It emphasizes a different ruling-class approach to maintaining effective power in the Lockean core of the transnational capitalist system—an approach that prioritizes the development of a real and substantial popular consent to capitalist legitimacy from classes and populations in these nation-states and blocs that don't share the same material interests as capital. The goal is to reestablish a more durable political and social equilibrium that limits challenges to the essential elements and basic interests of transnational capital. This objective of hegemonic dominance cannot be achieved or maintained by coercion and manipulation, although there will continue to be a good deal of both. Instead it depends on the successful expansion of general participation in social frameworks (parliamentary political parties and traditional trade unions) where the subordination of overwhelming majorities to tiny minorities has historically been effectively masked.

The manufactured consent and the hegemonic approach coexist and compete throughout the global system, with different relative strengths at different moments and in different locales. However, in the core capitalist blocs and states, the left should focus its politics on constructing a counterhegemonic alternative to ruling-class attempts to extend and consolidate the hidden, fetishized character of capitalist dominance. This will make the actual dimensions of accelerated state repression clearer and will provide a better basis for challenging it. In any case, it is important that the metropolitan left focus on understanding and countering those co-optative ruling-class strategic initiatives, actual and potential, that look to reconstitute a mass base for a capitalist legitimacy that doesn't rest on the TINA ("there is no alternative") mantra.

I want to be clear that this same priority does not necessarily hold for "second" and "third world" sectors of the transnational system. In these areas, a generalized repressive, and often militarized, authoritarianism is likely to provide the more substantial danger for revolutionary movements. While selective repression will be combined with most of these ruling-class initiatives to reconstitute its legitimacy, such repression in the capitalist core is unlikely to develop into a series of incremental steps toward a police state, toward "jailing the movement." Rather it will tend to be focused and limited, subordinated to advancing larger incorporative strategic goals that will provide a foundation for a cross-class, "antifascist" social compact that can defend and promote "democracy" and "good capitalism" as alternatives to "barbarism" and "exterminism." In fact, we should expect that in our current situation, major sectors of the ruling-class and state structure will increasingly emphasize a partially fabricated/partially real danger of "authoritarian populism"—or to use the liberal/left alternative terminology, a common enemy of "neoliberal fascism"—as a basis for their proposed "popular fronts."

This strategy will be implemented under circumstances of increasingly limited real possibilities for a return to the historic social democracy of material benefits, democratic participation, and class mobility. No "New" New Deal, decorated by the real, if terribly limited, benefits and dreams of "Fordism," is within the realm of possibility. This modern capitalist perspective will raise the potential for a "modern" social democracy that rests on narratives of common interests between rulers and ruled that evoke memories of World War II's flawed "antifascism." This will be a quasi-wartime social democracy, premised on obedience to authority and accommodation to austerity and explained and rationalized by fears of a fascist possibility that are partly a fabrication and partly a recognition of the real potential for Thompson's "exterminism."

The mass "popular" side of this compact will loosely cohere an array of reform constituencies into something like a social democratic movement. As the fascist danger can reasonably be presented as a global threat in some substantial ways, this resuscitated social democracy will have both national and supranational levels. However, since its practical focus will be confined within parliamentary and reformist frameworks that are by nature national, it will necessarily keep most of its politics confined within nation-states—although some details, like the specific characterization of "enemies" and the assessment of their strengths, may reference the international level. In any case, without some interventions in the struggle from the radical left, the main tendencies of this process will probably reflect the worst of the existent politics.

Such a cross-class compact can't function if it is only an exercise of ruling-class social engineering. We should be prepared for capitalist factions to employ a broad range of tactics, some of which are likely to be innovative and creative. Some of these ruling-class initiatives will be quite open, but many of the more important will be (and, in my opinion, already are) disguised and at least partially covert. It is extremely important that the left increase its capacity to recognize these approaches for what they are, and not confuse ourselves with hopeful, clichéd visions of what we might hope they would be.

Let me illustrate some issues by citing a few ruling-class comments that I think reflect this approach to capitalist hegemony. The first is from the Valdai Club, a liberal Russian ruling-class source, and deals with Macron's France (my emphasis):

> Macron is politically weakened. His only hope is a split in the opposition. The main condition for survival, the main insurance

of his presidency, is that his main opponent is Marine Le Pen.... Everything is being done in order to ... *convince people that Macron is the last line of defense against fascism.*[25]

Here's a similar analysis applied to the EU as a whole:

The nationalist and far-right parties across Europe are sensing an opportunity, particularly with European Parliament elections coming up later this month. The European Union, as a political force and option, is in turmoil. It is only a question of time before right-wing parties across Europe will replace the sporadic meetings of their leaders with a sort of coalition. Exploiting popular dissatisfaction with governments, right-wing parties are warning voters about globalization, stressing that holy national identities are endangered and stirring fear of the unknown (migrants).[26]

Finally, consider these grossly exaggerated possibilities for reformist cross-class cooperation based on illusory cross-class common interests:

In the United States, organizations like Indivisible, a progressive group created by former congressional staffers in the wake of the 2016 elections that now has five thousand local chapters, are not waiting for the political pendulum to swing by itself. They're already working hard to push politics back to the left—and their organizing produced results in the 2018 midterm elections when the Democratic Party retook the House of Representatives.[27]

A Better Approach to Resistance

On a theoretical level, an adequate response to these ruling-class politics should begin from Gramsci's concept of "organic crisis" ("State and Civil Society," *Prison Notebooks*). A recent *New Left Review* article on the French Yellow Vests gives a good restatement of the Gramsci position that illustrates its current relevance (my emphasis throughout):

The concept of the organic crisis, formulated by Gramsci in the 1930s, has served to orient a number of analyses of the recent conjuncture. Here it will suffice to recall that Gramsci was referring to a radical rupture in the links between representatives and the represented. A collapse in support for the traditional parties may be the most visible symptom of an organic crisis, but it extends throughout the mediating organizations of civil society. Though its expressions will vary, *it essentially involves a crisis of hegemony* of the dominant class, the breakdown of its ability to maintain its leading role within the social formation—in other words, *a generalized failure of consent.*

Gramsci distinguishes this from a revolutionary crisis, which is characterized by a qualitative rise in the activity of the masses, forming a collective will in opposition to the ruling bloc—a situation of dual power. By contrast, an organic crisis appears at a moment when the *subordinate classes have shown their incapacity to polarize the situation in their favour.* Typically, their response to the crisis is uneven—as Gramsci put it: they are not all capable of orienting themselves equally swiftly, or with the same rhythm. Meanwhile, despite their weakened hegemony, the traditional ruling classes still have important reserves at their disposal: the coercive and bureaucratic apparatuses of the state, as well as its intellectual strata—"intellectual" in the Gramscian sense, denominating also technical expertise and leadership capacity. The organic crisis unleashes a recomposition of political personnel, which can take diverse forms—from a Bonapartism, preserving the parliamentary facade, to the various Caesarisms and the "state of exception"—aiming to resolve the situation in the interests of the dominant bloc. The field is therefore open to solutions of force, represented by Gramsci's "men of providence."[28]

Our current political context resembles such an "organic crisis" of capital, including on the political level, "a generalized failure of popular consent"[29] where the "subordinate classes" have "shown their incapacity to polarize the situation in their favour." It is most certainly a "crisis [that] consists precisely in the fact that the old is dying and the new cannot be born; in this interregnum where … a great variety of morbid symptoms appear" (Gramsci, *Prison Notebooks*).

I've argued that in these circumstances, the core capitalist societies will attempt to manage their crisis by reactivating the political consent they receive from the classes and social groupings that they oppress and exploit. Although this approach will certainly be augmented by police force, the most crucial ruling-class political initiatives will be those that attempt to repair the fractured connections between "the representative and the represented," not those that are aimed at enforcing authority over the popular classes through administrative and military power.

Within the sociopolitical and geographical limits that I have indicated, the co-optative approach is likely to be the most attractive for the leading sectors of capital, and we should not lose sight of that reality. However, it's important to see all of these questions of strategy as open and with indeterminate answers that require that we consider all conclusions as tentative and provisional. Actual ruling-class behaviors must be constantly monitored and evaluated to determine the support for either of these major strategic alternatives (or for any other alternative, for that matter). Such evaluations will be made harder by the proliferation of "morbid symptoms" in ruling-class behavior that grow out of an elaborate mosaic of "accidents" and contingencies, many of which are not susceptible to rational explanation and are increasingly characterized by akrasia.

What Response?

So how should the revolutionary left respond to this political context—to "polarize the situation" in its favor? Might the lessons we can learn from the combination of state repression and political co-optation in our not-that-distant past help clarify some issues and problems? I think the answer is yes.

In this country, Badiou's injunction to revolutionaries to operate "at a distance from the state" is consistently ignored, and the great bulk of left radicalism focuses on intermediate "democratic" goals and "basic reforms" that, at least in this country at this time, generally combine support for some "(Green) New New Deal" with an opposition to postulated tendencies toward "neoliberal fascism." Despite various disclaimers, this is a perspective where the main struggles are reformist and parliamentary and the intermediate strategic goals involve capturing the levers of capitalist governance with a broad popular "front" that includes, implicitly or explicitly, a "progressive" and "democratic" sector of capital. This implies the opposite approach to the state from that suggested by Badiou. It is an alternative that fits comfortably with the state apparatuses and official state ideologies that are identified with the dominant sector of the transnational capitalist ruling class. Such approaches are widely advocated and pursued, despite the multiple failures of their political antecedents in this country over the past century plus—and despite their even clearer and more categorical failures throughout the rest of the capitalist core. If there are reasons and arguments for how a repetition of these defeats might be avoided, I'm not aware of them. In fact, these historic failures are seldom even raised within the US left, much less seriously evaluated.

Conclusion

I think there is clear evidence that major, possibly decisive, sectors of transnational capital and of its US components are more concerned with maintaining and extending the profitability and institutional stability of their *global* system of transnational capitalism than with maximizing the relative power of "their" national capitalisms. The existential threat that they fear is emerging from destabilizing nativist populisms and, most important, from the potential for transformed internationalist class conflict that exists beneath populist insurgencies. This sector of transnational capital is very aware of the need to strengthen its popular legitimacy to guard against these threats—and this is a need that will increase exponentially in the likely event of more serious global economic and political disruptions.

As the elements of crisis in the global system intensify, the different options facing transnational capital will become clearer. Whether the measures taken are repressive or co-optative, overt or covert, I think that the various *organized ruling-class efforts to implement them* will increase in importance. In my opinion, the initiatives with the most potential to successfully defend capital and seriously damage the revolutionary left will be those that tame reform coalitions to deal with some social costs of capitalist development within the framework of the continued dominance of capital—managing and mitigating any incidental risks that might be created for capitalist power and profits by keeping the reform struggle against capital in thrall to the postulated existential danger of "creeping" or perhaps "looming" "neoliberal fascism."

It's important that the left understand that this response from capital will include sophisticated class-conscious and strategically organized initiatives by ruling-class segments, some of which will be overt, and others of which will be at least partially covert. The short path to left suicide is to act within the framework of comfortable leftism, as though we are only dealing with spontaneous ruling-class responses to changing objective circumstances that are outside of any faction's direct control and that can be successfully challenged.[30]

Neera Tanden's "liberal democracy and the transatlantic partnership" is a current very public example of one version of this more sophisticated ruling-class approach.[31] This position advances conceptions of a "good," "reformable," "democratic" capitalism as an ally in a popular front against "fascism." To the extent that it gains some popular radical legitimacy, its exaggeration of the reactionary threat of "populisms" tends to eliminate the crucial distinctions between reform and revolution. The left should consider whether some recent organizational problems might have been impacted by the implementation of such ruling-class strategies.

This returns us to the issues of the state repression of previous decades that I raised early in this discussion. I think that some of the current repression and disruption of the left might be something more than it appears on the surface. The evidence is growing that a substantial proportion of the transnational ruling class is not inclined to risk its already shaky political legitimacy by supporting a generalized repression in the capitalist core, a step that could be a feature of an essentially fascist trajectory. However, it has access to effective repressive tactics that don't entail such risky options. While the transnational ruling class is providing significant cadre and many other resources to the official democratic "resistance" to existing reactionary movements—a number of which are widely seen as neofascist, sometimes with a bit of justification—it is also providing significant resources for taming potential sources of radical challenge.

The minority of ruling-class segments that might continue to support Trump and other quasi-populist tendencies are generally motivated by perceptions of their short-term, largely economic interests, not by some larger ideological purpose. The politics of such ruling-class strata are seldom clear and are usually opportunistic, far from an unchangeable given. They are very unlikely to retain much fervor for any type of populism, if and when a negative actual impact on their profits becomes apparent. These strata provide neither a stable base of support for reactionary populisms nor a serious challenge to them, and most of them have no intention of playing such roles in the foreseeable future.

Capital's main policies in the metropolis, at least prior to the emergence of more extended economic collapse, should be expected to emphasize the reformist parliamentary terrain while legitimating a range of formations that represent the "good capitalism" response to "populism." In this country, the Move-Ons, Onward Togethers, Quincy Institutes, Stand Up Republics, and others of similar ilk will be more significant threats to left insurgency than any ruling-class-sponsored movements that aim at an imposition of fascism by a coup from above—whether or not these have overt ruling-class sponsorship. In such conditions, it is a mistake to treat elements of confused quasi-populism and reactionary conservativism as fascist precursors, and an even greater mistake to see the "official" oppositions to such right-wing politics as building blocks for a viable antifascism. This is particularly important if there is evidence that such approaches are directly or indirectly, overtly or covertly, promoted by major ruling-class fractions.[32] *Such efforts should be seen for what they are: attempts to rescue capital by resuscitating a corrupt parliamentary reformism and an exhausted social democracy under the guise of an antifascist defense of democracy.*

Another major factor is based in the vast potentials for manipulation of social media that have emerged over the past two decades. In a recent comment, Matt Taibbi notes "the danger posed by Facebook, Google, and Twitter—under pressure from the Senate—organizing with groups like the Atlantic Council to fight 'fake news' in the name of preventing the 'foment of discord.'"[33] Taibbi primarily locates this issue as an element of the "manufactured consent" option that I previously argued is an important, although subordinate, element of ruling-class strategy. However, if social media can be manipulated to undermine institutional criticism and social debate under the guise of preventing the "foment of discord," as Taibbi and the Atlantic Council suggest, it can also be manipulated to actually "foment discord" within radical insurgencies. We should look forward to this being an important tool in modern repressive strategies.

In this context, it's certainly appropriate to note that the current rash of political implosions on the left reveal some definite patterns.

Accurately or not, the leftist and sectarian crimes and blunders of the more radical sectors that have been most seriously fragmented have been emphasized at the cost of eroding basic critiques of capitalist institutions and ideologies and crippling the concrete analyses of current conditions. When we can analyze these developments with the benefit of a few decades' hindsight, as we can now evaluate the half-century-old experiences of political repression of the past, it's not likely that this disintegration will appear to be all that accidental. However, whatever serious damage may have been done to the left, the problems of capitalism will also continue, and at least we will be guaranteed the opportunity to begin again—and to screw up again.

This article has reached the point where some indication of a viable alternative would be in order—an alternative extending beyond academic critiques and polemical exhortations, to include some plans of action. It's clear, at least to me, that the proper left response is to build an extraparliamentary anticapitalist social bloc that is intransigently hostile to all capitalist policy options and actively organizing against them at a "distance from the state." But how?

I'm sorry to have little to offer here beyond generalities. A minimum requirement for success in this undertaking will be the emergence of a left with sufficient organizational cohesion to think and act collectively as an actual radical force while taking proper care of its internal business. If my understanding of capital's strategic priorities is anywhere close to correct, major sectors of the transnational capitalist ruling elite are actively working to prevent such a development. Indeed, such efforts, both overt and covert, are probably well launched already.

Trump's Shaky Capitalist Support: Business Conflict and the 2016 Election

Matthew N. Lyons

Three Way Fight, February 17, 2019

What kind of support does Donald Trump have within the US ruling class? He is the first billionaire president of the United States, and his administration (despite the rhetoric about being an advocate for working-class Americans) has massively favored big business and the rich. Yet on a number of domestic and foreign policy issues he has gone against dominant neoliberal thought and has made many people in established elites deeply uncomfortable. And among big capitalists, it's not just centrist or liberal figures such as Tom Steyer and Michael Bloomberg who have opposed Trump, but also the Koch brothers, who just a few years ago were the most notorious funders of hard-line conservative politics but are now organizing against the president on immigration and trade policy.[1]

As a starting point to help make sense of Trump's relationship with US capitalists, I recommend the report "Industrial Structure and Party Competition in an Age of Hunger Games: Donald Trump and the 2016 Presidential Election," by Thomas Ferguson, Paul Jorgensen, and Jie Chen. Drawing on an intensively researched database of political contributions, the report (which I'll refer to as "Hunger Games" for short) analyzes the relative support the various 2016 candidates received from small and large contributors and, equally important, from specific industrial sectors within the business community.[2]

The Investment Theory of Party Competition

"Hunger Games" is based on Ferguson's investment theory of party competition, which argues that business interests hold most political power in capitalist societies, that electoral contests within and between political parties generally reflect conflicts between distinct blocs within the business community, and that these blocs tend to follow distinctions between specific industries (such as finance, mining, pharmaceuticals, etc.) and related economic characteristics (for example, labor-intensive versus non-labor-intensive industries, export-oriented firms versus firms oriented toward domestic markets, etc.). Ferguson, both alone and with various collaborators, has been using this approach for over thirty-five years to analyze political developments across much of modern US political history. For example, his book *Golden Rule* detailed the formation of a historical bloc of capitalists behind FDR's New Deal in the mid-1930s, while *Right Turn*, which Ferguson coauthored with Joel Rogers, traced the large-scale rightward shift of business interests in the 1970s, a development that pushed Jimmy Carter to the right, helped put Ronald Reagan in the White House, and contributed to the rise of what we now think of as neoliberalism.[3]

Before collaborating on the "Hunger Games" report, Ferguson, Jorgensen, and Chen previously analyzed the 2012 presidential race, in which Barack Obama won reelection over Mitt Romney. In many ways, 2012 was fairly typical of modern presidential elections: spending was similar for both big party nominees, but the Republican candidate enjoyed broader capitalist support overall, while the Democrat captured the greater share of small contributions (from non-rich voters). Broken down by sector, Romney received greater support than Obama from most industries, both in dollars and number of firms, with particularly strong support for Romney coming from "industries that have been heavily engaged in battles over climate change, alternative energy, and regulatory policy, including oil ..., mining ..., chemicals, paper, and utilities." But Obama received substantial backing from many of the other industries. Defense and aircraft manufacturers were evenly split between the two candidates, and Obama received the bulk of support from health insurance, telecommunications, computers, and software and web companies.[4]

Ferguson, Jorgensen, and Chen saw a key connection between the pattern of Obama's business support and the fact that his administration largely continued and in some respects expanded the national security policies initiated by Bush and Cheney. "Our study shows that national Democratic leaders are politically allied with many of the industries closely linked with the new national surveillance state"—i.e., "a system dominated by firms that want to sell all your data working with a government that seems to want to collect nearly all of it."[5]

2016: Small Contributors versus the Establishment

We don't need political scientists to tell us that the 2016 contest was different from 2012, and arguably from every other presidential race in US history. But "Hunger Games" helps us pinpoint and quantify some of what made it different. Two broad issues stand out. First, the report documents, in dollar terms, the revolt of ordinary voters against the established leadership in both major parties. In the Democratic primaries, the Bernie Sanders campaign represented "something we are confident is without precedent ... across virtually the whole of American history": "a major presidential candidate waging a strong, highly competitive campaign whose support from big business is essentially zero."[6] Aside from a few largish donations from labor unions, basically all of Sanders's funding came from small donors. But Donald Trump attracted a lot of small donations as well—a higher percentage of them, in fact, than Barack Obama did in 2012. Hillary Clinton, conversely, drew a smaller share of small donations than Mitt Romney did four years earlier. To Ferguson and his coauthors, for a Republican to attract more small money than the Democratic nominee is "the equivalent of forcing water suddenly to flow up hill." Based on the groundswells for both Trump and Sanders, they suggest that "the major parties appear to be breaking down as mass organizing vehicles."[7]

The "Hunger Games" authors trace popular support for both Sanders and Trump to the rise of what they call a "dual economy" in the US: the "extreme polarization of income and wealth over the last generation in the U.S. and many other developed countries, even while real earnings for most workers stagnated."[8] They devote several pages to detailing the dynamics, scope, and depth of this development. By 2016, they argue, the pressures of the dual economy had reached a tipping point—"a point where, quite literally, daily existence for many had become close to unlivable." "When two politicians broke through the big money cartels that dominate both major parties, popular enthusiasm surged almost overnight to seismic levels, shocking elites in both parties and flummoxing the entire American establishment."[9] I agree that the dual economy fueled the populist upsurge in both major parties, although on its own it doesn't tell us why some antiestablishment voters saw the main problem as concentrated wealth while others saw the main problem as Mexican and Muslim immigrants.

Capitalists Rally to Clinton

The other broad issue that set 2016 apart from most modern presidential elections is that capitalists sided heavily with the Democrats. Unlike 2012, the Democratic nominee received much more campaign spending overall than the Republican: $1.4 billion for Clinton compared with $861 million for Trump. The chronology of Trump's fundraising is significant. During the primaries, his campaign relied mainly on small contributions and his own money. As Ferguson et al. comment, "His money gave him both the means and the confidence to break the donors' cartel that until then had eliminated all GOP candidates who didn't begin by saluting the Bush family for starting the Iraq War, incessantly demanding cuts in Social Security and Medicare, and managing the economy into total collapse via financial deregulation.... He could say whatever he wanted."[10] Only in the summer, as the convention approached, did the Trump campaign begin to bring in significant money from major donors, ranging from coal mining companies to big banks to Silicon Valley firms such as Facebook. And capitalist donations to Trump didn't kick into high gear until after billionaire Rebekah Mercer persuaded Trump to put Steve Bannon and Kellyanne Conway in charge of the campaign, with a strategy to target white working-class voters in key swing states.[11]

The industrial pattern of political contributions was also dramatically different than it had been in 2012, when the Republican nominee received a majority of business contributions in most industries. In 2016, Clinton retained majority support from those industries that had sided with Obama (high tech and health insurance), but she also gained the bulk of contributions from defense and aerospace firms, which had split evenly between the two major parties in 2012, and she gained majority support from many industries that had backed Romney, including chemicals, electronics, pharmaceuticals, health care, utilities, general insurance, and both commercial and investment banking. Clinton enjoyed the broadest and deepest capitalist backing of any Democratic presidential candidate since 1964, when Lyndon Johnson defeated the "extremist" Barry Goldwater in a landslide. Clinton won this support, the "Hunger Games" authors argue, by reaching out to moderate Republicans and neoconservatives. She defended Wall Street in the face of Trump's populist rhetoric, moved to Obama's right on major foreign policy issues such as Syria, and (distancing herself firmly from Sanders) emphasized personal qualifications over policies. Clinton's strategy to reassure elites rather than speak to popular anger was, as the authors conclude, "a miscalculation of historic proportions."[12]

Despite Clinton's stronger business support overall, Trump did get majority backing from several industries, including mining (especially coal mining), casinos, agribusiness, rubber, steel, and gun and ammunition manufacturers. He also received a large proportion of support from food, chemicals, oil (especially big oil companies), transportation, and certain financial services sectors, especially private equity firms ("the part of Wall Street which had long championed hostile takeovers as a way of disciplining what they mocked as bloated and inefficient 'big business'").[13] As the "Hunger Games" authors argue, Trump's call for deregulation and climate change denial appealed to firms in many of these industries, while a few industries, notably steel and rubber, liked his economic protectionism. The gun industry was predictably hostile to Democrats.

Trump's Unstable Coalition
In their conclusion, Ferguson, Jorgensen, and Chen emphasize the deep ongoing tensions between President Trump and his party's establishment. They argue, moreover, that Trump's capitalist support base was not only much smaller than the Republican norm, but also "extremely unstable":

> It is made up of several layers of investor blocs with little in common other than their intense dislike of existing forms of American government. The world of private equity, intent on gaining access to the gigantic, rapidly growing securities markets of China and the rest of Asia or casinos dependent on licenses for their lucrative businesses in Macau are likely to coexist only fitfully with American industries struggling to cope with world overcapacity in steel and other products or facing twenty-first century mercantilist state targeting.[14]

Ferguson, Jorgensen, and Chen's analysis—particularly including this point about Trump's "extremely unstable" business support—bolsters and sheds light on points I made about the Trump administration in *Insurgent Supremacists*. I noted that Trump's candidacy alienated not only many Republican officials but also many business leaders. "Yet because he lacked an organizational base of his own, Trump was immediately forced not only to work with establishment figures in the Republican Party but also to bring them into his own administration. As a result, from the beginning Trump's presidency rested on an unstable coalition of right-wing factions both opposed to and aligned with conventional conservatism."[15]

This shaky coalition, I argued, brought together both supporters and opponents of neoliberalism, the ideology of deregulation, privatization, relatively open borders, and free trade that has dominated both major parties for about four decades. During the campaign, Trump advocated a form of nationalist populism embodied in the slogan "America First," which challenged neoliberal orthodoxy on trade and immigration and also called into question the establishment's related consensus around military interventionism and traditional alliances overseas. Trump brought some America Firsters into his administration, such as Steve Bannon, Jeff Sessions, Michael Flynn, Peter Navarro, and Stephen Miller, but they were never the dominant force there.

From the beginning, the majority of Trump's high-level appointees were not nationalist-populists, but conventional conservatives of various stripes. Some were Christian rightists or Tea Partiers, some were veterans of the Republican political establishment, and some were known mainly for their experience in the military or in business. From early on, America Firsters clashed with neoliberals and establishment figures in the administration and in Congress on issues such as trade policy, which contributed to an unusual degree of chaos and lack of clear direction. The issues on which the different factions agreed, and on which the Trump administration moved forward most effectively, basically represented a hard-line version of neoliberalism's domestic agenda: dismantle environmental regulations and consumer protection rules, open up public lands to corporate exploitation, "reform" the tax system to further redistribute wealth from low- and middle-income people to the rich, make the judicial system more punitive, and speed up militarization of the police. To a large extent, the result seemed to be policies that benefited narrow capitalist interests, such as military contractors, private prison operators, and energy companies, as well as the Trump family's own businesses, more than a coherent unified program.[16]

I think this image of an unstable coalition remains a useful framework. Since I wrote the passage above (in September 2017), the Trump administration's America First faction has lost ground, several of its leading members are gone, and some critics have concluded that the president is just continuing neoliberal policies while overlaying them with xenophobic rhetoric to appease his popular base.[17] But this doesn't adequately get at the administration's inconsistent, conflicted character, as when Trump announced a troop withdrawal from Syria that most of his own advisers opposed, or forced a government shutdown only after his right-wing base demanded no compromise on the border wall.[18] It doesn't explain why neoliberal measures have been interspersed with echoes of paleoconservative Pat Buchanan (who declared "we will put America first" over twenty-five years ago), as when Trump imposed steel and aluminum tariffs on Europe and Canada, launched a trade war with China, or railed against NATO allies. Buchanan's 1992 campaign in the GOP presidential primaries was one of the first major right-wing challenges to neoliberalism, and it drew support from some of the same business sectors that later backed Trump's candidacy.[19]

I don't have detailed information on how capitalists' views of Trump may have shifted since the 2016 election, but in broad terms, the dominant business voices have supported his administration on taxes and deregulation of industry, while opposing it on immigration and trade. For example, the Business Roundtable (BR), which includes the CEOs of most big US corporations, praised the 2017 tax "reform" law and testified that the Trump administration was "taking major steps" to achieve "smart regulation." But in September 2018, BR reported that two-thirds of CEOs feared recent tariffs and expected trade tensions would negatively affect their capital investment decisions, and in August 2018, sixty BR members, including some of the country's most prominent CEOs, signed a letter expressing "serious concern" over the administration's immigration policy changes.[20]

To sum up: Neoliberalism (and the related internationalist/interventionist foreign policy stance) still enjoys majority support within the US ruling class and among political elites in both major parties, but its ability to rally popular support is in crisis (as it also is, for example, in many European countries). Right-wing nationalist populism has a large popular constituency, but it lacks a coherent, independent organizational infrastructure and its capitalist support is relatively weak. These factors enabled Donald Trump in 2016 to defeat establishment candidates in both the Republican primaries and the general election, but he attracted a relatively small and internally divided array of business supporters. As president, despite his strong personal inclinations toward nationalist populism, Trump has been forced to bring many establishment figures into his administration and to implement elements of both neoliberalism and nationalist populism, or at least to oscillate between them.

This is a volatile situation, which Trump's authoritarian impulses won't fix, and it's hard to know how it will be resolved in the long run. Maybe transnationally oriented capitalists will find a way to reconnect with popular support, as Don Hamerquist has suggested.[21] Maybe (if the United States' global economic position weakens further) nationalist populists will gain greater and more organized ruling-class backing, thus expanding their ability to govern without neoliberal partners. In the meantime, the situation seems likely to feed not a calculated march toward dictatorship, but a sharpening mix of repression and instability. As the political collective Research & Destroy forecast shortly after Trump's inauguration, "In many of the futures we can see from here, the state will be both turbocharged and weak; its oppressive mechanisms will churn in higher gears without being highly functional, as jurisdictional and factional disputes proliferate."[22] There are openings here for the left—but also for the far right.

Trump's Election and Capitalist Power: An Exchange

Don Hamerquist and Matthew N. Lyons

Three Way Fight, March 28, 2019

This is a follow-up to Lyons's essay "Trump's Shaky Capitalist Support: Business Conflict and the 2016 Election," also published in this volume.

Don Hamerquist Comments

I agree with Matthew's emphasis on the "shaky" character of Trump's capitalist support. He points out that

> Trump has been forced to bring many establishment figures into his administration, and to implement elements of both neoliberalism and nationalist populism, or at least to oscillate between them.... [However] neoliberalism (and the related internationalist/interventionist foreign policy stance) still enjoys majority support within the US ruling class and among political elites in both major parties.... The situation seems likely to feed not a calculated march toward dictatorship, but a sharpening mix of repression and instability.[1]

This is quite distinct from the prevailing narrative on the North American left. Consider, for example, Henry Giroux's version of the "fascist creep" thesis, which pictures Trump as "a fusion of the worst dimensions and excesses of gangster capitalism with the fascist ideals of white nationalism and racial supremacy."[2]

However, while accepting most of Matthew's political conclusions, I have reservations about the Ferguson "investment theory of party competition" that is incorporated in his argument. In my opinion, such approaches are useful—but only within clear limits. (I would make similar criticisms of Gilens and Page's argument supporting their conception of oligarchy.)[3] Ferguson's campaign contribution metrics can roughly measure the efforts of particular capitalists to gain access to and influence on government, but they gloss over important contradictions that underlie alternative ruling-class approaches to the strategic direction of society. To adequately understand the organizational cohesion and the political "will" of the ruling-class fractions that support and/or oppose "Trump," it's important to avoid reducing class politics to financial and technical self-interest within an essentially "given" national framework.

US capitalism is part of a developing transnational system with an institutional and ideological trajectory and momentum that transcends national politics. The changing relationship between class profit and class power in the global capitalist system overdetermines the political, economic, and ideological posture of particular capitalist fractions—at times transforming them dramatically. This leads to the hollowing of capitalist state institutions and to growing challenges to capitalist hegemonic ideology—to a broad range of popular grievances and a heightened and more generalized instability. While capitalist fractions will continue to pursue narrow national and corporative interests through the parliamentary process, the more significant strategic elements of the ruling-class response to the problems confronting capital increasingly will be shaped in global economic and political institutions and processes outside this framework—where the left challenge should be located as well.

In 2008, at the depths of the global financial crisis, the factors setting the politics of capitalist fractions in this country were quite different from 2016, when Trump had his improbable triumph in the late stage of a capitalist recovery. These factors are likely to be very different again in 2020. In 2008, the destabilizing risks of concessions to nationalist populism—even concessions that were mainly symbolic or rhetorical—would have been overwhelming. In 2016, nearly a decade after capital had responded to its existential crisis with generalized austerity and mammoth institutional bailouts, a very different set of potential risks and responses had emerged. The overall system was no longer enmeshed in crisis—although there were warnings on the horizon—and the limited elements of nativist populism hinted at by Trump posed minimal risks for capital. Concessions in this direction might provide something of a release valve for mass discontent—a ruling-class feint with potentials to preempt more disruptive oppositions before the business cycle took its next dive.

In this view, "Trump" appears as something of an accident, like Brexit, but that also doesn't adequately explain the dynamics at work. The elements of "populism" in "Trump" have been almost totally eclipsed by the embrace of neoliberal economics and garden-variety capitalist reaction. The MAGA nationalism is likely to wilt if it is confronted with any indication of major problems in the global economy. Despite this, the most noteworthy feature of current politics is the frantic way a major sector of capital and much of the institutional weight of capitalist state power are organizing against Trump, notwithstanding his remarkably incompetent "populism" and his routine vanilla conservatism. Certainly this indicates a ruling-class fear of major pending dislocations in the global system, including an expectation of more substantive populist challenges. This dictates an accelerated need for a transnational ruling-class perspective that can enforce a capitalist consensus on competitive sectors of the ruling elites and develop some better tools to incorporate and defuse potential mass oppositions from both left and right. Trump is a distracting infection in the emergence of a global ruling class. The overreaction of ruling elites to the Trump phenomenon is an element of the birth pangs of a capitalist new world order.

Matthew N. Lyons Replies

I appreciate Don's comment and I think his criticism is very helpful. I agree that Ferguson's "investment theory" is not an adequate framework for analyzing ruling-class politics and internal conflict, and agree in particular that we need to bring in the international dimension. Still, I want to offer a couple of caveats. First, while Ferguson's quantitative analysis is limited, to me it's a welcome contribution in a context where so many leftist analyses of capital are based only on selective use of anecdotal evidence, or on out-and-out distortion. (I'm thinking for example of Floris D'Aalst's recent piece in *Insurgent Notes*, where he claims that the Koch brothers are Donald Trump's allies, although in fact they have consistently and very publicly opposed Trump on both immigration and trade issues.)[4]

My other caveat is that while Ferguson's framework here is indeed national, it would be a mistake to see his investment theory as just "reducing class politics to financial and technical self-interest." Ferguson and his coauthors combine the data from electoral campaigns with other evidence to develop larger analytic themes. For example, in their article about the 2012 presidential election, they draw a connection between Obama's cordial relationship with high-tech firms and his active continuation of the "national surveillance state" policies he inherited from George W. Bush.[5] One of the main reasons I got interested in Ferguson to begin with is because of his work from the 1980s on intracapitalist debates around FDR's New Deal. Ferguson argued that firms and sectors that had relatively low labor costs (and thus had more flexibility to negotiate with organized labor), and/or were oriented toward international markets, formed the core of a new historical bloc that backed FDR, restabilized US capitalism, and created a new hegemonic set of policies that persisted for forty years.[6] This analysis is far better than anything else I've seen on the subject.

Again, I think we need to look beyond Ferguson's approach—to examine, for example, how "the changing relationship between class profit and class power in the global capitalist system overdetermine the political, economic, and ideological posture of particular capitalist fractions," as Don puts it. One of the questions that Ferguson et al. pose—and by their own admission aren't really equipped to answer—is why Trump's (and Sanders's) politics captured mass support in 2016 and not earlier. I'm partly sympathetic to Don's suggestion that "in 2008, the destabilizing risks of concessions to nationalist populism … would have been overwhelming," whereas in 2016 the system had restabilized to the point that it could allow and benefit from "a release valve for mass discontent." However, to me this raises a question: What is the mechanism whereby "the system" makes these choices? Do they reflect conscious strategic decisions by sections of the ruling class, and if so where do these happen and what evidence do we have for them? Or is there some other "objective" mechanism at work? Either way, I'm wary of ascribing too much rationality to the system. I think the system has a tremendous capacity to adapt to unexpected pressures, and this seems like one of those times that the ruling class was blindsided and had to scramble to adapt. On this question, I would ask Don if he could elaborate on his somewhat cryptic comment that "'Trump' appears as something of an accident … but that also doesn't adequately explain the dynamics at work."

Don Hamerquist Replies

I wouldn't speak of "mechanisms," "system," and "rationality" in this context. The US nation-state is a rapidly changing complex entity that is impacted by a range of conflicting and contradictory interests and forces, some essentially internal and some not so much, many of which aren't clearly delineated or competently advanced. These are expressed within an array of structures that have their own weight and momentum, and they are mediated through a range of ideologies with their histories, fans, and fanatics.

Rather than "conscious strategic decisions by sections of the ruling class," political outcomes and policy stances in capitalist states are the result of a variety of different factors that interact at various levels and in different ways. Financial and commodities markets both determine and are determined by changing state policies—at times via conscious ruling-class intervention and at times in spite of it. A definite inertia and momentum is provided by the internal state and quasi-state bureaucracies and apparatuses that have developed to implement capital's control but that increasingly fail to reflect the interests of particular capitalist fractions in a stable and continuing fashion. The increasing weight of transnational capitalist institutions and policies that deal with trade, finance, countercyclical policy, and various accumulated social costs of capitalist development provide another set of causal factors that have real effects on internal politics, independently of the relative political strengths of domestic capitalist fractions—generally overriding them in most countries, and sometimes even here.

As you point out, US capitalism has a well-demonstrated capacity to adapt—or to say it differently, it is a system fortunate to have produced oppositions with demonstrated capacities to self-destruct. But despite its good fortune in enemies, US capital has no clear adaptive path. Its various efforts will "work" in places and at times, but usually at the cost of worsening problems elsewhere or, perhaps, later. This leads to a daunting multitude of unavoidable problems and adds to the difficult gestation of a legitimate transnational capitalist elite.

Nevertheless, the process is not all chaos and confusion. There are certain strands of policy that are clearly embraced and enforced by the dominant sectors of transnational capital. The most important of these is their organized opposition to any of the destabilizing populisms of either the right or the left that threaten to emerge from the dilemmas of global capital. These policies are developed at Davos and Valdai, and in the think tanks of Washington, Brussels, and London, and we will shortly see, I think, from Moscow and Beijing also. These are shared visions of a capitalist global order with common ideas about what forces and tendencies would be problematic for that order and a common concern with maintaining both the power and the legitimacy of transnational capital. I recognize the importance of differences over the significance of sovereignty and between visions of a unipolar or multipolar structure for the global system; however, these have strategic importance mainly for relatively weaker capitalist interests that are more reliant on access to specific elements of state power.

It's possible to discern the potential elements of a global strategy for capital in this framework. In the first place, it includes developing viable transnational institutions and understandings to deal with the predictable effects of the reversal of the business cycle and, more important, to deal with the increasingly critical aspects of secular crisis in capitalist production and bourgeois civilization. In the second place, it requires developing some basis of "consent" from among the masses that will not be among the beneficiaries of any global capitalist order.

The imperatives of this strategy underlie ruling-class attitudes toward Trump, toward Brexit, toward Bolsonaro. You say about Trump, "I think this was one of those times that the ruling class was blindsided and had to scramble to adapt." I agree for the most part, but what I think is most important is the content that the "adapting" scramble assumed. Perhaps we will have to argue this point elsewhere, but, beginning with the presidential primary and continuing through the first half of Trump's term, I think that it has taken the form of a thinly disguised attempted coup that risks the viability of the party system and parliamentary structure in this country. It's difficult to explain the magnitude and urgency of the organized ruling-class effort to displace Trump, who was swiftly neutralized into an ordinary reactionary—if he was ever something more. What calculation explains this effort against Trump, more of a comic figure than a populist demagogue?

V

MAKING SENSE OF TRUMPISM IN REAL TIME

Trump, the Far Right, and the Return of Vigilante Repression

Matthew N. Lyons

Three Way Fight, September 1, 2020

I've been revisiting the articles I wrote about Trump during the 2016 presidential campaign, taking stock of what's the same and what's different, as a way to get some perspective on what we're facing now.

One key piece of the picture is Trump's relationship with the forces of the US far right, by which I mean those rightists who are fundamentally disloyal to the existing political order, because they want to replace it with something even worse. In the 2016 campaign, Trump had a symbiotic relationship with the far right that was unprecedented—unlike anything any major-party presidential candidate had ever had in US history, as far as I can tell.[1] The relationship was centered particularly on the alt-right, which played an important role in helping the Trump campaign, particularly in the primaries but also in the general election, through its effective and innovative use of social media to attack Trump's opponents. In return, the alt-right got a lot more visibility and recognition and validation by having this connection with a rising and ultimately triumphant political figure.[2]

Looking at the current situation, it's still true that Trump has an unprecedented symbiotic relationship with far-right forces, but the specifics and the character of that relationship have changed.

In 2016, the alt-right was the far right's most dynamic sector.[3] After the election, they declared themselves to be the vanguard of the Trump coalition, and in 2017 they made a big push to capitalize on their success and create a broader, militant street-fighting coalition of right-wing forces.[4] The push failed and the alt-right suffered a dramatic decline. The murderous Unite the Right rally in Charlottesville exposed the brutality at the core of their politics for

everyone to see. That setback—followed by a strong countermobiliza-
tion by antifascists, deplatforming by media companies, and a series of
internal conflicts—left the alt-right much weaker and more isolated.[5]
Since the end of 2017, the alt-right has had little capacity to mobilize
much of anything.

Today, the most dynamic sector of the far right is the Patriot
movement—the people who brought you citizen militias, conspiracy
theories about globalist elites, and a militarized ideology of individual property rights. Unlike the alt-right, which is white nationalist
(meaning they literally want an all-white nation), the Patriot movement
has always encompassed a range of positions on race and a tension
between explicit calls for white dominance and what's been called
"color-blind racism"—the ideology that protects racial oppression by
denying it exists.[6]

The Patriot movement was probably a lot bigger than the alt-right
in 2016, but it was relatively quiet after the collapse of the Malheur
Wildlife Refuge occupation early that year. By contrast, 2020 has seen
a series of political mobilizations with politics much closer to Patriot
ideology than to alt-right white nationalism, notably the gun rights
rally in Richmond, Virginia, back in January and the antilockdown
protests in April and May.[7] While the alt-right in 2016 made powerful
use of internet memes and online harassment campaigns, the Patriot
movement in 2020 has demonstrated a capacity to put hundreds, thousands, or even tens of thousands of people in the streets in cities across
the country, something the alt-right was never able to do.

It's not just that a different branch of the far right is on the
upswing now compared with 2016. It's also that the Patriot movement has developed a different relationship with Trump and with the
established political system than the alt-right has had.

In 2016, most alt-rightists supported Trump enthusiastically, but
they were always clear that he wasn't one of them. They said: Trump
doesn't share our politics, but he is useful to us; he's creating openings
for us to promote our message, he's attacking a lot of our enemies—
including the conservative establishment—and he's buying time for
the radical changes we need. The alt-right saw Trump's anti-immigrant
and Islamophobic politics as slowing down the supposed process of
"white genocide," but they never expected him to dismantle the United
States or create a whites-only society. And as his administration went

on, many alt-rightists were deeply disappointed by what they saw as Trump's betrayal of his America First promises and his capitulation to establishment conservatism.[8] You see this shift most starkly on the *Occidental Dissent* blog, where alt-rightist Brad Griffin ("Hunter Wallace") once supported Trump but now writes about him with loathing and contempt.[9]

The Patriot movement doesn't call for a white ethnostate, but it has developed its own ways of delegitimizing the existing political system, such as claiming that local governments can veto or ignore federal laws, and even creating new bodies, such as "common law courts," that claim to have legal authority. In 2014, hundreds of Patriot activists with guns successfully faced down a large contingent of armed federal officers at Cliven Bundy's Nevada ranch in a dispute over Bundy's refusal to pay grazing fees on federal lands.[10] It's hard to think of another instance of armed rightist defiance of the US government on that scale since federal troops went after the Reconstruction-era Ku Klux Klan in the 1870s.

Yet the Patriot movement has, with exceptions, been more staunchly and consistently supportive of President Trump and his efforts to expand federal policing than the alt-right ever was. Patriot activists engage in ideological gymnastics that dismiss undocumented immigrants, refugees, and leftist protesters as tools of a sinister elite conspiracy to impose world government. This framework enables them to rationalize support for Trump's repressive measures as defense of a populist upsurge against an elite-sponsored campaign to suppress it.

In December 2015, I suggested that one way to read Trump's friendly relationship with much of the far right was that "Trump's campaign is co-opting far rightists into, if not renewed loyalty, at least suspending their disloyalty to the existing political order."[11] That co-optation has had limited effect on alt-rightists and other white nationalists, but it's had a strong pull for the Patriot movement.

So it's not surprising that Patriot activists—associated with Three Percenters, Oath Keepers, militias, and related groups—have played a major role in the wave of vigilante repression that's crashed over Black Lives Matter protests this year. Bolstering brutal police crackdowns, armed far rightists have dogged BLM demonstrations hundreds of times in 2020. Since George Floyd's murder in late May, right-wingers have physically attacked protesters over a hundred times and have killed at least three people.[12] Urged on by racist cops and Trump's "law and order" rhetoric, these activists have been functioning implicitly or explicitly as vigilantes, helping the police to crack down on radical dissent.

Previous right-wing mass killers such as Dylann Roof (Charleston, 2015) or Patrick Crusius (El Paso, 2019) have generally framed their violence in terms of white nationalist or neo-nazi ideology.[13] But Kyle Rittenhouse, who murdered two protesters in Kenosha last week, says he is a member of a local militia protecting local businesses; he is almost a caricature in his adoration for the police. Also unlike Roof or Crusius, Rittenhouse has been endorsed by figures such as Tucker Carlson and Trump himself.[14] It's true that some of the recent vigilantes have been white nationalists, but white nationalists have tended to be ambivalent about whether to support cops or not, while Patriot groups have rallied to them more consistently. Closely aligned with Patriot groups have been the Proud Boys, a misogynistic organization that is "Western chauvinist" but multiracial, and that has consistently tried to position itself as vigilante allies of the police, as well as Patriot Prayer, a northwest regional group with politics similar to the Proud Boys.[15]

If internet activism was the linchpin of Donald Trump's symbiotic relationship with the far right in 2016, physical violence and harassment play that role today. Whether they intimidate Black Lives Matter protests or intensify them, far-right vigilantes dramatize Trump's claims that extraordinary measures are needed to combat lawlessness. In return, his fearmongering offers Patriot activists and other paramilitary rightists validation, increased attention, and political focus.

Vigilante repression as an adjunct of state power is nothing new—it's been integral to the United States from the country's beginning. For most of US history, the state repressive apparatus was relatively small, and the people in power relied heavily on nonstate forces of armed white men to keep subject populations—Indigenous, Black, Mexican, and Asian—terrorized and under control. During the key period of industrialization from the 1870s to the 1930s, capitalists also relied heavily on private armies such as the Pinkerton National Detective Agency to intimidate, beat, or kill workers who tried to organize unions or go on strike.[16] As recently as the 1970s, federal security agencies sponsored right-wing vigilante organizations such as the Legion of Justice and the Secret Army Organization to spy on, vandalize, and physically attack leftists. In 1979, an undercover agent of the US Bureau of Alcohol, Tobacco and Firearms helped to plan the operation that resulted in the Greensboro Massacre, in which a coalition of Klansmen and nazis murdered five leftists at an anti-Klan rally.[17]

Overall, however, vigilante repression has tended to decline over the past half century or more, as traditional outfits such as the Ku Klux Klan became a liability to the ruling class, large sections of the white supremacist movement abandoned loyalty to the state for white nationalism, and the state's own repressive apparatus became much bigger and more powerful. But now we're seeing a new push to bring back vigilante repression alongside the modern security state.

Today's resurgence of right-wing vigilantism is unstable and conditional, because it's driven by a situation of unprecedented volatility. On one side, we have a wave of protests, uprisings, and strikes against police violence and white supremacy beyond anything the US has seen in decades. On the other, we have a president who promotes supremacist politics, routinely subordinates governmental functions to his own personal interests, and both threatens and celebrates violence against his opponents. Armed Patriot activists and some other far rightists are rallying to the police partly because they're afraid of Black-led working-class revolt, and partly because, despite reservations, they still see Trump as a populist leader at war with entrenched elite power. Their de facto loyalty to the system could shift into support for efforts to keep Trump in power by extralegal means, or armed opposition if they give up on Trump or he leaves office.[18]

Lockdowns, the Insurgent Far Right, and the Future of Antifascism: A Conversation with *Three Way Fight*

It's Going Down, December 30, 2020

This interview with Matthew N. Lyons and Xtn Alexander was conducted during the period after the November 2020 presidential election but before the January 6, 2021, attack on the US Capitol.

It's Going Down: Matthew, almost four years ago, you joined us right as Trump was coming in. At this point, how do you think that your predictions or the analysis that you had coming into this administration matches up to what you've seen?

Matthew: During the 2016 presidential campaign, and really since then, it's been an ongoing discussion about the question of Trump's relationship with fascism. Many people have argued that Trump is a fascist or is promoting a fascist agenda. That's something I've really taken issue with. The position I put forward in 2016 was that Trump was not a fascist, although he certainly was promoting certain elements of fascist politics and sort of paving the way or potentially laying the groundwork for more of a full-fledged fascist movement. I think that's really been borne out. There were two elements I argued were key to fascism that I did not see in Trump's coalition or in his administration. One was an overriding vision to systematically transform society according to a certain ideology, whether that be a white supremacist vision or more of a nationalist vision. Trump has promoted certain elements of that, but I don't think that he is really interested in systematically transforming society. He's interested in promoting his own interests and his own self-aggrandizement. Everything else is kind of subordinate to that.

And then another piece that I see as key to fascism that is missing is the need to build an independent organizational base in order to dismantle or systematically transform the political system. Trump has never tried to do that. He has mobilized people, he has gathered people behind him, but he has always worked within the framework of the Republican Party even though he's been at odds with its leadership. In the recent period, things have moved in a different direction, potentially, but basically, as far as the character of Trump's administration, I would say, again, fascistic elements but not a fully developed kind of fascist approach.

Xtn: We were always wondering what was on the horizon with Trump, and I and some of the people who are broadly in the three way fight camp looked at Trump as an opportunist, kind of a reactionary bourgeois capitalist wannabe politician, but ultimately an opportunist. But enough of the fascists, the far right and specifically national socialist groupings saw enough in Trump that they welcomed his entrance into the electoral arena and used it as an opportunity to build their base in ways that we haven't seen before. The whole explosion of far-right and fascist groupings was a challenge for all of us. I don't think we as a movement really expected to see the growth that happened. It's been an intense five years, lots of violence, lots of struggle, people being murdered, repression from the state, as well as ongoing attacks from the far right. And now antifascism, radical antifascism, is more part of the popular discourse, action, and activity than ever before. That's a positive thing. That said, antifascism is often all over the place, it's very diffuse, it can be contradictory. I think with projects like *Three Way Fight* as well as It's Going Down and fellow travelers in our camps, we need to continue to try to analyze what's going on, make sense of what's happening, and hopefully give some ideas to our movements. I agree with Matthew on the general characterization of Trump, but I wouldn't want that to diminish the real world organizing that fascists have actually done in the last five years. That's been significant and scary.

Matthew: Trump was certainly unique among presidents or even major presidential candidates in that he formed this kind of symbiotic and mutually beneficial relationship with elements of the far right. Initially that centered on the alt-right, with their use of online activism to promote his candidacy and getting a lot of visibility and recognition in return. Recently it's centered on more street-level activism with Patriot groups and others.

It's Going Down: A lot of what we'll be talking about today is what do we expect to see out of these formations, especially as Trump is saying that "wild protests" are going to be happening in January, and he continues to poke around and see if he can change the results of the election. And groups like the Proud Boys definitely seem to be growing or are pretty strong.

But first, we're going to turn to what happened in Salem the other day, and I think this is going to inform a lot of what we talk about. Yesterday in Salem, people associated with the group Patriot Prayer—which is a pan-far-right group that includes everything from white nationalists who'll show up to their events to people in groups like the Proud Boys to people associated with the Three Percenters and the general Patriot movement—they attempted, with several of them armed, to storm the capitol. This is a couple hundred people, in the town of Salem, Oregon. There was a closed session and this was framed as an antilockdown protest. People smashed out the windows or damaged the windows at the capitol, they clashed with police, there was a lot of bear mace and pepper spray being used on both sides. Police brought out BearCats [armored vehicles] and stuff. Notice that there were a lot of people saying things like, "Should we burn our Blue Lives Matter flags?"—people getting in arguments with the police. We've seen a lot of these things play out whenever these types of groups come up against the reality of the violence of the state.

Tucker Carlson that night did a segment. The banner read, "Is force now more important than voting?" There was one live streamer who did this thing while they were filming. This is somebody on the right, and they said, "Show up in black bloc." They were encouraging antifa to come out and said, "Get on your apps. Are you guys really standing against tyranny? Come out and stand with us. If you're really trying to make the world a better place and make citizens more free, stop this tyrannical government taking your rights and stand with us." This is definitely a lot of what we've already seen, but what's different about this is the inclusion of property destruction and clashing with the police and this antagonistic view of law enforcement. I would guess that as Biden comes into office, we will see more of a sort of boogaloo boi–type stance that law enforcement is not this grandiose thing that they make it out to be because their president is no longer in office, and perhaps they will take on more of an "anti–law enforcement" stance, even though they are at their basis very, very pro–law enforcement. They just want their people to be the ones with the guns. What is your take on what happened in Salem?

Matthew: To frame my thoughts, I want to back up for a moment and say a little more about the general perspective. Something that I've been focusing a lot on in recent years is this division that I see running through the right in the US between system-loyal forces and oppositional forces. It's a question of whether you accept or reject the legitimacy of the existing political system. You see this cutting across ideological divisions. So within white supremacist forces there are those who want to achieve white dominance within the existing political framework. And there's others who say, no, what we need to do is form a separate all-white nation. You also see it within the Christian right and other sectors. It's not to say that these are totally separate positions, because they're very much interacting. In some situations, oppositional rightists will clash with system-loyal rightists; in others, they will work together, but they're always interacting and influencing each other.

One thing that's important about Trump is that he in various ways strengthened the connections between system-loyal and oppositional rightists and to some degree blurred that distinction. Earlier this year, we saw Patriot movement forces—which in recent years have often clashed with law enforcement and have actually shot and killed police officers in a number of instances—we saw Patriot movement forces being co-opted, largely through their loyalty to Trump, into a much more system-loyal position. But now what we're seeing in the wake of the election is a shift in the other direction, with huge swaths of the right shifting from basically a system-loyal position into an oppositional position. This is very much spurred by Trump's refusal to accept the outcome of the presidential race—basically saying that the electoral process, the electoral system that put him in the White House, that that system is illegitimate. The fact that large sectors of the Republican Party have gone along with this is very significant. It means that the oppositional right has gone from maybe several million people in this country to suddenly tens of millions of people. It's literally an order of magnitude difference. How long that will remain and whether that is a stable long-term shift, or whether it's something temporary and unstable, that remains to be seen.

That's a lot of the context in which I look at events such as those in Salem, where you see supporters of the sitting president clashing physically with the forces of the state and, as you cited, even calling on leftists to join them. How sincere they are about that is another question, but just the fact that they're even raising that as an issue, that's a pretty dramatic change. So, I do see it as something that's emblematic of a much larger shift in the political situation in this country.

Xtn: I think what's important is that we're seeing the question being raised from the right, if it's time for extralegal action and a break with legality. It's a moment when the far right, and perhaps a growing sector of the right broadly speaking, is less tethered to the US state in its current form. And I think going into the next administration, we're gonna see that detethering even more, at least from the right in regard to what they perceive as a liberal administration. We should really be asking if there is a growing sense on all sides that the state is becoming more—or being seen as more—illegitimate in all its branches and attached institutions. I think a certain fragmentation of state hegemony and a growing crisis of state authority and governance is happening. And what flows from that, for me, is: (a) in this crisis there's going to arise an array of autonomous or semi-autonomous groups, movements, and tendencies across the political spectrum, and (b), and this goes to the live streamer's comments from Salem on antifa joining in, our side can't concede direct action or insurgent politics to the right or the fascists. We have to be developing, maintaining, and helping to expand class and social movements that are independent of the state. And not just independent of the state, but movements that are defined by liberatory visions, that are directed popularly and democratically, that have an intransigence to the system, and that are militant.

To some people it looks attractive, like, "Oh, there's people who are fighting the police. They're fighting the state. They're taking on the rule of the government." That's dangerous if we think through any kind of shared militancy there can be a connection. We have to resist that. We have to be offering up our own ideas, visions, and programs. But what's happened in Salem is really important. It's not the first time, but we need to be thinking more about that kind of situation.

It's Going Down: On the tip you were talking about not ceding these tactics or politics to the right; what do you think is incumbent upon autonomous anticapitalist movements then? The growth of things we've seen around either mutual aid or the growth of things like tenant associations has been really great, but that's almost overshadowed by this spectacular kind of violence like what we saw at the capitol in Salem. Do you see a danger that people who are angry at the lockdowns over justifiable class reasons would get sucked into these right-wing movements? And therefore, do we need a kind of left-wing answer to that? And what would that look like?

Xtn: Yes. I think that there is a danger there. People are angry. And I think a lot of mutual aid and tenant associations and various solidarity organizing is essential, it's important, but it's a component of a broader social movement that we need. And that's an ongoing thing to organize for. In the interim, though, people are going to be looking at these antilockdown protests, and the militancy and anger, and even if they don't agree with all of the players and actors and political tendencies that are part of that, I think people will on some levels be sympathetic to it. That's the danger. And because of that there's a need to constantly articulate and pose an alternative. I'm a medical worker, and I work in the emergency room. And our emergency rooms and our ICUs are just flooded. I mean, we are near full capacity. When I am out, I take all my precautions, masks and everything. When I'm out, I see people in bars, and it makes me angry. On the other hand, so many people in our movements, friends, families, how many people do we know who are servers? How many people do we know whose lives depend on being able to work in restaurants, bars, whatever it might be? There are no easy answers to the situation. I wish there were.

It's Going Down: With Biden coming into office, do you think that we will see more of an insurgent sort of anti–law enforcement or even "anti-state" vibe, coming into either things like the Patriot movement or the far right in general? Or even things like the Proud Boys from kind of like the boogaloo boi side? Will Biden, as the head of the state, make everything else "communist," and therefore, they'll be more apt to have an antisystem message that maybe they wouldn't have had under Trump, or do you think that it will basically stay the same?

Matthew: I think there's likely to be an upsurge of right-wing militancy. To some extent, there's a larger pattern there that when Democratic administrations come into power a section of the right tends to shift from simply supporting the Republicans into a more

militant stance. We saw that in the Nineties under Bill Clinton, we saw
it under Barack Obama when you had the sudden rise of the Tea Party
movement and also a resurgence of the Patriot movement that had been
dormant under George W. Bush. To some extent, this is following that
same pattern. What's different this time, I think, is that there's been
this larger shift of a large section of the right which had been system
loyal into a much more directly oppositional stance of rejecting the
legitimacy of the system because they see the election that put Biden
on top as illegitimate, and that from their standpoint it robbed Trump
of his rightful position as president. There's no way to square that
with recognition of the electoral system as it exists in this country.
So, I think that one way or another it's going to lead to increased
militancy, increased violence from right-wing groups, and how well
organized that is, how well focused it is, that's an open question. But
it's definitely going to be ugly.

It's Going Down: In Arizona, they had to literally have the electoral vote in secret because there were so many threats. This stuff gets
reported on now and it's just kind of like, "Oh, this is the world that
we live in." How can the state allow that to become the norm? It seems
like that is such an affront to its monopoly of force and its sovereignty,
even if it's coming from Trump supporters, that it would need to smash
that. Even this thing in Salem, or, for instance, the Proud Boys burning
the Black Lives Matter signs in DC—to my understanding, outside
of some officials in DC, there hasn't been any major condemnation
of these actions from Biden. I haven't heard Biden or Kamala Harris
say anything like, "Oh, by the way, people are hiding in secret to vote
us into office." Will there be repression for the right and for everybody else coming in the future? They don't seem to be prepping the
population for what's to come. And is that emblematic of some sort
of strategy or just that they're really weak, and they're trying to just
let this stuff fly under the radar and not make too much of it?

Xtn: One thing that the Trump administration has done, that
Trump himself has done, is put out on full display the actual lack of
cohesiveness of the state. It isn't to say that the US state and empire
isn't strong. It isn't to say that it's not still the most dominant power
in the world. But it's in crisis. I wouldn't say that the state has lost
control, but it is being tested. And we're seeing a lot of fissures and
fractures—for instance, today versus the Patriot movement and the

Militia movement of the early 1990s, as Matthew indicated, with the tens of millions of people who are not just sympathetic but who see themselves as active players on the right, that is much more widespread than it was in '93, '94, '95. So how can the state realistically control tens of millions of people in an openly repressive way? I think that there's basically an attitude on all sides of, "What is the future of the US government going to be?" And various political forces are actively trying to reshape that, and that's putting stresses on the state. That's something we need to be thinking about more.

Matthew: This issue underscores the importance of offering a radical left alternative. This is a situation where, just as it would be dangerous to side with anti-state rightists against the state, it would also be dangerous to side with the forces of liberal repression, even if the initial target of that repression is far rightists. Because something that we've seen repeatedly in this country is that state repression, even in the guise of antifascism, is dangerous to our movements. The classic example of that was during World War II, when 125,000 Japanese Americans were rounded up and imprisoned in the name of antifascism, as well as various other repressive measures that were carried out, strikebreaking and so on. But there have been a number of other instances since then where that same dynamic has played out. I'm not asking people to shed tears of sympathy when neo-nazis get arrested and when plots get exposed and broken up, but we need to look beyond this sort of short-term gratification to look at how did those kinds of incidents play into a larger agenda of building the overall security apparatus and who are the main targets and victims of that kind of apparatus.

It's Going Down: In the past month, we've seen Stop the Steal, the pro-Trump demonstrations, growing into these antilockdown protests. And we've seen a large role being played in the protests by groups like the Proud Boys, Three Percenters, and also the Groypers, who are led by Nick Fuentes and are sort of American Renaissance–style white nationalists. What do we make of these protests, and what does it say about the state of the far right and the broader kind of MAGA movement that all of these groups swim in?

Matthew: It points to a certain ideological diversity within the far right. Just thinking about the groups that you listed, clearly they have important things in common, but they also have some significant differences. There's a significant difference between groups like the Groypers, who come out of an explicitly white nationalist kind of politics, versus something like the Proud Boys, who certainly have a friendly relationship with white nationalists but have charted a different position. Their line is Western chauvinism, which is playing a subtle game. It's something that white nationalists can get behind, but it's something that has enabled them to recruit men of color too. Not in large numbers, but in significant numbers. That's a dynamic that we see in various sectors within the far right. You see that within the Patriot movement; you see that within the theocratic wing of the Christian right. Look at the New Apostolic Reformation movement, which has something on the order of three million people. It doesn't get talked about a lot in antifascist circles, but it's a huge force in the Christian right, and it includes significant numbers of people of color.

This is worth underscoring if you look at the results of the recent presidential election. The one major demographic group that Trump lost support with was white men. He gained support among Black and Latino voters, he gained support among white women, he gained support among Muslim voters, LGBT voters. Again, we're not talking large numbers, but for him to not only hold his own but increase his support in all of these demographics, to me that says that while white supremacist politics and misogynist politics are important elements in Trumpism, they're not the whole story. And if we want to understand the dynamics of the far right and what makes it the kind of broad-based movement that it is, we can't simply reduce everything to white nationalism or white supremacism or misogyny. It's a more complex kind of political dynamic playing out.

It's Going Down: Trump is saying that "wild protests" are going to happen on January 6 and beyond. There's also calls supposedly for rallies to take place leading up to January 20. There have been screenshots and stuff circulating saying that there'll be militias coming on the 20th. In some ways, this is reminiscent of what we heard from the Oath Keepers four years ago, which never really materialized. What do you think will come out of these far-right demos, especially if they're feeling their oats, like after Salem and these other Proud Boy mobilizations in DC? What do you think ultimately can come from "wild" far-right rallies? What is the danger, and what are we potentially up against here?

Xtn: It's difficult with Trump to know what is and what isn't going to happen. But if we remove Trump himself from this and look at this more as rightist and far-right movements, we've already been seeing a continuation from the elections up to now. Places like Minneapolis and St. Paul, they have Proud Boys and other right-wing groups rallying every weekend it seems. And that's happening across the country. So, to say something like that happens, wild protests on January 6 and beyond, we very much could see that, and it wouldn't be unexpected. Now that the call by him has been put out, it's going to embolden them more. What that means, I don't think we know. Maybe DC was a precursor or evidence of what might happen. I do think it's going to be difficult for these movements to continue to carry out weekly protests. On the other hand, maybe not. How many years have we seen ongoing protests, demonstrations, and campaigns and organizing in Portland? For years it seems. So, it's difficult to say what might happen January 6. The big thing is, though, our movements need to be thinking about how are we going to be planning to move forward, how are we going to react to this emergence of a broad-based far-right movement? And then how are we going to respond to the incoming administration and what kind of organizing do we need? What kind of structures, institutions, programs do we need? To me, that's going to be one of the most central and important things in the coming period. And it's got to be anti-state and it's got to be against fascism, it's got to be against the far right. It's a multipronged challenge for us.

Matthew: Far rightists are looking to demonstrate that they can put on a show of strength, that they can put people in the streets. They want to test how much they can get away with, how many people they can stab, before they get the cops to go after them. That's not clear, and it may vary from one city to another. I think in the short term, these kinds of protests are likely to be not particularly well organized, but that is going to be an open question. And something that people on the far right are probably looking at is how do we not just tap into people's anger, how do we not just get people to turn out, but how do we start to forge something that's more disciplined, more organized, something that we can really mobilize and deploy more strategically? That's when you know things can really shift from simply an impulsive use of violence to something that is more calculated and ultimately more dangerous.

It's Going Down: A lot of people have been asking themselves, in this post-Biden-elected world where a lot of liberals and progressives seem deactivated right now, something that people in DC are talking about, it's been harder to get thousands of people out on the streets. And some people are asking, is it worth it to mobilize against the far right at a time when we can't get forty thousand people like we could a couple of weeks after Charlottesville? Especially when we're also organizing all these other things we were just talking about, whether it's in the streets against police brutality, mutual aid tenant associations, all these other things people are working around. I'm curious to know your thoughts in general on continued antifascist mobilization in this period.

Xtn: The last couple of years have just been nonstop, and I think a lot of people in our movements, and the movements themselves, are getting worn out. It's been constant fighting, constant organizing, mass arrests; people have been facing felony charges as well as real violence to themselves and the others out in the streets. I think people are asking real questions about to what extent does it make sense to keep confronting the fascists. The old Anti-Racist Action slogan, "we go where they go, never let the fascists have the street," it's powerful. We should never underestimate the importance of having a radical antifascist movement present in the streets taking and defining space. But we should maybe not overestimate our ability to hold that space without massive risks and danger. Attached to that is this kind of social polarization which is happening and will continue. It's going to mean more and more sectors of society are in motion, they're more engaged with what I was saying a little bit ago. We need to be working to create radical blocs and united fronts that can defend against both far-right attacks and state repression, which are sometimes linked but sometimes separate. And then, too, carving out and expanding geopolitical space with the politics of opposition to the system. It's valuable if we can keep an antifascist movement, a radical antifascist movement, in all of its forms and in the streets, but we can't pretend that there aren't significant risks all around for doing that. And we have to be more thoughtful and pragmatic in our strategizing.

Matthew: I listened to part of the It's Going Down interview with the antifascist folks in Salem talking about their struggle to maintain a presence in a very, very difficult situation.[1] I really salute the courage and dedication of those folks. They're facing real isolation and real physical danger. As Xtn said, it's important to be realistic and not overestimate our movements' capacity to protect ourselves or control situations when the right is rising in this way. So, it's important to confront them but it's also important to protect ourselves and not be suicidal about it.

Xtn: I agree with Matthew, and this is an important conversation that I'm not sure we'll actually do justice to because it's ongoing. On the flip side of that, though, I do think we need to have a politics and organizing that's bold and audacious and militant, and as Emma Goldman said, to the daring belongs the future. It gets back to the earlier conversation we were having about these antilockdown protests: Is there a risk of them being attractive to people? I do think people want something better in their lives. And many people feel to get that under these present circumstances we have to fight, you have to fight individually and you have to fight collectively. How do we do that? How do we have antifascist actions, activity, movements, social justice movements from below? How do we do all that, recognizing the risks but not giving up the fight out of fear or any kind of conservatizing security concerns? There's some tension there, but I'm always for a kind of bold antifascist activity, maybe to a fault sometimes, but it's also how you win people over—you know, pragmatism and taking a stand. That's really attractive to people.

It's Going Down: Trump is continuing to meet with his advisers like Mike Flynn who were calling for him to declare a state of emergency and hold recount votes in states that were swing states. This continues to go back and forth. Every day there's a new story in the news cycle. Sometimes it seems like Trump is just this helpless buffoon; other times it seems very scary. This has been going on for months now. I'm curious of you-all's take on what's going on in terms of Trump continuously trying to figure out if a coup is possible.

Matthew: It's Going Down and *Three Way Fight* and a lot of other people in the weeks leading up to the election warned about the dangers of a potential coup, some kind of effort to set aside or overturn or disrupt the electoral process in order to keep Trump in power.[2] Our worst fears of what that might look like were not realized. Certainly the intent has been there, but Trump has not, for whatever reason, succeeded in making effective use of the levers of power available to him in order to stay in power. It's hard to imagine any situation where he could avoid being kicked out of the White House next month.

Bart Gellman in the *Atlantic* described Trump as a weak authoritarian,[3] which is a good phrase that I think others have used too. Trump is somebody who doesn't have the patience or the capacity to be an effective organizer, whether we're talking about political movements or organizing forces even just within the state. He's a disrupter and a skillful user of social media, but not an organizer. But characterizing him as a weak authoritarian, it also speaks to something larger, and this is part of the context for his failure to carry out an effective coup. His administration from the beginning was built on an unstable coalition of different political forces that were largely in disagreement. You had, in the very broadest terms, neoliberals and fierce opponents of neoliberalism in the cabinet, in the White House, and in the administration competing for power, competing for favor with the president, and so on. Trump has advanced capital's interests but has not enjoyed support from the majority of the big capitalists. In 2016, the bulk of the ruling class supported Hillary Clinton. And certainly that was true again in 2020.

Now, 2016 showed us that the ruling class doesn't simply dictate political outcomes, but it certainly can influence the room to maneuver that a president has. And the ways that you saw important, prominent figures within the Republican Party supporting Biden or organizing against Trump, that spoke to some important weaknesses within his support, and the things like the high-ranking military figures making clear that they were not going to intervene in the electoral process. Those are things that I'm sure made a difference in his calculations. This gets back to the point that Xtn made earlier, about the state being in crisis and the tensions and conflicts and fissures within the state apparatus being exposed. Trump could readily mobilize Homeland Security agents and deploy them in major US cities, but he could not rely on the US military to keep him in office. I think that's part of the landscape that future right-wing figures are going to have to navigate.

It's Going Down: The journal *Hard Crackers* recently did a report where somebody went to the Staten Island bar that was recently closed down due to COVID rules, and they were asking what are the lines of class and the political project being put forward, and is there any possible common struggle with these instances of people holding protests against the lockdown?[4] Is there something that could be built here in terms of fighting shared class enemies? This was interesting, because they walked away and they said pretty much no. That these people aren't really interested in having a broader class analysis and they were squarely on the right, very anti-leftist, even describing themselves as opposed to Black Lives Matter or any other kind of street movements.

Xtn: *Hard Crackers* have put out a lot of articles trying to report on and think through what's going on in terms of the rebellion and the pandemic. And in particular it's taking a closer, harder look at the right and the far right and the fascists. A lot of these articles and the one that you cite, I was really impressed with that. It presents real situations where the rightist currents are functioning in a much more confrontational way against the state. From our view, it would seem like there's a generalized liberal attitude out there, and this allows the far right to get a hearing, to navigate easier in these situations. And with that, perhaps we're seeing the far right and radical reactionary politics and movements become much more of a hegemonic current, socially, politically, or at least there's the potential for that. I think there's much more than just potential, but, like in Salem, Oregon, as we were discussing previously, it's another example of rightist and far-right and fascist actions positioning themselves against the government, and to me these actions are a mix of real grievances along with a lot of confusion about the pandemic and government policy regarding lockdowns on the economy.

So, we've got to figure out ways to connect with these struggles around grievances and needs and material demands, but with an approach that's rooted in an antifascist opposition politics. There absolutely cannot be unity over seemingly shared militancy. All that said, Staten Island demonstrates a complex situation that we can't reduce down to any kind of simple far-right characterization. Is it co-optation? What is it? Is it just something in the DNA, the kind of social DNA right now, pop culture DNA, you have right-wingers taking on names like autonomous zone or whatnot. There's a certain adaptation of what had been the left—far left, anarchists, militant antifascists—for a while now, including the black bloc. We see rightist kinda quasi–black blocs now at times. I don't want to reduce it to co-optation, but there are developments that we need to be much more acutely tuned into and trying to figure out what they are, and then what's our take and what's our alternative to confused contradictory demands and realities, but nonetheless also containing real grievances.

Matthew: There's a long history of right-wingers appropriating elements of leftist politics and offering them back in some kind of distorted form. And so, in that article about the Staten Island "autonomous zone," one of the participants uses the phrase that they were "using the left's concepts against them." I was reminded of one of the slogans of Tom Metzger, the recently deceased neo-nazi leader. Tom Metzger used the slogan "take the game away from the left." And he did that in the name of Third Position politics, which claims to be against both communism and capitalism and takes a lot of seemingly leftist positions but puts them within a fascist framework. Third Positionism has continued to be a significant force within the far right in the US, but it hasn't been a significant organized force since the Traditionalist Worker Party fell apart a couple years ago. Anyway, I think it's going to be interesting to see whether we see some kind of resurgence of Third Positionism in this country.

It's Going Down: We had somebody from Leonard Zeskind's think tank[5] on this podcast, Mr. Devin Burghart, who laid out something that I thought made a lot of sense. He feels that Trump is obviously on his way out, but a new kind of movement will form around him. And we'll see a lot of the stuff that we've been seeing, whether it's QAnon or these antilockdown protests, morph into a new Tea Party type thing. I think a lot of people are thinking along the same lines, especially if Trump goes on to run in 2024, which of course remains to be seen. But it does seem like he's going that way, and if he continues to be a player on the far right, then there could really be a continued kind of Trumpist MAGA current with him as the figurehead. What do you see in terms of that, and especially what do you see in terms of this continuing relationship between the far right on the streets and this Trumpian wing of the Republican Party, which may or may not split off from the GOP?

Matthew: In one way or another, he's going to continue to be a presence, whether it's just as a symbol and a sort of mythical figure that conspiracy theorists and so on can invoke, or whether he continues to be an active political player. I think he probably would like to. The way that he seems to be falling apart right now, it's unclear that he would be able to continue to function as this effective political power, but maybe he can pull it together. For the right, there's pluses and minuses to that. In some ways, he's certainly a galvanizing figure. He's somebody who people can hang a lot of imaginary great stuff around. And the alt-right a few years ago, they would do it kind of tongue in cheek, calling him the God Emperor and so on, sort of making fun of themselves but also being serious about it. The current crowd doesn't really seem to have that kind of self-mockery. But he's also somebody who can really get in their way. He's not an effective organizer. He's not somebody who has the character or the capacity to build a well-organized movement. He really has a very limited repertoire of things that he's good at. He's very good at skillful use of social media within certain limits, and at causing chaos. So I am in some ways more concerned about the prospect of some other unifying figure arising who has the skills and the strengths that Trump does but who is also a good organizer and can build something that will not be dependent on the conservative establishment, not dependent on the Republican Party leadership in the same way. I don't know whether that's going to happen; I don't have a candidate in mind. But I'm sure there are people on the right who are thinking about this.

It's Going Down: Anything else you want to say on what people should be thinking about in terms of the far right as a whole? And also, anything you'd like to add in terms of the major tasks for the antifascist movement right now?

Matthew: In terms of the far right as a whole, one of the things that we've alluded to but haven't focused on is, the far right in this country is something that's developed largely in reaction to neoliberalism. When people talk about "neoliberal fascism," it's really glossing over some huge, profound conflicts within the right. There are major differences on issues about trade and immigration, and the United States' role on the international stage, that put far rightists at odds with neoliberalism. This is important because neoliberalism, as a strategy of the ruling class and as a system of control, is in profound crisis. It's failing most people in this country, not to mention other parts of the world, and it's getting harder and harder for its proponents to patch that over. And the far right knows that, and that's where a lot of their energy and dynamism comes from, because they speak to those grievances that people have about being hung out to dry by the capitalist system and by a state that has pretty much dismantled social programs on a massive scale. To me, that speaks to the need for a radical alternative that refuses to cede the oppositional role to the far right, that says we can build an opposition that is based on liberatory principles, that is dynamic, that speaks to people's needs in a way that is based on solidarity rather than supremacism and exclusion and genocide.

Xtn: The question that you were asking for our side, for antifascists, that's the big question. First off, I'm not sure *Three Way Fight* has great answers, and we definitely don't have any unified take, even though we're probably in general agreement on most positions, and we're in enough agreement that we are trying to work things out when we look around. But the important thing is that there's been a growing, popular, diverse antifascist current, which is an opportunity for those of us with specific perspectives and approaches of radical and revolutionary antifascism. Masses of people have been in motion for this last period, and that's important. The movements have a lot of direct experience, and we need to be sorting through these histories and making sense of them, learning lessons and developing new approaches. Our side has to have expanding notions of organizing, and not just of antifa or autonomous forces, but of a broader popular class struggle and social solidarity approach to organizing. I point to examples over the last couple of years, from the General Defense Committees that emerged to the Popular Mobilization—the PopMob in Portland—to the Solidarity & Defense Network in Michigan in the Midwest. None of these are complete or sufficient, and there's been a lot of challenges for all these projects, but I think these are some real examples of radical antifascism in practice, rooted in the class, rooted in social struggle politics and attempting to develop some programs of community self-defense.

Matthew: And they're projects that have had significant successes also.

Xtn: Yes! Like when we talk about the TWP [Traditionalist Worker Party] or the end of the alt-right, that came about because those organizations, in conjunction with others, put real pressure on the alt-right and the nazis and brought them down. Spencer said, "Antifa have won." Well, it didn't come about because he got tired, it's because it was impossible for him to organize anymore. And that came through real planning, real strategizing, and it comes from building a radical popular antifascism. We need to be looking at that.

The difficulty is and always has been, how do we develop a distinct pole of radical and revolutionary thought and practice within the struggles and not get our projects sucked up or contained or co-opted or liquidated—sometimes liquidated consciously by ourselves for whatever strategic reasons—but how do we prevent our projects from getting sucked into broader popular fronts to save the state or the system? There's that conservatizing pull, and it's always there and it's always a threat. How do we resist that? How do we posit independent organizing campaigns and movements? We're going to have to be sharper. We're going to have to be more critical while constructive. We're going to have to be more determined in articulating and putting forward more of our maximal and revolutionary ideas, visions, and programs as antifascists and as those who know there's got to be a better, a free, a humanist way forward out of this friggin' mess that we're all in.

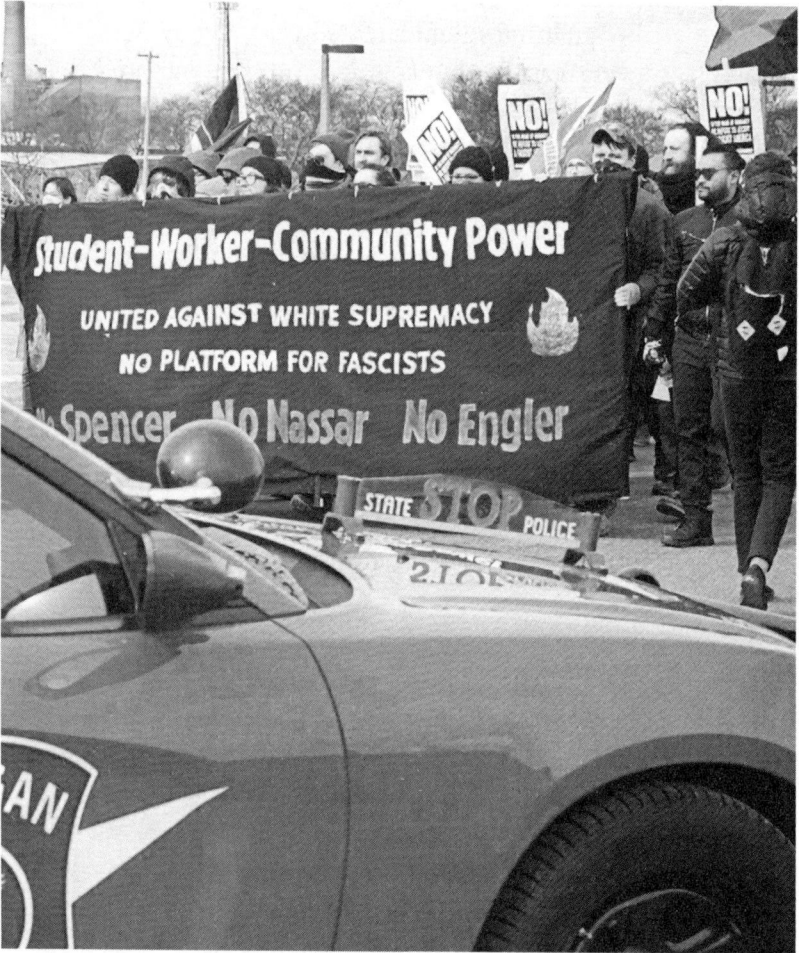

March 5, 2018. Mass mobilization in East Lansing, Michigan, against Richard Spencer and alt-right forces. Spearheaded by the Solidarity & Defense Network, the protests connected the antifascist struggle to broader political and social fights, including local university administrators' cover-up of the decades-long sexual abuse and rape of female student-athletes by a university sports doctor. The March 5 mobilization ended Richard Spencer's attempts at public organizing and contributed to the alt-right's strategic defeat.

Broken Windows Fascism

Three Way Fight

Three Way Fight, January 6, 2021

1. When Donald Trump was first running for president in 2015–16, a lot of alt-rightists supported him not because they thought he could win, but because they hoped he would help destroy the Republican Party. He hasn't quite done that, but he has created a serious crisis within the party, which is now deeply divided between those who accept and those who reject the legitimacy of the existing electoral system. A broken GOP might sound like cause for celebration, but it's likely to benefit the far right most of all. Today's physical assault on the houses of Congress was the militant edge of a much larger movement, and while it will alienate or frighten some sympathizers it will galvanize and embolden others.

2. In broader terms, Trump's insistent denial of the November election results has spurred a massive political shift within the US right, as millions of people have moved—at least temporarily—from system loyalty into system opposition, as symbolized by Proud Boys stomping on a Thin Blue Line flag. We should expect this oppositional right to remain active and violent long after the current fight over the presidency has died down, as Natasha Lennard argued yesterday. And as Robert Evans documents, the oppositional right is a meeting place where different rightist currents and ideologies—such as neo-nazism and QAnon—converge and interact.[1] It remains to be seen how unified or well organized the oppositional right will be, what kind of strategies and tactics they will use, and whether or not Trump himself will continue to play an active role.

3. The attack on the US Capitol is, as many have described it, an attempted coup.[2] It dramatizes Donald Trump's authoritarianism, demagoguery, and repudiation of the electoral system that put him in the White House, but it also highlights one of the key limitations that separated the Trump administration from fascism. Fascism requires an independent mass organization in order to carry out its attack on the established political order.[3] Trump has never tried to build such an organization. He has skillfully used social media and rallies to mobilize supporters, but organizationally he has relied on existing institutions, above all the Republican Party, which is part of why his administration was a coalition between America Firsters and conventional conservatives of various kinds. Now that coalition is falling apart. And Trump's control over the federal security apparatus also proved to be quite limited. He could mobilize Homeland Security agents and US marshals to crack down on Black Lives Matter protesters last summer, but he failed to deploy any federal agents to help him overturn the results of the 2020 election. Today's mob of Trump supporters never had a chance of seizing power, but they did bring Congress to a complete standstill for hours. With better organization and leadership, the movement they represent could quickly turn into something far more dangerous.

4. A question for the coming months and years is: To what extent will the state repressive apparatus be used to crack down on the oppositional right? Certainly, cops aren't likely to go after MAGA activists and Proud Boys the way they go after Black Lives Matter and antifa, but there's a long history of federal security forces targeting far rightists, especially through covert operations.[4] Joe Biden likes to talk about unity, but it's not hard to imagine his administration reviving and expanding FBI and Homeland Security capabilities for tracking white supremacists and other far rightists. It's also not hard to imagine some conventional conservatives actively supporting this effort. Let's remember that the federal government's most serious and systematic effort to crack down on oppositional rightists in the past forty years— from the Order to the Lyndon LaRouche network—took place under Ronald Reagan. And let's remember, too, that in the hands of the capitalist state, antifascism can be a powerful rationale for

building the repressive apparatus—which ends up getting used mainly against oppressed and exploited groups. Even when the cops and the Klan don't go hand in hand, neither one is our friend.

5. Instead of looking to the state to bring things under control, there's an urgent need for broad-based militant action on two fronts: to combat both the openly supremacist forces of the oppositional right and the less blatant but still deadly systems of established privilege and power. The past four years have been nightmarish in lots of ways, but they've also been a time of dynamic liberatory activism on a large scale. There are a lot of powerful examples of militant, creative organizing we can look to for lessons and inspiration.

Insurgent Movement, Government Complicity, or Both?

Xloi and B. Sandor

Three Way Fight, January 13, 2021

We wrote this after discussing last week's events on January 6 and watching this video [which has since been removed] from a protester who goes by "Insurgence USA." Our sense is that he is right wing but poses as also being pro–Black Lives Matter.[1] His footage captured the front of the line throughout the storming of the Capitol and a close-up of the woman being shot by the US Capitol Police. It was gruesome, but provided an account of the events firsthand.

We cannot assume that the movement that stormed the Capitol on January 6 was at large anti-state or solely an insurgent movement from below. While elements of the movement were insurgent, this movement was egged on by Trump and other key people in his administration and in Congress. What this means is that instead of just understanding this as a right-wing assault on "democracy," it needs to be understood as both internal to our so-called democracy while simultaneously having elements that are insurgent and anti-state. A main contingent of this movement to "Stop the Steal" would have gone home if the announcement had been made that Trump would stay in office. Therefore, the insurgent components and government complicity at play here should be understood and confronted as such.

We saw political violence last Wednesday. We saw Confederate flags and people flaunting nazi tattoos in the Capitol. We saw armed masses (mostly men) break through lines of police, albeit with Blue Lives Matter flags.[2] We know storming the Capitol was an organized and thought-out action, although they were probably as surprised as we were that it actually worked. In footage from the front lines, you can hear protesters screaming, "Criticism of the government isn't enough, we need action," while running to storm the Capitol, and another exclaiming, "This is a revolution," once they break through a couple of police lines. Regardless, there was no cohesive strategy for what they would do once they actually entered the Capitol. If there was, you would have heard in the videos at least some discourse on the different thought-out plans.

The mixed responses from the protesters to the police were notable, as Jarrod Shanahan discusses in his article "The Big Takeover."[3] One protester shouted to a line of police, "Over the summer, we backed you when no one else did." Another screamed, "Now no one likes you, Black people and white people." In other moments, protesters try to win over the police, saying, "We have your back. We get it. We're on your side." There will continue to be major splits within the far right over alignment with the police, with many becoming politicized against the police because of what happened that day. It is also key to address the amount of ex-military and former police within the ranks of far-right militia, paramilitary, and street-fighting gangs that were clearly present at the Capitol.

The next logical question is, why were there so few Capitol police, given that the FBI and researchers around the country knew for months that protesters were planning on storming the Capitol that day? More details are coming out about the Capitol police and the Trump administration's possible complicity and lack of preparation. From Ibram X. Kendi to so many others, people are commenting on how little force was used relative to BLM protests and that if the Capitol was stormed by people of color, there would have been an entirely different plan in place.[4]

While the protesters transgressed police lines, some lines were as sparse as only five to ten officers, leaving even middle school students commenting on the relative lack of protection of a federal building. But, very quickly, many used this argument as a justification and immediate demand for more military and police, forces that will ultimately target innocent people and the left. Lawmakers are already using the events at the Capitol to introduce legislation to increase police presence at protests and adopt measures to further criminalize all dissent.[5] What is this political amnesia that we have? Within a moment, the momentum and political consciousness gained after years of antipolice struggles that culminated in the mass movements against the murder of George Floyd seemingly went in reverse. We must still recognize our enemies in blue.[6]

Narratives that bill Wednesday as a violent protest or insurrection, while failing to acknowledge the violence from police (against Black lives, but also against the right), reinforce the argument that the left and the state need to come together to defeat the far right, rather than pose a liberatory alternative to both.

We know cops take orders. Maybe they had been given orders to be lenient and use soft policing tactics. Until a Capitol police officer shot and killed the woman protester, the Capitol police attitude toward protesters looked mixed. Some looked intent on holding the line, others looked mortified, and some seemed to back down seamlessly. More investigations will uncover why, for example, the Pentagon initially refused to back up the Capitol police after requests from their chief for the military to step in. Previous investigations show that far-right militias look to former national security advisers to the Trump administration for intelligence.[7] There's still a lot we don't know. We will soon learn more about what was and wasn't done and why.

We do know there was clear tactical leadership on the part of the movement to enter the Capitol and stop the counting of the votes on Wednesday, but not much beyond that. Some wanted to critique the powers that be, some wanted to stop a so-called stolen election, some wanted to restore the Confederacy, some wanted Pence's head, and some wanted to smear shit on the walls. This lack of cohesion could tear the movement apart when there is no one person for them to unite behind. They are also already facing sharp repression, with arrests as far away as Arizona.[8] Few movements can withstand the kind of repression they are about to face, not to mention the likelihood that the movement is already widely infiltrated by state forces. Many new so-called movement leaders will eventually be exposed as undercover state operatives. Either way, under the banner of "Stop the Steal," right-wing forces will be claiming victory for years.

We are grappling with what the three way fight looks like in action in this moment. We think we should be developing a political pole that opposes both insurgent and government-backed far-right forces, while also reinforcing movements against the police like those that took off across the country over the summer. We need an antifascism that doesn't ultimately back up the state or ignore the right altogether in the hopes that the state will simply smash it. While we might not yet have the capacity as a movement to really do both, it is imperative to understand that one without the other will be fatal.

VI

THE GEORGE FLOYD REBELLION

Abolition and the Movement against Police Brutality

Twin Cities Workers Defense Alliance

August 27, 2020

The heroic Minneapolis Uprising, provoked by the public lynching of George Floyd, has shaken the entire world. Things that seemed impossible just a couple of months ago are now openly discussed and debated at all levels of society.

A prime example is the slogan "Abolish the Police"—which arose with the flames and smoke from the militant protests on Lake Street. "Abolish the Police" was the major, defining slogan of the uprising. It served as a marker of how radical and defiant the movement had become—and how unwilling the young people were to accept the usual kind words and crumbs from the politicians.

The role of police in society should be clear—it is to protect the rich and powerful and preserve the status quo. This is why Black police chiefs, training programs, and civilian oversight have never made a real difference—the underlying purpose of the police is still the same. When you know the history of the police in the United States, from the slave patrols to the deputized thugs who harassed and intimidated the immigrant working class, to today's riot police and assassins—it all starts to makes sense. The Minneapolis Police Department (MPD) is not on our side and never could be. We should focus on building the capacity of working-class communities to resist the police and defend our neighborhoods—not tweak the existing repressive apparatus.

The Workers Defense Alliance supports the slogan "Abolish the Police." Our predecessor organization, the General Defense Committee—and also our comrades in the former IWW African Peoples Caucus—both raised this slogan in the militant protest movements for Justice for Jamar Clark and Philando Castile over four years ago.

Issue number 1 of *The Defender*, the newsletter of the Twin Cities Workers Defense Alliance.

We promoted abolition as part of our approach of building both militant street resistance to police brutality and organizing "working-class defense groups" to help communities protect themselves from the police and antisocial community violence. For us, the slogan helped explain the role of the police in our society and the folly of trying to reform it into something better. We did not propose "Abolish the Police" as a legislative measure to go lobby liberal politicians, but as the result of the revolutionary struggle of the working class.

Reformist Abolition?

Since the struggles around Jamar and Philando, other abolitionist groups have become more prominent in the Twin Cities. Some of them, like MPD150, have produced excellent materials detailing the brutal history of the MPD and inviting the community to envision a world without police.[1] New groups like Black Visions Collective and Reclaim the Block have been effectively challenging the power structure to justify any funding of the murderous MPD. But these new abolitionist groups have also pretty much removed revolution from the equation of how to get rid of the police. Instead of preparing the fighting capacity of the working class and oppressed communities, the focus is on "organizing the politicians" to defund and (maybe) dismantle the police.

The debate around abolishing the MPD now regrettably centers around the strategy of several Minneapolis city councilors to amend the city charter and take out the provisions that mandate a police department and a minimum number of cops. They say they want to replace the MPD with a new "public safety department" that would emphasize social services but still retain a smaller number of law enforcement officers. This new agency would be under great pressure to evolve back into the same kind of repressive apparatus the MPD was. If it couldn't do that fast enough, the Hennepin County sheriff and private security forces would start to fill the gap for the power structure.

Clearly this is not the kind of "abolition" that abolitionists and revolutionaries fight for, even if it does show the power of the uprising to change the debate. Unfortunately, the longer-term community-based and left-wing anti–police brutality groups—all of which have made major contributions to the struggle against police murders and violence—are not providing a solid alternative to abolition-lite.

[A section that critiques the specific counterproposals and delaying tactics of several local reformist organizations has been omitted.]

Our Approach

So what should our approach be to the city council's maneuvers? First, we should avoid getting bogged down in the lobbying at city hall. These efforts are designed to pull activists off the street and into the logic of system politics. It was the uprising that put this discussion on the table, not the politicians. Let's keep our focus on the communities and class that carried out the rebellion. Second, we should aggressively promote the concept of abolition of the police—not in a watered-down, reformist way, but in a clearly argued revolutionary framework that includes building up working-class defense organizations and expropriating needed resources from the rich. We should expose attempts to label things "abolition" that are clearly not. We should also get better at discussing and debating the real questions, concerns, and criticisms many people have about abolition of the police. Third, and most importantly, we must push ahead with the building up of working-class defense organizations and other autonomous spheres of working-class power.

Theses on the George Floyd Rebellion

Shemon Salam and Arturo Castillon

Ill Will, June 24, 2020

> The working class in every country lives its own life, makes its
> own experiences, seeking always to create forms and realize
> values which originate directly from its organic opposition to
> official society.
> —C.L.R. James, Grace Lee Boggs, and Cornelius Castoriadis,
> *Facing Reality*

1. The George Floyd Rebellion was a Black-led multiracial rebellion. This rebellion cannot be sociologically categorized as exclusively a Black rebellion. Rebels from all racialized groups fought the police, looted, and burned property. This included Indigenous people, Latinx people, Asian people, and white people.

2. This uprising was not caused by outside agitators. Initial arrest data shows that most people were from the immediate areas of the rebellions. If there were people driving in from the "suburbs," this only reveals the sprawling geography of the American metropolis.

3. While many activists and organizers participated, the reality is that this rebellion was not organized by the small revolutionary left, and neither by the so-called progressive NGOs. The rebellion was informal and organic, originating directly from working-class Black people's frustration with bourgeois society, particularly the police.

4. Not only was the police state caught off guard by the scope and intensity of the rebellion, but civil society also hesitated and wavered in the face of this popular revolt, which quickly spread to every corner of the country and left the police afraid and in disarray.

5. The police displayed many weaknesses during the rebellion. Up against a few hundred protesters, departments were easily overwhelmed and forced to concentrate their forces in particular hot spots. Once police arrived in one area of conflict, people would retreat and move on to another location to do more damage. Conventional warfare, with its emphasis on superior weaponry and technology, failed to counter a series of flexible, decentralized, rapid maneuvers focused on property destruction.

6. The militant phase of the rebellion was from May 26 to June 1. After June 1, the rebellion was not only repressed through military force, but also politically repressed. Aside from the police, military, and vigilante crackdown, the uprising was politically repressed by elements of the left, which reacted to the riots by blaming them on outside agitators. In some places, "good protesters" went so far as to detain "bad protesters" and hand them over to the police.

7. Black NGOs, including the Black Lives Matter Foundation, had no relationship to the militant phase of the rebellion. In fact, such organizations tended to play a reactionary role, often preventing riots, looting, and attacks on the police from spreading. Black NGOs were the spearhead of the forces dividing the movement into good and bad protesters. The social base of Black NGOs is not the Black proletariat but the Black middle class and, most importantly, a segment of the radicalizing white middle class.

8. This rebellion was about racist police violence and racial inequality, but it was also about class inequality, capitalism, COVID-19, Trump, and more.

9. This rebellion opens up a new phase in the history of Turtle Island. A new generation of people have experienced a powerful movement, and in the face of ongoing inequalities and crises people are unlikely to sit back and accept them. The rebellion has produced a new political subjectivity—the George Floyd rebel—initiating a set of processes with many possible outcomes which will be determined by class struggles in the present. The American proletariat has finally emerged and entered history.

10. This rebellion is the tip of the spear in the struggle against the pandemic. The rebellion shows the world that revolutionary struggle can happen even during a pandemic. The pandemic is

only going to worsen the living conditions of people around the world, and as a result, we can expect more rebellions across the planet.

11. The George Floyd Rebellion has been put down for the time being. Many NGOs and middle-class people will make a buck off the brave efforts of the rebels who fought during that week. But these rebellions will return. They are part of the ongoing class struggles that have been happening in the United States and at a global level since the last global recession (2008–13). Now the world economy is once again in recession.

12. The ongoing daytime protests are a contradictory product of the rebellion, drawing in large crowds, more middle-class and more white. This composition certainly helps to create a nonviolent and "good protester" type of atmosphere, but that is inseparable from the Black leaders who advocate this type of politics. At the same time, the expansion of the daytime protests allows for greater participation, which is important.

13. The nighttime riots had a limit in the sense that they did not draw larger sections of society into their activity. Riots, looting, and attacking the police are a young people's and poor people's activity. Many working people had sympathy with it but stayed at home. This shows that riots by themselves are not enough.

14. Many important struggles have merged with this movement, including transit workers refusing to collaborate with the police. Still, it is unclear how this rebellion connects to the simmering workplace struggles, prison struggles, and housing struggles which are unfolding in the context of the pandemic. It seems there are historical and future connections to be made. To what extent were those involved in the prior workplace struggles involved in the riots? To what extent will the rioters go back to work and continue the struggle at work?

15. Unions often view police and prison guards as workers in need of protection, instead of seeing them as the armed thugs of the bourgeoisie that they are. Despite the long history of police being strikebreakers, much work remains to be done on the labor front when it comes to police and prison abolition. Without the transit workers, logistical workers, sanitation workers, medical workers, and others, the abolitionist struggle is doomed.

16. Considering the low unionization rates, many workplace struggles will be chaotic, explosive, and unmediated by unions or any other kind of official organization. Unions will come in and attempt to control them and co-opt them. Can the struggles in the workplace feed back into the struggles in the streets? If they do, we will enter a new phase of struggle.

17. In order to reconsolidate its power and prevent revolution, the bourgeoisie scrambles to grant reforms and concessions. Some police get fired and charged; the budgets of some police departments get cut; some schools and universities cancel their contracts with police; some racist statues are removed; Trump signs an executive order providing more resources for police accountability; the Minneapolis City Council votes to disband its police department. This sequence follows a common pattern in capitalist history—the ruling class responds to revolutionary crises by reorganizing and restructuring itself in a way that allows it to stay in power.

18. What must be done through the self-activity of the proletariat, other elements of society are attempting to do through petitions, voting, legislation, and policy change. Reforms are a commendable goal in a racial capitalist system that clearly prioritizes policing over life. However, we must keep in mind that bourgeois society wants to keep this rebellion as narrow as possible: making it only about George Floyd, about slashing police budgets and redistributing the budget to other areas of society. But this rebellion is about something much more. It is about the deep injustice felt by a people, which no amount of reform can extinguish.

19. Abolition entails the material destruction of the range of policing infrastructures built during the era of racial capitalism. Abolition occurred from May 26 to June 1. As a result of widespread rioting, more has happened in a week to discredit and limit police power than has occurred in many decades of activism. Here we see the potential of abolition in its fullest sense, opening up a brief moment of solidarity between the different racialized fractions of the proletariat, causing a national crisis, and cracking open the door to a new world for a brief moment.

20. Not everything that took place during the uprising was empowering and liberating. The same problems that existed before continued during the rebellion—racism, transphobia, homophobia,

competition for meager resources. All of that doesn't suddenly disappear in a rebellion. The crucial work of building a new world remains to be done.

21. We have yet to answer the full meaning of this rebellion. Is the content of Black Lives Matter only about those who are racialized as Black, or does the Black struggle take on a larger content?

22. Comparisons of this rebellion to 1968 are wrong. This rebellion is different on many levels. It is Black mayors and Black police commissioners who govern in many cities. It was a multiracial proletariat which rebelled.

23. Can the Black proletariat lead the other racialized fractions of the proletariat in the upcoming years? This is a question that goes back a century, with Du Bois, Haywood, James, Jones, and Hampton all trying to devise various coalitions with other fractions in this country or overseas in an attempt to defeat racial capitalism and empire. They all knew that the Black proletariat could spark a broad rebellion but could not defeat its enemies on its own.

24. The unification of the proletariat in a common struggle to eliminate capitalism is the only hope humanity has of saving itself and the earth. This counterpower is based on all people coming together to fight against racism, patriarchy, and everything that capitalism brings with it.

25. The desire for multiracial solidarity is always fraught, as the histories of racism have shown. The development of solidarity will be tense and difficult and will depend on objective circumstances and strategic choices. Of greatest concern is that solidarity might come at the expense of Black liberation. To prevent this, efforts must be made to respect and support the autonomy of the Black revolutionary struggle.

People taking the streets in Minneapolis during the George Floyd
Uprising of May 2020. Photographer unknown.

Five I's for a City beyond Policing: A Message to Defense Groups in Minneapolis

Twin Cities Workers Defense Alliance

August 27, 2020

In the wake of the murder of George Floyd, the wrath of the people of Minneapolis, St. Paul, and surrounding communities has been unleashed. As plans to defund and (perhaps) abolish the Minneapolis Police Department continue, the police have withdrawn their active presence from some parts of Minneapolis. This is to be welcomed. The police never really protected the majority of us and our neighbors, especially those of us marginalized by race, poverty, country of origin, gender, and/or sexuality. It is literally, legally (by repeated court decision), not their job to protect the people, and for a long time now, they have been actively harming people with no repercussions whatsoever.

Let's be clear: reforming and regulating the police is not what we want. We can do much better than prolonging the life of this doomed, repressive institution, but to do better, we need to plan how to do better.

Many people's attention is now turning to the formation of armed self-defense groups to protect our communities. This development should be welcomed and encouraged. It is the legal and moral right of the people to bear arms in legitimate self-defense. However, this needs to be done right if it's going to be done at all. Here are a few guidelines to consider.

Inspiration. Our motivation should be to protect all of the people in our communities, and especially those marginalized in society at present. No exceptions. Protecting the people means shielding them from physical harm as well as conflict and emotional trauma, not swaggering around with weapons in a misguided display of machismo. We don't look for trouble. We look to keep trouble away from our neighbors and loved ones. We deescalate conflicts by open, humble, and generous communication with our neighbors. Whenever possible and practical, without putting others at greater risk, we retreat before resorting to any kind of physical force. We are not there to be cops. We are there to be friends and to build peaceful communities through friendship and trust.

Similarly, we cannot and should not ever use lethal force to defend private property, except against attacks that endanger the lives of the people who live and work there. Black Lives Matter. Property does not.

Independence. Community self-defense groups should have no ties with law enforcement, with politicians, or with nonprofit corporations. We all know that the Republicans serve the racists and the rich, but the Democrats are not our friends either. The Democratic Party in particular hands out millions of dollars in loans, development aid, and tax breaks to large and small businesses that prey on low-income workers in our communities, while repeatedly trying to end the freedom of the people to protect themselves through the legal possession and carry of firearms. We have no business allying ourselves with Democrats, and I suspect they wouldn't want us anyway. Similarly the police. We cannot simultaneously cooperate with, and oppose the existence of, the people and the institution who violently murdered George Floyd, Philando Castile, Jamar Clark, Fong Lee, and many others.

Insurance. Without any particular respect for the police, politicians, or courts of law, we nonetheless must follow the letter of the law in order to minimize our vulnerability when practicing armed community self-defense. If we choose to carry firearms, we must purchase them legally and obtain carry permits from the State of Minnesota. We must be aware of the legal limits for use of deadly force by private citizens. We must seek out instructors and train diligently, both by dry-firing weapons at home with dummy rounds and by regularly visiting the shooting ranges that Minneapolis will not allow within city limits. If we are going to be out on the streets in a security role, we should try to buy and wear body armor to reduce the risk of fatal gunshot wounds. No one should be carrying firearms, let alone serving in a security role, when under the influence of alcohol or drugs.

Inclusiveness. People from every part of our neighborhoods must be encouraged to take part in community defense and to give their consent to it, even if they choose not to be personally involved. This must be true regardless of their race, age, gender, family status, religion, ethnicity, or nation of origin. Priority must be given to the involvement of those who are marginalized by the capitalist system, especially Black, Indigenous, and other formerly or currently colonized people.

Some Black, Indigenous, and other people of color may prefer to form their own groups with others of a common experience. This is a natural, healthy part of decolonization and should be encouraged and supported. There is nothing preventing an inclusive, neighborhood-oriented group from working together in coalition with identity-focused groups that prefer to maintain their independence.

Improvement. Personally, collectively, neighborhood-wide, and movement-wide, we all need to be continually improving our abilities and capacity. We learn to carry first aid kits as well as pistols. We study first aid and CPR as well as firearms use. We learn deescalation and conflict resolution as well as physical self-defense. We memorize and teach the four cardinal rules of firearm safety and the four Ds of threat response: Deter, Detect, Delay/Deescalate, and Defend Deliberately and Decisively.

As the police fade out and disappear, we can build strength, community, solidarity, and security in Minneapolis in a way that they never could.

States of Incarceration: A Discussion

Interview with Zhandarka Kurti and Jarrod Shanahan by Tobi Haslett

Brooklyn Rail, October 2022

Tobi Haslett (*Brooklyn Rail*): Zhandarka Kurti and Jarrod Shanahan's new book, *States of Incarceration*, is a report, an analysis, and a critique.[1] A report of what actually happened in the streets in 2020, an analysis of the carceral state that digests the thickening genre of abolitionist scholarship, and a critique, delicately constructed, of the positions and ideologies that have delivered us into a contradictory moment marked by blooms of possibility and ruthless, forceful closure. This book, perhaps the most synthetic and ambitious look at the George Floyd Rebellion, is an attempt to view the events of 2020 from the perspective of complete social transformation—which is to say, revolution.

Let's start with the purpose of the book and the shape you wanted your intervention to take. The text begins with a rousing, scene-by-scene description of some of the most bursting, spectacular moments in the rebellion itself, in the spring and summer of 2020. This is less to thrill the reader or capture the ecstasies of the crowd—though perhaps that's part of it—than to point to specific forms of militancy, particular tactical innovations, which would define the uprising and distinguish it from the first wave of BLM. Why was that important to you? Is this fastidious, blow-by-blow retelling meant as a corrective to the liberal account? It also reads like a stab at a theory that could be adequate to the praxis of 2020.

Zhandarka Kurti: Our book is coming out two years after the most militant rejection of the status quo in recent American history. We wrote what became the first chapter of the book initially as an article for *Brooklyn Rail* two weeks into the rebellion. Jarrod and I wanted to capture as much as possible its militant spirit as it unfolded and the variety of tactics we witnessed, because they signaled a giant leap from the previous protest movements that have defined our generation. But unfortunately, within months the militancy of the rebellion was forgotten and willfully erased. With this book we wanted to recuperate the militancy of the George Floyd Rebellion from the liberal amnesia that currently plagues us.

Jarrod Shanahan: Idris Robinson predicted very early on that the liberal strategy of counterinsurgency was going to rely heavily on redefining the rebellion as peaceful and within the framework of civil disobedience. I think something that you did very well, Tobi, in your essay "Magic Actions," is argue that we would not be having any conversations about this rebellion if it hadn't been for the illegal activity, the riots, the looting, and the attacks on carceral infrastructure and the cops themselves.[2] All of this set the table for whatever came next. Regardless of how one feels about those forms of political participation, the reality is these tactics lent the rebellion impetus and caused it to resonate worldwide. So we wanted to craft an account of the rebellion that was faithful to how it actually went down.

Our work has long examined the US punishment system, alongside the social movements of the last decade or so, especially Occupy and Black Lives Matter. In the rebellion, these threads converged neatly. We recognized very early on that its focus—which could have been about unemployment, lack of health care, racial disparities in home ownership, or a myriad of other injustices—zeroed in on the cops and on carceral infrastructure. In a moment of great despair and uncertainty, something about the sight of violent state agents disposing of a working-class Black man's life in such a callous way spoke to the fears and anxieties of tens of millions of people, including large numbers of non-Black people. From the most militant components of the rebellion, which directly attacked cops and carceral infrastructure, to the more social-democratic aspects, which were calling for procedural reforms to them, the central figure of the rebellion was the US carceral state, and in particular, the situation of the working-class Black people who are the most powerless in its hands.

To us, this choice of target was no coincidence; it suggests a collective sense of the need to radically address the role that police, jails, prisons, and courts play in our society. And the great urgency and stridency of this movement, along with its timing in the middle of such an unprecedented social crisis, and the radical conclusions many of its participants drew about the need to restructure our society, all suggest to us that this thread can be traced to a larger picture of just about everything that's wrong with American life. So in the book we begin with the rebellion and then work backward through a political-economic account of how we got to this moment, when suddenly tens of millions of people were out on the street, saying: "We've had enough."

Kurti: The George Floyd Rebellion provided an opportunity to express a collective fury that had reached a tipping point. Let's be real, most people will not participate in street protests unless they see their fate directly related to what is at stake. The COVID-19 pandemic not only put the spotlight on deeply embedded structural inequalities but made evident how vulnerable everyday life was for most Americans (save for the super rich). There was a general sense of helplessness as we watched the most vulnerable Americans die before our eyes while the Trump administration fueled conspiracy notions about the deadly virus. In those first months of the pandemic, the future for millions of people had never felt more uncertain. And on top of this COVID-19 mayhem, the police decided to strangle a Black man to death in broad daylight over an alleged counterfeit twenty-dollar bill. For a significant number of people, these contradictions became too much to bear.

The rebellion also turned up the dial in terms of tactics from the last large-scale Black Lives Matter protests. By the summer of 2020, Trump's tweets, actions, and policies had destroyed the Obama-era dreams of a postracial society, including that of police reform. Instead of another toothless legislative bill, the most enduring image from the summer of 2020 is the smoldering flames of Minneapolis's Third Precinct. When was the last time our generation witnessed something like that?

We are also very clear that the entire world was moved by the murder of George Floyd. The rebellion had widespread global reso-nance. In the Middle East, protesters compared the George Floyd uprising to the Arab Spring protests of 2011. Brazil erupted in soli-darity protests that made connections to the racism and state violence in the favelas and the right-wing politics of Bolsonaro. The George Floyd Rebellion struck a chord around the world, and it offered us a glimpse of international mobilizations that we can hope to see more of going forward.

Rail: One thing that I tried to do (so it's nice to finally place this burden on someone else) was give an account of the "diversity" of the crowd. Racial diversity, yes, but also class diversity. Which is to say, within the very American category of "working people"—a blurry term that I think can sometimes have a kind of pragmatic utility—there are different stripes and conflicting fractions, all of whom felt interpellated at different levels of severity to participate in what was a variegated but explosive social phenomenon: a rebellion. But a rebellion whose rhetorical engine was Black liberation. How do you explain that?

Shanahan: In my own experience, the Occupy movement represented a real turning point in American politics. In a country where much of official society is arranged to erase the existence of class and to assure just about everybody that they are "middle class," you suddenly saw the explosion of a visceral kind of rudimentary class politics. And this was not due to the genius ideas of any individual people, although there were lots of smart people involved. It was a direct reflection of the 2008 fiscal crisis and the widespread sense among the so-called middle class, and the upper tiers of the working class, that they would not be able to enjoy a standard of living superior or even equal to what their parents had enjoyed. As we know, the 2008 crisis was a particular disaster for Black people in terms of home ownership and employment. That particularly steep downward slope, coupled with the state's racially selective management of the crisis by the violence of cops and prisons, played no small part in the emergence of the Ferguson Rebellion, the Baltimore Riots, and the attendant 2014–15 Black Lives Matter movement. These are movements against the violence of so-called austerity, which is just a polite word we use to describe the draconian lengths capitalism is willing to adopt to protect itself amidst the protracted crises that are part of its nature.

So, while the structural violence of austerity is felt most bluntly and devastatingly in working-class Black America, typified by the barbaric murder of George Floyd in broad daylight, it is also part of a more generalized crisis attendant on capitalism's profound inability to sustain human life. From the explosion of apocalypse-themed stories in popular culture to the rise of demented extremists like Trump and DeSantis, there is a general sense of doom permeating our society. And this is where all those white people come in. There's a standard "white ally" line from 2020—"We are out here because we're standing in solidarity with people who are oppressed, exploited, and suffering, unlike us, who have it great"—and I don't believe it. I know why people say that: because they don't want to "center themselves" and so forth. But I don't believe that anybody takes the kinds of risks we saw in 2020, is willing to hurl themselves into harm's way at the hands of violent cops and murderous vigilantes, simply out of a kind of moral responsibility to alleviate somebody else's suffering. If human beings were so benevolent, we'd already live in a perfect world. But in this one, people typically take action only when their own liberation hangs in the balance.

Kurti: From my experience and from speaking to participants and also reading accounts of the rebellion, millennials and Generation Z dominated in the streets. And certainly one can say this was partly due to the fact that older people were more vulnerable to COVID-19 so they avoided joining the protests. But the 2008 crisis and Black Lives Matter movement in particular have politicized millennials and Generation Z.

A lasting effect of the 2008 crisis was the creation of the gig economy. The rise of Uber, Lyft, and Airbnb can all be traced to the 2008 crisis. Millennials make up the largest share of gig workers, and the COVID-19 pandemic exposed the vulnerabilities of this precarious and contingent workforce. The kinds of job protections afforded to some regular workers are nonexistent for gig workers who rely on day-to-day wages. The pandemic closed down most of the service industry save for certain types of work deemed "essential." Millions were left unemployed, and young people especially felt that they had nothing to lose. All of this had an effect on what we saw unfold: widespread looting, destruction of carceral infrastructures, and graffiti slogans on boarded-up businesses targeting the rich. I thought it was interesting how during the rebellion dining out became seen as a sign of privilege by protesters who heckled the brunch crowds. Eat the rich, indeed!

The fact that some white people heckled the rich and fought off cops while others cried about being unable to dine outside fancy places and the worst of the lot traveled across distances to take up arms and defend property gives us a small glimpse into the morbid symptoms of whiteness today. In tandem with the violence of austerity that Jarrod mentioned are the transformations of whiteness which we should pay more attention to. Historically, whiteness has been a cross-class alliance, "the original sweetheart deal" in the words of Noel Ignatiev, which ensured that a section of the American working class would comply with the racial order that defines American life at the expense of solidarity with Black and Brown workers, thus forsaking any possible shot at human liberation. Trump's ascendancy awakened many to the potential destruction of aggrieved white people. He gave them a scapegoat for their wretched lives: Mexican immigrants, Black people, Muslims, leftists. In 2016, Trump won over sixty million Americans to his dystopian vision of the world. So in the summer of 2020, for a brief moment, the George Floyd Rebellion offered a utopian antidote. Millions of people rejected the status quo not only in large cities, but across suburbia and small towns in America. And for a brief moment in the streets, white allies were turned into accomplices and became the targets of both police and white vigilante violence.

Rail: This question is related to my last one. There are a lot of unresolved paradoxes inherent to the rebellion: how it grew, how it died, the subsequent political responses. But we're still marveling at this moment of generalized disorder, when an unprecedented number of people flung themselves at carceral and policing infrastructure, all under the discursive auspices of Black struggle—its history, its moral force. But abolition is a universal program. It relies on a universal and necessarily *total* critique of how this society is bolted together and reproduces itself every day. It has been nourished by Black militancy and sets its sights on a transformation at the broadest and deepest level. Is there, say, a conceptual space between the particularist prompt of the rebellion (Blackness) and the scale of the problem to be tackled? And do you think that space has to be closed or transcended? Do you foresee militants learning to talk differently, proceed differently? How can the specific, vital contribution of Black struggle withstand the temptations of liberal antiracism? History will answer these questions one way or another. But I thought it might be worth the effort to guess.

Kurti: It goes beyond 2014. From nineteenth-century Abolitionism, through Civil Rights and Black Power, to the George Floyd Rebellion, the radical political involvement of large numbers of Americans has been shaped by the demands of Black liberation struggles. The televised images of police dogs mauling Black children in Birmingham politicized a new generation to fight against white supremacy. The women's liberation movement of the 1960s and 1970s was inspired by the Black liberation struggle for self-determination. The list goes on and on. However, within this history of Black liberation struggles there was also an affirmation of race that you may be alluding to. We have not escaped that, because no Black liberation movement to date has been successful in overthrowing the racial order. Ultimately, the struggle will be successful if it can abolish, not reaffirm, race.

I am not sure if it's just the explicit invocation of race that rendered the George Floyd Rebellion vulnerable to liberal antiracism. As we discuss in the book, the spontaneity of the rebellion also hit real limits, not all of which can be blamed on outside forces and institutions. Even as it was a spectacular rejection of the status quo, the political imagination and the willpower did not exist to connect to areas of American social life that produce the ills that police and prisons manage. As soon as the rebellion subsided, everyone returned to their segregated neighborhoods. It is hard to destroy hundreds of years of race-making through riots alone. In such moments, liberal antiracism is successful because it's easier for people to imagine that racism can be dismantled by crafting more good white people or diversifying leadership positions rather than abolishing the system that makes it possible.

It's worthwhile mentioning that the participation of whites in Black-led rebellions is still a relatively new phenomenon. Also, the boundaries of race are not fixed; they are constantly being remade in ways that will undoubtedly influence future struggles.

Rail: In a few places you cite "Onward Barbarians," an essay published by the Endnotes collective, in which the authors deploy (or rather adapt) the term *con-fusion* to discuss what's sometimes called identity politics. That is, fusion and confusion: the jagged new constituencies and forms of identification that have sprung from recent uprisings across the planet. Is that line of thinking helpful to you? And does it get us even part of the way to solving strategic problems?

Shanahan: I mean, speaking in purely abstract terms, the universalist solution is, of course, correct: we set aside our differences and struggle for some mythic unifying working-class interest, and then we win! But in terms of how struggles for liberation have actually played out, even in the heat of battle we appear to be stuck with some version of the way that capital has divided us. If you look at movements like Occupy, which attempted to posit a false universal—a whopping 99 percent of the population have the same interests!—you can glimpse valiant yet ultimately doomed efforts to abstract from the hard work of politics waged in perhaps the most complexly divided society in world history.

While many people like to blame "identity politics" and other convenient scapegoats for these difficulties, I tend to think the divisions are real—rooted in the longstanding division of labor within the US and also on a global scale, in which you have lots of different classes of people who are exploited to varying degrees, but don't have identical interests, to say nothing of lived experiences and entry points into politics. On the flip side, due to the constant turbulence of capitalism, the meaning and significance of different positions in the division of labor is always changing. The racial, ethnic, gendered, and sexual divisions that haunt us today were not born in people's heads, but ossified in patterns of social reproduction, housing availability, employment opportunities, the use of public space, treatment by the law, and so forth. As capital churns the productive base of our world, these practices are always changing, sometimes strengthening some of the identities based in them, such as the incorporation of ethnic Europeans into "whiteness" in the twentieth century, but also threatening to undercut ways we have been traditionally divided.

Think about the consequences, for instance, of traditional conceptions of working-class masculinity, in a period when much of the industrial and manual work for a "breadwinner" salary that once defined it has been eliminated, and men from working-class backgrounds increasingly end up in the service industry, clerical work, and other "feminized" and precarious occupations. The old masculinity doesn't make much sense anymore for a large number of its contemporary adherents. They can beat their chests at sporting events watching others excel in athletics, buy massive trucks with flatbeds that will forever remain pristine, and join reactionary groups of the emasculated and aggrieved like the Proud Boys, but these activities are confined to leisure time and cannot define a subjectivity foisted on them by the dictates of their productive life. Important cracks have emerged, most notably in the gender binary itself. We have to be a bit more careful talking about the racial division of labor, because in economic and cultural terms, the color line is far more stubborn in the United States than the division between supposed genders has proven to be, but what it means to be white or Black, categories which come to us not from discourses but practices inherent to the division of labor, is not static, and we can expect it to change as modes of work and social reproduction are altered. As Zhana just said, more attention needs to be paid to the idea that the so-called races might not make as much sense as they once did.

The most effective movements of the last decade have pushed against the inherited categories, not from a position of dismissing them outright, but pressing within them until they explode. This was true of the move from a fairly class-blind conception of Blackness in 2014–15 to the class-struggle politics of abolitionism that emerged in 2020, which entailed a lot of class struggle within Black activist circles against the nonprofits and political elites who would happily corral all of that activity into the Democratic Party. Following this example, I think that it is worthwhile to spend less time figuring out false universals that will unite us all in a think piece, slogan, or party program that subsequently fails spectacularly in practice, and more time taking seriously the ways we are divided, and pushing the contradictions within these divisions.

Rail: Let's talk about disorganization. You talk about the ultimate disorganization of the forces on the ground in 2020 as being Janus-faced. On the one hand, this was a (momentary) strength, in that the situation on the ground was completely, incontrovertibly ungovernable. Despite the organizing in Minneapolis and elsewhere that predated the rebellion, at a certain point it became clear that the militants answered to nothing and no one: no figurehead, no organization, no ideology. There was only self-propelling, autonomous force. But inevitably that became a limitation. Praxis needs a politics.

But you also caution against the attempts to mediate or to lodge the rebellion too snugly within a vocabulary or political frame. That leads to your very sophisticated and thorough canvassing of the abolitionist literature, and of abolition as a *political* project. You acknowledge the various strands of opinion within abolitionism and pay close attention to how its discourse has come to function in the aftermath of the riots. I saw the book as trying to register a paradox: on the one hand, you recognize that the absence of a coherent politics is a weakness to be transcended, but you also insist on your own wariness of "politicization" and mediation.

Shanahan: It's a great question, and I think that it might be impossible to answer on a purely intellectual level, because it's simply the terrain that any communist politics worthy of the name needs to inhabit: striking a balance between a praxis rooted in the way that working people all around you are already struggling, with the need to orient that toward a revolutionary horizon.

And this is why we spent so much time enumerating the tactics and the various forms the rebellion took in the first chapter. I actually assigned this chapter to my students, and some of them informed me, much to my dismay, that it was a little boring.

Rail: What are their other assignments? I assume they're not getting a master's in urban guerrilla warfare, but what do I know?

Shanahan: Yeah, they only want to read about revolutions that were successful. But that's why we spent so much time with the concrete ways that people were struggling. Because I really think that any serious communist politics must begin not with its imaginary version of how people should be struggling but with how people are already struggling in the real world. It therefore becomes necessary to develop a working practical relationship to struggle, as it all already exists, with an eye toward a possible revolutionary horizon. You might agree that the book's final chapter hinges around the absent figure of revolutionary organization. There are some cool groups and microsects in the United States that are attempting to work through this in practice. And without professing to have the winning program in mind, I do think that if we're talking about bridging the spontaneous aspects of struggle with a long-term revolutionary effort, it's unavoidable that, in a country firmly rooted in individualism and anti-organizational politics, we have to take revolutionary organization much more seriously.

The winning organizational form might not look like the statist parties of the twentieth-century left, which have now become kind of parodies of themselves in the US, performing a historical moment that has long since passed. But we certainly need organized networks and structures facilitating coherence and consistency over time, which is how I define organization. This is why we focus so much on the role abolitionism played in the rebellion.

Kurti: What I appreciate about abolitionists is that they have demystified the role and function of police and prisons in simple terms.

Since the 1970s, prison abolitionists have consistently argued that reform of the system is not possible because the system is not broken but instead functioning just as it was intended to. Police and prisons are not there to protect or create safety, abolitionists remind us, but instead to manage the contradictions and social ills of a highly unequal society. This is an important rejection of liberal reforms. However, it was the rise of Black Lives Matter and the failures of liberal police reforms that pushed abolitionism out of academia and smaller organizing milieus into a larger mainstream view. Up until the summer of 2020, much of abolitionist organizing focused on the important struggles of fighting back jail and prison expansion and addressing community harm through transformative justice. The George Floyd Rebellion provided an important opportunity for abolitionists to reflect more deeply on what it would take to abolish the conditions that police and prisons manage. And we wrote this book to engage with this very important question.

Shanahan: In the summer of 2020, abolitionists throughout the United States provided an example of how an organized revolutionary force could orient to a rebellion. Thanks to decades of organization on the local and national level, they had achieved a remarkable degree of theoretical and practical unity on key political questions. Abolitionists who may have never met each other or have been aware of each other's existence were able to mobilize effectively throughout the country and to help focus and define the rebellion. People often are compelled to actions by forces that might be outside of their immediate perception. A lot of folks you talk to in moments of great upsurge say something like: "Wow! I never thought I would do something like this!"

Often it's not so much that precise political ideas catalyze actions, but these big movements become bitter struggles between competing political definitions of why people are doing *what they are already doing*. In 2020, abolitionists were in a place to help people make sense of the actions that they were taking and to help them orient toward a future political horizon. And that, in my mind, is the exact role that could be played by a more explicitly revolutionary organization or tendency.

Rail: That's a clarifying way to phrase it. But the concept of organization leads me to my next question, in which I'll come out as the flavor of leftist subjected to your very comradely critique. My view is that any political organization capable of wielding worthwhile power in a conjuncture defined by a writhing, hydra-like working class will have to bind, or "articulate," several disparate strands of struggle. Here I'm thinking of a great essay by Salar Mohandesi, "Party as Articulator." The advantage of a party is not simply that it offers a "line" that you can chain yourself to, but that the organization serves as both a place for struggles to meet and a repository for movement history. The party cultivates a sense of memory and can offer a *coordinated*, partisan counter to bourgeois discourse—for instance, the rhetorical bleaching of the George Floyd Rebellion.

Among this panoply of struggles is the current redistributionist one—the preoccupation of what you call the "Keynesian" left. The Marxist critique of simple redistribution goes very far back, of course. But I think a lot of people involved in struggles around budgetary policy and universal benefits don't see it as a mere repotting of the fiscal soil, but as a way to build class power. There are probably some who believe that a painless hydraulic process will allow us to reform our way to utopia, but I think a lot of people see "social-democratic" issues as class struggle pitched on a particular terrain. What do you make of that position? And can you explain, for a moment, how this debate factors into your book?

Kurti: This is a good point. It is heartening that in my lifetime, I see so many Americans recognizing that the system we currently have in place is extremely unequal and wanting to do something to change it. Thousands of people have joined what is an explicitly socialist organization, the Democratic Socialists of America (DSA). Growing up in New York City in the 1990s, I never thought this would be possible.

I think you are right to say that leftists who push for social-democratic reforms are doing so because they truly believe that pursuing this path will build class power. And while I am sympathetic to this vision, I am not entirely convinced by how it is unfolding. And that is mostly because I am seeing mostly (not all!) a very narrow way of building class power that has historically proven a huge failure not only in America but in the European countries some leftists want to emulate. In Chicago, where I now live, most of the energy is poured into supporting the election of socialist politicians who can help pass reformist bills and legislation. I wonder what would happen if, instead of pursuing an electoral path, the focus was on building power inside and outside workplaces, in Black and Brown neighborhoods that have faced decades of disinvestment, the list can go on. I don't have the answers, but I certainly don't believe the answer lies in electoral politricks. For example, cities that were the hotbed of militant protests during the George Floyd Rebellion have today capitulated to the conservative rhetoric of public safety and politics that emphasize a "law and order" response to crime. Despite all their virtue signaling, the Democrats (including the more progressive wings of the party) did not succeed at the municipal and local level to pass policies that would divest money from the police and reinvest it in poor communities of color. The position among certain socialists that insists on pushing Democrats to the left has proven to be a failure over and over again.

The George Floyd Rebellion and the rise of abolitionist politics is forcing us to think more about what it takes to build power. Is the state a neutral actor that we can mold into whatever we want? This is an important question that we pose in the book, especially in the last chapter. One of the lessons of previous moments of heightened struggles, whether in the 1930s or 1960s, has been the need of radical movements to maintain their independence from the official institutions of liberal bourgeois society and to rely on mass direct action as a means of forcing reforms instead of pursuing the usual dead-end channels of electoral politics. We saw how the rebellion forced the hands of ruling elites to find extra money to add to our stimulus checks. But it was a moment of mass direct action that forced a reform. I think the strength of the George Floyd Rebellion was that for a brief moment it made the question of "reform or revolution" less abstract and more concrete.

Shanahan: To be clear, some of my proudest political moments have been in demand-based campaigns, especially the ongoing struggle for faculty pay parity and free education at the City University of New York. These are surely not demands for immediate proletarian revolution—although I certainly wouldn't have minded if the struggle went that way! As far as I'm concerned, there's nothing inherently wrong with economistic struggles, for the reasons you outline, Tobi, and especially because they can quickly escape their predetermined bounds if the time is right. But, echoing Zhana, we see building power as a means and not as an end in itself. It is possible to sacrifice the revolutionary content of the struggle as a precursor to building so-called power.

For instance, beginning with the New Deal and the National Labor Relations Act of 1935, the mainstream US labor unions pledged loyalty to the capitalists' labor law, supported US imperialism and the color line, and ceded control over working conditions to the bosses, all in the name of building "class power"—understood as synonymous with expanding the size and political connectedness of business unions. This strategy proved inadequate even to these narrow ends, of course, as time soon told, but it lives on to the present day, long after it should have been abandoned, through what Mike Davis called the "barren marriage" of labor and the Democratic Party. This doesn't mean that revolutionary struggle cannot originate within workplace struggles, but as long as struggle remains confined within a legalistic trade union structure, the most you can probably hope for is a raise that keeps pace with inflation, as your union bargains away the future of the next generation of workers to keep you happy. The revolutionary potential of organized labor has been undercut at countless junctures in US history by the advocates of this form of "class power."

There is a parallel within abolitionism today, where you see an unresolved contradiction over the vital question of how we can bring about a world without prisons and cops. On the one hand, you have folks like *End of Policing* author Alex Vitale who advocate a technocratic, parliamentary path toward abolition, suggesting that we can achieve cop-free social democracy in the United States through convincing bourgeois politicians to abolish an arrangement of social forces that serves as the basis of their power. If you believe that capitalism requires cops and prisons, as many abolitionists do, this amounts to the old canard that you can abolish capitalist society through bourgeois politics. On the other hand, you have folks like the Revolutionary Abolitionist Movement, who draw on revolutionary abolitionism and the tradition of Black anarchism in particular to argue that the ruling class will never willingly redistribute its power to us, and there's no peaceful or legal route to abolition. This latter camp also likely includes many people who have not left a discursive footprint but took bold and decisive action in 2020 by attacking the cops and their infrastructure.

So the intervention that we are trying to make in this book is to force a little bit of reckoning. Do we imagine abolition realized through the mechanisms of the bourgeois state, or through its overthrow? Is there some alternative to this binary, and if so, what is it?

Will the realization of a world without prisons and cops require the end of capitalism? And if so, what will it take to end capitalism? What will replace it? No matter how abstract these questions may seem, I really can't imagine more important distinctions to make at the basis of a liberatory politics.

To be clear, we do not believe that the vast majority of abolitionists served a recuperative role in the 2020 rebellion. As we argue in the book, the success of Defund came more within a vacuum vacated by the more militant street fighters than from co-opting their momentum. But could a legalistic, parliamentary vision of abolitionism be used to disorient and destroy an extraparliamentary, actually revolutionary one, speaking the language of "nonreformist reforms" all the way? Of course it could! Especially now that abolitionism is in vogue, and the procapitalist nonprofit industrial complex is adopting its language. That's why if we are seriously thinking about a society that would not require prisons or cops, to say nothing of a society beyond capitalism, we need a reckoning on what exactly we think needs to happen to get there. Building power is a laudable goal, but what exactly are we building this power to do?

VII
ORGANIZING AND STRATEGY

Clinic Defense in the Era of Operation Rescue

Suzy Subways

Hard Crackers, July 22, 2022

In the early Nineties, anarchists and other feminists defended clinics with our bodies and taught each other how to do abortion techniques such as menstrual extraction safely. As the Christian right bombed hundreds of clinics, killed health care providers and patients, and mobilized its base to swarm clinics and shut them down, grassroots reproductive freedom activists stood against this terror, building a powerful and exciting movement. But liberal feminist nonprofits rejected this grassroots mass movement, choosing to rely on the police and courts for protection. Since then, the Christian right has continued to attack and harass people at clinics, mobilizing its own grassroots activists to shame people getting health care and shut down clinics one by one. Their local, bottom-up strategy took the long view and is now winning at the highest levels of government. If today's movement for reproductive freedom is to win, it must return to the grass roots.

The militant antiabortion group Operation Rescue was founded in 1986 to mobilize thousands of people to physically block and shut down clinics across the country. The well-funded and -staffed organization presented an image of the Christian right as peaceful activists guided by a deep moral outrage, although some of its leaders had signed a pledge defending the assassination of abortion providers and were active in the right-wing Militia movement. Reproductive freedom activists, led by people with the capacity to get pregnant, mobilized to protect clinics with our bodies. On the ground, Operation Rescue was aggressive, and sometimes the space in front of clinics erupted into hand-to-hand combat as antiabortion activists shoved people and tried to crawl through their legs.

Clinic Defense: Using Our Bodies to Protect Our Lifesaving Spaces

I did clinic defense a few times, when I was eighteen and nineteen. As a student at Antioch College in 1992, I went to Columbus, Ohio, with some friends on a few Saturdays. We'd wake up super early and stand in formation in front of the clinic with dozens of others to protect it. We saw these health centers as precious places. People going through trauma after sexual assault and through abusive relationships, very young people, and married women trying to keep their lives from getting unmanageable were taking control of their health despite their vulnerability in those moments. As protectors, we took our role seriously, and we bonded with each other as we stood against the enemy. This was the source of the passion that grew a powerful movement from below.

My dear friend Kathy became a legend at Antioch one day for her response to a vile Christian right protester who harassed her for hours outside the clinic. Kathy was a hot butch lesbian who grew up on a farm and didn't take shit, although she was quiet most of the time. This man kept telling her, "You should be married and having children," until finally, she pulled out her bloody pad, put it in his hand, and said, "Put this in your petri dish and grow it!"

This was the vibe at clinic defense. We were taking back our power and control of our bodies, and the energy this ignited in us as a collective body grew exponentially. There's something about being there when your life-giving space is under attack, being able to defend it successfully, and doing it together. Using our bodies to defend our bodily autonomy.

Operation Rescue targeted my hometown of Philadelphia during summer 1993. With at least a hundred people on our side—maybe hundreds—we kept the clinic open. Operation Rescue had about half as many people and stood on the sidewalk across the street. I remember following a crew of badass anarchist lesbians who I admired around the corner and a few blocks away as they chased a male leader of Operation Rescue, yelling at him and surrounding him. They got in his face, and he cowered. Our power took a visible, audible, unstoppable form: Get out of our town.

Back outside the clinic, I saw a friend on the other side of the street, with the antiabortion activists. She had been the first to welcome me to my new school when I'd moved to Philly. I felt my face get hot and looked away. I almost felt remorse for the confrontation along with my disappointment. Should I pretend I didn't see her?

I decided to cross the street and say hi. Sheepishly but warmly, she returned my friendly greeting. It looked like she was there with a church group. A woman standing next to her cast me some snide vibes, saying, "Shouldn't you be over there?" My friend and I ran out of things to say and I went back, but I felt better knowing she hadn't rejected me. Decades later, we reconnected on social media, and she is living happily as a lesbian with a wife and kids.

Thinking of that day reminds me of the value of my brilliant, late comrade Joel Olson's favorite saying: "Peace to the villages—war to the palaces." A little kindness goes a long way with people we can win over, but we can't let politeness and decorum get in the way of wielding our power against those who would take our power away.

A Betrayal: Liberal Feminist Nonprofits Tell Defenders to Go Home

In 1995, I moved to New York City and joined Love and Rage Revolutionary Anarchist Federation. In the August/September issue of our national newspaper that year, Laura from Bay Area Coalition for Our Reproductive Rights (BACORR) wrote:

> Fight Back Network members from BACORR, Refuse & Resist Minneapolis, and Love and Rage went to LA May 25th–28th to try to keep the clinics open and to blast OR's efforts to define themselves in the media as non-violent-peaceful-ba-by-lovin'-Christians. BACORR had been in touch with WAC LA (Women's Action Coalition) and a Southern California NOW chapter that welcomed our support and involvement.[1]

Unfortunately, the Fund for the Feminist Majority, a national nonprofit, was in charge at the scene. As reported by Laura, the fund had put a lot of resources into electing Bill Clinton as president and lobbying for a law that passed in 1994 to make it a federal crime to block clinic doors. The fund had decided to let Operation Rescue and a group calling themselves Missionaries to the Preborn shut down the clinics in LA that day, in order to bring the FACE (Freedom of Access to Clinic Entrances) law into the courts as a test case. Laura continued:

Saturday, the day of the hit, hundreds of pro-choicers were at the clinics around LA. Many had followed the OR caravan from its church meeting-point earlier in the morning. The Fund's "official leaders" made it clear from the get-go that they would offer no resistance to OR if they rushed the door, and were depending on the police to move the anti's away and level federal charges.

In a nutshell, the anti's were permitted to sit down in front of the doors, creating the image of non-violent anti-abortion protest. They kept the clinic shut down for two hours. The Fund's main office lied to BACORR and to Palm Springs NOW, who they knew was working with BACORR, about OR's where-abouts—telling us they had lost the caravan and had no idea where it was. . . . A local reporter told us that she had interviewed pro-choice people who were standing at the door when the hit went down who were told not to stop the anti's and to move away from the door.[2]

Operation Rescue got their dream media opportunity, and police beat and injured Laura and a friend after fund staff told police they had nothing to do with the official pro-choice response. The fund didn't alert legal support that Laura and her friend had been arrested, and they implied to the media that the two had deserved it. Operation Rescue and Missionaries to the Preborn were arrested gently at their sit-in, creating a widely broadcast spectacle of peacefully praying dissent, but they were never even charged under the FACE law.

How the Christian Right Won

While the Fund for the Feminist Majority and other liberal femi-nist nonprofits ordered clinic defenders to stop protecting clinics and simply hold a "Keep Abortion Legal" sign on the sidelines, the Christian right supported and honored its grassroots movement. They energized large numbers of people, and they inspired many, many more who followed their actions. While the pro-choice establishment dismantled our movement, grassroots activists of the Christian right have never stopped protesting outside clinics. Even in major liberal cities, they harass and shame people who are just trying to get health care. This grassroots, on-site shaming campaign has made abortion something people feel like they need to be ashamed of, feel guilty about, and not talk about—in contrast to the first decade after legalization in the US, when people interviewed about their abortions mostly talked about how relieved they felt. This grassroots movement in local areas across the country has grown stronger over the past three decades, getting clinics closed one by one, winning at the state level and now at the national level, proving to us on the left what we already knew: power comes from below.

Since the 1990s, anytime there's an upsurge in support of abortion access, it's been brief and has felt kind of abstract. Young people need an inspiring, direct-action movement to jump into with all their heart and their bodies—they won't be inspired by getting told to carry a sign through the biggest street in their town. Maybe once or twice, but then it dies down. It's hard to build a base when you're not at the place where harm is being done, able to stop it. Or at the place where lives are being saved, able to protect that space.

There's an honest argument to be made that health clinics should never have to be battlegrounds, that patients in moments of vulnerability shouldn't have to walk through such a war. But they've been walking through a gauntlet of shame all these years anyway, because clinic defenders haven't been there to shield them from the hate. And in the Nineties, clinic defenders used our creativity and joy as a buffer between patients and attackers. The Church Ladies for Choice brought their drag queen brilliance, and our queer kiss-ins outside right-wing churches freaked out the Christian right activists to the point they would avoid getting near us.

As a strategy, anarchists and other revolutionaries in the reproductive freedom movement have consistently—as in, for more than fifty years—demanded the repeal of all abortion laws. Not more state involvement from the police and courts, but a removal of all state power from our reproductive lives. We call it "reproductive freedom" because it's about more than abortion; it's about the history of forced and coerced sterilizations of Black, Latinx, and Native American women and other people with the capacity to bear children. It's about the population control tactics used against poor people and those who use drugs.

People don't have the ability to "choose" whether to have a kid or not when wages are too low, childcare is not accessible, and the rent is too damn high. Medicaid hasn't paid for abortions since the Hyde Amendment in 1977. Giving a baby up for adoption—or being adopted—can be deeply traumatizing, especially under our current unsupportive system. And it's worse for children of color adopted by white parents. But "choice" has been our battle cry since the 1980s. Why? This "choice" versus "life" debate has allowed the Christian right to control the narrative and make it about their idea of morality. It's been a successful wedge strategy from the right, dividing people who could be united in coalitions.

Can We Still Win Now?

If the Christian right won by building their grassroots movement and letting its power grow across the decades, so must we. If our power is strongest at the location of our bodily autonomy—in the places where we are able to exercise our reproductive freedom—then we must build our movement there. A full strategy also includes fighting for our demand to repeal all abortion laws and going on the offensive against the Christian right, but that's beyond the scope of this essay. I want to leave you with some ideas of how to channel the spirit of clinic defense into strategy and tactics today.

Abortion pills and menstrual extraction (which can be done in our homes by trained people who don't have to be medical professionals) allow us to take care of ourselves on our own territory. This is our strongest position strategically and what the right fears most. They are using surveillance by state power and vigilantes to track, hunt down, and punish whoever provides and receives these medications and treatments, because they can't just rely on hospital and doctors' records. Every home could be an abortion clinic. It's a scary situation, but it also makes clear our advantage.

So it seems clear that the reproductive freedom movement's strategy now is to protect these sites of health care and resistance by building powerful antiracist and queer-positive coalitions involving hundreds of thousands of people. We need as many people involved as possible in order to keep the most vulnerable safe and also to make this health care accessible. If it's limited to those in the know—people who are already activists and people who are able to find out about the support networks they need—that will exclude the people who need it most.

Some of these coalitions and support networks need to be underground, and some need to be above ground. Some need to be sharing information with people who need abortions about how to get abortion pills and what to say if they need to go to the emergency room ("I think I'm having a miscarriage"—don't mention abortion). Some need to be driving people to appointments, providing emotional support, following up and making sure people are okay. Some need to be talking to the media and educating, agitating, and organizing in our communities and workplaces. Some will need to fundraise for legal support and organize demonstrations in solidarity with reproductive freedom's new political prisoners. This work is direct action, because you're meeting a basic human need in defiance of those who'd prefer that we die.

Militant Tactics in Antifascist Organizing

Interview with Kieran

Against the Grain (KPFA Radio), February 14, 2017

The interview was conducted for KPFA Radio's *Against the Grain* by the program's coproducer, Sasha Lilley, and was broadcast on February 14, 2017. The following transcription, by Clarissa Rogers, was posted to *Three Way Fight* on April 26, 2017.

Kieran was one of the founders of Anti-Racist Action, a youth-based direct action movement that organized against nazi skinheads, the Ku Klux Klan, and the white power music scene from the 1980s to the 2000s. He's now chief steward in a local union of telecom workers and is a member of the Industrial Workers of the World's General Defense Committee, which has taken on antifascist work in a number of cities. In late January, a member of the General Defense Committee of the IWW was shot at a Milo Yiannopoulos event in Seattle. *Against the Grain*, a program of radical ideas originating from KPFA Radio, spoke with him after demonstrators closed down Yiannapoulous's event at UC Berkeley on February 1.

Against the Grain: Kieran, many liberals and leftists believe that the right of free speech is paramount. As you know, protesters using militant tactics shut down a Milo Yiannopoulos event at UC Berkeley, which is the home of the Free Speech Movement. Why don't you think that the right of free speech should be extended to fascists and the far right?

Kieran: There are a couple of points to this. I think there's both a question of strategy and tactics. I think that all of this is with the understanding that what we're opposing is not the free speech of fascists, or the speeches of fascists. What we're doing is opposing the organizing of the fascists. So, for instance, in my workplace, I work with workers with a whole range of opinions on all different kinds of questions. And occasionally you're going to run into people who are influenced by far-right politics. In those circumstances, it doesn't make sense for me to start a fight, a physical fight with a coworker, since they raised some perspective that comes from that background.

But that's totally different than a situation where you have an organization or a personality who's using the framework of a public speech or an event, a forum, in order to advance political goals. And so the way we look at it is the way we would look at any kind of organizing done by that group with those aims.

In the case at UC Berkeley, this outright celebrity and provocateur, Milo Yiannopoulos, very clearly is trying to advance a certain kind of politics and more and more is trying to shape it into a movement. Our understanding is that he was planning to out undocumented students at Berkeley for the sole purpose of putting them under attack by Trump's immigration forces. And, so, in that circumstance, we can't let that attack go unchallenged. And I think that when you look at it from that perspective, it makes sense to try to oppose it.

If we just wait until they've created the groundswell, or created the base of support for these aggressive actions to take place, it can be too late. And so the way we approach fascist organizing or right-wing organizing is not really focused on the question of free speech but is focused on whether or not we're going to let them organize to implement their program. And our perspective is that we're not. We're going to challenge it. We're going to try to stop it. We're going to try to stop them.

Against the Grain: Let's talk about the stakes. On the night of Inauguration Day, a member of the Industrial Workers of the World was shot in the stomach by a Milo Yiannopoulos supporter in Seattle. What do we know about what happened there and the condition of the man who was shot?

Kieran: Yeah, that's correct. On the night of the inauguration, Yiannopoulos was speaking at the University of Washington in Seattle, and there was a mass demonstration against him that included a range of political forces. And there were also a number of supporters of Trump and Yiannopoulos who were there as well. So there was a fairly confrontational scene happening outside of Yiannopoulos's talk. And in that situation, my understanding—I wasn't there, but my understanding is that one of the right-wingers started to spray Mace or another chemical at the anti-Trump, anti-Yiannopoulos forces, and that a member of the IWW and the General Defense Committee tried to intervene to stop that person from doing that and was shot in the stomach, as you said.

It was a life-threatening injury. He was in the ICU for many days. He's incurred at least two surgeries. So it was a potentially deadly attack. And as of now, there have been no charges brought against the person who did it. Again, our understanding from media reports is that the person who shot him went to the police and gave a statement and was released without any charges. And so, of course, this is sort of a bad sign for where things are at right now, that we take very seriously. Because as it stands what it appears is that some people are going to walk away from this with the idea that antifascists can be shot without consequences. And that's very dangerous.

Against the Grain: And in fact, that's been the case. This past summer, there was a confrontation between white supremacists and radicals in Sacramento, California, where a number of people were stabbed and there were no consequences.

Kieran: Right. I think that just points to a broader point, which is that we can't rely on law enforcement, on the state, to either defend our communities or defend antifascists. Some antiracists have a perspective of wanting to try to call on the state to carry out justice, and our approach is a little different. We come from it with an understanding that the state is not neutral. That the state is built on a foundation of a history of exploitation and oppression, and that it represents the folks who are at the top of that system and defends their interests. So when we're organizing, we don't do so from the point of view of trying to get the state or the police to protect us or to find justice for us, but instead we try to build movements that are self-reliant and are based on community self-defense, on popular self-defense.

Against the Grain: There's been a lot of debate among progressives and leftists about the use of militant tactics. Some of this is a continuation of debates that came out of Occupy, some of this goes even further back, but there are a lot of conflicting opinions. There's no unity whatsoever among the left about the use of militant tactics, whether property damage or shutting down an event. Are there times when militant tactics aren't called for? Do they need to be considered strategically among other possible tactics?

Kieran: Yeah, I think all of this is a question of tactics. That being said, I think we have some underlying principles as well. And that those inform the tactics that we would draw from in order to organize effectively. And you can imagine lots of different situations where you're encountering the right or the fascists, where either you don't have the means to effectively disrupt their activity and their organizing or you want to sort of put a larger emphasis on trying to undermine their ability to develop their base. And so there's a few things, and it's never been just a question of militant tactics. Militant tactics is a part of our strategy, but it's not the only part.

A big part of it is a battle for the hearts and minds that the fascists are trying to recruit for their base. So we've always, along with militant tactics against their organizing, have also tried to engage with the communities that the fascists are targeting. And that can be from interviews or leafleting, to building cultural events like shows with bands, to trying to connect with the people in those communities who already have an antifascist impulse, possibly because of their identity or how they see the world. But we try to bring a message that this program that the right wing and the fascists are selling is not in our interest as working-class people. And that it is a dangerous and divisive one, and that it's going to lead to a common catastrophe if enacted. And in fact, many of the concerns people have would be better served by organizing a united multiracial, multicultural, antifascist movement that challenges the system.

Against the Grain: One of the things that comes up in these debates—and not just from liberals, but also from others on the left— is that militant action can actually be alienating for those who would like to build larger grassroots opposition to the right. How would you respond to that?

Kieran: I've heard those arguments a lot. And I think it's true that sometimes there's militancy that's poorly organized or not well thought out. But I hear that argument oftentimes from people who are really upset with how the mainstream media covers us. Or how the more moderate tendencies within the social movements react to it. While those things are important to be mindful of, I think that there's also a question of people beyond the current left. People in working-class communities. People who are already suspicious of what the mainstream media tells us. And I just think that it's a fact that most working-class people respect folks who stand up and are willing to defend themselves and are willing to take risks. And so, you can watch a news report in which antifascists, or anarchists, or radicals are being condemned, but people receive that information in all different kinds of ways. People who are already suspicious of the way the mainstream media talks about anything are likely to have a more positive response seeing a group of people standing up and fighting back.

So I think that we have to be really careful about arguments like that, because I think they tend to try to reduce all of our tactics to whatever the most moderate elements within the movement are willing to support. And that's just not a recipe for building the kind of movement that we need. And it's not a recipe for bringing in the most marginalized people, the people who are feeling sort of the knife's edge of the system the most, because those folks already have an antagonistic attitude toward the system and toward these racists. And so if we're serious about including those folks in our movements, then we can't take a moderate attitude toward them. When the racists and fascists are organizing, we have to be ready to stand up and fight.

Against the Grain: I'd like to ask you about Anti-Racist Action, a youth-based militant direct-action movement which organized against nazi skinheads in the white power music scene and which you cofounded. It was started in the 1980s and lasted through the 2000s. How broad was it? And what sort of work did it do? There's a renewed interest in it now.

Kieran: It started out sort of spontaneously in this sense. In the mid to late Eighties, largely within the punk scene in the US and Canada, there was a polarization politically that happened. And so, around the same time in many cities there were white supremacists and nazi gangs that formed. They were influenced by Skrewdriver (which was a nazi skinhead band) and the fascist politics of the National Front in Britain. And in response to that, or sometimes ahead of that, there were groups that considered themselves militantly antiracist and antifascist, and these two sets of groups could not coexist for long within alternative scenes, within the punk scene.

So there was a struggle that went on simultaneously in a number of cities, and the antiracists—who often started off as antiracist skinheads and some punks and some anarchist activists—found each other after a while, either through touring with bands or through the letters column in *Maximum Rocknroll*, or by corresponding with each other, and started to network, started to build. So Anti-Racist Action was the organizing expression of that spontaneous organizing that happened in the youth culture scenes in North America.

Then, over the years, it broadened out to include people who didn't come from those scenes but who came from other subcultural scenes like graffiti, or young feminists, or hip-hop. It started to take on other issues too, related to racism and white supremacy. So you had Anti-Racist Action chapters that organized Copwatch patrols against police brutality, participated in protests against police violence, helped defend abortion clinics from the far-right Christian right, and a number of other fronts that Anti-Racist Action was active in. At its peak, it included several thousand mainly young people in North America who were self-organizing in their cities and in their scenes, and putting out zines and holding benefit concerts, and really, anytime the fascists tried to make a move, resisting them.

At one point in the Nineties, one of the major Ku Klux Klan groups tried to organize a series of rallies across the Midwest. They did this over the course of a few years, in little towns and big towns in Ohio and Indiana, Wisconsin, Michigan. Anti-Racist Action was key to organizing resistance in all of those places. That meant, also, being in those small towns and talking to people, mainly young people in those towns and trying to connect with them. That was successful.

There were a number of ARA chapters in small towns as well as the big cities where the left is stronger. I think Anti-Racist Action, which had plenty of problems as all movements do, can really say that it helped restrain and deliver some defeats to fascist organizing in the US.

Against the Grain: How seriously did the far right take the work of Anti-Racist Action? Did they see it as a genuine threat to their organizing?

Kieran: Absolutely. We were the major force that they had to deal with in terms of opposition on the streets. So they were very conscious of Anti-Racist Action. In every locality there would be conflicts, and there were many people who were harassed or intimidated, who might have gotten their homes graffitied, or phone calls to their parents with threats from the fascists. They definitely saw us as an obstacle, especially to their ability to organize openly and in public, in contested public space.

I suppose the peak of this was in Las Vegas in 1998, on the Fourth of July weekend. A couple of antiracist skinheads, one who was African American and one who was white, both of whom were well known in the scene and active in Anti-Racist Action, were kidnapped by a gang of white supremacists and tortured and killed and left in the desert. So there were people who died fighting, being a part of this movement. That really hangs heavy for me and the other people who have been part of this, as does the shooting in Seattle, when you hear people complaining about the possible violation of Milo Yiannopoulos's rights.

Against the Grain: Let me ask you a question of clarification. You've mentioned antiracist and antifascist skinheads several times. I think for a lot of people, when they hear the term *skinhead* they assume that's synonymous with fascist and racist, and not antifascist and antiracist.

Kieran: Yeah, sure. Skinhead culture came to the US mainly from the influence of British music bands. The initial skinhead cultural scene from England, and the bands that were most popular within it, was a multiracial scene, heavily influenced by Jamaican immigrants to England. So the skinhead identity has always been contested. Antiracist skinheads make a strong claim that in fact the original skinhead identity was not a racist one but was a multiracial one. In the US, among the original chapters of Anti-Racist Action, and the original fighters against white supremacist skinheads, were a number of youth of color. So there were African American skinheads. In Chicago, there were Puerto Rican skinheads. There were Native American skinheads in Minneapolis, and they were a big and important part of the struggle against the racists.

Against the Grain: Let's take things up to the present, looking at the lessons that can be drawn from the decades of work of Anti-Racist Action for the current situation where, with the Trump administration in power, you have an emboldened far right. Part of that far right, the alt-right, is operating less on the streets and more on the level of propaganda on the internet, but then there are certainly groups on the ground as well. Can you tell us about the General Defense Committee of the Industrial Workers of the World and your political approach to countering fascist and racist forces on the ground?

Kieran: Definitely. I think you're right in describing the situation right now—that we've gone from a situation where we were concerned about the growth of particular fascist and white supremacist organizations and their movement-building to a situation where all of a sudden, particularly through the alt-right, there's suddenly this mass propaganda and mass distribution of fascist ideas. So it's no longer just about the growth of a neo-nazi group in a certain town, but it's the fact that the college Republicans on your campus are peddling alt-right ideas. Also, that that's circulating on social media and that it's become a part of the public debate in a way that the neo-nazi groups and Ku Klux Klan groups could never quite achieve in the past couple of decades.

So that is a serious situation, and I think the thing that the GDC brings to this, is trying to formulate, is trying to connect the ideas of community self-defense, popular self-defense, popular antifascism with the idea that we need to cultivate a working-class base. That it can't just be a squadron of elite antifascists carrying out a technical operation that's going to win this. That we need to get the masses of working-class people in our milieus from all different kinds of communities and identities together. That's what it's going to take to defeat the politics that Trump is putting forward and the system that gave birth to it.

I think that while we are proud to be militant antifascists, and we take that identity seriously, and we take those tactics seriously, we don't want to marginalize ourselves, we don't want to be what Lorenzo Kom'boa Ervin called a "vanguard versus vanguard," where people just see two street gangs fighting with each other and don't really see their needs or demands met by either one of them. Instead, we want to try to organize ourselves and our coworkers and our neighbors into a popular response to the fascists. One that, when we take action, we're not just doing it on behalf of a small cadre of people but that it's really an expression of a community and of the working class as a whole.

Against the Grain: How do you do that in practical terms?

Kieran: Well, I think, in many ways, it's how we talk about it. It's who we try to involve in our actions. It's the way we report about and the way that we sum up our actions. The way we decide if we're successful or not. So it's not just purely a question of are we able to disrupt their organizing on this day—it's also a question of were we able to help develop a base within this community or within this working class that is going to be able to continually be able to confront the fascists and make it a hard place for the fascists to organize and grow.

Some concrete examples of that might be when neo-nazis planned to organize against an antiracist program that was being held by a local YWCA in Minneapolis a few years ago. We took that as an attack on the community. We organized leafleting in the neighborhood. We encouraged neighbors to come out, the community to come out. We held a public meeting. So we gave people from the neighborhood and from different other organizations a chance to become part of the organizers of the counteraction. There were some reformist leftist groups that came and really argued against any militancy. We argued with them in the open meetings so that there could be a community judgment about which tactics were best.

Myself, I coached soccer—youth soccer—in the parks here in Minneapolis and I let other parents from the folks that I coached with, let them know about this, since it was in our neighborhood. And I distributed information about it at work and brought out coworkers to it. So our attitude is that we want to build a popular defense against this. The fascists attack not just a small group of people, but really are against huge communities, and against the class as a whole. It weakens the class as a whole. So we want to have a popular response.

I think some folks, many folks—on both sides—try to divide the concept of a mass response from a militant response. That it's only possible to do one or the other.

I think we really want to challenge that. We think that what's needed is both. And that's not easy. There's no simple formula for it. We're going to need to experiment. We're going to get some things wrong. We're going to bend the stick too far one way or the other, undoubtedly. But that's our goal: to build a mass militant movement that includes lots of people and that uses lots of tactics in order to confront this threat.

Against the Grain: Frequently, when people are involved in militant actions, they wear masks or take other steps to keep from being identified by the police or the far right. But what if that anonymity allows people to become vigilantes, unaccountable to other radicals for their actions? In your experience, how has this tension between militant action and accountability been addressed?

Kieran: The question of masks is one that there has been some debate around within the General Defense Committee and the broader circles we participate in. But I'm not sure that accountability is the main issue. I agree that there should be some kind of accountability by individuals and groups to the broader movement (and, I would say, to the working-class base) but what that accountability is, is open to debate. For instance, some sections of the movement insist on a strictly legalistic framework and use the argument that anything outside of a strict legalism threatens the most vulnerable and oppressed. We should challenge that argument. When real, sustained militancy erupts, it is almost always from those who feel the pressure the most. If others join in, that is an important act of solidarity. And we should reject "accountability" to the law or to forces inside the movement who would turn people over to the authorities.

But it is true I think that groups and individuals should be answerable in some form for their tactical decisions—but this is not just true of masked-up militants but of everyone in an action. People should be accountable for working with the police (an act that endangers us) or for the political line that they project on banners, flyers, or chants, etc. In other words, *all* tactics should be open to debate and criticism.

To get further into the specifics of your question, masks may hide an individual's identity and therefore prevent that particular individual from being "accountable," but generally people in political movements, especially if they've been around for a while, have an idea of the different forces involved, and not knowing an individual's name has never stopped folks from (rightly or wrongly) criticizing actions.

The question we've been debating here about masks is a little different. We've been debating whether they are actually effective for security. Now, we aren't arguing about whether they are effective at concealing your identity—let's say they are. But we've noticed that if you are a smallish group of people all masked up in a larger demo, the police will actually focus on you—instead of becoming camouflaged, you are actually in the spotlight. The cops may not immediately know who you are, but if they focus on the masks, they can just wait until an opportune time and surround and detain the masked-up people and ID or arrest them. We've seen this happen a couple of times.

This speaks to what actually provides security—I would say it is having a real working-class base of support for your organizing, for your projects. Regular people who have a stake in the organizing, who understand the need for militant action, who are willing to stand up and defend each other, both politically and physically, who give a shit if one of their friends or comrades is attacked or arrested—this is a much more important, much more real form of security, but it often gets lost in the aesthetic desire for a certain militant "look" that includes masks.

Another related consideration is that masks can make it harder to further develop a base—to talk to people at an action or other event, to have discussions and arguments. There is also the very real factor that folks can get confused as to what people in the masks stand for—and not just liberal pacifists either. The GDC's experience in participating in the struggle for Justice for Jamar Clark (a young unarmed African American worker killed by the Minneapolis Police in 2015) was that many times people from the Northside community where Jamar was from, who were quite militant, were also very suspicious of people in their midst with masks on. This was exacerbated by the fact that a group of masked-up white supremacists attacked the protest occupation, shooting and seriously wounding four people. So there were a couple of times where people from the community tried to evict masked-up activists from street demos—and this wasn't the "peace police" types, but neighborhood militants. We spent time arguing with people over evicting them, we defended those wearing masks—but I started thinking, "Is this really effective? Is this the best use of our time?"

In saying all that, we should never rule out masks. It's a tactical choice. For all the above negative examples, there are also counterexamples of folks from different scenes sharing masks at mass actions that turn militant, where masks handed out were appreciated and seen as an asset. The point is that we should think through tactical choices, weigh the pros and cons—with one of the main considerations being will this help build/expand a militant working-class base to fight fascism, to fight exploitation and oppression.

Against the Grain: You're the chief steward at a union local in Minneapolis that represents telecom workers. What do you think labor's role should be in battling the forces of the right? Most unions are, of course, not the Industrial Workers of the World. They don't self-identify as radical. But even though unions only represent a small portion of the working class, they still are the only membership-based organizations of the working class. Is there a role for unions? And is it realistic to expect them to be involved in such militant action against the right?

Kieran: I think so. If we look at where there have been mass confrontations, going back to the Eighties and Nineties where some Klan rallies provoked big responses, where large numbers of people came out in Michigan and Ohio and Pennsylvania and Indiana, lots of times you're going to run into union members who come out against that stuff. We need to turn it away from just being individual actions of individual union members to more of an organized expression.

So I think you're right that unions, along with churches and other houses of worship, are some of the few mass membership organizations out in the class. We need to go to the unions. And if the union leadership wants to avoid it or doesn't take this seriously, then we need to build rank-and-file groups that are willing to take this seriously.

My experience is, actually, that people in workplaces are incredibly interested in this stuff. If the Klan is coming to your town, or if there are fascists organizing in your city, people—more people than one might expect—are interested in opposition to that. And I think we need to build on that. And I think that hopefully the GDC, with its origins in the labor movement, can play a role in bringing on board some unions, or groups of rank-and-file workers from the unions, who can be a part of this movement.

Against the Grain: Let me end by asking you perhaps the hardest question, which is: In thinking about opposing the right and the very serious threats that people are facing in the United States right now, is the greatest threat from fascist groups on the ground, or is the repression of the state a much more serious issue, as we're seeing with the deportations of the undocumented, first under Obama, of course, and now under Trump? And if that's the case, how do we fight that?

Kieran: That's a good question. I don't think that it's either/or. I think that the state is becoming increasingly oppressive. And part of what is allowing that to happen is, even though Trump lost the popular vote, and millions more people didn't vote for either of the candidates, the fact that he did have millions of voters allows him to present a mandate to carry out these actions.

I read a recent article about how Trump was very keen on using his Twitter to unleash action. This wouldn't be formally state action;

he's not necessarily calling on the FBI to go harass one of his critics. But by using social media he's able to unleash a torrent of abuse on whoever he's decided is the enemy of the moment, by his supporters.

So I think that there are two things. There's the danger of increased deportations, increased raids, attacks on the ability of women to get reproductive health care. There are attacks on so many fronts that are going to come from the state, and some moving back by both parties. We have to be aware of that. So we're going to need to form resistance to that.

And then, at the same time, one of the big dangers is that the forces on the ground, people who we might live next to or work with, are going to be organized into right-wing and fascist formations, or at least be soft support for that taking place. I think that some of our tactics and our strategies are similar for both, though. When we talk about organizing community self-defense, that's not just against the fascists, or just against the state, but against whatever attacks come. Even from attacks within the community, from antisocial or sexist or racist elements within the community. So I think that a strategy that we've set for the near term, which is organizing community self-defense, is the method that's needed for both.

For an Antifascist, Revolutionary Unionism

African Peoples Caucus of the Twin Cities Industrial Workers of the World

April 2, 2017

Fascism is a concept that has grown a lot of particular interest since the election of Donald Trump and the failure of neoliberalism. While we don't consider Trump himself to be a fascist but a right-wing populist, we do recognize that he has mobilized a broad coalition of the right, which includes some fascists. However, reactionary violence is nothing new to black and African people living in the United States. Our communities have seen firsthand the terror campaigns of proto-fascist groups such as the KKK, and other kinds of organized white supremacist violence. Our oppression and exploitation have been central to the establishment of modern capitalism in the Americas. This also means we have been fighting back since we were brought here. Our stake in antifascism is not an academic question.

Fascism needs to be defined for our context: right now this is a smaller element participating within a popular front of the right wing. Most notable of this multitendency white nationalist milieu is the alt-right, who believe in atrocities such as "white" ethnic cleansing, misogyny, violence against a perceived "other" (minorities, refugees, Muslims, women, LGBTQIA, Jews), and overwhelming worship of authority and class-based hierarchies. What allows this to spread is that neoliberal economic policies under capitalism cause the working class to suffer, and they are given scapegoats and offered false and authoritarian solutions. The reactionaries' influence within the state will be strengthened, which will increase the suffering of black and African people at the hands of the police, prison, and poverty.

While fascism sometimes spreads using political opportunists like the electoral right wing, it is also an independent movement of the insurgent right wing and has an agenda separate from and opposed to the current state. Fascists also recruit through entryism into popular cultures and subcultures (music, arts, internet groups, faith-based, etc.). Today's fascists have improved the ability to hide within "legitimate" conservative political and social groups. Its spread is international and evident in the Western turn away from neoliberalism toward economic nationalism, Islamophobic motives surrounding Brexit, and the state literally assassinating drug users in the Philippines. Trump is a big piece of this, but definitely not the only one. In addition to being aware of fascists attempting to turn the repressive state apparatus against us, we also have to prepare to defend ourselves against reactionaries like George Zimmerman and Dylann Roof, who have terrorized us with direct extralegal violence since we got here.

It's important that we not let our history of struggle be claimed by the liberal narrative that the Civil Rights era was built on a dogmatic commitment to "nonviolence." Black and African people have had to physically, mentally, and emotionally defend their communities from state and white supremacist terror, and it was organized. Groups like the Deacons for Defense, Black Liberation Army, and Black Panther Party understood why a self-defense approach in the face of police and reactionaries was necessary. If a person knows the bloodshed that occurred at the height of the labor movement, one must also acknowledge there has been consistent violence against black and African people for centuries. Labor organizers and specifically the IWW have long opposed class traitors like the Ku Klux Klan. White supremacists despise the radical left because of their commitment to solidarity with all oppressed people. The IWW will remain a target of the state and the far right, especially as our activity gains momentum and size. The General Defense Committee has been and can continue to be an excellent vehicle to grow the antifascist movement. Antifascism needs to grow into an extremely popular movement in order to win. Communities that build their capacity for organized defense against the state and organized hate will be major contributors to the fight against capitalism.

We black and African workers face this threat in many places within and beyond our workplaces, and a fascist threat to any of the working class is a threat to the entire class. We have no choice but to confront organized white supremacists, just as we have no choice but to struggle against the bosses in our workplaces. We are calling on our comrades in the IWW and elsewhere to join us in confronting white nationalists organizing to direct further violence against our people. We are calling on the General Administration to give our rank-and-file militants the support we need to organize in defense of ourselves and our class on the ground. We believe that the slogan "an injury to one is an injury to all" should also be demonstrated by our white comrades who feel as though confronting fascism is optional or of little importance.

For an antifascist, revolutionary unionism!
Twin Cities IWW African Peoples Caucus

Tigertown Beats Nazis Down: Reflections on Auburn and Mass Antifascism

Three Members of the Atlanta General Defense Committee

Lifelong Wobbly, May 4, 2017

"Outside Agitators"—but Who's Agitating?

The scene in Auburn, Alabama, when we showed up was one of the most bizarre we've ever seen in a political context.[1] Neo-nazi spokesperson Richard Spencer had just been allowed to begin his speech in Foy Hall, after a local judge negated Auburn University's decision to cancel his event. The live stream showed a packed audience, though some were opponents. Outside, there was a large crowd of students and onlookers. Standing in the crowd, looking to our left and right, it was often impossible to tell if our neighbors were spectators, trolls, anti-Spencer Auburn students, college Republicans, or fascists.[2] We were able to identify some people in the crowd as fascists due to their MAGA hats or giant American flags, but they did a much better job of blending in than many of the antifascists did.[3] Many of the antifascists were dressed in black and were armed with helmets and other aspects of the "uniform" that made them stand out from anyone from Auburn.[4] The most visible fascists themselves were already in the auditorium, which meant that for the next several hours, the only visible "outsiders" for the crowd were the antifascists. For people in the crowd, antifascism looked like a specialized thing, while the fascists themselves were abstract and out of sight.

Before we talk more about what happened, let's talk about Alabama and Auburn. It seems unlikely that many antifascists were familiar with Auburn before Spencer's speech was announced or had ever spent time in Alabama. We don't mean to score cheap points here. Obviously, most of us have not been to all parts of the US, and we may not have heard of every city. However, we think that the US left simultaneously ignores and scorns the South in general and the Deep South in particular. Furthermore, Auburn—home to one of Alabama's two main universities—has its own particular culture and significance within Alabama. Think of the biggest deal you can imagine people making about college football—double that, and add a little more for good measure. That's how important football is for Alabama, and Auburn is their number two school. To say the town's culture revolves around football, and the state's culture revolves around the football of the University of Alabama and Auburn University, would be an understatement. Alabama head coach Nick Saban has been called "the most powerful man in Alabama," and that's probably not an exaggeration.[5] Indeed, it seems that one of the biggest missteps Spencer took in Auburn was to speak against Black football players and berate people for supporting them—attacking Auburn football may have galvanized the school and the town against him in a serious way.[6]

There is a dominant stereotype that white people in the Deep South are ignorant conservatives. This stereotype comes from liberal institutions (think of the character Kenneth on *30 Rock*), and it carries over into the left if it is not consciously challenged (which it usually isn't). Of course, this contributes to a hostile or skeptical attitude from Alabamians when there is any engagement. There hasn't been any meaningful left presence in Alabama since the Seventies, and very few attempts by contemporary left groups to engage seriously with Alabama.[7] When the US left spends decades ignoring the Deep South, we are telling ourselves and the rest of the world that we don't believe there's any meaningful organizing to be done there. The right wing doesn't make the same mistake. In Alabama, groups like the League of the South have open meeting halls and billboards by the highway and have announced the formation of a "Southern Defense Force."[8]

This is important because it heavily influences how we approach a situation like this. For those of us who believe in a mass-based, working-class-oriented antifascism, it comes down to some central questions. Can we imagine a mass antifascist movement in Alabama? Can we actually imagine that large numbers of Alabamians would agree with our program and strategy for fighting fascism? Or do we basically think that mass antifascism might theoretically work elsewhere, but not in a place like Alabama?

These questions deserve attention, because they had a huge impact on our orientations toward this situation. Entering unfamiliar terrain with preconceptions about the political territory set up a situation that would characterize the rest of the night—a theatrical production of specialized antifascists versus specialized fascists, where everyone else was just in the way.[9] We saw little talk beforehand about how Auburn students might engage or how we might relate to them. It seems that all of us (present authors included) made decisions based to some degree on a lack of faith in the possibility for mass antifascism in Alabama. Most of us would probably say that we think mass antifascism is an ideal, preferable to a "squad-versus-squad" style of antifascism.[10] However, in practice we tended to write off the possibility that large numbers of Alabamians might actually agree with our program for fighting fascism if we actually presented it to them. If we want to stop the normalization of fascism, then we have to normalize antifascism—even (maybe especially) in places like Alabama.

There were some attempts on our side to preemptively address some of these concerns. We had designed flyers to explain our positions to the crowd, but due to haste and confusion these were not distributed. There had been some attempts on Reddit and elsewhere to connect with folks in Auburn ahead of time, which was a good start, but we should have followed up on them more systematically. By the time Spencer's speech was starting, the damage had been done—the bloc was isolated and pressed between a police barricade and a crowd ranging from indifferent to hostile. Onlookers, potential allies, and low-key fascists were all intermingled in an incoherent mass, with police scattered throughout. Furthermore, it was getting dark, making it harder to talk with people and less likely that people would read or care about flyers. The only clear distinction was between the black-clad antifascist activists (who were visibly not from Auburn) on the one hand and the jumble of people with illegible politics (but generally from Auburn or looking like they could be) on the other.

In short: we treated them like "others" who might get in our way and ruin things for us; is it any wonder they treated us the same?

Auburn's "White Students Union" had been agitating against "Atlanta Antifa" ahead of time. They put up posters around campus warning people against "Atlanta Antifa" as scary outsiders who might attack bystanders. The spectacle that the black bloc provided played right into this.

On the other hand, we have to recognize that there were low-key fascists blended in with the crowd, at some points agitating or "trolling" us quite effectively.[11] This was separate from a noticeable trend of random individuals who had come out to troll for less clear reasons: there were some individuals who seemed to be mostly trying for jokes, but others were in small groups, wearing MAGA hats or carrying flags, and communicating closely with each other. In other words, the fascists attempted to seize the possibility for agitation that we had abandoned. In fact, at some points it did seem that the fascists or trolls were able to influence the crowd, but because they were blending in well, it was tough to determine exactly when this was happening.

"Spectators" Only Exist When Spectacles Produce Them

As we were arriving, we were seeing messages that people felt "trapped" by the crowd, that the crowd was full of "trolls" and "spectators" and "stupid liberals." This seemed improbable to us. When we arrived, we saw more context.

There were several hundred people in the crowd, most of whom looked like traditional Auburn students. Interspersed were small pockets of people dressed in all black. Shortly after we arrived, one of the black-clad people started walking through the crowd, shouting and attempting to agitate it. The crowd quickly felt like it was being yelled at by a person who had obviously marked themselves as separate from the crowd, and it subsequently tensed up.[12] People began to crowd around and heckle this person, filming them at the same time. At one point as tensions rose, it seemed like there could be a fistfight between this white punk-looking antifascist person and a Black person in the crowd—which would have been an absolute disaster the moment it hit the internet.

This was just one early example that antifascists were treating the crowd as the "other" and were displaying antifascism as a specialized activity, not something for Alabamians unfamiliar with urban political scenes to take up and make their own.

The bloc continued to make these kinds of decisions throughout the night—at one point the bloc had managed to maneuver out of the middle of the crowd and down a street. Other people, many of whom looked like frat members, followed closely behind the bloc, seemingly looking for excitement. We worried that as the bloc tried to disperse, some of the people following them might try to pick fights. Luckily, some pigs on bikes zoomed in a divergent direction and led those followers astray, buying the group time and space. The bloc deliberated and decided to head straight back into the crowd, placing themselves again in the middle of things and riling the crowd up in its procession. This time we were sure that violence would break out—only a Holocaust denier stole the show and locals congregated around him instead, mostly to confront him. The bloc consistently reinserted itself into the crowd and made itself the object of spectatorship rather than something the crowd could engage with or, at the very least, accept and act alongside. The spectacle of specialized antifascism undermined the concrete possibility of mass antifascism.

Possibly the most dangerous moment came when about twenty or so people in black were chanting together and were getting hemmed in by the larger crowd. Some of the crowd may have been spectating, some hostile—it's hard to tell. The vibe was already tense when the group began chanting what sounded like "Atlanta, Atlanta, Antifascista."[13] In response, someone in the crowd began an Auburn fight song that none of the out-of-towners knew. Everyone from Auburn immediately joined in, fists pumping, and those of us from out of town were conspicuously silent, confused, vastly outnumbered, pressed in, and scared. It felt like the situation was on the razor's edge of a brawl, which would have ended very, very badly for everyone wearing black. By showing ourselves as outsiders, we handed the MAGA bros an opportunity to throw a punch and start a brawl, potentially with popular support. Luckily, they didn't seize this opportunity. After Berkeley, that would have been an absolute disaster, and a demoralizing turn on the national level.

Tigertown Beats Nazis Down—but the Black Bloc Doesn't

Eventually the fascists had to leave Foy Hall. The police had barricades set up so that the crowd was all along the edge of the path that the fascists took toward the edge of the campus. This was part parade, part walk of shame. As the fascists were parading out in full insignia, our people took the opportunity to rile the crowd up and remind them that these were actual, flesh-and-blood nazis, helping to stir up militant chants along the route. It seems that allowing people to actually see that the nazis were real, not abstract and not a joke, did a lot to reorient the tensions—antifa were no longer the only people who were visibly not from Auburn.

At a certain point, the barricades ended, and the nazis and the crowd met. A confrontation developed directly between some students and the fascists. Some fascists, outnumbered and overpowered, had to flee at a sprint from the students.[14] There were some antifascists there when this started, but they were far outnumbered by the students who chased the fascists off campus and into the downtown area. The militant vanguard of the students seemed to be "good ol' boys," the same type that we had been writing off or at least vaguely wary of the whole night. They not only ran the nazis off campus, they caught up to some of them in the town and pushed, beat, or taunted at least a few of them to chants of "Tigertown beats nazis down." This sudden militancy of the crowd was a victory salvaged from the jaws of defeat; the militant posture of the black bloc was not only completely ineffective, but at several points it led to the edge of disaster. We have to wonder at this point whether the presence of the black bloc had any positive impact.

Pride of Alabama: Victory Belongs to the Auburn Students, Not Us

Before the events, outsiders traveling to Auburn had discussed goals and the roles we could we play as outside militants. At one meeting, we discussed that shutting down the event would probably not be likely. Other goals we discussed were to maintain a radical space and presence and defend it if need be (presumably in some kind of bloc formation). One of us had raised ideas of being among the crowd, with the goal of promoting militancy and resiliency among the crowd, explaining our positions, and building links for future organizing, but this idea did not receive much interest. It seems that the "default" option of going as the bloc was never seriously challenged. In reflection, we think that these goals all assumed that we would be the most militant force present, the most organized and able. We also note that the goals didn't include anything about building relationships with students who were coming out to oppose fascism. Each goal we could imagine, stated or unstated, we failed to meet that day.

We failed, but the Auburn students did not. They were the most militant, the most able. While they weren't organized in any political fashion, loose social networks and an identity around their school allowed them to move quickly and decisively to chase out the fascists from the campus and run them out of town.

This was fundamentally different than previous experiences of "spontaneity" we've witnessed—and parts of it are difficult to reckon with.[15] This was not a preconceived political act from an organized body, nor was it a spontaneous action of oppressed people who feel powerful in a moment. This was mostly "bro"-looking football fans—many of whom we suspect initially attended as spectators—suddenly catapulted into a political act.[16] It's likely that the scene of organized, decked-out neo-nazis riled some students up—they realized this was real, these were really neo-nazis. It's possible that some out-of-town antifascists in the crowd were able to effectively encourage a more militant approach toward the nazis at this point. It's likely many students broke into a run simply because others were running. And it's also possible that the scene of any visible "outsiders"—be it the black bloc, the fascists, or another football team's fans—could have roused a similar sentiment: this is our campus, our town, and outsiders are not welcome.[17]

But what happens when a group of students, with little understanding of the current threat of fascism, with little experience with political protests, not "activists" or even necessarily politically concerned, and many not directly affected by the current threat, find themselves suddenly thrust into a political act? Activity changes consciousness. Many of these students now have an experience of running fascists out of town, an experience they identify with and which will impact their consciousness in unexpected ways in the future.[18]

Lessons
Auburn Ain't Atlanta
One of the central principles of mass antifascism is that "we don't cede territory." This means that we should not just assume that the far right has a monopoly on places like rural Alabama, but instead we should actively seek allies, build relationships, and support the development of an organized anticapitalist, antiracist militancy. Many of us are still defaulting to squad-versus-squad skirmishes, but the fascists are not. The speaking events of Milo or Spencer are about recruiting and

building a mass base for fascism. *We think the most promising way to prevent the development of mass fascism is through mass antifascism. The worst thing we can do right now is to keep insisting on the black bloc as the default tactic. This is the path toward catastrophic failure.*

In order to make friends, we'll have to understand the limits of certain tactics. Black bloc is a tactic, not a strategy or an identity, and a single tactic should never be our default. Instead, we'll have to put our goals up front, then decide on a strategy to achieve those goals, and tactics that might be useful as part of that strategy. Furthermore, those who insist on bringing the "black bloc" identity, regardless of the local context, will end up being obstacles to building a mass antifascist movement. They have to be struggled with, or left behind.[19]

One alternative tactic is to just dress in clothing that won't stand out and mingle throughout the crowd, not appearing to be an organized force.[20] This can provide safety, so that no small group is singled out by police or hostile forces; it can also allow space for comrades to build relationships with people in the crowd, to feel out the mood, and to try to raise the militancy throughout the crowd. We should take seriously the old Maoist idea of being among the people "like fish in the sea." This is something that at least some of the fascists were doing in Auburn, and we can't cede that space to them.

This doesn't mean that the black bloc tactic will never be useful in some situations. Keep a bandanna in your literal and figurative back pocket—or keep two in case someone else needs one. But otherwise, we think we might begin by dressing in a way that doesn't immediately set us apart from the rest of the crowd.

Recovering the Art of the Agitator

Agitating a crowd in a political context isn't the kind of skill that any of us are born with or develop accidentally. When there have been successful labor or socialist movements in the past, this was a skill that movements deliberately trained people in.[21] This is something that we have been mostly ignoring for decades, and we are paying for it now. But we have to begin somewhere.

The picket/guard training that has been developed by the General Defense Committee identifies some possible roles that can apply in a mass public action, such as picket captain, marshal/security, and MC. We think "agitator" should be added to this list as a possible useful role, especially for actions like this one in Auburn or anywhere else where we will be acting within a larger crowd and trying to raise the militancy and resiliency within it. We envision that agitators can work in pairs throughout the crowd, in coordination with each other and other parts of the group, with the goal of raising the temperature of the crowd, encouraging it to defend itself, or supporting any other goals. Working in pairs allows for immediate feedback if something seems not to be working, or to be working well, and also allows for better debriefing (and security). Of course, like with any other "role" there should be some fluidity—it's not to say that only some specialized people will try to agitate the crowd while others don't at all. Rather, it's that some people would be focusing on this while others are focusing on other useful tasks.

A mass approach requires a higher level of coordination. If we're serious about confronting fascism—and doing so in a way that allows for mass engagement and helps develop mass militancy—then we'll need to get serious about group cohesion, group discipline, and accountability. As we mentioned above, at one point there was one person trying to "agitate" the crowd but who only succeeded in agitating them against the black bloc. The movement that we need now has to move beyond that kind of individual, unaccountable behavior.

Communications: One Big Signal Group Isn't Working

It seems that the only plan for communication in Auburn was to put everybody who was coming to town on one Signal group and leave it at that. What this meant was that there was a lot of confusing chatter and there was no plan about how to keep communication focused on essential topics. Furthermore, many people did not know each other, so it was often unclear who was giving certain information or ideas. There were a lot of texts like "Who is 867-5309?" and there were times when it felt like the conversation was totally hijacked by one or two people. Furthermore, if we didn't check it for a few minutes, there might be a hundred messages waiting to be read. It wasn't totally useless, but often close. This should be assessed before future actions. There should be plans for smaller communication groups over a variety of apps and mediums, including walkie-talkie apps or physical walkie-talkies, as well as people who are designated as "runners." Of course, all of this requires actual organization ahead of time.

Avoiding False Lessons

It's Going Down wrote that "it was the ability of the police to control the crowd that allowed Spencer to speak—not the ability of the Alt-Right to hold their ground."[22] Although the article was generally good, we disagree with that point. We don't think the police played the only critical role in controlling the crowd in this situation. Another major factor was the inability of antifascists to actually engage with the crowd. Berkeley and Auburn both require some serious self-criticism and evaluation of our strategies up to this point, and probably a total overhaul of the way we engage in antifascist organizing. We've tried to outline what we think are some key points above, and we'll summarize them again.

First, to prevent fascism from normalizing, we have to normalize antifascism and make it something that people who are not already activists can identify with and find a way to participate in.[23] We have to ditch the black bloc as a uniform. We have to assess each situation in its own context, but we think the default should be to dress like how we expect the crowd to dress, while keeping the bandannas in our back pockets.

Second, to keep fascism from developing a mass base, we need to build a mass base for antifascism. To a large degree, that means organization, both in the day-to-day when we are not physically confronting fascists and on the more tense days when we are. We should approach any confrontation with fascists by setting goals and figuring out the strategy and tactics that will achieve them. This means being organized ahead of an action to apply that strategy. The picket/guard training from the General Defense Committee has a good framework for how to approach this.

We still have the possibility to develop a mass antifascist movement in the US. But time is not favoring us, and if we continue to apply old strategies like always showing up in black bloc, we will begin to see worse and more demoralizing defeats. On the other hand, if we develop our mass approach, we could end up being really surprised by how many people might be open to it. If even Southern, white football "bros" are open to running fascists out of town, then our approach and program could inspire and unite a lot more people than we expect.

Gaming's Three Way Fight: Why Antifascists Should Organize in and around Video Games

M., Roberto Santiago de Roock, and Joel D. Lovos, Members of the Abolitionist Gaming Network

Three Way Fight, February 20, 2023

We're all people who love to play video games. We're also the kind of people who fascists want to run out of video games because we're not straight white men. Recently, some cops and their academic allies have claimed they are going to save us from the fascists in video games; for example, the Department of Homeland Security awarded almost $700,000 in grant money to researchers who are studying how to confront "extremism" in gaming, with a focus on stopping white nationalist recruitment in digital games and the online communities associated with them.[1] We are abolitionists, people who want to abolish police, prisons, and related forms of oppression like digital surveillance, given their role in confining and controlling Black and Indigenous people, working-class people, queer people, and to some degree the rest of society. Given that, we don't think that the cops at the Department of Homeland Security will save anyone from fascists—they're just gonna make the situation worse.

Recently in Atlanta, the police and politicians have used this "confronting extremism" framework to raid and arrest abolitionist activists who are trying to defend the Atlanta forest and stop the development of a militarized police training facility. Several protesters are facing domestic terrorism charges, and one of them, Tortuguita, was murdered by the cops.[2] Antifascists should not support a "confronting extremism" political framework, in games or elsewhere, because it just adds more funding and legitimacy to this kind of repression.

We need to imagine better ways to confront fascists in video games, which are a crucial space of social, cultural, and economic struggle.

However, these spaces are mostly overlooked and often dismissed by abolitionists, antifascists, and other radical activists. We hope to change that.

We see the situation as a three way fight: a conflict between (1) the capitalist carceral state, (2) insurgent fascists challenging that state, and (3) abolitionists and other revolutionaries who need to challenge both the state and the fascists. The authors of the *Three Way Fight* blog point out, for example, that capitalist antifascism isn't necessarily liberatory and "repression isn't necessarily fascist—anti-fascism itself can be a tool of ruling-class repression (as was the case during World War II, when anti-fascism was used to justify strike-breaking and the mass imprisonment of Japanese Americans, among other measures)."[3] We think that abolitionists should organize to oppose *both* fascist recruitment in games *and* capitalist policing of games. In doing so, we can also better leverage the radical histories and possibilities of video games as an arena of abolitionist organizing.

Why Focus on Video Games?

Fascists and cops understand something that the majority of abolitionists and antifascists have not figured out yet: games are an important terrain of political conflict and organizing. As the grant announcement on the Department of Homeland security website puts it,

> Over the past decade, video games have increasingly become focal points of social activity and identity creation for adolescents and young adults. Relationships made and fostered within game ecosystems routinely cross over into the real world and are impactful parts of local communities.... Correspondingly, extremists have used video games and targeted video game communities for activities ranging from propaganda creation to terrorist mobilization and training.[4]

They are not wrong about the political importance of video games. They are just wrong in defining the problem as "extremism" and "terrorism" rather than as fascist mobilization, and of course their solution is just more surveillance and policing. That solution just adds to the problems, since, as we know, surveillance and policing always end up disproportionately targeting marginalized communities instead of fascists.

The left is the only part of the three way fight that's (mostly) not taking games seriously; fascists and the state have both been using games to organize, surveil, etc., as they fight each other and as they fight us. Antifascists should take gaming seriously as a space for learning, organizing, building friendships, imagining liberated futures, practicing skills needed in these futures, and mobilizing both online and in the real world. If we don't do it, the fascists and cops will use games against us.

The left is currently preoccupied debating about Twitter, about whether or not it should be surveilled and controlled and how to stop it from being a haven for white supremacist mob organization. Meanwhile, young people spend far more time on gaming platforms than they do on Twitter.[5] If the left is taking Twitter this seriously, they should be taking games and their related social media platforms even more seriously. Digital gaming has expanded rapidly during the pandemic, and it's been a long time since it was a fringe subcultural phenomenon. At this point, calling oneself a gamer is like calling oneself a music listener or movie watcher. In their report on the rise of extremism in gaming, the Anti-Defamation League asserts, "Gaming plays a huge role in American life: according to the Entertainment Software Association, 75% of American households include at least one gamer, and the video game industry generates more money annually than the film and music industries combined." Among teens, a staggering 97 percent of boys and 83 percent of girls in the US play video games.[6]

Given this rapid expansion of gaming, it's likely that many of the young people who participated in the 2020 George Floyd uprising against police violence probably play games and use them to think, imagine, learn, and socialize. Shouldn't antifascists be trying to connect with them in these scenes and spaces?

Fascists Are Organizing in Games

On the other two sides, mass shooters with fascist white supremacist ideologies have developed their ideologies and tactics in gaming-related platforms like Discord and Twitch. This includes the white supremacist who opened fire at a Buffalo supermarket in May 2022, killing ten. The US military is also increasingly focusing recruiting efforts on video-game-playing teenagers, uses video games for training and morale-building, and developed a series of video games over the last two decades "intended to inform, educate, and recruit prospective soldiers."[7]

Playing games and politics are more closely linked than they first appear, especially when people are using games to practice and train for real-world activities. Given the relative lack of political moderation, fascists who used to organize on broader social media platforms are turning to games as a space to regroup after many of them got kicked off platforms like Facebook. Steam, for example, is the main platform used for buying PC games while also serving as a platform for gamer communities and game content creation, with around 120 million monthly active players. The parent company, Valve, only employs around 360 people. It has very little moderation and so has ended up full of fascist-leaning or outright fascist individuals and groups, including those celebrating school shooters and neo-nazis, among other racist, homophobic, and antisemitic content. Even child-oriented games like *Minecraft* or *Roblox* have become playgrounds for fascists. One survey found that among those who play online multiplayer games, 23 percent were exposed to extremist white supremacist ideology while playing. It is widely known that players with marginalized identities encounter consistent hate and harassment within games and many gamer communities.[8]

Fascists go beyond sowing terror in online games. They also have lots of tactics for organizing within video games and their associated communities. Recruitment is sometimes done through creating new games or game content depicting fascist violence. These games might be stand-alone, modified versions of existing games (mods), or experiences within game-creation platforms like *Roblox* or *Minecraft*. Fascists also use mainstream games. For example, they join a chat, are deliberately provocative, see who responds positively, and then seek to recruit them:

> You'll often get a cell of extremists who will go into a gaming chat room or a party chat in Fortnite or a group in Call of Duty, for instance, and they'll use racial slurs or some other type of extremist content.... They'll monitor the people in those group chats and see who is responding positively with laughter, maybe asking questions about the certain use of these specific extremist terms. And then the people who respond well to that will be invited into a deeper group chat.[9]

The discussions then move onto other platforms, often gamer-adjacent Discord, in which young people are offered membership in a hierarchy—whites against all others—and quickly oriented toward blood-soaked ideology and action.[10] Even when members are not recruited through games, gaming serves as a powerful common ground and reference point, and gamified online harassment "raids" (semi-organized targeted harassment) a popular tactic of terror.

Grassroots versus Capitalist Antifascism

This fascist organizing is being opposed in various ways. Historically, antifascism has been found in an array of grassroots movements associated with broader social dynamics. These have included Black liberation groups like the Black Panther Party and Black Liberation Army, anticolonial movements, insurgent and grassroots movements against US-supported dictators, and class struggle organizations like the Industrial Workers of the World (IWW), along with anarchist, queer liberation, communist, and radical feminist movements throughout the world.[11] Contrary to what Donald Trump and the far right say, antifascism (including antifa) is not an organization; it is an activity that people from many different backgrounds and politics (organized and unorganized) participate in. During the Trump years, antifa was a grassroots movement intertwined with rebellions against the system of racialized capitalism; for example, it was an expression of the George Floyd Rebellion against policing, when people in the streets defended themselves against fascists who attacked them.

While Trump called for violent repression of antifa, the Democratic Party and the liberal wing of the capitalist ruling class have been trying to co-opt antifascist organizing, even as their cops, courts, and prisons still harm people when they actually fight fascists. These ruling-class forces have been trying to refashion themselves as people "defending democracy" from "far-right extremism," asking people to imagine them as a new version of Franklin Delano Roosevelt's Democratic Party that fought the Nazis in World War II. We see this with Biden's speech in fall 2021, which framed Trump's Make America Great Again movement as a fascist threat to democracy. We also see it in some of the rhetoric around the congressional and court investigations into the January 6 riots at the Capitol. In fall 2021, someone influenced by far-right ideologies attacked Democratic Party politician Nancy Pelosi's husband, and in the wake of the attack, the liberal wing of the capitalist class has become more and more aggressive about stopping "domestic extremism."

Many antifascists are trying to resist this co-optation by capitalist politicians. For example, the *Three Way Fight* blog has pointed out how this reemerging capitalist antifascism can become its own form of authoritarianism.

Content moderation and surveillance measures on social media have become major points of political contestation within this emerging conflict between the fascists and the liberal capitalists. We see this of course with the debates over Twitter and calls for the federal government to step in to prevent far-right groups from using the platform to organize now that Elon Musk has allowed them back onto it.

Grassroots versus Capitalist Antifascism in Video Games

This conflict over social media is now beginning to spill over into conflicts over video games. Several prominent researchers have received grants from the Department of Homeland Security to "counter extremism" among young people in video games.[12] The goal seems to be to push the video game industry to implement some kind of content moderation system similar to what Meta has and what Twitter has but seems to be losing under Elon Musk. The far-right media outlet Breitbart wrote a piece calling this left-wing censorship, defending the legacy of Gamergate (a coordinated far-right campaign against women in gaming, which gave the alt-right its blueprint for coordinated online harassment).[13] Game industry leaders are also discussing how to improve content moderation systems based on player feedback and systems for reporting "toxic" behavior, and Maggie Hassan, a member of the Senate's Homeland Security Committee, recently demanded that Valve address the neo-nazi content in its platforms.[14]

Internationally, UNESCO views violent extremism as an issue in need of resolution. Most important to our argument is UNESCO's focus on the internet and social media as solutions, given the ways we view gaming and game-related spaces as powerful social media platforms.[15] While many people look to formalized organizations for guidance, specifically to combat "extremism" in social media (and in this case, video games and game-related spaces), we find their guidance lacking. UNESCO's very own resources seem to point to 404 error pages, which is quite reflective of the ways games are discussed as solutions for fascism—the actual solutions are nonexistent. UNESCO engages with video games as powerful tools, but its engagement is toward "peace and sustainability" or to highlight the learning possible.[16] While these arguments about games are important, so too is addressing the violence that can result from fascism present in games. Thus, video games should not just be about peace, given that this peace is already disrupted by fascism. They can and should be about disruptive combat, a direct tussle with fascism. Furthermore, we can learn alternative ways of combating fascism, particularly from abolitionist gamers, educators, and other antifascist efforts seen in pop culture history.

Problems with Capitalist Antifascism

Researchers who want to be antiracists "doing the work" are suddenly rebranding themselves as "extremism" researchers. Do they realize the implications of what they're getting into?

While it is good to see people taking the issue of fascist mobilization in gaming seriously, we are wary that these interventions could accelerate the surveillance and repression involved with capitalist antifascism. While many of the researchers and game industry leaders leading these efforts are experts in gaming, they are not experienced antifascists with an understanding of the three way fight dynamics outlined above, and they are intervening primarily on behalf of their funders, who want to maintain ruling-class interests: the funders' goal is to secure the profitability of gaming platforms while stabilizing the US racial capitalist state. The researchers are inserting themselves into a potentially armed conflict between the far right and the state without the necessary training or preparation. As a result, they are likely to be manipulated by government and corporate interests who want to make a name for themselves through the grift, corruption, and public posturing associated with decades of War on Terror politics. Such careerist maneuvering may play a role in the repression of the Atlanta forest defenders, which has now escalated into an outright assassination of an environmental/abolitionist protester.[17] The consequences are matters of life and death.

The Role of AI in Surveillance and Content Moderation

There's a debate going on about whether such moderation and surveillance should be done by humans or by artificial intelligence (AI), not just in video games but across the tech industry. This is expressed in a Federal Trade Commission report to Congress, "Combatting Online Harms through Innovation":

> Facebook reportedly uses AI, combined with manual review, to attempt to understand text that might be advocating for terrorism, find and remove terrorist "clusters," and detect new accounts from repeat offenders. YouTube and TikTok report using machine learning or other automated means to flag extremist videos, and Twitter indicates that it uses machine learning and human review to detect and suspend accounts responsible for TVEC [terrorist and violent extremist content]. Moonshot (a tech company) and Google's Jigsaw use the "Redirect Method," which uses AI to identify at-risk audiences and provide them with positive, de-radicalizing content, including pursuant to Google searches for extremist content.[18]

The FTC report points out that academics and government entities have raised concerns about potential invasions of privacy, lack of accuracy, and biased datasets involved in these tools.

Ruha Benjamin, a sociologist at Princeton, has warned that people are essentially creating new forms of racist AI surveillance and algorithmic policing in the name of using AI to counter racism online. She argues it's part of a transition toward decentralized incarceration, or policing through digital platforms and apps. The Stop LAPD Spying Coalition is similarly warning that the whole framework of "countering extremism" is being used against Black, Indigenous, and environmental activists, not just the far right. They've linked that to their organizing against the LAPD's AI-based "predictive policing" model, which uses big data and machine learning to allocate where to send officers based on predicted crime patterns. They have shown how the algorithms are biased and racist.[19]

The FTC report reviews AI research showing that increases in racist speech in online forums in certain cities predicts racist violence in those cities. Some researchers and government officials consider this kind of research a possible use case for AI, allowing people to predict possible waves of real-world violence associated with online hate speech. However, the report ends up doing exactly what Stop LAPD Spying Coalition warns against: it treats antipolice protesters and abolitionists as creators of hate speech and violence, lumping them in with fascists and white supremacist groups who were threatening to kill protesters and sometimes carried out those threats through car attacks and gun violence:

> Internal Facebook documents show that analysts worried that hateful content on the platform might be inciting real-world violence in connection with Minneapolis protests occurring after the police killing of George Floyd. Although it is not clear what precise tools they used, these analysts discovered that "the largest and most combative demonstrations" took place in two zip codes where users reported spikes in offensive posts, whereas harmful content was only "sporadic" in areas where protests had not yet emerged.[20]

That quote cites an article by Bloomberg which says Facebook had a "heat map" of speech it flagged as offensive, and staffers watched as the map turned red in Minneapolis and then eventually turned red across the country as the protests spread. Yet at the same time, Facebook refused to prevent Trump from openly calling for the murder of protesters, when he posted, "When the looting starts, the shooting starts."[21] The attempt to equate the violence of protesters with the violence of the state and fascists who oppose them just plays into the violent repression of abolitionist organizing that Trump and others attempted.

While digital gaming platforms are moderated by humans and algorithms, it seems they are not as strictly moderated as other social media platforms like Facebook. This might be because they are not yet widely seen as political spheres and forms of social media, even though they are. Most moderation is focused on improving or maintaining the quality of gameplay experience. It usually does this only for some players, leaving others, e.g., Black lesbian players, subjected to racist and homophobic interactions during multiplayer gameplay, as game researcher Kishonna Gray has documented extensively.[22]

Toward Abolitionist Antifascism in Gaming

At the grassroots level, gamers are already resisting fascism in various ways; for example, as Kishonna Gray has documented, Black and LGBTQIA+ players have organized themselves to play together in ways that shield each other as much as possible from racist, sexist, and homophobic attacks in multiplayer game forums. In Brazil, people organized to deplatform a fascist gamer group that openly shared contempt toward a Black Brazilian journalist for celebrating Black representation in *Valorant*. This opened up avenues of harassment by the fascist group's fanbase and ultimately led to the mobilization of gamers, journalists, and game developers around the goal of getting the group banned from platforms such as Twitch and YouTube.[23] It's important to note the strategies used, which included protesting in live streams on Twitch, using Twitter to post and share hashtags about the movement, and ultimately sending emails and complaints to the CEO of Xbox and the Brazilian Public Ministry.

While these grassroots efforts are important, they need to go further, building autonomy from the state and capitalist antifascism. We encourage abolitionists and antifascists to engage with games in creative and strategic ways. Here are some possibilities we would like to propose.

Antifascists have a long history of seeing music scenes as important spaces for social and political life, spaces that must be defended and kept free from fascist appropriation and infiltration. For example, antiracist punks and folk fans have tried to run fascists out of their own scenes, and this has provided a sense of community that has enlivened broader antifascist organizing and mobilization in the streets. But if games are just as widespread as music these days, shouldn't they also be contested in similar ways? For example, Anna Anthropy said that making indie games is the new form of zine-making.[24]

Grassroots abolition efforts in fields like education also highlight alternative pathways for abolitionist and antifascist coalition building. While the Abolition Teaching Network focuses on addressing the injustices in schools specifically, its guiding principles on racial injustice and abolitionist social and emotional learning help us imagine and think through tangible abolitionist practices in the classroom, which could be combined with educators' growing efforts to use games as equipment for critical learning and teaching. These efforts are more fruitful than, say, what UNESCO is trying to do.[25]

Anticapitalists can also make our own abolitionist and antifascist games and media, and we can create spaces where more people—especially young people—can learn to do this. These could be video games, tabletop games, theater games, and so on. We can also modify ("mod") existing games to play them in more abolitionist ways, e.g., playing pro-cop riot simulation games with the goal of making the cops lose. The games we make could prompt players to imagine and conjure unpoliced futures, like the abolitionist video game *Kai Unearthed*. Or they could be strategy games that simulate direct actions and ways of avoiding police repression, like the tabletop game *Bloc by Bloc*.[26] They could also help people practice skills needed in abolitionist organizing, including antifascist organizing. Augusto Boal said theater games are "rehearsal for revolution," and the same could be said of video games and tabletop games. We should not make fun of people for LARPing (live action role playing) as revolutionaries, as long as they know when a situation is a game and when it is a real-life conflict with life-or-death consequences (e.g., an actual riot or an actual street brawl with fascists). LARPing in low-stakes settings can be a way for people to practice and to learn from their mistakes so they'll be more prepared to handle situations that are not games, where the consequences for failure are much higher.

For example, a game could model and simulate the three way fight itself. There could be three teams: the capitalist state versus revolutionaries versus insurgent fascists. Each team needs to decide whether to get involved in conflicts between the other two or whether to sit back, observe, and learn from the conflict. Conflicts between each of the three sides can influence the outcome of conflicts between the other two. For example, the state winning against fascists might increase their capacity to win against revolutionaries. Revolutionaries winning against the state might create openings for fascists to practice fighting the state. Conflicts between revolutionaries and insurgent fascists might be used by the state as a pretext to criminalize and repress both. This is just one way that a game could model a revolutionary struggle against fascists and the state.

Closing Thoughts

Abolitionists and antifascists face a daunting task when it comes to the three way fight that is tearing up digital media, including games. Do we organize ourselves to transform existing corporate platforms, or do we build our own digital infrastructure? Do we try to deplatform fascists from these networks, and if so, how? How do we relate to AI in all of this? While these questions may be overwhelming for many, we don't need answers to all of them right away, and we don't need to be advanced hackers, coders, or expert designers to begin to take games seriously. Anyone can choose some games you and your friends like and organize an abolitionist game night, playing the games together in ways that prompt discussions about abolishing police and prisons. And with a range of free and increasingly accessible game design tools like Twine, Unity, and Figma now available, it is easier than ever to learn how to make your own abolitionist game that you can share with your friends. If enough people start doing this sort of thing, we can build robust abolitionist gaming networks that can reclaim games from both the fascists and the capitalists/cops.

From games to the streets, fuck the police!

There Will Always Be More of Us: Antifascist Organizing

Paul O'Banion

Three Way Fight, September 16, 2021

The events of August 22 (A22) in Portland, Oregon, were a clear victory, with hundreds of people turning out all afternoon on the downtown waterfront to confront the fascists—until it suddenly wasn't.

The Proud Boys' last-minute change of location—away from the waterfront to a parking lot a half-hour drive away (and even longer on the bus)—resulted in only a relatively small group in bloc engaging in a courageous but ill-considered attempt to confront them: going where they go, but without the necessary preparation and coordination. It turned into, at best, a shit show. Proud Boys smashed up a couple of vehicles, flipping one on its side, beat the shit out of some folks, and engaged in sustained attacks. Our side mobilized a black bloc of roughly thirty; covered Tiny, one of the far right's main instigators, head-to-toe in paint, stopping his club-wielding charge in its tracks; and attacked a photographer. Despite the relative success of the earlier waterfront mobilization, we didn't end the day looking very good. It's controversial, but optics matter. The narrative that is created about actions we are involved in is critical to our long-term success.

The events of A22 starkly illustrate the limits of fighting fascists on purely military or tactical grounds. For five years, we have battled various fascists, the fascist-adjacent, and fascist-enabling in the Pacific Northwest, with the most brutal part of the whirlwind being Portland (and not for the first time!). Antifascists have done a remarkable job tirelessly defending against incursions, provocations, and attacks by the far right, especially since the 2016 election of Donald Trump. There have been more mobilizations against Patriot Prayer, the Proud Boys, and other knuckleheads than one can remember. Established organizations, such as Rose City Antifa and the Pacific Northwest Antifascist Workers Collective, various crews, affinity groups, and collectives have done exemplary work. Yet, at best, we have achieved a kind of stalemate; at worse, in the larger national and international picture, we are losing.

So how do we start winning? In order to defeat the fascists in a decisive way, we need to subsume our tactical struggle to the political one. Contextualizing street fights as one component of a larger effort keeps our focus on our long-term work to build a free, mutualistic, and egalitarian society. We need people on the front lines with skills in martial arts, first aid, and communications. We need people with hacking and doxing skills. And we need to continue developing material support infrastructure and mutual aid efforts for mobilizations. All of this is essential. But A22 showed us that, in and of itself, all of this will never be enough.

If we only develop the skills to make us a better fighting force, the fascists will outmaneuver us on the larger terrain and continue to build their movement. To complement our ability to deny the fash the streets and public platforms, we need to better contest their attempt to win sympathy for their ideas. This means continuing the longer-term, less glamorous work of organizing, talking with other working-class and oppressed people, developing ideas together—in short, creating a broad, popular movement aimed at fundamentally remaking society, getting at the roots of what gives rise to fascism in the first place. We should be able to respond to the questions that the far right is answering with our own alternative: a movement and liberatory culture that is so attractive to everyday people that they can't resist the urge to become involved. Efforts toward establishing "everyday antifascism" as commonplace is one example.

Politics partly involves developing a shared narrative that helps people make sense of the world. This is what the fascists are doing: they are providing stories that help people understand what is going on, providing a sense of meaning and belonging that is both comforting and supports taking action in the world. We too need to keep our focus on the big picture, on winning in the long term. Our goal should be creating a broad-based popular movement to help create a nonfascist society. By developing our politics together and collectively envisioning what we want and how we think we can best get there, perhaps we will also gain more discipline as a movement—the kind of discipline that allows us *not* to rush into situations unprepared, disorganized, and uncoordinated, to fight the fash on terrain they chose. We need the power and momentum to pick our battles.

What happens in the street is essential. Fascists, on principle, should not be allowed to gather, organize, or speak publicly. But *how* we do that will determine whether we win the larger war, not just one particular battle. How these confrontations play out to those watching from their workplaces, neighborhoods, bars, and homes is of the utmost importance in determining whether the majority of folks side with us or support state and fascist violence against us.

The antifascist struggle in Germany is more practically and theoretically advanced, mainly because they've been doing it longer. As Bender, an autonomous antifa militant active in Berlin since the 1980s, says,

> The most important step [is] to get organized in groups, which would have regular meetings and a clear membership ... a common basis of understanding and common goals, and a clear name. These groups would be approachable for others outside the group, and capable of and willing to engage in alliances, they also could take better care of new, interested people.... The groups would also represent their positions publicly in a way that was open to participation.

Bender continues that antifascists should not fight fascists alone, stressing the importance of "temporary alliances with other groups outside the autonomous movement, such as other leftist groups, trade unions ... and so on." But in collaborating with groups that may not share all of our politics, it is necessary "to maintain *our* positions and *our* forms in these alliances. That means to have—at least on a symbolic level—an autonomous standpoint and a radical expression, for example at demonstrations, by using the politics and tactics of the black bloc."[1]

Those in autonomous antifa came to realize that they were becoming marginalized and isolated and that the larger narrative matters, which led them to understanding "the importance of better public relations and being concerned with media representation." Bender suggests that we can recognize the role media plays in maintaining the status quo and institutional power while still engaging it "to produce

pictures for the public, which nowadays has become, due to the mechanism of media and politics, part of the 'society of the spectacle.'"[2]
This requires us to be smart about how society works, how people
come to form opinions, and how everyday working people come to
be willing to take risks to fight fascism. It doesn't mean toning down
the level of militancy but better understanding the dynamics of how
these confrontations are represented.

An International Struggle

With the dizzying momentum of authoritarian movements around the
world and, closer to home, the relentless march of far-right Trumpist
Republicans, we need to understand our struggle as not only local, but
national and international. This requires us, as the far right is doing,
to mobilize and organize a mass, popular movement. In this practical
struggle and war of ideas, the fact that being antifascist or believing
that Black lives matter are even controversial positions indicates that
we are not even close to winning. One of our tasks is to develop antifascism as the "common sense." If we do this, we can marginalize and
limit the growth of fascism, better enabling us to defeat it.

There are plenty of historical examples we can learn from in developing the antifascist movement. We can look at the organizing that
brought out hundreds of thousands of people to defend the largely
Jewish East End of London against a fascist march in 1936: the famous
"Battle of Cable Street." At that time, members of the Jewish and
Irish communities, local workers and Labour and Communist Party
members, anarchists, antifascists, socialists, and pissed-off Londoners
all came out to the streets to fight Oswald Mosley, leader of the British
Union of Fascists (BUF), and his three thousand Blackshirts, not to
mention the six thousand police marshaled to protect them. The
reason up to three hundred thousand people mobilized and stood up
to Mosley and his fascists on that day is made clear in *The Battle of
Cable Street: An Account of Working Class Struggles against Fascism*,
published by the London Trades Union Council SERTUC:

> A common cause of hatred of Fascism brought people together.
> Charlie Goodman made a name for himself during the battle
> when he climbed up a lamp post, exhorting people to fight back
> as they began to waver, and described one alliance: "it was not

just a question of Jews being there, the most amazing thing was to see a silk-coated Orthodox Jew standing next to an Irish docker with a grappling iron. This was absolutely unbelievable. Because it was not a question of … a punch up between the Jews and the Fascists, it was a question of people who understood what Fascism was."[3]

We can also look at how Rock Against Racism organized, also in England, this time in the late 1970s against the National Front, working with the Anti-Nazi League to turn out tens of thousands of people in antiracist festivals that made being against fascism part of popular culture, doing so in a fun, engaging, and welcoming way. This is also the approach of today's PopMob (Popular Mobilization) in Portland, Oregon, an organization that has succeeded on several occasions in turning out large numbers of people in part by creating a welcoming and safe place for new and uninitiated folks to come and take a stand. All this complements and backs up frontline fighters and those in bloc, which PopMob is explicit about. As PopMob spokesperson Effie Baum points out,

> Without the black bloc, we would not be safe out there because they are the ones who are protecting us from both the violence of the far right as well as the violence from the police, because they are the brave ones who put their bodies between us and those threats. So, the reason that we also have this big tent approach is because we do include that in our diversity of tactics. And I want folks … when they're out there, they will also see firsthand the truth, which is that they are being protected by people who are engaged in community defense and that it's not what they're seeing on TV.[4]

We can better win our battles with fascists in part by turning out far greater numbers than them. To do this well, we need to reach out beyond those already convinced of the need for militant antifascism, going outside our scenes and comfort zones, having difficult conversations, developing politics with a wider group of people than are currently involved.

Examples of what this approach looks like on the ground here in the US include the broad-based antifascist mobilization against the

Unite the Right rally in Charlottesville, Virginia, in 2017, which turned out thousands of people; the work in the Bay Area that saw ten thousand folks, including a huge black bloc, show up to confront the "No to Marxism" rally planned in Berkeley later that same month; and in Portland, in August 2018, when well over a thousand people marched against Patriot Prayer and other fascists behind a well-organized black bloc of several hundred.

Always Be More of Us

The first time I physically confronted nazis was in Minneapolis in the early 1990s. I was strolling through the streets of Uptown with two comrades I was just getting to know. Our afternoon was suddenly interrupted when a teenager ran up and said, "Hey Kdog, you used to be a Baldie, right?" Kdog responded, "I still am a Baldie!" Our young friend excitedly told us he was just hanging out on the train tracks when two older dudes showed him their swastika tattoos and told him to "tell his friends that they are back." This was just after the Baldies, an antiracist skinhead crew that helped initiate Anti-Racist Action (ARA), had successfully kicked nazi boneheads out of Minneapolis. Kdog quickly rounded up a crew of twenty people, and we headed to the train tracks. Scouts up ahead spotted the nazis, shouting back to the rest of us. The nazis hightailed it up and off the tracks and back into the streets. We finally surrounded them in a grocery store parking lot; I had a half brick in my hand, and we backed them into the store.

In that moment, with everyday American life swirling all around us, I thought how strange this was: a running battle between us, a motley crew of anarchists, punks, antiracist skins, and disaffected youth, versus a couple of scraggly older nazis. I felt a connection to the historic struggle between antifascism and fascism that has flared up across the last century, mobilizing millions. But here we were, on this warm sunny afternoon, a few dozen of us with crude improvised weapons in a grocery store parking lot, confronting nazis while complacent America went about its business. That confrontation between a handful of antifascist militants and a couple of nazis has now grown far larger. We need to adjust accordingly. The street fights that Anti-Racist Action once engaged in now play out on a national and international level. These fights are no longer only between fascist and antifascist subcultures. They involve all of society.

Our task is to better relate to the larger working class and other oppressed communities, listen to what they are also going through, and develop solidarity, mutual aid, and common understandings while building power together. We can crush the fascists with numbers, sharing a collectively generated vision of a new society, figuring out how we get there along the way. Our fight against fascism is political, against *their* politics and for *ours*. We need to better develop and clarify just what our politics are.

The ongoing discussions and debates among antifa, and in sympathetic aligned movements such as anarchism, Indigenous resistance, queer and trans liberation, and the environmental movement, in addition to fora such as this, need to spread among our coworkers, neighbors, friends, and family.

During that altercation in Minneapolis, those two disheveled nazis briefly emerged through the automatic doors of the grocery store to show us their faces and yell, "The only reason you won is 'cause there's more of you than us!" To which Kdog immediately responded, "There'll always be more of us than you!" And that's what we should remember: there will always be more of us than them, but only if we out-organize them.

Afterword

Michael Staudenmaier

For these concluding thoughts, I want to go back to the beginning. That is, to the origins of the three way fight framework: the horrors of September 11, 2001, and their terrifying aftermath. For those of us who lived through those shocking experiences as militant antifascists, many previous assumptions had to be reconsidered. Most pivotally, instead of defaulting to an us-versus-them mindset in which antiracists faced off against racists, we quickly realized we were confronted with a world of "Them, Them, and Us," in the words of the BRICK Collective, which I had helped found a year earlier.[1]

At the time, I was also a member of the Chicago branch of the Anti-Racist Action Network (ARA), which rapidly began to comprehend that a suddenly new and radically different era had begun on September 11. Many anti-imperialists in the North American left failed to ask, much less attempt to answer, what it meant that the most significant attack on the global power of the United States in at least a generation came from the right, not from the left.[2]

ARA, however, was struck by this unexpected reality and immediately recognized it needed to oppose both al-Qaeda and US imperialism. A brief formal statement from the network, approved at its annual conference in October 2001, pointed out that "historically, fascism is built from above and below" and stated bluntly that "we do not believe that the perpetrators on September 11 acted in the real interests of the people, and we do not believe that [President George W.] Bush is acting to protect anyone from terrorism with this war, itself an act of terror against the Afghani people."[3]

Still, geopolitical analysis is not the same thing as real-world understanding, and the days after 9/11 offered painful, practical experience of the impact of the three way fight for those of us active in Chicago ARA. Starting the day after the September 11 attacks, the Mosque Foundation, a site of worship in the diverse, working-class Chicago suburb of Bridgeview, became a target for Islamophobic attacks. Hundreds of angry young men, most white and many waving American flags, were blocked by police as they tried to march on the mosque.[4]

The protests continued for a few more nights, and Chicago ARA speculated that some of the instigators might well have been members of the local fascist groups which we monitored and opposed. In hopes of documenting and denouncing their involvement, and also perhaps lending modest public support to the mosque's membership in the face of rampant Islamophobia, a dozen members of Chicago ARA mobilized in multiple cars to drive to Bridgeview on the night of Thursday, September 13.

Upon arrival, we realized the crowd was massive and volatile. Most of us did not even attempt to leave our vehicles, viewing it as too dangerous. A handful of small confrontations took place, including the confiscation by a Chicago ARA member of a Confederate flag held by one of the protesters. But recognizing that we could not effectively defend ourselves, particularly several members of color who could easily have been targeted with racist violence by the mob, much less provide any assistance to the mosque or its members, we retreated to the parking lot of a strip mall a few blocks away and eventually went home.

The whole experience was upsetting, scary, and depressing, but it was also instructive. The white supremacist mob gathered in Bridgeview that night was a premonition of the white nationalism that has become ubiquitous since the Trump era. As with the alt-right, the protesters' relationship with the institutional guardians of white supremacy was confused. They waved hundreds of United States flags (and, as noted above, at least one Confederate flag) proudly, while militantly confronting local police, who in turn took on the task of preventing them from attacking the mosque.

Importantly, however, the crowd in Bridgeview remained "system loyal" on a global level, as the prominence of the US flag made crystal clear. They offered a full-throated endorsement of violent retribution by the US military against pretty much any target in the broader Arab and Muslim worlds. Meanwhile, the long global shadow of al-Qaeda loomed over our local reality, demonstrating the danger of revolutionary insurgencies from the right, aiming to disrupt US imperialism not in service of liberation but instead in furtherance of an ultrareactionary and violent theocracy.

Caught in the crossfire, ARA struggled to respond. What we witnessed in Bridgeview, alongside many other challenges in the aftermath of 9/11, helped several of us begin to think about fascism differently. The ideas we and others explored in the following years proved controversial, as many antifascists preferred to stick to their binary frameworks.

More than two decades later, it is worth revisiting the politics of the three way fight, reexamining the relationships between Them, Them, and Us. The essays in this book will serve us well as we undertake this effort. Beyond the many powerful insights contained elsewhere in these pages, I'd like to close with a couple of suggestions for contemporary antifascists trying to navigate this complicated terrain.

First, the far right today, globally and in North America, is larger, more dynamic, and far more dangerous than it was at the time of 9/11. To fight it successfully will require the collective action of masses of people against the threat of fascism and reaction. If the three way fight has value, it will be demonstrated in real-world struggles.

Second, don't behave as if you know everything or that you have some special access to a correct analysis. The three way fight is not an ideology or a fixed political line. It is a framework that can be used to interpret a world in flux, in service to a revolutionary struggle for a truly free society.

The years ahead are likely to feature yet more unanticipated changes that will force militant antifascists to again rework our theory and our practice. Hopefully, the three way fight will help us continue to think critically and carefully, and to act collectively and courageously, in the conflicts to come.

Notes

Editors' note: When a note is written in the first person, it is in the voice of the essay's author(s).

Introduction

1   Three Way Fight, "About Three Way Fight," *Three Way Fight*, July 15, 2013, updated November 12, 2017, http://threewayfight.blogspot.com/p/about.html.

2   See Shannon Clay, Lady, Kristin Schwartz, and Michael Staudenmaier, *We Go Where They Go: The Story of Anti-Racist Action* (PM Press, 2023).

3   Sojourner Truth Organization, "Theses on Fascism," April 1981, published in *Urgent Tasks*, no. 13 (Spring 1982), reprinted in this volume. On STO see Michael Staudenmaier, *Truth and Revolution: A History of the Sojourner Truth Organization, 1969–1986* (Oakland: AK Press, 2012).

4   J. Sakai, *Settlers: The Mythology of the White Proletariat from Mayflower to Modern*, 4th ed. (Montreal: Kersplebedeb Publishing, and Oakland: PM Press, 2014); Butch Lee, *The Military Strategy of Women and Children* (Montreal: Kersplebedeb Publishing, 2003); Butch Lee and Red Rover, *Night-Vision: Illuminating War & Class on the Neo-colonial Terrain*, 2nd ed. (Montreal: Kersplebedeb Publishing, 2017); and Bromma, *Exodus and Reconstruction: Working-Class Women at the Heart of Globalization* (Montreal: Kersplebedeb Publishing, 2012), http://kersplebedeb.com/posts/exodus.

5   See Wayne Price, "A History of North American Anarchist Group Love & Rage," *Northeastern Anarchist*, no. 3 (Fall 2001), available at https://theanarchistlibrary.org/library/wayne-price-a-history-of-north-american-anarchist-group-love-rage.

6   See Sara Diamond, *Spiritual Warfare: The Politics of the Christian Right* (Boston: South End Press, 1989); Sara Diamond, *Roads to Dominion: Right-Wing Movements and Political Power in the United States* (New York: Guilford Press, 1995); Chip Berlet, *Right Woos Left: Populist Party, LaRouchite, and Other Neo-fascist Overtures to Progressives, and Why They Must Be Rejected* (Cambridge, MA: Political Research Associates, 1994); and Chip Berlet and Matthew N. Lyons, *Right-Wing Populism in America* (New York: Guilford Press, 2000).

7   "International Militant Anti-fascist Network Launch Statement," *Anti-Fascist Forum*, no. 3 (1998): 42–44, available at https://issuu.com/randalljaykay/docs/antifaforum1998number3124. See also Mark Bray, *Antifa: The Anti-fascist Handbook* (Brooklyn, NY: Melville House, 2017), 59.

8   Anti-Fascist Forum, ed., *My Enemy's Enemy: Essays on Globalization, Fascism and the Struggle against Capitalism*, 3rd ed. (Montreal: Kersplebedeb Publishing, 2003).

9   Don Hamerquist et al., *Confronting Fascism: Discussion Documents for a Militant Movement*, 2nd ed. (Montreal: Kersplebedeb Publishing, 2017).

10   See the following articles on *Three Way Fight*: C. Berneri, "Brief Report on Toledo Anti-NSM Protest," December 12, 2005, http://threewayfight.blogspot.com/2005/12/this-was-forwarded-to-us.html; "Roundup of Lansing Anti-NSM News," April 24, 2006, http://threewayfight.blogspot.com/2006/04/round-up-of-lansing-anti-nsm-news.html; Larry Bradshaw and Lorrie Beth Slonsky, "Eye Witness Accounts by Two Paramedics in New Orleans: Hurricane Katrina—Our Experiences," September 6, 2005, http://threewayfight.blogspot.com/2005/09/i-received-following-article-from.html; "Info on Iraqi Federation of Trade Unions (IFTU) and UFPJ Tour," June 17, 2005, http://threewayfight.blogspot.com/2005/06/info-on-iraqi-federation-of-trade.html; and "Women Protest in Iran—Call for Rights," June 13, 2005, http://threewayfight.blogspot.com/2005/06/women-protest-in-iran-call-for-rights.html.

11   See the following articles on *Three Way Fight*: Don Hamerquist, "Responding to Stan Goff's 'Debating a NeoCon,'" December 15, 2004, http://threewayfight.blogspot.com/2004/12/responding-to-stan-goffs-debating.html; "Interview from Beating Fascism: Anarchist Anti-fascism in Theory and Practice," October 26, 2005, http://threewayfight.blogspot.com/2005/10/interview-from-beating-fascism.html, originally published as "Anti-fascism Now, Kate Sharpley Library, Class War and 'Three Way Fight,'" in *Beating Fascism: Anarchist Anti-fascism in Theory and Practice*, ed. Anna Key (London: Kate Sharpley Library, 2005); Francis, "'¡Que se Vayan Todos': Venezuela's Anarchists and the Three-Way Fight," July 28, 2005, http://threewayfight.blogspot.com/2005/07/que-se-vayan-todos-venezuelas.html; and Matthew N. Lyons, "Notes on Women and Right-Wing Movements," pts. 1 and 2, September 27, 2005, and October 1, 2005, http://threewayfight.blogspot.com/2005/09/notes-on-women-and-right-w_112787003380492443.html and http://threewayfight.blogspot.com/2005/10/notes-on-women-and-right-wing.html.

12   See the following on *Three Way Fight*: RX, "France on Fire: North African Youth Riots," November 4, 2005, http://threewayfight.blogspot.com/2005/11/france-on-fire-north-african-youth.html; RX, "Revolt in Oaxaca," October 31, 2006, http://threewayfight.blogspot.com/2006/10/revolt-in-oaxaca.html; Francis, "Hindu Fascism," December 8, 2006, http://threewayfight.blogspot.com/2006/12/hindu-fascism.html; Matthew N. Lyons, "Hindu Nationalism: An Annotated Bibliography of Online Resources," June 3, 2008, http://threewayfight.blogspot.com/2008/06/hindu-nationalism-annotated.html; C. Alexander, "Election Spurs 'Hundreds' of Race Threats, Crimes," November 17, 2008, http://threewayfight.blogspot.com/2008/11/election-spurs-hundreds-of-race-threats.html; and C. Alexander, "Militant Anti-abortion Activity, the Patriot Movement, & the Christian Right," June 4, 2009, http://threewayfight.blogspot.com/2009/06/militant-anti-abortion-activity-patriot.html.

13   See the following on *Three Way Fight*: Matthew N. Lyons, "Defending My Enemy's Enemy," August 3, 2006, http://threewayfight.blogspot.com/2006/08/defending-my-enemys-enemy.html; Don Hamerquist, "Islamic Radicalism and the Left," August 9, 2006, http://threewayfight.blogspot.com/2006/08/on-islamic-radicalism-and-left.html; Matthew N. Lyons and Bromma, "Islamic Fundamentalism and the Three-Way Fight: An Exchange," October 14, 2007, http://threewayfight.blogspot.com/2007/10/islamic-fundamentalism-and-three-way.html; Don Hamerquist, "Capitalism in Crisis?," September 25, 2008, http://threewayfight.blogspot.com/2008/09/capitalism-in-crisis.html; "Dave Ranney Comments on 'Capitalism in Crisis?,'" October 2, 2008, http://threewayfight.blogspot.com/2008/10/dave-ranney-comments-on-capitalism-in.html; C. Alexander, "Potentials and Pitfalls: Debate on the Global Economic Crisis and the Three Way Fight," October 10, 2008, http://threewayfight.blogspot.com/2008/10/potentials-and-pitfalls-debates-on.

html; and Don Hamerquist, "Thinking and Acting in Real Time and a Real World," January 27, 2009, http://threewayfight.blogspot.com/2009/01/thinking-and-acting-in-real-time-and.html.

14 See for example the following on *Three Way Fight*: Matthew N. Lyons, "Frazier Glenn Miller, Nazi Violence, and the State," May 8, 2014, http://threewayfight. blogspot.com/2014/05/frazier-glenn-miller-nazi-violence-and.html; Matthew N. Lyons, "Far Rightists Divided on Coronavirus and Trump," March 19, 2020, http:// threewayfight.blogspot.com/2020/03/far-rightists-divided-on-coronavirus.html; Three Way Fight, "Multiracial Far Right: A Conversation with Daryle Lamont Jenkins and Cloee Cooper," September 14, 2019, http://threewayfight.blogspot. com/2019/09/multiracial-far-right-conversation-with.html; Matthew N. Lyons, "Review of Robyn Marasco's 'Reconsidering the Sexual Politics of Fascism,'" July 14, 2021, http://threewayfight.blogspot.com/2021/07/review-of-robyn-marascos-reconsidering.htm; Matthew N. Lyons, "Liberalism's Limits: A Review of Burghart and Zeskind's Tea Party Nationalism," May 30, 2011, http://threewayfight.blogspot. com/2011/05/liberalisms-limits-review-of-burghart.html; and Matthew N. Lyons, "Major Report on Red-Brown Alliances from New Anarchist Website," February 4, 2018, http://threewayfight.blogspot.com/2018/02/major-report-on-red-brown-alliances.html.

15 RX, "Cursory Thoughts on Armies, Insurrection, and the Sixth," *Three Way Fight*, August 4, 2005, http://threewayfight.blogspot.com/2005/08/cursory-thoughts-on-armies.html.

16 Matthew N. Lyons, "Rightists Woo the Occupy Wall Street Movement," *Three Way Fight*, November 8, 2011, http://threewayfight.blogspot.com/2011/11/rightists-woo-occupy-wall-street.html; Matthew N. Lyons, "Occupy Movement: Anticapitalism versus Populism," *Three Way Fight*, December 6, 2011, http://threewayfight.blogspot. com/2011/12/occupy-movement-anti-capitalism-versus.html; and Matthew N. Lyons, "Feds + Corporate America versus the Occupy Movement," *Three Way Fight*, January 1, 2013, http://threewayfight.blogspot.com/2013/01/fbi-versus-occupy-movement.html.

17 See Matthew N. Lyons, "Oath Keepers, Ferguson, and the Patriot Movement's Conflicted Race Politics," *Three Way Fight*, August 28, 2015, http://threewayfight. blogspot.com/2015/08/oath-keepers-ferguson-and-patriot.html; Matthew N. Lyons, "Cooptation as Ruling Class Strategy," *Three Way Fight*, June 23, 2020, http://threewayfight.blogspot.com/2020/06/cooptation-as-ruling-class-strategy. html; and Ben Lorber, "A Constellation of Threats: Far Rightists Respond to the Black-Led Uprising," *Three Way Fight*, July 19, 2020, http://threewayfight.blogspot. com/2020/07/a-constellation-of-threats-far.html. The boogaloo bois were a loose far-right paramilitary network that sought to provoke a civil war in the United States and engaged in physical attacks on police. Some members of the network were white supremacists, some avoided taking a position on race, but others presented themselves as supporters of Black Lives Matter.

18 See for example the following articles by Matthew N. Lyons on *Three Way Fight*: "Trump's Impact: A Fascist Upsurge Is Just One of the Dangers," December 22, 2015, http://threewayfight.blogspot.com/2015/12/trumps-impact-fascist-upsurge-is-just.html; "Trump: 'Anti-political' or Right Wing?," March 15, 2016, http:// threewayfight.blogspot.com/2016/03/trump-anti-political-or-right-wing.html; and "Some Thoughts on Fascism and the Current Moment," July 7, 2019, http:// threewayfight.blogspot.com/2019/07/some-thoughts-on-fascism-and-current.html.

19 See the following articles by Matthew N. Lyons: "AlternativeRight.com: Paleoconservatism for the 21st Century," *Three Way Fight*, September 10, 2010, http:// threewayfight.blogspot.com/2010/09/alternativerightcom-paleoconservatism. html; "Rising Above the Herd: Keith Preston's Authoritarian Anti-statism," *New*

Politics, April 29, 2011, https://newpol.org/rising-above-herd-keith-prestons-authoritarian-anti-statism; "Jack Donovan on Men: A Masculine Tribalism for the Far Right," *Three Way Fight*, November 23, 2015, http://threewayfight.blogspot.com/2015/11/jack-donovan-on-men-masculine-tribalism.html; "Calling Them 'Alt-Right' Helps Us Fight Them," *Three Way Fight*, November 22, 2016, http://threewayfight.blogspot.com/2016/11/calling-them-alt-right-helps-us-fight.html; "Alt-Right: More Misogynistic than Many Neonazis," *Three Way Fight*, December 3, 2016, http://threewayfight.blogspot.com/2016/12/alt-right-more-misogynistic-than-many.html; "Ctrl-Alt-Delete: The Origins and Ideology of the Alternative Right," Political Research Associates and Kersplebedeb Publishing, January 2017, https://politicalresearch.org/2017/01/20/ctrl-alt-delete-report-on-the-alternative-right; and "An Alt Right Update," Political Research Associates, August 7, 2017, https://politicalresearch.org/2017/08/07/an-alt-right-update.

20   Niko Georgiades, "Ex-Marine Linked to Minneapolis Mass Shooting Shared War Gore and Murder Fantasies after Trial," *Unicorn Riot*, April 26, 2019, https://unicornriot.ninja/2019/ex-marine-linked-to-minneapolis-mass-shooting-shared-war-gore-and-murder-fantasies-after-trial; Associated Press, "Portland: Man Convicted of Murder in Stabbing Deaths of Two Men on Train," *Guardian*, February 22, 2020, https://www.theguardian.com/us-news/2020/feb/22/portland-train-stabbing-jeremy-christian-convicted-murder; and Twin Cities General Defense Committee, "Shooter of Unarmed Anti-racist Walks Free; Authorities Silent," Twin Cities General Defense Committee, January 25, 2017, https://twincitiesgdc.org/2017/01/25/seattleshootingpr2.

21   Christopher Mathias, "After Fights and Arrests, Richard Spencer Speaks to Tiny Crowd at Michigan State," *HuffPost*, March 5, 2018, https://www.huffpost.com/entry/richard-spencer-michigan-state_n_5a9d8eafe4b0479c0255e2b6; Shane Burley, "The Fall of the Alt-Right Came from Antifascism," *Salon*, April 15, 2018, https://www.salon.com/2018/04/15/the-fall-of-the-alt-right-came-from-anti-fascism_partner; and R.J. Wolcott, "White Nationalist Richard Spencer Blames Violent Protesters for Small Crowd at MSU," *Lansing State Journal*, March 5, 2018, https://www.lansingstatejournal.com/story/news/local/2018/03/05/richard-spencer-michigan-state/397727002.

22   Three Way Fight, "Understanding A22 PDX: Discussion and Analysis for the Antifascist Movement," *Three Way Fight*, August 29, 2021, http://threewayfight.blogspot.com/2021/08/understanding-a22-pdx-discussion-and.html, and following posts, including Paul O'Banion, "There Will Always Be More of Us: Antifascist Organizing," *Three Way Fight*, September 16, 2021, reprinted in this volume, and Matthew N. Lyons, "Strategies to Defend Abortion Access: Three Essays," *Three Way Fight*, July 19, 2022, http://threewayfight.blogspot.com/2022/07/strategies-to-defend-abortion-access.html.

23   See "From the Perspectives on Anarchist Theory Journal Collective, an Interview with German Antiauthoritarian Antifascists," *Three Way Fight*, August 29, 2019, http://threewayfight.blogspot.com/2019/08/from-perspectives-on-anarchist-theory.html; Matthew N. Lyons, "Rape, the State, and the Far Right in India," *Three Way Fight*, February 10, 2013, http://threewayfight.blogspot.com/2013/02/rape-state-and-far-right-in-india.html; and Matthew N. Lyons, "Threat or Model? U.S. Rightists Look at China," *Three Way Fight*, April 20, 2020, http://threewayfight.blogspot.com/2020/04/threat-or-model-us-rightists-look-at.html, reprinted in this volume.

24   See for example Kristian Williams, "Comment on Foucault and the Iranian Revolution: The Philosopher and the Ayatollah; 'A Perplexing Affinity,'" *Three Way Fight*, February 28, 2020, http://threewayfight.blogspot.com/2020/02/comment-on-foucault-and-iranian.html.

25   Michael Staudenmaier and Anne Carlson, "Of Chavistas and Anarquistas: Brief
      Sketch of a Visit to Venezuela," Anarkismo.net, July 3, 2005, https://www.anarkismo.
      net/newswire.php?story_id=839&region=southamerica&results_offset=20; Francis,
      "'¡Que se Vayan Todos': Venezuela's Anarchists and the Three-Way Fight"; Bromma,
      "Notes on XXIst Century Socialism," *Three Way Fight*, August 2, 2007, http://
      threewayfight.blogspot.com/2007/08/notes-on-xxist-century-socialism.html; and
      Matthew N. Lyons, "Far Rightists Divided over Hugo Chávez," *Three Way Fight*,
      March 24, 2013, http://threewayfight.blogspot.com/2013/03/far-rightists-divided-
      over-hugo-chavez.html.
26   See the following articles by Matthew N. Lyons on *Three Way Fight*: "Defending
      My Enemy's Enemy," August 3, 2006, http://threewayfight.blogspot.com/2006/08/
      defending-my-enemys-enemy.html; "Further Thoughts on Hezbollah," August 26,
      2006, http://threewayfight.blogspot.com/2006/08/further-thoughts-on-hezbollah.
      html; and "Right-Wing Anti-imperialists Are Not Promoting Feudalism: A Reply to
      Michael Karadjis," October 10, 2006, http://threewayfight.blogspot.com/2006/10/
      right-wing-anti-imperialists-are-not.html. For critical responses to "Defending My
      Enemy's Enemy," see Max, "Hizbullah Victorious Again," *Ideas for Action*, August
      16, 2006, http://ideasforaction.blogspot.com/2006/08/hizbullah-victorious-again-
      to-get.html; Rami El-Amine, "Anti-Arab Racism, Islam, and the Left," *MR Online*,
      September 3, 2006, https://mronline.org/2006/09/03/anti-arab-racism-islam-and-
      the-left. See also the exchange between Michael Staudenmaier and Rami El-Amine,
      "The Three Way Fight Debate: Challenges for the Left," *Upping the Anti*, no. 5
      (October 2007): 115–42; and Matthew Lyons, "Defending the Three Way Fight
      Perspective" (letter), *Upping the Anti*, no. 6 (May 2008): 14–17.
27   See the following articles by Matthew N. Lyons on *Three Way Fight*: "Ukraine's
      Upheaval: Between Fascists, Neoliberals, and Kremlin Tools," February 28, 2014,
      http://threewayfight.blogspot.com/2014/02/ukraines-upheaval-between-fascists.
      html; "Who Are Ukraine's Fascists?," March 4, 2014, http://threewayfight.blogspot.
      com/2014/03/who-are-ukraines-fascists.html; and "U.S. Fascists Debate the
      Conflict in Ukraine," March 12, 2014, http://threewayfight.blogspot.com/2014/03/
      us-fascists-debate-conflict-in-ukraine.html.
28   Three Way Fight, "Antifascist Resources on Ukraine," *Three Way Fight*, March
      2, 2022, updated April 3, 2022, http://threewayfight.blogspot.com/2022/03/
      antifascist-resources-on-ukraine.html; and Matthew N. Lyons, "No Longer a
      Gendarme for the West: Simon Pirani on Russia's Invasion of Ukraine," *Three
      Way Fight*, June 11, 2022, http://threewayfight.blogspot.com/2022/06/no-longer-
      gendarme-for-west-simon.html.
29   As a reflection of this disagreement, when It's Going Down posted a debate on
      whether anarchists should support the Ukrainian resistance to Russia's invasion,
      both sides in the debate referenced three way fight politics or authors to bolster
      their arguments. See "No War but Class War: Against State Nationalism and Inter-
      imperialist War in Ukraine," It's Going Down, April 13, 2022, https://itsgoingdown.
      org/no-war-but-class-war-against-state-nationalism-and-inter-imperialist-war-in-
      ukraine; and "A Response on Ukraine and 'No War but Class War,'" It's Going Down,
      April 14, 2022, https://itsgoingdown.org/a-response-on-ukraine.
30   See Don Hamerquist, "New Stuff from an Old Guy—Part 2," *Three Way Fight*,
      October 28, 2018, http://threewayfight.blogspot.com/2018/10/new-stuff-from-
      old-guy-part-2.html.
31   See the following by Don Hamerquist on *Three Way Fight*: "Thinking and Acting in
      Real Time and a Real World," January 27, 2009; "Barack, Badiou, and Bilal al Hasan,"
      January 24, 2010, http://threewayfight.blogspot.com/2010/01/barack-badiou-and-
      bilal-al-hasan.html; and "New Stuff from an Old Guy—Part 1," October 23, 2018,
      http://threewayfight.blogspot.com/2018/10/new-stuff-from-old-guy-part-1.html.

32 Don Hamerquist, "Distinguishing the Possible from the Probable: Contending Strategic Approaches within and against Transnational Capitalism," Kersplebedeb, June 14, 2020, https://kersplebedeb.com/posts/distinguishing-the-possible-from-the-probable-contending-strategic-approaches-within-and-against-transnational-capitalism, reprinted in this volume.

33 Hamerquist, "Thinking and Acting."

34 Don Hamerquist, "Fascism & Anti-fascism," in Hamerquist et al., *Confronting Fascism*.

35 Don Hamerquist, "New Stuff from an Old Guy—Part 3," *Three Way Fight*, November 12, 2018, http://threewayfight.blogspot.com/2018/11/new-stuff-from-old-guy-part-3.html.

36 See for example Coordinating Committee of Bring the Ruckus, "A Three-Cornered Fight: Tasks of American Revolutionaries in the Twenty-First Century," Bring the Ruckus, December 1, 2003, available at https://theanarchistlibrary.org/library/coordinating-committee-of-bring-the-ruckus-a-three-cornered-fight; and Geert Dhondt, Joel Olson, et al., "Debates on Fascism," Bring the Ruckus, October 10, 2008, available at https://theanarchistlibrary.org/library/ruckus-collective-debates-on-fascism.

37 See for example It's Going Down, "Lockdowns, the Insurgent Far Right, and the Future of Antifascism: A Conversation with *Three Way Fight*," It's Going Down, December 3, 2020, reprinted in this volume.

38 See for example Rebel Jay C. Cornelius and Insurgente s.c. Rocinante, "Three-Way Fight: Armed Resistance and Militant Anti-fascism," Anarkismo.net, November 3, 2006, https://web.archive.org/web/20170314114047/http://www.anarkismo.net/newswire.php?story_id=4091 and its revised version, J. Clark, "Three-Way Fight: Revolutionary Anti-fascism and Armed Self-Defense," in *Setting Sights: Histories and Reflections on Community Armed Self-Defense*, ed. scott crow (Oakland: PM Press, 2018), 49–67; Devin Zane Shaw, *Philosophy of Antifascism: Punching Nazis and Fighting White Supremacy* (London: Rowman & Littlefield, 2020); Paul Bowman, "Fascism and the Three-Way Fight," *Medium*, February 4, 2022, https://eidgenossen.medium.com/fascism-and-the-three-way-fight-4a05b87a4eec; Natasha Lennard, "Far-Right Violence Is Going to Be a Threat with or without Trump's Calls to Action," *Intercept*, January 5, 2021, https://theintercept.com/2021/01/05/trump-rally-far-right-violence; Shane Burley, ed., *¡No Pasarán! Antifascist Dispatches from a World in Crisis* (Chico, CA: AK Press, 2022); and Paul Messersmith-Glavin, "Interview with Shane Burley," Institute for Anarchist Studies, October 28, 2022, https://www.anarchistagency.com/critical-voices/paul-messersmith-glavin-interview-with-shane-burley-editor-of-no-pasaran-antifascist-dispatches-from-a-world-in-crisis.

39 CrimethInc., "CrimethInc. West Coast Tour: December 2019," CrimethInc., November 19, 2019, https://crimethinc.com/2019/11/19/crimethinc-west-coast-tour-december-2019-from-democracy-to-freedom-the-new-upheavals; Steven Gardiner and Tarso Luís Ramos, "Capitol Offenses: January 6 2021 & the Ongoing Insurrection," Political Research Associates, January 12, 2022, https://politicalresearch.org/2022/01/12/capitol-offenses-january-6th-2021-ongoing-insurrection. See also Matthew N. Lyons's response to Gardiner and Ramos, "Caution Doesn't Make Us Safe: A Review of PRA's Report on the MAGA Movement," *Three Way Fight*, February 17, 2022, http://threewayfight.blogspot.com/2022/02/caution-doesnt-make-us-safe-review-of.html.

40 The Race Traitor political tendency, associated with the journal *Race Traitor* (1993–2005), centers on the idea that abolishing the white race (as a socially constructed system of privileges) is strategically crucial for human liberation in the United States.

Fascism and Antifascism: A Decolonial Perspective

1 This essay has been revised for publication in this volume. The website has recently

been retitled the Spectral Archive and can be found at https://onkwehonwerising. wordpress.com.

2   Roger Griffin and Matthew Feldman, *Fascism: Critical Concepts in Political Science* (London: Routledge, 2004).

3   Georgi Dimitrov, "The Fascist Offensive and the Tasks of the Communist International in the Fight for the Unity of the Working Class against Fascism," in *The Fascist Offensive & Unity of the Working Class* (Paris: Foreign Languages Press, 2020), 1–79.

4   Zak Cope, *Divided World, Divided Class: Global Political Economy and the Stratification of Labour under Capitalism* (Montreal: Kersplebedeb Publishing, 2015), 294.

5   Communist International, *The Programme of the Communist International, Together with the Statutes of the Communist International* (London: Modern Books, 1932).

6   Cope, *Divided World*, 294.

7   Gilles Dauvé, "Notes on Trotsky, Pannekoek, Bordiga," Theory and Practice, 1973, available at https://libcom.org/article/notes-trotsky-pannekoek-bordiga-gilles-dauve; Leon Trotsky, "What Is Fascism: Extracts from a Letter to a Comrade," *Militant* 5, no. 3 (1932): 4; and Leon Trotsky, *Fascism: What It Is and How to Fight It* (New York: Pathfinder Press, 1996), 34. While Dimitrov represented the official line of the Comintern under Stalin's leadership, many dissident Leninists held to analyses of fascism that were quite similar in their basic arguments. Leon Trotsky, for example, while emphasizing the particular role of the middle classes as a mass base of fascism, concludes similarly to Dimitrov in noting that the "historic function of fascism is to smash the working class, destroy its organizations, and stifle political liberties when the capitalists find themselves unable to govern and dominate with the help of democratic machinery" and that it is "directed and financed by big capitalist powers." Similarly, the Italian left-Leninist Amadeo Bordiga argued that fascism and democracy were merely variations on the theme of rule by capital, and that democracy both bred fascism and called it to its rescue.

8   Don Hamerquist, "Fascism & Anti-fascism," in *Confronting Fascism: Discussion Documents for a Militant Movement*, by Don Hamerquist et al., 2nd ed. (Montreal: Kersplebedeb Publishing, 2017), 28.

9   Hamerquist, "Fascism & Anti-fascism."

10   J. Sakai, "The Shock of Recognition: Looking at Hamerquist's Fascism & Anti-fascism," in Hamerquist et al., *Confronting Fascism*, 96.

11   Sakai, "Shock of Recognition," 115.

12   Matthew N. Lyons, "Two Ways of Looking at Fascism," *Socialism and Democracy* 22, no. 2 (2008).

13   Matthew N. Lyons, *Insurgent Supremacists: The U.S. Far Right's Challenge to State and Empire* (Oakland: PM Press, and Montreal: Kersplebedeb Publishing, 2018), ii–iii.

14   Lyons, *Insurgent Supremacists*, iii.

15   Cope, *Divided World*, 294.

16   Aimé Césaire, *Discourse on Colonialism* (New York: Monthly Review Press, 2000), 13.

17   Césaire, *Discourse on Colonialism*, 14.

18   Hamerquist, "Fascism & Anti-fascism"; Cope, *Divided World*; Sakai, "Shock of Recognition."

19   Lorenzo Veracini, *Settler Colonialism: A Theoretical Overview* (London: Palgrave Macmillan, 2014); and Patrick Wolfe, "Settler Colonialism and the Elimination of the Native," *Journal of Genocide Research* 8, no. 4 (2006): 387–409.

20   Wolfe, "Settler Colonialism," 393.

21   Stephen Pearson, "'The Last Bastion of Colonialism': Appalachian Settler Colonialism

and Self-Indigenization," *American Indian Culture and Research Journal* 37, no. 2 (2013): 165–84.

22   Ward Churchill, *A Little Matter of Genocide: Holocaust and Denial in the Americas, 1492 to the Present* (San Francisco: City Lights Books, 1997).

23   Nicolás Juárez, "To Kill an Indian to Save a (Hu)Man: Native Life through the Lens of Genocide," *Wreck Park*, no. 1 (2014).

24   Juárez, "To Kill an Indian."

25   Patrick Wolfe, *Traces of History: Elementary Structures of Race* (London: Verso, 2016), 40–41.

26   Audra Simpson, "The State Is a Man: Theresa Spence, Loretta Saunders and the Gender of Settler Sovereignty," *Theory & Event* 19, no. 4 (2016).

27   Leslie G. Espinoza and Angela P. Harris, "Embracing the Tar-Baby: LatCrit Theory and the Sticky Mess of Race," in *Critical Race Theory: The Cutting Edge*, ed. Richard Delgado and Jean Stefancic, 2nd ed. (Philadelphia: Temple University Press, 2000), 440–47; Saidiya V. Hartman, *Scenes of Subjection: Terror, Slavery, and Self-Making in Nineteenth-Century America* (New York: Oxford University Press, 1997); Frank B. Wilderson, *Red, White & Black: Cinema and the Structure of U.S. Antagonisms* (Durham, NC: Duke University Press, 2010); Lewis R. Gordon, *Bad Faith and Antiblack Racism* (Atlantic Highlands, NJ: Humanities Press, 1995); and Ruth Wilson Gilmore, *Golden Gulag: Prisons, Surplus, Crisis, and Opposition in Globalizing California* (Berkeley: University of California Press, 2007).

28   Loïc Wacquant, "Deadly Symbiosis: When Ghetto and Prison Meet and Mesh," *Punishment & Society* 3, no. 1 (2001): 95–133; and Loïc Wacquant, "Class, Race & Hyperincarceration in Revanchist America," *Daedalus* 139, no. 3 (2010): 74–90.

29   Wilderson, *Red, White & Black*.

30   Gordon, *Bad Faith and Antiblack Racism*.

31   Karl Marx, *Capital, Volume 1* (New York: Vintage, 1977), 915.

32   Glen Sean Coulthard, *Red Skin, White Masks: Rejecting the Colonial Politics of Recognition* (Minneapolis: University of Minnesota Press, 2014), 8–9; Peter Kropotkin, *The Conquest of Bread and Other Writings* (Cambridge: Cambridge University Press, 1995), 221; Rosa Luxemburg, *The Accumulation of Capital* (London: Routledge, 2003), 348–49.

33   Wolfe, "Settler Colonialism," 388.

34   Chris Chen, "The Limit Point of Capitalist Equality: Notes toward an Abolitionist Antiracism," *Endnotes*, no. 3 (2013).

35   Jodi A. Byrd, *The Transit of Empire: Indigenous Critiques of Colonialism* (Minneapolis: University of Minnesota Press, 2011), 38.

36   Stephen Pearson, "'Enter the Amerikaner Free State': The Alt Right and Settler Colonialism," *Journal of Labor and Society* (forthcoming).

37   Pearson, "'Enter the Amerikaner Free State.'"

38   Amadeo Bordiga and Edek Osser, "Against Anti-fascism: Amadeo Bordiga's Last Interview," *Storia Contemporanea*, no. 3 (1973).

39   Eve Tuck and Wayne K. Yang, "Decolonization Is Not a Metaphor," *Decolonization: Indigeneity, Education and Society* 1, no. 1 (2012): 1–40.

40   Amílcar Cabral, *Revolution in Guinea: Selected Texts* (New York: Monthly Review Press, 1972).

Antifascism against Machismo: Gender, Politics, and the Struggle against Fascism

1   Ana Maria Tijoux, "We Can't Think of a Feminism, an Anti-patriarchy, without Anti-capitalism," Committee on US-Latin American Relations, March 8, 2017, https://cuslar.org/2017/03/10/ana-tijoux-we-cant-think-of-a-feminism-an-anti-patriarchy-without-anti-capitalism.

2   "How Anti-fascists Won the Battles of Berkeley—2017 in the Bay and Beyond: A Play-by-Play Analysis," CrimethInc., January 3, 2018, https://crimethinc.com/2018/01/03/how-anti-fascists-won-the-battles-of-berkeley-2017-in-the-bay-and-beyond-a-play-by-play-analysis.

3   Liz Fekete, "Anti-fascism or Anti-extremism?" *Race & Class* 55, no. 4 (2014): 29–39.

4   Jason Wilson, "What Do Incels, Fascists and Terrorists Have in Common? Violent Misogyny," *Guardian*, May 4, 2018, https://www.theguardian.com/commentisfree/2018/may/04/what-do-incels-fascists-and-terrorists-have-in-common-violent-misogyny.

5   Greg Wilford, "Heather Heyer: Charlottesville Neo-Nazi Rally Organizer Describes Protester's Death as 'Payback,'" *Independent*, August 20, 2017, http://www.independent.co.uk/news/world/americas/jason-kessler-charlottesville-virginia-white-supremacist-rally-heather-heyer-payback-communist-a7903381.html.

6   Maya Oppenheim, "GoDaddy Bans Neo-Nazi Site Daily Stormer for Defaming Charlottesville Victim Heather Heyer," *Independent*, August 14, 2017, http://www.independent.co.uk/life-style/gadgets-and-tech/daily-stormer-godaddy-bans-charlotteville-victim-heather-heyer-victim-fat-slut-defame-uva-neo-nazi-a7891856.html.

7   Cloee Cooper and Julia Taliesin, "White Nationalist Groups Turn Up at 2018 Women's Marches," Political Research Associates, February 2, 2018, https://politicalresearch.org/2018/02/02/white-nationalist-groups-turn-up-at-2018-womens-marches.

8   Roy Batty, "Womyn Throw Protest on International Womyn's Day," *Daily Stormer*, 2018, https://dailystormer.name/womyn-throw-protest-on-international-womyns-day (site discontinued).

9   Maja Sager and Diana Mulinari, "Safety for Whom? Exploring Femonationalism and Care-Racism in Sweden," *Women's Studies International Forum* 68 (2018): 149–56.

10   "We Are Not Afraid: Chilean Feminism Rises in the Face of Fascist Attacks—Black Rose/Rosa Negra Statement on Opposing the Fascist Attacks and Stabbing of Three Feminist Activists in Chile," Black Rose Anarchist Federation, July 26, 2018, http://blackrosefed.org/we-are-not-afraid-chilean-feminism.

11   Joseph Luger, "Cultural Marxism is the #1 Enemy of Western Civilization," *Western Mastery*, March 23, 2017, http://www.westernmastery.com/2017/03/23/cultural-marxism-is-the-1-enemy-of-western-civilization.

12   Nicole Loroff, "Gender and Sexuality in Nazi Germany," *Constellations* 3, no. 1 (2011): 49–61.

13   Matthew N. Lyons, "Ctrl-Alt-Delete: The Origins and Ideology of the Alternative Right," Political Research Associates, January 20, 2017, https://politicalresearch.org/2017/01/20/ctrl-alt-delete-report-on-the-alternative-right.

14   Theodore Koulouris, "Online Misogyny and the Alternative Right: Debating the Undebatable," *Feminist Media Studies* 18, no. 4 (2018): 755.

15   Spencer Sunshine, "Three Pillars of the Alt Right: White Nationalism, Antisemitism, and Misogyny," Political Research Associates, December 4, 2017, https://politicalresearch.org/2017/12/04/three-pillars-of-the-alt-right-white-nationalism-antisemitism-and-misogyny.

16   Matthew N. Lyons, "The Alt-Right Hates Women as Much as It Hates People of Colour," *Guardian*, May 2, 2017, https://www.theguardian.com/commentisfree/2017/may/02/alt-right-hates-women-non-white-trump-christian-right-abortion.

17   Aja Romano, "How the Alt-Right's Sexism Lures Men into White Supremacy," *Vox*, April 26, 2018, https://www.vox.com/culture/2016/12/14/13576192/alt-right-sexism-recruitment.

18   Angela Nagle, *Kill All Normies: Online Culture Wars from 4chan and Tumblr to Trump and the Alt-Right* (Alresford, UK: Zero Books, 2017).

19   Lyons, "Ctrl-Alt-Delete."

20 Matthew N. Lyons, "Alt-Right: More Misogynistic than Many Neonazis," *Three Way Fight*, December 3, 2016, http://threewayfight.blogspot.com/2016/12/alt-right-more-misogynistic-than-many.html.

21 Romano, "How the Alt-Right's Sexism Lures Men into White Supremacy."

22 Matt Lees, "What Gamergate Should Have Taught Us about the 'Alt-Right,'" *Guardian*, December 1, 2016, https://www.theguardian.com/technology/2016/dec/01/gamergate-alt-right-hate-trump.

23 Amelia Tait, "Spitting out the Red Pill: Former Misogynists Reveal How They Were Radicalized Online," *New Statesman*, February 28, 2017, https://www.newstatesman.com/long-reads/2017/02/reddit-the-red-pill-interview-how-misogyny-spreads-online.

24 Lyons, "Ctrl-Alt-Delete."

25 Nagle, *Kill All Normies*, 91.

26 Nagle, *Kill All Normies*, 88–89.

27 It's Going Down, "The Rich Kids of Fascism: Why the Alt-Right Didn't Start with Trump, and Won't End with Him Either," It's Going Down, December 16, 2016, https://itsgoingdown.org/rich-kids-fascism-alt-right-didnt-start-trump-wont-end-either.

28 Alex DiBranco, "Mobilizing Misogyny," Political Research Associates, March 8, 2017, https://politicalresearch.org/2017/03/08/mobilizing-misogyny.

29 Nagle, *Kill All Normies*, 92.

30 Nagle, *Kill All Normies*, 92–93.

31 Jeff Sparrow, "From Misery to Misogyny: Incels and the Far Right," *Overland*, April 27, 2018, https://overland.org.au/2018/04/from-misery-to-misogyny-incels-and-the-far-right.

32 Zoe Williams, "'Raw Hatred': Why the 'Incel' Movement Targets and Terrorises Women," *Guardian*, April 25, 2018, https://www.theguardian.com/world/2018/apr/25/raw-hatred-why-incel-movement-targets-terrorises-women.

33 Zack Beauchamp, "Incel, the Misogynist Ideology That Inspired the Deadly Toronto Attack, Explained," *Vox*, April 25, 2018, https://www.vox.com/world/2018/4/25/17277496/incel-toronto-attack-alek-minassian.

34 Nellie Bowles, "Jordan Peterson, Custodian of the Patriarchy," *New York Times*, May 18, 2018, https://www.nytimes.com/2018/05/18/style/jordan-peterson-12-rules-for-life.html.

35 Bromma, *Exodus and Reconstruction: Working-Class Women at the Heart of Globalization* (Montreal: Kersplebedeb Publishing, 2012), http://kersplebedeb.com/posts/exodus.

36 Hannah Gais, "The Alt-Right Doesn't Know What to Do with White Women," *New Republic*, October 17, 2017, https://newrepublic.com/article/145325/alt-right-doesnt-know-white-women.

37 Sunshine, "Three Pillars of the Alt Right."

38 Matthew N. Lyons, "Jack Donovan on Men: A Masculine Tribalism for the Far Right," *Three Way Fight*, November 23, 2015, http://threewayfight.blogspot.com/2015/11/jack-donovan-on-men-masculine-tribalism.html.

39 *The Unquiet Dead: Anarchism, Fascism, and Mythology* (self-pub., 2017), 11.

40 Shane Burley, *Fascism Today: What It Is and How to End It* (Chico, CA: AK Press, 2017), 51.

41 Burley, *Fascism Today*, 91.

42 Matthew N. Lyons, "Notes on Women and Right-Wing Movements—Part One," *Three Way Fight*, September 27, 2005, http://threewayfight.blogspot.com/2005/09/notes-on-women-and-right-w_112787003380492443.html.

43 Lyons, "Jack Donovan on Men."

44 Jack Smith, "The Women of the 'Alt-Right' Are Speaking Out against Misogyny. They'd Prefer Absolute Patriarchy," *Mic*, December 8, 2017, https://www.mic.

com/articles/186675/the-women-of-the-alt-right-are-speaking-out-against-misogyny-theyd-prefer-absolute-patriarchy.

45   George Michael, "David Lane and the Fourteen Words," *Politics, Religion & Ideology* 10, no. 1 (2011): 43–61.

46   Kathleen M. Blee, "Women in the 1920s' Ku Klux Klan Movement," *Feminist Studies* 17, no. 1 (1991): 57–77.

47   Loroff, "Gender and Sexuality in Nazi Germany," 50.

48   Helen Zia, "White Power Women," *Washington Post*, April 7, 1991, https://www.washingtonpost.com/archive/opinions/1991/04/07/white-power-women/a30050ed-cf61-46e2-a11f-3b2df977ea08.

49   Southern Poverty Law Center, "National Socialist Movement," Southern Poverty Law Center, accessed January 31, 2023, .

50   Women for Aryan Unity, "Mission Statement," Women for Aryan Unity, no date, archived at https://web.archive.org/web/20190305201827/http://www.wau14.com/mission-statement. The phrase "Race and Revolution" was later changed on the WAU website to "Folk and Revolution." See "About WAU," Women for Aryan Unity, accessed December 1, 2022.

51   Dean Cornish, "Whining Men: 'We're Blamed for Everything,'" News.com.au, July 4, 2018, https://www.news.com.au/lifestyle/real-life/true-stories/whining-men-were-blamed-for-everything/news-story/e2c27c0f6e5590e9f0373cd08cc09340.

52   @proudboysgirls, Twitter, https://twitter.com/proudboysgirls (account suspended).

53   David Futrelle, "'Gina Tingles' and the Elders of Zion: Do Alt-Rightists Hate Women as Much as They Hate Jews?" *We Hunted the Mammoth*, June 14, 2017, https://www.wehuntedthemammoth.com/2017/06/14/gina-tingles-and-the-elders-of-zion-do-alt-rightists-hate-women-as-much-as-they-hate-jews.

54   Lyons, "Alt-Right: More Misogynistic than Many Neonazis."

55   Gais, "Alt-Right Doesn't Know What to Do With White Women."

56   Posts on the *Daily Stormer* website argue things such as: women who have sex with Black men deserve "swift and rapid extermination" via death squads; Brown men are "deranged savages" who are indefensible except in cases where they "beat the shit out of" their "bitch" girlfriends; men need the right to beat their daughters so they don't become "dumb sluts"; and "women have become complete sociopaths that collectively deserve to be punished and punished severely."

57   Lyons, "Ctrl-Alt-Delete."

58   Donna Minkowitz, "Hiding in Plain Sight: An American Renaissance of White Nationalism," Political Research Associates, October 26, 2017, https://politicalresearch.org/2017/10/26/hiding-in-plain-sight-an-american-renaissance-of-white-nationalism.

59   Sunshine, "Three Pillars of the Alt Right."

60   Minkowitz, "Hiding in Plain Sight."

61   Chris Schiano, "Leaked: A Year inside the Failed Neo-Nazi Traditionalist Worker Party," *Unicorn Riot*, April 5, 2018, https://www.unicornriot.ninja/2018/leaked-a-year-inside-the-failed-neo-nazi-traditionalist-worker-party.

62   A.C. Thompson, "Inside Atomwaffen as It Celebrates a Member for Allegedly Killing a Gay Jewish College Student," *ProPublica*, February 23, 2018, https://www.propublica.org/article/atomwaffen-division-inside-white-hate-group.

63   James Kirchick, "A Thing for Men in Uniforms," *New York Review of Books*, May 14, 2018, https://www.nybooks.com/online/2018/05/14/a-thing-for-men-in-uniforms.

64   Clay Bodnar, "Gay Men and the Alternative Right: An Overview," *Hope Not Hate*, April 11, 2018, https://hopenothate.org.uk/2018/04/11/gay-men-alternative-right-overview.

65   Johann Hari, "The Strange, Strange Story of the Gay Fascists," *Huffington Post*,

October 21, 2008, updated May 25, 2011, https://www.huffpost.com/entry/the-strange-strange-story_b_136697.

66 Laurie Marhoefer, "Queer Fascism and the End of Gay History," *Notches*, June 19, 2018, https://notchesblog.com/2018/06/19/queer-fascism-and-the-end-of-gay-history.

67 Hari, "The Strange, Strange Story of the Gay Fascists."

68 Michael Abernethy, "Oxymorons: Gay Nazi, Gay Aryan, Gay Supremacist," *Pop Matters*, March 22, 2009, https://www.popmatters.com/72054-oxymorons-gay-nazi-gay-aryan-gay-supremacist-2496038330.html.

69 Bodnar, "Gay Men and the Alternative Right."

70 NYC Antifa, "New York's Alt Right (Part II)," NYC Antifa, December 6, 2016, https://nycantifa.wordpress.com/2016/12/06/new-yorks-alt-right-part-ii.

71 Donna Minkowitz, "How the Alt-Right Is Using Sex and Camp to Attract Gay Men to Fascism," *Slate*, June 5, 2017, https://slate.com/human-interest/2017/06/how-alt-right-leaders-jack-donovan-and-james-omeara-attract-gay-men-to-the-movement.html.

72 Kirchick, "Thing for Men in Uniforms."

73 James J. O'Meara, "The Rebirth of the Männerbund in Brian De Palma's *The Untouchables*," Counter-Currents Publishing, April 11, 2012, https://www.counter-currents.com/2012/04/brian-de-palmas-the-untouchables.

74 Lyons, "Jack Donovan on Men."

75 Minkowitz, "How the Alt-Right Is Using Sex and Camp."

76 Rose City Antifa, "The Wolves of Vinland: A Fascist Countercultural 'Tribe' in the Pacific Northwest," Rose City Antifa, November 7, 2016, https://rosecityantifa.org/articles/the-wolves-of-vinland-a-fascist-countercultural-tribe-in-the-pacific-northwest.

77 Nora Caplan-Bricker, "How a Bunch of Clowns Shut Down Anti-migrant Vigilantes in Finland," *Slate*, February 1, 2016, https://slate.com/human-interest/2016/02/a-bunch-of-clowns-shut-down-anti-migrant-vigilantes-in-finland.html.

78 Cindy Casares, "Trump's Repeated Use of the Mexican Rapist Trope Is as Old (and as Racist) as Colonialism," NBC News, April 7, 2018, https://www.nbcnews.com/think/opinion/trump-s-repeated-use-mexican-rapist-trope-old-racist-colonialism-ncna863451.

79 Jamelle Bouie, "The Deadly History of 'They're Raping Our Women,'" *Slate*, June 18, 2015, https://slate.com/news-and-politics/2015/06/the-deadly-history-of-theyre-raping-our-women-racists-have-long-defended-their-worst-crimes-in-the-name-of-defending-white-womens-honor.html.

80 Johannah May Black, "When Women Bear the Nation's Honour: Fascism and the Woman-as-Symbol under Trump," *Revolutionary Anamnesis*, February 3, 2017, https://johannahmayblack.com/2017/02/03/when-women-bear-the-nations-honour-fascism-and-the-woman-as-symbol-under-trump.

81 Suvi Keskinen, "The 'Crisis' of White Hegemony, Neonationalist Femininities and Antiracist Feminism," *Women's Studies International Forum* 68 (2018): 157–63.

82 Angela Davis, *Women, Race & Class* (New York: Random House, 1983), 107–8.

83 Davis, *Women, Race & Class*, 109.

84 Jackie Wang, "Against Innocence: Race, Gender, and the Politics of Safety," *LIES: A Journal of Materialist Feminism* 1 (2012): 164.

85 Andrea Smith, *Conquest: Sexual Violence and American Indian Genocide* (Durham, NC: Duke University Press, 2005), 10.

86 Smith, *Conquest*, 23.

87 Joane Nagel, "Ethnicity and Sexuality," *Annual Review of Sociology* 26 (2000): 122.

88 Caitlin Carroll, "The European Refugee Crisis and the Myth of the Immigrant Rapist," *Europe Now Journal*, July 6, 2017, https://www.printfriendly.com/p/g/wmsRa6.

89 "Italian and Polish Neo-Nazis Join Forces to Patrol Beaches to 'Protect Women from Migrants,'" *Freedom*, July 6, 2018, https://freedomnews.org.uk/2018/07/06/

italian-and-polish-neo-nazis-join-forces-to-patrol-beaches-to-protect-women-from-migrants.

90 Miriam Lafontaine, "La Meute Cancels Protest at Montreal Mosque Friday," *Link*, December 14, 2017, https://thelinknewspaper.ca/article/la-meute-cancels-protest-at-montreal-mosque-friday.

91 Minkowitz, "How the Alt-Right is Using Sex and Camp."

92 Sally R. Munt, "Gay Shame in a Geopolitical Context," *Cultural Studies* 33, no. 2 (2019): 223–48.

93 Shon Faye, "'We're Here, We're Queer, We're Racists," Zed Books, February 15, 2017, archived at https://web.archive.org/web/20210516031659/https://www.zedbooks.net/blog/posts/were-here-were-queer-were-racists.

94 Christine Hanhardt, *Safe Space: Gay Neighborhood History and the Politics of Violence* (Durham, NC: Duke University Press, 2013), 223.

95 *The Unquiet Dead*, 7.

96 Isabelle Richet, "Women and Antifascism: Historiographical and Methodological Approaches," in *Rethinking Antifascism: History, Memory and Politics, 1922 to Present*, ed. Hugo García et al. (New York: Berghahn Books, 2016), 152–66.

97 CeCe McDonald is a Black transwoman who was attacked by a nazi in June 2011. McDonald and a group of friends were confronted by another group of people spewing racist and transphobic remarks at them. One of the women in the other group smashed a glass in McDonald's face and punched her. After a fight between the two groups broke out, the woman's ex-boyfriend assaulted McDonald, whose face was already bleeding from the glass, and threw her into the street. The man, with fists clenched, began pursuing McDonald. She quickly pulled a pair of scissors from her purse and stabbed the man in the chest as he lunged toward her. The man died. He was later found to have a swastika tattooed on his chest. She went to prison for nineteen months of her forty-one-month sentence, despite having obviously been defending herself against a racist, transphobic nazi who was threatening her life.

98 This dynamic of disregarding women's political activities is made worse by the fact that there is generally less documentation of women's involvement. Women were more likely to be illiterate and thus unable to write down their ideas and experiences. And even if they were literate, they were less likely to have the opportunity or time to record their thoughts. Furthermore, so much of antifascist history (at least in the period around the Second World War) was recorded by traditional political organizations and their leaderships, from which women were most often excluded.

99 There are so many amazing stories of queer antifascists. While outside of the scope of this article, I wanted to include at least one demonstrative example. Raad van Verzt (Resistance Council) was a group in the Dutch antifascist resistance. The group was founded by the gay artist Willem Arondeus and comprised many openly queer members, including the well-known lesbian cellist Frieda Belinfante. The group engaged in a variety of activities but focused primarily on forging documents for the Jewish community in Amsterdam to help them escape Nazi persecution. While they had initial success with forging records, they eventually encountered a problem—the forged documents could be discovered as fakes by cross-referencing their information with the records kept in the Amsterdam Public Records Office. In response, late one evening the group burned the Public Records Office to the ground and, in the process, destroyed a key resource used by the Nazis to hunt Jews and other "degenerates." Following this sensational act, the group was hotly pursued by Nazis forces and, tragically, many of them were quickly arrested and executed. Right before his execution, Willem Arondeus passed these final words to his lawyer: "Let it be known that homosexuals are not cowards."

100 Ingrid Strobl, *Partisanas: Women in the Armed Resistance to Fascism and German Occupation (1936–1945)* (Oakland: AK Press, 2008), xv.

101 Molly Crabapple, "Hidden Fighters: Remembering America's Black Antifascist Vanguard," *Baffler*, no. 35 (June 2017), https://thebaffler.com/salvos/hidden-fighters-crabapple.

102 Aregawi Berhe, "Revisiting Resistance in Italian-Occupied Ethiopia: The Patriots' Movement (1936–1941) and the Redefinition of Post-war Ethiopia," in *Rethinking Resistance: Revolt and Violence in African History*, ed. Jon Abbink, Mirjam de Bruijn, and Klaas van Walraven (Boston: Brill, 2003), 100.

103 Minale Adugna, *Women and Warfare in Ethiopia: A Case Study of Their Role during the Campaign of Adwa 1895/96, and the Italo-Ethiopian War, 1935–41*, Gender Issues Research Report Series, no. 13 (Addis Ababa, Ethiopia: Organization for Social Science Research in Eastern and Southern Africa, 2001), 24.

104 Adugna, *Women and Warfare*, 31.

105 Adugna, *Women and Warfare*, 32.

106 Adugna, *Women and Warfare*, 2.

107 Adugna, *Women and Warfare*, 4.

108 Adugna, *Women and Warfare*, 26.

109 Adugna, *Women and Warfare*, 26.

110 Denise Lynn, "Fascism and the Family: American Communist Women's Anti-fascism during the Ethiopian Invasion and Spanish Civil War," *American Communist History* 15, no. 2 (2016): 179.

111 Neelam Srivastava, "Anti-colonialism and the Italian Left: Resistances to the Fascist Invasion of Ethiopia," *interventions* 8, no. 3 (2006): 427.

112 David Featherstone, "Black Internationalism, Subaltern Cosmopolitanism, and the Spatial Politics of Antifascism," *Annals of the Association of American Geographers* 103, no. 6 (2013): 1406–20.

113 Crabapple, "Hidden Fighters." Organized by the Communist International, the Abraham Lincoln Brigade was the battalion of volunteers from the United States who traveled to Spain to resist fascism and fight in the civil war. Similar battalions organized by the Comintern throughout the world were known collectively as the International Brigades.

114 Lisa Lines, *Milicianas: Women in Combat in the Spanish Civil War* (Lanham, MD: Lexington Books, 2015), 49.

115 Mary Nash, *Defying Male Civilization: Women in the Spanish Civil War* (Denver: Arden Press, 1995), 63.

116 Nash, *Defying Male Civilization*, 78.

117 Martha Ackelsberg, *Free Women of Spain: Anarchism and the Struggle for the Emancipation of Women* (Bloomington: Indiana University Press, 1991), 115.

118 Ackelsberg, *Free Women of Spain*, 135.

119 Ackelsberg, *Free Women of Spain*, 147.

120 Chiara Bonfiglioli, "Women's Political and Social Activism in the Early Cold War Era: The Case of Yugoslavia," *Aspasia* 8 (2014): 1–25.

121 Jelena Batinic, "Gender, Revolution, and War: The Mobilization of Women in the Yugoslav Partisan Resistance during World War II" (PhD diss., Department of History, Stanford University, 2009), 2.

122 Bonfiglioli, "Women's Political and Social Activism," 5.

123 Strobl, *Partisanas*, 53.

124 Strobl, *Partisanas*, 53–54.

125 Bonfiglioli, "Women's Political and Social Activism," 5.

126 Strobl, *Partisanas*, 54.

127 Batinic, "Gender, Revolution, and War," 126.

128 Strobl, *Partisanas*, 54.

129 Batinic, "Gender, Revolution, and War," 127.

130 Batinic, "Gender, Revolution, and War," 126.

131   Batinic, "Gender, Revolution, and War," 128.
132   Batinic, "Gender, Revolution, and War," 97.
133   Batinic, "Gender, Revolution, and War," 126.
134   Strobl, *Partisanas*, 55.
135   Batinic, "Gender, Revolution, and War," 130.
136   Rob Jackson, "There Is No Such Thing as Revolutionary Inheritance," Louise Michel Library Project, February 12, 2019, https://louisemichellibraryproject.wordpress.com/2019/02/12/there-is-no-such-thing-as-revolutionary-inheritance.
137   Romina Akemi and Bree Busk, "Breaking the Waves: Challenging the Liberal Tendency within Anarchism," Perspectives in Anarchist Theory, June 29, 2016, https://anarchiststudies.org/breaking-the-waves-challenging-the-liberal-tendency-within-anarchist-feminism-by-romina-akemi-and-bree-busk.
138   Anna Bravo, "Armed and Unarmed: Struggle without Weapons in Europe and in Italy," *Journal of Modern Italian Studies* 10, no. 4 (2005): 468–84.
139   Seattle Ultras, "Class Combat," *Ultra*, August 4, 2017, http://www.ultra-com.org/project/class-combat; and It's Going Down, "On Ultras and Militant Structures," It's Going Down, April 22, 2017, https://itsgoingdown.org/on-ultras-and-militant-structures. As part of this critique, I would also include the aggrandizement of particular aesthetics. It's fine to be into a certain style or subculture, but they can present limits. A sleek Adidas sports jacket, a crisp Fred Perry polo shirt, etc.—at least in some spaces antifascism has a particular European-influenced aesthetic. Inherited from the white-dominated punk subcultures from which modern antifa emerged, this aesthetic can function to hinder struggle if antifascism is exclusively thought of or associated with a specific dress code. Aesthetics should not be a stand-in for, nor should it be prioritized over, politics.
140   Antifascist gyms are great, and antifascist football clubs can be useful. But what about an antifascist neighborhood association? Or antifascist storytelling time for children, or an antifascist food program? Or maybe, antifascist day at the nail salon or an antifascist roller derby league? The list could go on.
141   Sarah Jaffe, "The Long History of Antifa," interview with Mark Bray, *Progressive*, September 13, 2017, https://progressive.org/latest/the-long-history-of-antifa-jaffe-170913.
142   Ashoka Jegroo, "Fighting Cops and the Klan: The History and Future of Black Antifascism," *Truthout*, February 21, 2017, https://truthout.org/articles/fighting-cops-and-the-klan-the-history-and-future-of-black-antifascism.
143   There are countless examples of Black antifascism. Before the height of the Civil Rights movement, Black activists like Mabel and Robert Williams worked to arm Black people and taught them how to defend themselves against the Ku Klux Klan. The Black Panthers held a national conference in 1969 on antifascism (the National Revolutionary Conference for a United Front against Fascism). Many Black intellectuals have theorized the role of fascism in America and also done much to highlight (and organize against) police as key perpetrators of fascist violence.
144   Editorial Committee, "Building Everyday Anti-fascism," *Upping the Anti*, no. 19 (February 2, 2017), http://uppingtheanti.org/journal/article/19-building-everyday-anti-fascism.
145   Strobl, *Partisanas*.
146   For example, there's no distinction made between different tendencies on the right; everyone from a self-identified neo-nazi to a Christian conservative is a fascist and must be confronted in the same manner.
147   I mostly mean this bar fight reference figuratively, but I also know lots of examples of dudes going out drinking to the bar and purposefully looking for fascists to fight. In this case, there literally is an "antifascist bar fight." This usually looks like men who identify as antifascist getting into a bar fight with those perceived to be

fascists, though this sometimes get muddled (e.g., is the guy wearing that T-shirt of a fascist metal band actually a fascist, or does he just like the band and not know anything about its politics?).

Seven Theses on the Three Way Fight

1   Georgi Dimitrov, *The Fascist Offensive & Unity of the Working Class* (Paris: Foreign Languages Press, 2020), 4. Don Hamerquist discusses in passing how anarchist definitions of fascism during this time were similar to Dimitrov's line. See Don Hamerquist, "Fascism & Anti-fascism," in *Confronting Fascism: Discussion Documents for a Militant Movement*, by Don Hamerquist et al., 2nd ed. (Montreal: Kersplebedeb Publishing, 2017), 30.

2   The Black Panther Party, "Call for a United Front against Fascism," in *The U.S. Antifascism Reader*, ed. Bill V. Mullen and Christopher Vials (London: Verso, 2020), 269.

3   See Dimitrov, *Fascist Offensive*, 6: "Fascism is able to attract the masses because it demagogically appeals to their most urgent needs and demands."

4   See Enzo Traverso, *The New Faces of Fascism: Populism and the Far Right* (London: Verso, 2019); Samir Gandesha, "Posthuman Fascism," *Los Angeles Review of Books*, August 22, 2020; and Alberto Toscano, "The Long Shadow of Racial Fascism," *Boston Review*, October 28, 2020. I have criticized Toscano in more detail in Devin Zane Shaw, "On Toscano's Critique of 'Racial Fascism,'" *Three Way Fight*, December 30, 2020, http://threewayfight.blogspot.com/2020/12/on-toscanos-critique-of-racial-fascism.html.

5   See for example Mark Bray, *Antifa: The Anti-fascist Handbook* (Brooklyn, NY: Melville House, 2017), Daniel Sonabend, *We Fight Fascists: The 43 Group and Their Forgotten Battle for Post-war Britain* (London: Verso, 2019); and Hilary Moore and James Tracy, *No Fascist USA! The John Brown Anti-Klan Committee and Lessons for Today's Movements* (San Francisco: City Lights, 2020). Note that this list does not include antifascist approaches developed by groups that framed their struggle in terms of national liberation, though they are certainly worthy of study as well.

6   Bray, *Antifa*, 172.

7   As Matthew N. Lyons notes, "repression … can even come in the name of antifascism, as when the Roosevelt administration used the war against the Axis powers to justify strikebreaking and the mass imprisonment of Japanese Americans." See *Insurgent Supremacists: The U.S. Far Right's Challenge to State and Empire* (Oakland: PM Press, and Montreal: Kersplebedeb Publishing, 2018), ix.

8   See Devin Zane Shaw, Philosophy of Antifascism: Punching Nazis and Fighting White Supremacy (London: Rowman & Littlefield, 2020) and Devin Zane Shaw, "Between System-Loyal Vigilantism and System-Oppositional Violence," *Three Way Fight*, October 25, 2020, http://threewayfight.blogspot.com/2020/10/between-system-loyal-vigilantism-and.html.

9   Dimitrov, *Fascist Offensive*, 4.

10   Hamerquist, "Fascism & Anti-fascism," 41.

11   T. Derbent, *The German Communist Resistance, 1933–1945* (Paris: Foreign Languages Press, 2021), 99. Despite the repeated assertions by paternalistic liberals that fascism is a working-class movement, even liberal historians acknowledge that workers "were always proportionally fewer than their share in the population." See Robert O. Paxton, *The Anatomy of Fascism* (New York: Vintage, 2004), 50.

12   Lambert Strether, "The Class Composition of the Capitol Rioters (First Cut)," *Naked Capitalism*, January 18, 2021.

13   Hamerquist argues, for example, that fascist labor policy under the Nazis extended beyond "the genocidal aspect of continuing primitive accumulation that is part of 'normal' capitalist development.... The German policy was the genocidal

obliteration of already developed sections of the European working classes and the deliberate disruption of the social reproduction of labor in those sectors—all in the interests of a racialist demand for 'living space'" ("Fascism & Anti-fascism," 43); see also Lyons, *Insurgent Supremacists*, 255.

14   Lyons, *Insurgent Supremacists*, ii.

15   Lyons, *Insurgent Supremacists*, 28.

16   Lyons, *Insurgent Supremacists*, ii.

17   In *Confronting Fascism*, Hamerquist and Sakai both criticized the assumption that fascism (even in North America) will continue to be necessarily white supremacist. Within the discussions of the three way fight, the meaning of nonwhite participation in far-right movements remains an open debate. In my view, we must assess the degree of nonwhite participation while also providing an explanation as to why this participation remains at the present moment marginal (for most individuals within ostensibly white supremacist movements or as autonomous organizations) within the broader far-right milieu. That account is provided in these theses.

18   W.E.B. Du Bois, *Black Reconstruction in America: An Essay Toward a History of the Part Which Black Folk Played in the Attempt to Reconstruct Democracy in America, 1860–1880*, ed. Henry Louis Gates Jr. (Oxford, UK: Oxford University Press, 2007), 573–74.

19   Ken Lawrence, "The Ku Klux Klan and Fascism," *Urgent Tasks* 14 (Fall/Winter 1982), 12, reprinted in *The U.S. Anti-fascism Reader*, ed. Bill V. Mullen and Christopher Vials (London: Verso, 2020).

20   Sakai, "The Shock of Recognition," in Hamerquist et al., *Confronting Fascism*, 130.

21   Cheryl Harris, "Whiteness as Property," *Harvard Law Review* 106, no. 8 (June 1993), 1714.

22   Indeed, Tammy Kovich (pseudonym Petronella Lee) contends, in a point that applies both to the creation of a broader antifascist culture and to the use of the diversity of tactics, that "we cannot focus almost exclusively on physical activities and/or traditionally male-dominated spaces. It's important to have spaces, roles, and activities that account for the variety of diversity of social life—for example, considering things like ability and age." Nor should we perpetuate gender stereotypes in organizing community self-defense. See *Antifascism against Machismo* (Montreal: Kersplebedeb Publishing, 2023), 68, reprinted in this volume.

23   Robert F. Williams, *Negroes with Guns* (Detroit: Wayne State University Press, 1998), 4.

Principal Enemy: Demystifying Far-Right Antisemitism

1   Campbell Robertson, Christopher Mele, and Sabrina Tavernise, "11 Killed in Synagogue Massacre; Suspect Charged with 29 Counts," *New York Times*, October 27, 2018, https://www.nytimes.com/2018/10/27/us/active-shooter-pittsburgh-synagogue-shooting.html; Maggie Fox, "Police Killings Hit People of Color Hardest, Study Finds," NBC News, May 27, 2018, https://www.nbcnews.com/health/health-news/police-killings-hit-people-color-hardest-study-finds-n872086; Melissa Jeltsen, "Who Is Killing American Women? Their Husbands and Boyfriends, CDC Confirms," *HuffPost*, July 21, 2017, https://www.huffpost.com/entry/most-murders-of-american-women-involve-domestic-violence_n_5971fcf6e4b09e5f6cceba87; and Samantha Allen, "2018 Is Shaping Up to Be Another Terrible Year for Trans Murders," *Daily Beast*, July 2, 2018, https://www.thedailybeast.com/2018-is-shaping-up-to-be-another-terrible-year-for-trans-murders.

2   Antiracistantizionist, "Not Quite 'Ordinary Human Beings'—Anti-imperialism and the Anti-humanist Rhetoric of Gilad Atzmon," collective statement signed by over 100 people, *Three Way Fight*, March 2012, http://threewayfight.blogspot.com/p/atzmon-critique_09.html; Cloee Cooper, "Kevin Barrett: Repackaging Antisemitism," *Political*

Research Associates, October 23, 2017, https://politicalresearch.org/2017/10/23/kevin-barrett-repackaging-antisemitism; Élise Hendrick, "CounterPunch or Sucker Punch?," *Meldungen aus dem Exil*, July 19, 2015, https://meldungen-aus-dem-exil.noblogs.org/post/2015/07/19/counterpunch-or-suckerpunch; Spencer Sunshine, "The Left Must Root Out Antisemitism in Its Ranks," *Forward*, June 1, 2017, https://forward.com/opinion/373577/leftists-must-root-out-anti-semitism-in-its-ranks; and April Rosenblum, *The Past Didn't Go Anywhere: Making Resistance to Antisemitism Part of All of Our Movements* (self-pub., 2007), https://www.aprilrosenblum.com/_files/ugd/4dc342_10d68441b6c44ee0a12909a242074ca6.pdf.

3   Eric K. Ward, "Skin in the Game: How Antisemitism Animates White Nationalism," *Public Eye* (Political Research Associates), Summer 2017, https://politicalresearch.org/2017/06/29/skin-in-the-game-how-antisemitism-animates-white-nationalism; Jews for Racial & Economic Justice, *Understanding Antisemitism: An Offering to Our Movement* (pamphlet), Jews for Racial & Economic Justice, November 15, 2017, https://www.jfrej.org/news/2017/11/understanding-antisemitism-an-offering-to-our-movement; Ben Lorber, "Understanding Alt-Right Antisemitism," *Doikayt*, March 24, 2017, https://doikayt.com/2017/03/24/understanding-alt-right-antisemitism (site discontinued); and Rachel Tabachnick, "The New Christian Zionism and the Jews: A Love/Hate Relationship," *Public Eye* (Political Research Associates), Winter 2009/Spring 2010, https://politicalresearch.org/2010/01/18/the-new-christian-zionism-and-the-jews-a-lovehate-relationship.

4   Ward, "Skin in the Game."

5   Robertson et al., "11 Killed in Synagogue Massacre."

6   Ward, "Skin in the Game."

7   Ward, "Skin in the Game."

8   Jews for Racial & Economic Justice, *Understanding Antisemitism*, 9.

9   Matthew N. Lyons, "Not Just a Smear Tactic," review of *The Past Didn't Go Anywhere* by April Rosenblum, *Upping the Anti*, no. 5, November 19, 2009, https://uppingtheanti.org/journal/article/05-not-just-a-smear-tactic.

10   Jews for Racial & Economic Justice, *Understanding Antisemitism*, 15.

11   Jews for Racial & Economic Justice, *Understanding Antisemitism*, 26, 28.

12   Abram Leon, *The Jewish Question: A Marxist Interpretation* (Mexico City: Ediciones Pioneras, 1950), available at https://www.marxists.org/subject/jewish/leon/index.htm.

13   Jews for Racial & Economic Justice, *Understanding Antisemitism*, 17.

14   Lorber, "Understanding Alt-Right Antisemitism."

15   Moishe Postone, "Anti-Semitism and National Socialism," in *Germans and Jews since the Holocaust*, ed. Anson Rabinbach and Jack Zipes (New York: Holmes and Meier, 1986), available at https://libcom.org/article/anti-semitism-and-national-socialism-moishe-postone.

16   Postone, "Anti-Semitism and National Socialism." In a comment on the original blog version of this essay, Don Hamerquist argued that the false dichotomy between productive industry and parasitic finance doesn't fully capture current views of capital among fascist antisemites. His point is well taken: while banker-bashing remains important, antisemitism takes different forms and uses different forms of scapegoating, such as targeting "globalists" who threaten "national sovereignty" or denouncing a "universalism" that suppresses "biocultural diversity." In the same comment, Hamerquist also argued that "the global capitalist framework that has emerged over the past few decades has dramatically subordinated industrial capital to financial capital" and noted, rightly, that radicals need to be able to discuss this without automatically being accused of antisemitism.

17   Matthew N. Lyons, "Jack Donovan on Men: A Masculine Tribalism for the Far Right,"

Three Way Fight, November 23, 2015, http://threewayfight.blogspot.com/2015/11/jack-donovan-on-men-masculine-tribalism.html.

18   Lorber, "Understanding Alt-Right Antisemitism."

19   Lorber, "Understanding Alt-Right Antisemitism."

20   Tabachnick, "The New Christian Zionism and the Jews."

21   Tabachnick, "The New Christian Zionism and the Jews."

22   Tabachnick, "The New Christian Zionism and the Jews."

23   Jack Jenkins, "Jewish Groups Decry Messianic Jewish Rabbi's Prayer at Pence Rally," Religion News Service, October 31, 2018, https://religionnews.com/2018/10/31/jewish-groups-decry-messianic-jewish-rabbis-prayer-at-pence-rally.

24   Matthew N. Lyons, *Insurgent Supremacists: The U.S. Far Right's Challenge to State and Empire* (Oakland: PM Press, and Montreal: Kersplebedeb Publishing, 2018), 38–39.

25   Tabachnick, "The New Christian Zionism and the Jews."

Threat or Model? US Rightists Look at China

1   This essay has been edited for length.

2   Leah Asmelash, "With the Spread of Coronavirus Came a Surge in Anti-Asian Racism Online, New Research Says," CNN, April 10, 2020, https://www.cnn.com/2020/04/10/us/sinophobic-racism-rise-coronavirus-research-trnd/index.html; and Hanna Kozlowska, "How Anti-Chinese Sentiment is Spreading on Social Media," *Quartz*, March 25, 2020, https://qz.com/1823608/how-anti-china-sentiment-is-spreading-on-social-media.

3   Quoted in Alexander Saxton, *The Indispensable Enemy: Labor and the Anti-Chinese Movement in California* (Berkeley: University of California Press, 1971), 244.

4   Charlotte Brooks, "Numbed with Fear: Chinese Americans and McCarthyism," *American Experience* (PBS), December 20, 2019, https://www.pbs.org/wgbh/americanexperience/features/mccarthy-numbed-with-fear-chinese-americans.

5   Veronica Stracqualursi, "10 Times Trump Attacked China and Its Trade Relations with the US," ABC News, November 9, 2017, https://abcnews.go.com/Politics/10-times-trump-attacked-china-trade-relations-us/story?id=46572567.

6   Alan Rappeport and Ana Swanson, "Peter Navarro, Trump's Trade Warrior, Has Not Made His Peace with China," *New York Times*, December 26, 2019, https://www.nytimes.com/2019/12/26/us/politics/peter-navarro-china-trade.html; and Zeeshan Aleem, "I Read Trump's Trade Adviser's Anti-China Book. It's Wilder Than You Can Imagine," *Vox*, April 6, 2017, https://www.vox.com/world/2017/4/6/14697762/china-trump-trade-navarro.

7   Scott Morefield, "Tucker and Former Clinton Adviser Clash over Whether Russia or China Is the Greatest Threat," *Daily Caller*, December 2, 2019, https://dailycaller.com/2019/12/02/tucker-carlson-richard-goodstein-russia-china.

8   Benjamin Haas, "Steve Bannon Compares China to 1930s Germany and Says US Must Confront Beijing," *Guardian*, September 11, 2017, https://www.theguardian.com/us-news/2017/sep/11/steve-bannon-compares-china-to-1930s-germany-and-says-us-must-confront-beijing; "Former Trump Strategist Steve Bannon: 'COVID-19 Is a Communist Party Virus,'" *ADN Cuba*, March 22, 2020, https://adncuba.com/english/steve-bannon-covid-19-communist-party-virus-trump; and Dale Owens, "Steve Bannon, China and the 2020 Presidential Election," *InsideOver*, December 19, 2019, https://www.insideover.com/politics/steve-bannon-china-and-the-2020-presidential-election.html.

9   Committee on the Present Danger: China, "Guiding Principles," Committee on the Present Danger: China, accessed December 1, 2022, https://presentdangerchina.org/guiding-principles; and Stracqualursi, "10 Times Trump Attacked China."

10   Lili Loofbourow, "The Real Reason Trump Started Calling the Virus 'Chinese,'"

Slate, March 21, 2020, https://slate.com/news-and-politics/2020/03/trump-calling-coronavirus-chinese-virus.html.

11   Brenda Walker, "Senator Tom Cotton: America Must Re-evaluate Its Relationship with China," VDare, March 18, 2020, https://vdare.com/posts/senator-tom-cotton-america-must-re-evaluate-its-relationship-with-china; Michelle Malkin, "Red China's Infection of US Classrooms," *American Renaissance*, January 29, 2020, https://www.amren.com/commentary/2020/01/chinese-immigrants-us-security-michelle-malkin.

12   Robert Hampton, "Sympathy for the Dragon," Counter-Currents, March 2020, https://www.counter-currents.com/2020/03/sympathy-for-the-dragon.

13   F.C. Comtaose, "Teaching White Nationalism in a Chinese University," Counter-Currents, September 2016, https://www.counter-currents.com/2016/09/teaching-white-nationalism-in-a-chinese-university.

14   F.C. Comtaose, "The Excellence of the White Race & the Chinese Question," Counter-Currents, October 2019, https://www.counter-currents.com/2019/10/the-excellence-of-the-white-race-the-chinese-question.

15   Riki Rei, "The Chinese Question & Trump Supporters," Counter-Currents, January 2017, https://www.counter-currents.com/2017/01/the-chinese-question-trump-supporters.

16   Thomas Jackson, "The Mind of the Chinese," review of *Hegemon: China's Plan to Dominate Asia and the World*, by Steven Mosher, *American Renaissance*, February 2001, https://www.amren.com/news/2019/10/hegemon-steven-mosher-china-vs-the-west; Jonathan Peter Wilkinson, "Chinese Racism as a Huge Force Multiplier," *Amerika*, March 29, 2017, http://www.amerika.org/politics/chinese-racism-as-a-huge-force-multiplier; and Andrew Anglin, "So, I've Figured Out the Agenda: ZOG Is Planning a War with China," *Daily Stormer*, April 4, 2020, https://dailystormer.su/so-ive-figured-out-the-agenda-zog-is-planning-a-war-with-china (site discontinued).

17   Matt Pearce, "What Happens When a Millennial Goes Fascist? He Starts Up a Neo-Nazi Site," *Los Angeles Times*, June 24, 2015, https://www.latimes.com/nation/la-na-daily-stormer-interview-20150624-story.html; and Anglin, "Figured Out the Agenda."

18   Hunter Wallace, "The Alt-Right, President Trump, and China," *Occidental Dissent*, November 17, 2016, http://www.occidentaldissent.com/2016/11/17/the-alt-right-president-trump-and-china.

19   Hunter Wallace, "Steve Bannon: We're in an Economic War with China," *Occidental Dissent*, May 17, 2019, http://www.occidentaldissent.com/2019/05/07/steve-bannon.

20   Wallace, "The Alt-Right, President Trump, and China."

21   Wallace, "Steve Bannon."

22   Bethany Allen-Ebrahimian, "Lyndon LaRouche Is Running a Pro-China Party in Germany," *Foreign Policy*, September 18, 2017, https://foreignpolicy.com/2017/09/18/lyndon-larouche-is-running-a-pro-china-party-in-germany; and Helga Zepp-LaRouche, "Anti-China Hysteria Is Very Dangerous, and Very Stupid," LaRouche PAC, April 16, 2020, https://larouchepac.com/20200416/anti-china-hysteria-very-dangerous-and-very-stupid.

Moscow Conference Draws Fascists, Neo-Confederates, US Leftists

1   Special thanks to Michael Pugliese for pointing me to much of the information in this article, and to Andrew Pollack for permission to quote from his UFPJ-Activist memo.

2   "Moscow Conference Stands in Solidarity with Novorossiya, Palestine and Black America," International Action Center, December 17, 2014, updated January 7, 2015, archived at https://web.archive.org/web/20150423124329/https://iacenter.org/actions/moscow-conf010715; and Ali Abunimah and Hussein Ibish, "Serious

Concerns about Israel Shamir," *Ibishblog*, April 16, 2001, archived at http://web.archive.org/web/20111002073436/http://www.ibishblog.com/article/2001/04/16/serious_conserns_about_israel_shamir.

3   Alexander Ionov, "Declaration: The Right of Peoples to Self-Determination and Building a Multipolar World," *Truthout*, January 21, 2015, https://truthout.org/articles/declaration-the-right-of-peoples-to-self-determination-and-building-a-multipolar-world.

4   "Alexander Dugin: For Our People and the Truth," interview by Natella Speranskaja, Open Revolt!, May 6, 2012, archived at https://web.archive.org/web/20160201184418/openrevolt.info/2012/05/06/alexander-dugin-for-our-people-and-the-truth.

5   Marlene Laruelle, "Aleksandr Dugin: A Russian Version of the European Radical Right?," Kennan Institute Occasional Paper no. 294 (Washington, DC: Woodrow Wilson International Center for Scholars, 2006).

6   Tishreen, "Russian Parliamentarians: 'Syrian Opposition' Intransigence Key Obstacle to Convening Geneva II," *Tishreen*, December 11, 2013, archived at https://web.archive.org/web/20150515062338/http://tishreen.news.sy/tishreen/public/print/302400.

7   Anti-globalization Movement of Russia, "Faces of Globalization," Anti-globalization Movement of Russia, accessed January 15, 2015, http://anti-global.ru.

8   Anti-globalization Movement of Russia, "About," Anti-globalization Movement of Russia, accessed January 15, 2015, http://anti-global.ru/?page_id=160&lang=en.

9   Anti-globalization Movement of Russia, "About."

10   "Protest against Same-Sex Marriage Being Prepared in Moscow," Interfax-Religion, July 9, 2013, http://www.interfax-religion.com/?act=news&div=10609 (site discontinued).

11   Anton Shekhovtsov, "Aleksandr Dugin's Neo-Eurasianism: The New Right *à la Russe*," *Religion Compass* 3, no. 4 (2009): 697–716; and Alain de Benoist and Charles Champetier, "The French New Right in the Year 2000," *Telos*, no. 115 (Spring 1999): 117–44.

12   "Antiglobalism in Russia," Anti-globalization Movement of Russia, accessed January 15, 2015, http://anti-global.ru/antiglobalizm-v-rossii; and Natalia Vitrenko, "United States and EU, with Ukrainian Terrorists, Establish Nazi Regime," *Executive Intelligence Review*, February 28, 2014, https://larouchepub.com/other/2014/4109vitrenko_statement_nazi_regime.html.

13   "Moscow Election Cleared of Rodina," *Kommersant*, November 28, 2005, archived at https://web.archive.org/web/20150330093843/http://www.kommersant.com/p630171/r_500/Moscow_Election_Cleared_of_Rodina; Anton Shekhovtsov, "Italian Fascists from Millennium Ally with Pro-Russian Right-Wing Extremists," Anton Shekhovtsov's blog, June 11, 2014, http://anton-shekhovtsov.blogspot.com/2014/06/italian-fascists-from-millennium-ally.html; and l'Unità, "Milano, convegno estrema destra Scontri con gli antagonisti," l'Unità, January 17, 2014, archived at https://web.archive.org/web/20140119072357/http://www.unita.it/italia/milano-esterma-destra-a-convegno-br-scontri-con-gli-antagonisti-1.545727.

14   Ben Neal, "The Russian Far Right," *Project*, September 8, 2014, archived at https://web.archive.org/web/20140929032802/http://www.socialistproject.org/international/the-russian-far-right.

15   Michael Hill, "The League of the South Takes Its Southern Nationalist Message to Moscow," League of the South, September 13, 2014, https://leagueofthesouth.com/the-league-of-the-south-takes-its-southern-nationalist-message-to-moscow.

16   See Texas Nationalist Movement, https://tnm.me; and Jonathan Hutson, "Not Just Whistling 'Dixie': Peroutka Stands Up for Southern Secession," *HuffPost*, July 30, 2014, updated September 29, 2014, https://www.huffpost.com/entry/not-just-whistling-dixie_b_5636221.

17 Cynthia Meyer, "UNAC Published a Report on Their Trip to Russia," Stop-Imperialism. com, December 30, 2014, http://stop-imperialism.com/2014/12/30/4923.

18 Andrew Pollack, email to UFPJ-Activist listserv, January 18, 2015.

19 Joe Lombardo, email to UFPJ-Activist listserv, January 22, 2015.

20 Efe Can Gürcan, "NATO's 'Globalized' Atlanticism and the Eurasian Alternative," *Socialism and Democracy* 27, no. 2 (2013): 154–67; Matthew Lyons and Efe Can Gürcan, "Exchange on Eurasianism," *Socialism and Democracy* 28, no. 1 (March 2014): 165–71.

21 US Department of Justice, "Russian National Charged with Conspiring to Have U.S. Citizens Act as Illegal Agents of the Russian Government," Press Release 22-814, US Department of Justice, July 29, 2022, updated August 3, 2022, https:// www.justice.gov/opa/pr/russian-national-charged-conspiring-have-us-citizens-act-illegal-agents-russian-government; and Dan Sullivan et al., "FBI Investigating Russian Interference Possibly Linked to St. Petersburg Uhuru Movement," *Tampa Bay Times*, July 29, 2022, updated July 31, 2022, https://www.tampabay.com/news/ breaking-news/2022/07/29/federal-agents-serve-warrant-at-uhuru-house-in-st-pete; see also "Mr. Anti-Globalization," *Meduza*, May 20, 2021, https://meduza.io/ en/feature/2021/05/21/mister-anti-globalization.

Network Contagion Research Institute: Helping the State Fight Political Infection Left and Right

1 Costa-Gavras, dir., *Z* (Algiers: Office National pour le Commerce et l'Industrie Cinématographique, 1969).

2 Network Contagion Research Institute, "About NCRI," Network Contagion Research Institute, no date, archived at https://web.archive.org/web/20210509141102/https:// networkcontagion.us/about.

3 Alexander Reid-Ross et al., "A Contagion of Institutional Distrust: Viral Disinformation of the COVID Vaccine and the Road to Reconciliation," Network Contagion Research Institute, March 11, 2021, https://networkcontagion.us/ reports/a-contagion-of-institutional-distrust.

4 Alex Goldenberg and Joel Finkelstein, "Cyber Swarming, Memetic Warfare and Viral Insurgency: How Domestic Militants Organize on Memes to Incite Violent Insurrection and Terror against Government and Law Enforcement," Network Contagion Research Institute, February 7, 2020, https://networkcontagion.us/ reports/cyber-swarming-memetic-warfare-and-viral-insurgency-how-domestic-militants-organize-on-memes-to-incite-violent-insurrection-and-terror-against-go-vernment-and-law-enforcement.

5 Savvas Zannettou, Joel Finkelstein, et al., "A Quantitative Approach to Understanding Online Antisemitism," *Proceedings of the International AAAI Conference on Web and Social Media* 14, no. 1 (2020), 786–97, https://arxiv.org/abs/1809.01644; and Ross et al., "A Contagion of Institutional Distrust."

6 Lindsay Beyerstein, "Beyond the Hate Frame: An Interview with Kay Whitlock & Michael Bronski," *Public Eye* (Political Research Associates), Summer 2015, https://politicalresearch.org/2015/07/27/beyond-the-hate-frame-an-interview-with-kay-whitlock-michael-bronski.

7 Kay Whitlock, "We Need to Dream a Bolder Dream: The Politics of Fear and Queer Struggles for Safe Communities," *Scholar and Feminist Online*, no. 10.1–10.2 (Fall 2011–Spring 2012), https://sfonline.barnard.edu/we-need-to-dream-a-bolder-dream-the-politics-of-fear-and-queer-struggles-for-safe-communities.

8 Goldenberg and Finkelstein, "Cyber Swarming."

9 Finkelstein et al., "Network-Enabled Anarchy: How Militant Anarcho-Socialist Networks Use Social Media to Instigate Widespread Violence against Political Opponents and Law Enforcement," Network Contagion Research Institute,

September 14, 2020, https://networkcontagion.us/reports/network-enabled-anarchy.

10   Kristian Williams, "Intelligence Report on 'Extremism' Equates Anarchists with Right-Wing Militias," *Truthout*, April 7, 2021, https://truthout.org/articles/intelligence-report-on-extremism-equates-anarchists-with-right-wing-militias.

11   Finkelstein et al., "Network-Enabled Anarchy."

12   Network Contagion Research Institute, "About NCRI."

13   Emmaia Gelman, "The Anti-Defamation League Is Not What It Seems," *Boston Review*, May 23, 2019, https://www.bostonreview.net/articles/emmaia-gelman-anti-defamation-league; Richard C. Paddock, "New Details of Extensive ADL Spy Operation Emerge: Inquiry: Transcripts Reveal Nearly 40 Years of Espionage by a Man Who Infiltrated Political Groups," *Los Angeles Times*, April 13, 1993, https://www.latimes.com/archives/la-xpm-1993-04-13-mn-22383-story.html; and Josh Nathan-Kazis, "ADL Tells Cops to Infiltrate Antifa—and Film Protests," *Forward*, August 30, 2017, https://forward.com/news/381488/adl-tells-police-to-infiltrate-and-film-antifa-protests.

14   Philip Elliott, "Koch Network Mounts Grassroots Effort to Support Immigration," *Time*, July 20, 2018, https://time.com/5343074/libre-koch-congress-immigration.

15   Jeremy W. Peters, "One Republican's Lonely Fight against a Flood of Disinformation," *New York Times*, April 3, 2021, https://www.nytimes.com/2021/04/03/us/politics/denver-riggleman-republican-disinformation.html.

16   Reid-Ross et al., "A Contagion of Institutional Distrust"; and Alex Goldenberg et al., "The QAnon Conspiracy: Destroying Families, Dividing Communities, Undermining Democracy," Network Contagion Research Institute, December 15, 2020,

17   Alexander Reid Ross, *Against the Fascist Creep* (Chico, CA: AK Press, 2017); rowan, "The Alt-Creeps: A Review of *Against the Fascist Creep* and *Ctrl-Alt-Delete*," *Perspectives on Anarchist Theory*, no. 30 (2018/2019).

18   See for example Zannettou, Finkelstein, et al., "A Quantitative Approach to Understanding Online Antisemitism."

19   Faramarz Farbod, "Why Liberal Anti-fascism Upholds the Status Quo," *Common Dreams*, January 24, 2021, https://www.commondreams.org/views/2021/01/24/why-liberal-anti-fascism-upholds-status-quo.

20   Office of the Director of National Intelligence, "Domestic Violent Extremism Poses Heightened Threat in 2021," Office of the Director of National Intelligence, March 1, 2021, https://www.dni.gov/files/ODNI/documents/assessments/UnclassSummaryofDVEAssessment-17MAR21.pdf.

21   Williams, "Intelligence Report on 'Extremism.'"

Distinguishing the Possible from the Probable: Contending Strategic Approaches within and against Transnational Capitalism

1   Whatever is clear and useful in this piece owes a great deal to the critical assistance I got from Kristian Williams. (This essay has been edited for length. The original complete version can be found at https://kersplebedeb.com/posts/distinguishing-the-possible-from-the-probable-contending-strategic-approaches-within-and-against-transnational-capitalism.)

2   This category was developed by Kees Van der Pijl and is defined as follows by William Carroll in *The Making of a Transnational Capitalist Class: Corporate Power in the 21st Century* (London: Zed Books, 2013): The "region within the world-system in which capitalist internationalization was most intense, what [Van der Pijl] called the Lockean heartland, and the Atlantic ruling class that, over the course of three centuries, had come to form a hegemonic fraction."

3   David Ranney, *New World Disorder: The Decline of U.S. Power* (Oakland: PM Press, 2014).

4   Basav Sen, "The Terrifying Global Implications of Modi's Re-election," *CounterPunch*,
     May 27, 2019, https://www.counterpunch.org/2019/05/27/the-terrifying-global-
     implications-of-modis-re-election.

5   Basav Sen, "Why the Trump/Modi Relationship Is So Dangerous," *CounterPunch*,
     March 9, 2020, https://www.counterpunch.org/2020/03/09/why-the-trump-modi-
     relationship-is-so-dangerous.

6   I particularly question the application of Sen's approach to Brazil. Increasingly,
     Bolsonaro's subservience to the extractive wing of global capital and to neoliberal
     economics in general outweighs his regime's more classically fascist characteristics.
     Particularly since it appears likely that, despite some rhetoric to the contrary, this
     social base is not capable of a break with bourgeois parliamentarianism and legal-
     ism. This leaves Bolsonaro's regime essentially reversible in ways that wouldn't be
     possible in an actual fascism. See Forrest Hylton, "Brazil Undone," *London Review
     of Books*, March 27, 2020, https://www.lrb.co.uk/blog/2020/march/brazil-undone.
     Similar points are made by this earlier treatment of the changing status of the "Car
     Wash" prosecution: Glenn Greenwald, "Fearful of Lula's Exoneration, His Once-
     Fanatical Prosecutors Request His Release from Prison. But Lula Refuses," *Intercept*,
     October 4, 2019, https://theintercept.com/2019/10/04/fearful-of-lulas-exoneration-
     his-once-fanatical-prosecutors-request-his-release-from-prison-but-lula-refuses.
         I'd also recommend this article on the recently collapsed Italian "populist" coali-
     tion, particularly some of the later sections that detail the contradictions within the
     positions of both the Northern League and the Five Star Movement: Thomas Fazi,
     "The Revenge of the Elites," *Spiked*, October 4, 2019, https://www.spiked-online.
     com/2019/10/04/the-revenge-of-the-elites. Note that Salvini, the quasi-fascist
     leader of the temporarily victorious populist coalition, appears to be well on his
     way to jail. Similar arguments and evidence are relevant for most of the alleged
     "fascisms" in the Baltic and Balkan areas. It's hard to see how even quite reactionary
     regimes can be defined as fascist, when they can lose governmental control and/or
     have key policies reversed by "legal" parliamentary means. However, this appears to
     be a feature of the ambivalent and sometimes contradictory relationships of most
     of these right-wing populisms with capitalist globalism.
         (In my opinion, the key issue in forecasting the likely trajectories of these
     "populist" insurgencies and regimes is the presence or absence of an organized,
     autonomously radical reactionary mass base that can substantially define the polit-
     ical terrain. However, my factual knowledge in some of these cases is lacking, and I
     intend to avoid hasty negative generalizations—particularly in light of India, where
     the RSS does appear to provide such a mass social and ideological base for fascism.)

7   This is a paraphrase of Marx from *The Communist Manifesto*. The connection
     between this conception of essential limits for capital and Luxemburg's theme of
     "Socialism or Barbarism" is clear enough.

8   Edward Thompson, "Notes on Exterminism, the Last Stage of Civilization," *New Left
     Review*, June 1, 1980, https://newleftreview.org/I/121/edward-thompson-notes-on-
     exterminism-the-last-stage-of-civilization. I've taken the Thompson insight from
     some useful criticisms that Dave Ranney offered on an earlier article of mine that
     covered some of the same ground as this one does. See Dave Ranney, comment on
     Don Hamerquist, "New Stuff from an Old Guy—Part 3," *Three Way Fight*, November
     21, 2018, https://www.blogger.com/comment.g?blogID=13622622&postID=8912
     449938511451385&isPopup=true&.

9   This approach to capitalist power comes from Marx's conception of capitalism
     as a fetishized social order where an essential "expropriation" appears as "an
     exchange of equals" on the level of production, and the essential domination
     and subordination of those who are ruled occurs behind their backs, disguised
     by fictions of equality and democracy on the level of power. Also significant to

Marx's conception of capitalism is the opaque relationship between political rule and economic exploitation that is not a characteristic of other class societies. (See *Capital*, volume 1, p. 280.) The capitalist state functions to maintain and defend capitalism as a system, not as an appendage or tool of the capitalist class or some fraction of that class. Michael Heinrich is an important source for this position that challenges various instrumental conceptions of the capitalist state that are widespread among Marxists. For a good exposition of Heinrich's argument, see Nate Hawthorne, "State and Capital," LibCom.org, January 7, 2014, https://libcom.org/article/state-and-capital.

10   *The Turner Diaries*, a political novel by William Pierce, published 1978, is the classic (nazi) exposition of a fascist revolution in the US. It advocates the violent suppression of the "liberal" transnational sector of the capitalist class along with the destruction of capitalism's institutional framework and its consumerist culture. *The Turner Diaries* has been a major organizing document for US fascists, although its main theses are increasingly challenged by the more overtly anticapitalist (as contrasted with antibourgeois) Strasserite "Third Position" advocates.

11   Scott Atran, "From Christchurch to Colombo, Islamists and the Far Right Are Playing a Deadly Duet," *Guardian*, April 25, 2019, https://www.theguardian.com/commentisfree/2019/apr/25/christchurch-colombo-islamists-far-right-sri-lanka.

12   Andrew Edgecliffe-Johnson, "Why American CEOs Are Worried about Capitalism," *Financial Times*, April 22, 2019, https://www.ft.com/content/138e103a-61a4-11e9-b285-3acd5d43599e.

13   "Companies today face an existential choice. Either they wholeheartedly embrace 'stakeholder capitalism' and subscribe to the responsibilities that come with it, by actively taking steps to meet social and environmental goals. Or they stick to an outdated 'shareholder capitalism' that prioritizes short-term profits over everything else—and wait for employees, clients, and voters to force change on them from the outside." (Klaus Schwab, "Capitalism Must Reform to Survive," *Foreign Affairs*, January 16, 2020, https://www.foreignaffairs.com/articles/2020-01-16/capitalism-must-reform-survive.)

14   Business Roundtable, "Our Commitment," Business Roundtable, accessed January 15, 2023, https://opportunity.businessroundtable.org/ourcommitment. If there is any question about the general and specific attitudes of the US and global capitalist elites to such issues, check the signatories on the Business Roundtable statement. Here are a range of similar positions: Nick Hanauer, "The Dirty Secret of Capitalism—and a New Way Forward," TED talk, video, 16:54, accessed January 31, 2023, https://www.ted.com/talks/nick_hanauer_the_dirty_secret_of_capitalism_and_a_new_way_forward; Martin Wolf, "Martin Wolf: Why Rigged Capitalism Is Damaging Liberal Democracy," *Financial Times*, September 18, 2019, https://www.ft.com/content/5a8ab27e-d470-11e9-8367-807ebd53ab77; Ann Pettifor, "High Finance Is Wrecking the Economy and the Planet—but It Won't Reform Itself," *Prospect*, October 5, 2019, https://www.prospectmagazine.co.uk/magazine/high-finance-is-wrecking-the-economy-and-the-planet-but-it-wont-reform-itself-banking-wall-street-city-of-london; and Mark DeCambre, "Salesforce Founder Marc Benioff Says 'Capitalism as We Know It Is Dead,'" *MarketWatch*, October 4, 2019, https://www.marketwatch.com/story/salesforce-founder-marc-benioff-says-capitalism-as-we-know-it-is-dead-2019-10-04.

15   The FIRE sector is focused on monopoly-based "rents" and the revenue-generating capacities of speculative manipulations of Marx's "fictitious capital," not commodity production. In monetary terms, it is orders of magnitude larger than what has been termed the "productive" sector of capital, and the disproportion is rapidly increasing. Some have expressed this relationship in Marxist terms as the supplanting of M-C-M by M-M (Wolfgang Streeck).

16   "Joe Biden and the Party of Davos," *New York Times*, May 3, 2019, https://www. nytimes.com/2019/05/03/opinion/joe-biden.html.

17   Center for American Progress, "CAP and AEI Team Up to Defend Democracy and the Transatlantic Partnership," Center for American Progress, May 10, 2018, https://www.americanprogress.org/press/release-cap-aei-team-defend-democracy-transatlantic-partnership.

18   See Don Hamerquist, "New Stuff from an Old Guy—Part 3," *Three Way Fight*, November 12, 2018, http://threewayfight.blogspot.com/2018/11/new-stuff-from-old-guy-part-3.html.

19   Henry Giroux, "Pedagogical Terrorism and Hope in the Age of Fascist Politics," *CounterPunch*, May 10, 2019, https://www.counterpunch.org/2019/05/10/pedagogical-terrorism-and-hope-in-the-age-of-fascist-politics.

20   Giroux, "Pedagogical Terrorism."

21   The term *kakistocracy*, the "rule by the worst," gained public currency in 2018 when fired CIA head John O. Brennan noted the extraordinary level of collective and individual incompetence in the Trump administration and accused it of being a kakistocracy. Appropriately, Brennan opted for a tweet to make his point. (John O. Brennan, @JohnBrennan, "Your kakistocracy is collapsing after its lamentable journey," Twitter, April 13, 2018, https://twitter.com/johnbrennan/status/984803 286006951936?lang=en.)

22   Ranney expands on his notions of "flailing and churning" in his valuable book *New World Disorder*.

23   "In all evidence, Western rationality is reaching a new level that implies a leap in development. But it is also giving birth to new monsters. Modern technologies make it possible to penetrate human psyche much deeper and to install new identity. The economy is being dehumanized, while labor control efficiency grows exponentially. Modern workers are under tight surveillance, with their time clocked in seconds. Many other parameters can be monitored as well, from eye-pupil movements to brain activity. This efficiency is being gladly adapted to politics. Modern technologies can help alienate human beings from their proper nature and identity to an extent never envisaged by Marx, Fromm, Adorno, Marcuse and the critics of repressive rationality. While earlier Foucault's freak show was limited to the human body, today it is penetrating human psyche. The 'system' may know about us much more than we do ourselves." (Ivan Timofeev, "'Twilight of the West?' The New Totalitarianism, Reflection and Free Thought," Valdai Discussion Club, September 17, 2019, https://valdaiclub.com/a/highlights/twilight-of-the-west-the-new-totalitarianism.)

24   There is extensive current reporting on the use of such techniques in response to COVID-19. They all indicate that the techniques will certainly outlast the pandemic.

25   Julien Braun, "Forum 2018 du club Valdaï : Un exercice convenu et un Vladimir Poutine moins concerné," interview with Arnauld Dubien, Valdai Discussion Club, October 25, 2018, https://www.lecourrierderussie.com/international/2018/10/forum-2018-club-valdai-vladimir-poutine.

26   Mira Oklobdzija, "The New Kid on the Nationalist Block: Thierry Baudet," *CounterPunch*, May 14, 2019, https://www.counterpunch.org/2019/05/14/the-new-kid-on-the-nationalist-block-thierry-baudet.

27   John Feffer, "The Rising Tide of the Populist Right," *TomDispatch*, May 13, 2019, https://tomdispatch.com/john-feffer-the-rising-tide-of-the-populist-right.

28   Stathis Kouvelakis, "The French Insurgency," *New Left Review*, nos. 116/117, March–June 2019, https://newleftreview.org/issues/II116/articles/stathis-kouvelakis-the-french-insurgency.

29   Some elements of a crisis of profitability will have features that relate more or less directly to crises of legitimacy, e.g., a secular decline in the rate of profit, a rapid increase in social and economic inequality, and an increase in general indebtedness

propelled by financialization. The emergence of critical tipping points in capital's so-called externalities that are features of the deferred social and ecological costs of capital production will further sharpen the contradictions between the transnational economic content of current capitalism and the nation-state-based forms of its domination. The "generalized failure of popular consent" is, and will continue to be, the overdetermined impact of the combination of all such factors.

30   It was always a mistake for the antifascist movement to look at fascists as "boneheads," but it was widely done. It would be a similar mistake, but a much more serious one, to take a similar approach to the capitalist ruling class.

31   An elaborate version of the argument is presented by Ken Gude in an essay from the CAP/AEI's "Moscow Project": Ken Gude, "Russia's 5th Column," Center for American Progress, March 15, 2017, https://www.americanprogress.org/article/russias-5th-column.

32   Contradictions around "identity" might substitute for the left fault lines of the 1970s that were exploited so effectively in the repressive projects of that period. This points to the importance of paying attention to political formations that combine an advocacy of reformist electoral politics inside the general left with the promotion of various internal disruptions of more militant sectors of it—typically around some question of identity.

33   Matt Taibbi, "We're in a Permanent Coup," *TK News by Matt Taibbi*, October 11, 2019, https://taibbi.substack.com/p/were-in-a-permanent-coup.

Trump's Shaky Capitalist Support: Business Conflict and the 2016 Election

1   Brianne Pfannenstiel, "Billionaire Activist Tom Steyer Says He Will Focus on Impeaching Donald Trump," *USA Today*, January 9, 2019, https://www.usatoday.com/story/news/politics/2019/01/09/tom-steyer-focus-impeaching-donald-trump/2529896002; Abid Rahman, "Michael Bloomberg Slams 'Recklessly Emotional and Senselessly Chaotic' Trump," *Hollywood Reporter*, December 24, 2018, https://www.hollywoodreporter.com/news/politics-news/bloomberg-trump-1171584; Philip Elliott, "Koch Network Mounts Grassroots Effort to Support Immigration," *Time*, July 20, 2018, https://time.com/5343074/libre-koch-congress-immigration; and Jonathan Karl and Arlette Saenz, "Koch Brothers Taking on Trump with Free Trade Campaign," ABC News, June 4, 2018, https://abcnews.go.com/Politics/koch-brothers-taking-trump-free-trade-campaign/story?id=55637361.

2   Thomas Ferguson, Paul Jorgensen, and Jie Chen, "Industrial Structure and Party Competition in an Age of Hunger Games: Donald Trump and the 2016 Presidential Election," Working Paper No. 66, Institute for New Economic Thinking, January 2018, https://www.ineteconomics.org/research/research-papers/industrial-structure-and-party-competition-in-an-age-of-hunger-games.

3   Thomas Ferguson, *Golden Rule: The Investment Theory of Party Competition and the Logic of Money-Driven Political Systems* (Chicago: University of Chicago Press, 1995); and Thomas Ferguson and Joel Rogers, *Right Turn: The Decline of the Democrats and the Future of American Politics* (New York: Hill and Wang, 1986).

4   Thomas Ferguson, Paul Jorgensen, and Jie Chen, "Party Competition and Industrial Structure in the 2012 Elections: Who's Really Driving the Taxi to the Dark Side?" *International Journal of Political Economy* 42, no. 2 (Summer 2013): 3–41, https://modernmoneynetwork.org/sites/default/files/biblio/ferguson_jorgensen_chen_intl_journal_of_pol_econ_2013.pdf.

5   Ferguson, Jorgensen, and Chen, "Party Competition and Industrial Structure in the 2012 Elections."

6   Ferguson, Jorgensen, and Chen, "Industrial Structure and Party Competition in an Age of Hunger Games," 25.

7　Ferguson, Jorgensen, and Chen, "Industrial Structure and Party Competition in an Age of Hunger Games," 25, 3.

8　Ferguson, Jorgensen, and Chen, "Industrial Structure and Party Competition in an Age of Hunger Games," 25–26.

9　Ferguson, Jorgensen, and Chen, "Industrial Structure and Party Competition in an Age of Hunger Games," 28.

10　Ferguson, Jorgensen, and Chen, "Industrial Structure and Party Competition in an Age of Hunger Games," 38.

11　Jane Mayer, "The Reclusive Hedge-Fund Tycoon behind the Trump Presidency: How Robert Mercer Exploited America's Populist Insurgency," *New Yorker*, March 17, 2017, https://www.newyorker.com/magazine/2017/03/27/the-reclusive-hedge-fund-tycoon-behind-the-trump-presidency.

12　Ferguson, Jorgensen, and Chen, "Industrial Structure and Party Competition in an Age of Hunger Games," 47.

13　Ferguson, Jorgensen, and Chen, "Industrial Structure and Party Competition in an Age of Hunger Games," 45.

14　Ferguson, Jorgensen, and Chen, "Industrial Structure and Party Competition in an Age of Hunger Games," 48.

15　Matthew N. Lyons, *Insurgent Supremacists: The U.S. Far Right's Challenge to State and Empire* (Oakland: PM Press, and Montreal: Kersplebedeb Publishing, 2018), 200.

16　Lyons, *Insurgent Supremacists*, 204.

17　Marco Rosaire Rossi, "Trump's New Neoliberalism," *New Compass*, July 1, 2018, http://new-compass.net/articles/trumps-new-neoliberalism.

18　Karen DeYoung and Karoun Demirjian, "Contradicting Trump, Bolton Says No Withdrawal from Syria until ISIS Destroyed, Kurds' Safety Guaranteed," *Washington Post*, January 6, 2019, https://www.washingtonpost.com/world/national-security/bolton-promises-no-troop-withdrawal-from-syria-until-isis-contained-kurds-safety-guaranteed/2019/01/06/ee219bba-11c5-11e9-b6ad-9cfd62dbb0a8_story.html; and Eliana Johnson and Burgess Everett, "Pressure from Base Pushed a Flustered Trump into Shutdown Reversal," *Politico*, December 20, 2018, https://www.politico.com/story/2018/12/20/trump-budget-reversal-1071388.

19　Ferguson, *Golden Rule*, 334n28.

20　"Strong Businesses Invest in American Workers and Jobs," Business Roundtable, circa 2017, https://www.businessroundtable.org/policy-perspectives/tax-fiscal-policy/strong-businesses-invest-in-american-workers-and-jobs; Maria Ghazal, "Examination of the Effects of Regulatory Policy on the Economy and Business Growth," prepared statement, US Senate Committee on Homeland Security and Governmental Affairs Subcommittee on Regulatory Affairs and Federal Management, September 27, 2018, https://www.hsgac.senate.gov/imo/media/doc/2018-09-27%20TESTIMONY,%20Maria%20Ghazal.pdf; Ylan Mui, "Trump's Trade War Is Spooking CEOs into Scaling Back Investment Plans, According to a Business Roundtable Survey," CNBC, September 24, 2018, https://www.cnbc.com/2018/09/24/trump-trade-war-spooks-ceos-into-curbing-investing-business-roundtable-survey.html; and Chuck Robbins et al., letter to Kierstjen M. Nielsen, August 22, 2018, https://s3.amazonaws.com/brt.org/archive/letters/Immigration.Nielsen%20Letter%2008232018.pdf.

21　Don Hamerquist, "New Stuff from an Old Guy—Part 3," *Three Way Fight*, November 12, 2018, http://threewayfight.blogspot.com/2018/11/new-stuff-from-an-old-guy-part-3.html.

22　Research & Destroy, "The Landing: Fascists without Fascism," Research & Destroy, February 20, 2017, https://researchanddestroy.wordpress.com/2017/02/20/the-landing-fascists-without-fascism.

Trump's Election and Capitalist Power: An Exchange

1   Matthew N. Lyons, "Trump's Shaky Capitalist Support: Business Conflict and the 2016 Election," *Three Way Fight*, February 17, 2019, included in this volume.

2   Henry A. Giroux, "Neoliberal Fascism and the Echoes of History," Truth Dig, August 2, 2018, https://www.truthdig.com/articles/neoliberal-fascism-and-the-echoes-of-history.

3   "The U.S. Is an Oligarchy? The Research, Explained," ResearchUS, no date, https://act.represent.us/sign/usa-oligarchy-research-explained.

4   Floris D'Aalst, "Whither America? Class and Politics in the Era of American Decline," *Insurgent Notes*, February 24, 2019, http://insurgentnotes.com/2019/02/whither-america-class-and-politics-in-the-era-of-american-decline.

5   Thomas Ferguson, Paul Jorgensen, and Jie Chen, "Party Competition and Industrial Structure in the 2012 Elections: Who's Really Driving the Taxi to the Dark Side?" *International Journal of Political Economy* 42, no. 2 (Summer 2013): 3–41, https://modernmoneynetwork.org/sites/default/files/biblio/ferguson_jorgensen_chen_intl_journal_of_pol_econ_2013.pdf.

6   Thomas Ferguson, "From 'Normalcy' to New Deal: Industrial Structure, Party Competition, and American Public Policy in the Great Depression," in *Golden Rule: The Investment Theory of Party Competition and the Logic of Money-Driven Political Systems* (Chicago: University of Chicago Press, 1995), 113–172.

Trump, the Far Right, and the Return of Vigilante Repression

1   Matthew N. Lyons, "Trump's Impact: A Fascist Upsurge Is Just One of the Dangers," *Three Way Fight*, December 22, 2015, http://threewayfight.blogspot.com/2015/12/trumps-impact-fascist-upsurge-is-just.html.

2   Matthew N. Lyons, "Making America Worse," *Three Way Fight*, July 16, 2016, http://threewayfight.blogspot.com/2016/07/making-america-worse.html.

3   Matthew N. Lyons, "Ctrl-Alt-Delete: The Origins and Ideology of the Alternative Right," Political Research Associates, January 20, 2017, https://politicalresearch.org/2017/01/20/ctrl-alt-delete-report-on-the-alternative-right, also published in *Ctrl-Alt-Delete: An Antifascist Report on the Alternative Right* (Montreal: Kersplebedeb Publishing, 2017).

4   Matthew N. Lyons, "An Alt Right Update," Political Research Associates, August 7, 2017, https://politicalresearch.org/2017/08/07/an-alt-right-update.

5   Matthew N. Lyons, "'Racial Dissidents Have Lost the Ability to Organize Openly': Alt-Rightists on Trump, ICE, and What Is to Be Done," *Insurgent Notes*, August 4, 2018.

6   Spencer Sunshine et al., *Up in Arms: A Guide to Oregon's Patriot Movement* (Scappoose, OR: Rural Organizing Project, and Somerville, MA: Political Research Associates, 2016), https://rop.org/resources/up-in-arms-pdf-2; and Matthew N. Lyons, "Ammon Bundy, the Refugee Caravan, and Patriot Movement Race Politics," *Three Way Fight*, December 20, 2018, http://threewayfight.blogspot.com/2018/12/ammon-bundy-refugee-caravan-and-patriot.html.

7   Tay Wiles, "Malheur Occupation, Explained," *High Country News*, January 4, 2016, https://www.hcn.org/articles/oregon-occupation-at-wildlife-refuge; Lois Beckett, "Virginia: Thousands of Armed Protesters Rally against Gun Control Bills," *Guardian*, January 20, 2020, https://www.theguardian.com/us-news/2020/jan/20/virginia-gun-rally-activists-richmond; and "What and Who Is behind the US Anti-lockdown Protests?" *Al Jazeera*, April 21, 2020, https://www.aljazeera.com/news/2020/4/21/what-and-who-is-behind-the-us-anti-lockdown-protests.

8   Tess Owen, "The Alt-Right's Love Affair with Trump Is Over. Here's Why," *Vice*, July 9, 2019, https://www.vice.com/en/article/gy4ee7/the-alt-rights-love-affair-with-trump-is-over-heres-why.

9   Occidental Dissent, http://occidentaldissent.com.

10   Ryan Lenz and Mark Potok, "War in the West: The Bundy Ranch Standoff and the American Radical Right," Southern Poverty Law Center, July 10, 2014, https://www.splcenter.org/20140709/war-west-bundy-ranch-standoff-and-american-radical-right.

11   Matthew N. Lyons, "Trump's Impact."

12   "Mapping Paramilitary and Far-Right Threats to Racial Justice," Political Research Associates, June 19, 2020, updated October 27, 2021, https://politicalresearch.org/2020/06/19/mapping-paramilitary-and-far-right-threats-racial-justice; and Ben Lorber, "A Constellation of Threats: Far Rightists Respond to the Black-Led Uprising," *Three Way Fight*, July 19, 2020, https://threewayfight.blogspot.com/2020/07/a-constellation-of-threats-far.html.

13   Matthew N. Lyons, "Dylann Roof's White Nationalism," *Three Way Fight*, June 21, 2015, https://threewayfight.blogspot.com/2015/06/dylann-roofs-white-nationalism.html; and Farid Hafez, "The Manifesto of the El Paso Terrorist," Bridge: A Georgetown University Initiative, August 26, 2019, https://bridge.georgetown.edu/research/the-manifesto-of-the-el-paso-terrorist.

14   Dan Mihalopoulos, "Kenosha Shooting Suspect Fervently Supported 'Blue Lives,' Joined Local Militia," National Public Radio, August 27, 2020, https://www.npr.org/sections/live-updates-protests-for-racial-justice/2020/08/27/906566596/alleged-kenosha-shooter-fervently-supported-blue-lives-joined-local-militia; Caitlin O'Kane, "Tucker Carlson Draws Backlash after Saying 17-Year-Old Kenosha Shooting Suspect 'Maintain[ed] Order When No One Else Would,'" CBS News, August 28, 2020, https://www.cbsnews.com/news/tucker-carlson-kyle-rittenhouse-defense-shooting-suspect-backlash; and Carla Herreria Russo, "Trump Defends Kyle Rittenhouse's Deadly Shooting: 'They Attacked Him,'" *HuffPost*, August 31, 2020, https://www.huffpost.com/entry/trump-defends-kyle-rittenhouse-kenosha-shooting_n_5f4d71aac5b64f17e1419ba5.

15   Richard Houck, "Law Enforcement & the Hostile Elite," Counter-Currents, June 20, 2018, https://counter-currents.com/2018/06/law-enforcement-the-hostile-elite; Three Way Fight, "Multiracial Far Right: A Conversation with Daryle Lamont Jenkins and Cloee Cooper," *Three Way Fight*, September 14, 2019, https://threewayfight.blogspot.com/2019/09/multiracial-far-right-conversation-with.html.

16   Matthew N. Lyons, "Rising Above the Herd: Keith Preston's Authoritarian Anti-statism," *New Politics*, April 29, 2011, https://newpol.org/rising-above-herd-keith-prestons-authoritarian-anti-statism; and Christopher Mathias, "White Vigilantes Have Always Had a Friend in Police," *HuffPost*, August 28, 2020, https://www.huffpost.com/entry/white-vigilantes-kenosha_n_5f4822bcc5b6cf66b2b5103e.

17   Matthew N. Lyons, "Liberal Counterinsurgency versus the Paramilitary Right," *Three Way Fight*, November 27, 2012, https://threewayfight.blogspot.com/2012/11/liberal-counterinsurgency-versus.html; and Matthew N. Lyons, "Frazier Glenn Miller, Nazi Violence, and the State," *Three Way Fight*, May 8, 2014, https://threewayfight.blogspot.com/2014/05/frazier-glenn-miller-nazi-violence-and.html.

18   Highlighting that Patriot movement support for Trump is not a given, Oath Keepers, one of the most prominent Patriot groups, tweeted in August 2020, "We'll give Trump one last chance to declare this a Marxist insurrection & suppress it as his duty demands. If he fails to do HIS duty, we will do OURS." (Oath Keepers, @Oathkeepers, "The first shot has been fired brother," Twitter, August 30, 2020, available at https://twitter.com/shane_burley1/status/1300170228375068672/photo/1.)

Lockdowns, the Insurgent Far Right, and the Future of Antifascism: A Conversation with *Three Way Fight*

1   It's Going Down, "This Is America #133: Salem Antifascists Speak-out; Discussion

on COVID Deaths, Social Media & Civil War," podcast, It's Going Down, December 22, 2020, https://itsgoingdown.org/this-is-america-133-salem-antifascists-speak-out-discussion-on-covid-deaths-social-media-civil-war.

2   It's Going Down, "How Trump Is Consolidating His Forces to Hold On to Power," It's Going Down, August 17, 2020, https://itsgoingdown.org/message-in-a-molotov-election-trump; and Matthew N. Lyons, "Resisting Trump's Coup," *Three Way Fight*, September 27, 2020, http://threewayfight.blogspot.com/2020/09/resisting-trumps-coup.html.

3   Barton Gellman, "The Election That Could Break America," *Atlantic*, November 2020, https://www.theatlantic.com/magazine/archive/2020/11/what-if-trump-refuses-concede/616424.

4   A.M. Gittlitz, "Middle-Class War: A Visit to Staten Island's Autonomous Zone," *Hard Crackers*, December 20, 2020, https://hardcrackers.com/middle-class-war.

5   Institute for Research and Education on Human Rights, https://www.irehr.org.

Broken Windows Fascism

1   Kahron Spearman, "Video: Cops 'Turn On' Proud Boys, Far-Right Group Desecrates 'Blue Lives' Flag in Response," *Daily Dot*, January 3, 2021, https://www.dailydot.com/debug/police-proud-boys-salem-fight-videos; Natasha Lennard, "Far-Right Violence Is Going to Be a Threat with or without Trump's Calls to Action," *Intercept*, January 5, 2021, https://theintercept.com/2021/01/05/trump-rally-far-right-violence; and Robert Evans, "How the Insurgent and MAGA Right Are Being Welded Together on the Streets of Washington D.C.," *Bellingcat*, January 5, 2021, https://www.bellingcat.com/news/americas/2021/01/05/how-the-insurgent-and-maga-right-are-being-welded-together-on-the-streets-of-washington-d-c.

2   Matthew N. Lyons, "Resisting Trump's Coup," *Three Way Fight*, September 27, 2020, http://threewayfight.blogspot.com/2020/09/resisting-trumps-coup.html.

3   Matthew N. Lyons, "Some Thoughts on Fascism and the Current Moment," *Three Way Fight*, July 7, 2019, http://threewayfight.blogspot.com/2019/07/some-thoughts-on-fascism-and-current.html.

4   Matthew N. Lyons, "Liberal Counterinsurgency versus the Paramilitary Right," *Three Way Fight*, November 27, 2012, http://threewayfight.blogspot.com/2012/11/liberal-counterinsurgency-versus.html.

Insurgent Movement, Government Complicity, or Both?

1   Insurgence USA, "About," Insurgence USA, no date, https://www.insurgenceusa.com/about-insurgence-usa.html, archived at https://web.archive.org/web/20210111131145/https://www.insurgenceusa.com/about-insurgence-usa.html.

2   Jarrod Shanahan, "The Big Takeover," *Hard Crackers*, January 7, 2021, https://hardcrackers.com/the-big-takeover.

3   Shanahan, "The Big Takeover."

4   "'White Privilege Is on Display.' Ibram X. Kendi, Director of BU's Center for Antiracist Research, Sounds Off on US Capitol Attack," *BU Today*, January 7, 2021, https://www.bu.edu/articles/2021/ibram-x-kendi-us-capitol-attack.

5   Alleen Brown and Akela Lacy, "In Wake of Capitol Riot, GOP Legislatures 'Rebrand' Old Anti-BLM Protest Laws," *Intercept*, January 12, 2021, https://theintercept.com/2021/01/12/capitol-riot-anti-protest-blm-laws.

6   Kristian Williams, *Our Enemies in Blue: Police and Power in America*, 3rd ed. (Oakland: AK Press, 2015).

7   Glenn Thrush and Helene Cooper, "The Capitol Police Chief Says His Pleas for Backup Were Ignored by the Sergeants-at-Arms and the Pentagon," *New York Times*, January 11, 2021, https://www.nytimes.com/2021/01/11/us/capitol-police-backup-ignored.html; and Cloee Cooper and Sam Smith, "In the Lead-Up to

the Election, Special Forces Train Civilians for Insurgency," Political Research Associates, October 30, 2020, https://politicalresearch.org/2020/10/30/lead-election-special-forces-train-civilians-insurgency.

8   Marie Fazio, "Notable Arrests after the Riot at the Capitol," *New York Times*, January 10, 2021, updated July 23, 2021, https://www.nytimes.com/2021/01/10/us/politics/capitol-arrests.html.

Abolition and the Movement against Police Brutality

1   See MPD150, *Enough Is Enough: A 150 Year Performance Review of the Minneapolis Police Department*, expanded ed. (Minneapolis: MPD150, 2020), https://www.mpd150.com/wp-content/uploads/reports/report_2_compressed.pdf.

States of Incarceration: A Discussion

1   Jarrod Shanahan and Zhandarka Kurti, *States of Incarceration: Rebellion, Reform, and America's Punishment System* (London: Reaktion/Field Notes Books, 2022). This interview originally appeared in the *Brooklyn Rail* and is reprinted with permission.

2   Tobi Haslett, "Magic Actions: Looking Back on the George Floyd Rebellion," *n + 1*, no. 40 (Summer 2021), https://www.nplusonemag.com/issue-40/politics/magic-actions-2.

Clinic Defense in the Era of Operation Rescue

1   Laura, "Liberal Attack on Choice," *Love and Rage* 6, no. 4 (August/September 1995): 3.

2   Laura, "Liberal Attack on Choice," 24.

Tigertown Beats Nazis Down: Reflections on Auburn and Mass Antifascism

1   This piece was originally written and distributed locally. We are publicizing it in order to contribute to debate within the broader movement. At the time of writing, we had the benefit of a YouTube video made by two Auburn weight-lifting "bros" that reinforced many of our observations or suspicions. Unfortunately, that video has been removed. We have had to adjust some points as a result. "Tigertown" is another name for Auburn, after the mascot.

2   Most antifascist events don't have this kind of intermingling. The usual events include two camps, both standing on opposite sides of a barricade, with at least one line of cops in between them.

3   Many of the white men in the crowd were dressed like "good ol' boys": baseball caps, polo shirts, cargo shorts, and sandals. Most of the fascists were dressed the same. At the time we caught ourselves assuming that anyone dressed this way was conservative, but at several points they confronted the fascists most directly. (MAGA = Make America Great Again.)

4   Some images show a good example: someone in all black holding an Anti-Fascist Action sign and staring standoffishly into the distance behind black sunglasses, studiously avoiding interaction with anyone around them.

5   "The next most influential man in his state is probably Governor Robert Bentley. But Saban is Nos. 1 through 10 on the list of Alabama power brokers. He would be in the top 10 even without his three national titles with the Crimson Tide. The position itself—head football coach at Alabama—gives you a platform of power. But because of the program's wild success, Saban is the best-liked person in the state. He has the most visible job in the state, and given the religiosity with which Alabamians apply themselves to college football, Saban now has another title: the pontiff of pigskin." (Leada Gore, "Nick Saban, Not Gov. Robert Bentley, Is Most Powerful Person in Alabama, Paul Finebaum Writes: Do You Agree?" AL.com, August 11, 2014, https://www.al.com/news/2014/08/nick_saban_not_gov_robert_bent.html.)

6   It is not clear how much of the crowd was aware of this when it happened or how much this contributed to student anger in the moment. Some of this observation is coming from reading comments on reddit.com/r/auburn. Or, as the students in the video said, "He said we shouldn't watch football and came to Auburn—probably not a good idea."

7   Until recently, the only left organizations that had even tried to build a presence in Alabama were Socialist Alternative and the IWW. (The IWW came close to establishing a branch, but many of the key members walked away in disgust over what they perceived as a bureaucratic, authoritarian, and distant attitude from the executive board when they were chartering in 2015.) Recently, it seems that the Socialist Party and DSA have built groups in Alabama as well.

8   See Southern Poverty Law Center, "League of the South," Southern Poverty Law Center, accessed April 15, 2017, https://www.splcenter.org/fighting-hate/extremist-files/group/league-south.

9   In the General Defense Committee's picket/guard training, we learn to think of pickets, protests, or marches as a theatre performance, where many roles might be filled. In this case, we think that most antifascists generally tended to see people from Auburn as "spectators" of the theatre rather than participants in it; likewise, many students considered themselves spectators.

10 "Squad versus squad" or "vanguard versus vanguard" is shorthand for the kind of antifascism that was dominant in the Eighties and Nineties, where small, specialized groups of antifascist punks and skinheads engaged in street fights with small, specialized groups of fascist punks and skinheads. This is in contrast to "mass antifascism," which focuses on organizing as broadly as possible within the community to oppose fascists.

11 There are some interesting overlaps between agitation and "trolling"—this is beyond the scope of this piece, but worth thinking about, especially insofar as all of the time and energy that fascists spend trolling means that they are honing their agitational skills much more than we are.

12 The content of what they were yelling was also problematic. In form, it was antagonistic toward the crowd, treating the crowd as antagonists toward the black bloc. In content, it was about how the black bloc was there to "protect marginalized communities that couldn't protect themselves"—a racist and vanguardist attitude. At a recent debrief meeting, several of us agreed that we failed to intervene.

13 It's Going Down reported that the chant was "Alerta, Alerta, Antifascista," but many of us heard it as "Atlanta," and we suspect the crowd did as well. In contrast, we noticed that we got pretty good responses when we turned some of their football chants against Spencer. We might've missed a good opportunity for a "War Damn Antifa" banner. (See It's Going Down, "Auburn, AL: Students Chase Off Richard Spencer and Matthew Heimbach's Alt-Right Trolls," It's Going Down, April 19, 2017, https://itsgoingdown.org/auburn-al-students-chase-off-richard-spencer-matthew-heimbachs-alt-right-trolls.)

14 Several fascists have tried to claim that the crowd ran right through them, which is a lie. It's true that some groups escaped attention and were able to walk away, but the crowd did chase after several nazis, and those nazis did eventually have to escape the crowd under police escort.

15 We acknowledge that on this section in particular we are theorizing "blindly." There are many question marks. Was it totally spontaneous? Were there networks (fraternities, for example) that weren't visible to us that had planned for something like this? Did it start as a small scuffle that pulled in more students, or was there a large group ready to throw down already? Did any antifascists from outside Auburn play a role in the start of the scuffle? How much were the students looking to fight fascists, and how much would they have settled on any fight, for example with the black bloc?

16   We spoke to many people who explained, "I'm here to see what's going to happen. Some sh** might go down." Some brought up the potential for scuffles between antifa types and fascists; some planned to hit the bars after.

17   This is part of why we think the threat of a brawl between antifa and the crowd was real. We also have to point out here or elsewhere that to many of the students, the antifascists looked much more like the fascists (especially the "Traditionalist Worker Party," who were dressed in all black, with helmets, and keeping a bloc formation) than they looked like Auburn students. There were some times where even we couldn't easily tell which side people were on.

18   On the flip side—what would have happened if the students had had the "experience" of running antifascists out of town?

19   This problem of people who attach themselves to a movement precisely because of its irrelevance is not new. Harvey Swados nails it perfectly in *Standing Fast*, his excellent novel about American Trotskyists in the Thirties and Forties: "Let's be frank," Joe said. "There are guys who are in the Party now because we're small. If we really grew, if we really became an influence, they'd flee." (See Lionel Abel, "*Standing Fast*, by Harvey Swados," *Commentary*, December 1970, https://www. commentary.org/articles/lionel-abel-2/standing-fast-by-harvey-swados.)

20   Sometimes people talk about "gray bloc," but that isn't quite the same. That's more of a modified version of black bloc, and not what we're proposing.

21   *Standing Fast* also has some great descriptions of how agitators used to be trained deliberately, almost in an apprenticeship with an older, more experienced agitator.

22   It's Going Down, "Students Chase Off Richard Spencer."

23   To be clear, we mean something more akin to "popularize." When we say "normal" we put it in quotes because the concept of "normal" is gendered, sexualized, and racialized, and it's used against people. We really mean "people who do not dress in black bloc at actions, do not identify with a certain politics, and are unfamiliar with the political scenes specific to many large US cities."

Gaming's Three Way Fight: Why Antifascists Should Organize in and around Video Games

1   Matthew Gault, "DHS to Spend Almost $700,000 Investigating 'Radicalization in Gaming,'" *Vice*, September 16, 2022, https://www.vice.com/en/article/4ax4n3/ dhs-to-spend-almost-dollar700000-investigating-radicalization-in-gaming.

2   Stop Cop City, accessed February 23, 2023, https://stopcop.city; James Factora, "Queer 'Cop City' Protestor Tortuguita Fatally Shot by Law Enforcement in Atlanta," *Them*, January 23, 2023, https://www.them.us/story/tortuguita-shot-killed-atlanta-police-cop-city.

3   Three Way Fight, "About Three Way Fight," *Three Way Fight*, July 15, 2013, updated November 12, 2017, http://threewayfight.blogspot.com/p/about.html.

4   Center for Prevention Programs and Partnerships, "Targeted Violence and Terrorism Prevention Grant Program," US Department of Homeland Security, January 11, 2023, https://www.dhs.gov/tvtpgrants.

5   Stefan Wojcik and Adam Hughes, "Sizing Up Twitter Users," Pew Research Center, April 24, 2019, https://www.pewresearch.org/internet/2019/04/24/sizing-up-twitter-users.

6   Samuel Stewart, "Video Game Industry Silently Taking Over Entertainment World," *EJInsight*, October 22, 2019, https://www.ejinsight.com/eji/ article/id/2280405/20191022-video-game-industry-silently-taking-over-entertainment-world; Anti-Defamation League, "This Is Not a Game: How Steam Harbors Extremists," Anti-Defamation League, April 29, 2020, https:// www.adl.org/resources/report/not-game-how-steam-harbors-extremists; and Andrew Perrin, "5 Facts about Americans and Video Games," Pew

Research Center, September 17, 2018, https://www.pewresearch.org/fact-tank/2018/09/17/5-facts-about-americans-and-video-games.

7   Anthony Brooks and James Perkins Mastromarino, "Extremists Exploit Gaming Networks and Social Media to Recruit and Radicalize," *Here & Now*, WBUR, May 19, 2022, https://www.wbur.org/hereandnow/2022/05/19/video-games-extremists-recruit; John Yang, "U.S. Military Focuses Recruiting Efforts on Video-Game Playing Teenagers," *PBS News Hour*, September 1, 2022, https://www.pbs.org/newshour/show/u-s-military-focuses-recruiting-efforts-on-video-game-playing-teenagers; Katie Lange, "Military Esports: How Gaming Is Changing Recruitment & Morale," US Department of Defense, December 13, 2022, https://www.defense.gov/News/Feature-Stories/Story/Article/3244620/military-esports-how-gaming-is-changing-recruitment-morale; and US Army, "America's Army: Proving Grounds," video game, Steam, October 1, 2015, https://store.steampowered.com/app/203290/Americas_Army_Proving_Grounds.

8   Matthew Gault, "Steam Is Filled with Groups That Celebrate School Shooters," *Vice*, March 6, 2018, https://www.vice.com/en/article/d3w9ea/steam-is-filled-with-groups-that-celebrate-school-shooters; Will Carless and Aaron Sankin, "The Hate Report: Gaming App Has 173 Groups That Glorify School Shooters," *Reveal*, March 2, 2018, https://revealnews.org/blog/hate-report-gaming-app-has-173-groups-that-glorify-school-shooters; Emanuel Maiberg, "Steam Is Full of Hate Groups," *Vice*, October 19, 2017, https://www.vice.com/en/article/d3dzvw/steam-is-full-nazi-racist-groups; Cecilia D'Anastasio, "How Roblox Became a Playground for Virtual Fascists," *Wired*, June 10, 2021, https://www.wired.com/story/roblox-online-games-irl-fascism-roman-empire; Anti-Defamation League, "This is Not a Game"; and Anti-Defamation League, "Free to Play? Hate, Harassment, and Positive Social Experiences in Online Games," Anti-Defamation League, July 18, 2019, https://www.adl.org/resources/report/free-play-hate-harassment-and-positive-social-experiences-online-games.

9   Brooks and Mastromarino, "Extremists Exploit Gaming Networks."

10   Aoife Gallagher et al., "Gaming and Extremism: The Extreme Right on Discord," Institute for Strategic Dialogue, August 4, 2021, https://www.isdglobal.org/wp-content/uploads/2021/08/04-gaming-report-discord.pdf.

11   Dana M. Williams, "Black Panther Radical Factionalization and the Development of Black Anarchism," *Journal of Black Studies* 46, no. 7 (2015): 678–703; and Miriam Lafontaine, "The IWW Is Making Labour Anti-fascist Again: How Worker's Unions Are Involved in the Fight against Fascism," *Link*, April 3, 2018, https://thelinknewspaper.ca/article/the-iww-is-making-labour-anti-fascist-again.

12   Gault, "DHS to Spend Almost $700,000."

13   Aja Romano, "What We Still Haven't Learned from Gamergate," *Vox*, January 7, 2021, https://www.vox.com/culture/2020/1/20/20808875/gamergate-lessons-cultural-impact-changes-harassment-laws.

14   Adam Tanielian Sr., "Building Healthy Communities Summit," Electronic Arts, June 13, 2019, https://www.ea.com/news/building-healthy-communities-summit; and Matthew Gault, "Senator Asks Gabe Newell Why Steam Hosts So Much Neo-Nazi Content," *Vice*, December 16, 2022, https://www.vice.com/en/article/dy79na/senator-asks-gabe-newell-why-steam-hosts-so-much-neo-nazi-content.

15   UNESCO, "Preventing Violent Extremism," UNESCO, accessed February 23, 2023, https://www.unesco.org/en/preventing-violent-extremism.

16   Anamika Gupta, "Beyond the Zombie Apocalypse: Video Games for Peace and Sustainability," UNESCO Mahatma Gandhi Institute of Education for Peace and Sustainable Development (MGIEP), 2015, https://mgiep.unesco.org/article/video-games-for-peace-and-sustainability; and UNESCO MGIEP, "Games for Learning," UNESCO MGIEP, accessed February 23, 2023, https://mgiep.unesco.org/games-for-learning.

17   Eunus, "Clarifications: On the Arrest of Six Young People for 'Domestic Terrorism,'" *Ill Will*, December 16, 2022, https://illwill.com/clarifications.

18   Federal Trade Commission, "Combatting Online Harms through Innovation: Report to Congress," Federal Trade Commission, June 16, 2022, https://www.ftc. gov/system/files/ftc_gov/pdf/Combatting%20Online%20Harms%20Through%20 Innovation%3B%20Federal%20Trade%20Commission%20Report%20to%20 Congress.pdf.

19   Ruha Benjamin, *Race after Technology: Abolitionist Tools for the New Jim Code* (Hoboken, NJ: John Wiley & Sons, 2019); Stop LAPD Spying Coalition, accessed February 23, 2023, https://stoplapdspying.org.

20   Federal Trade Commission, "Combatting Online Harms through Innovation."

21   Naomi Nix and Lauren Etter, "Facebook Privately Worried about Hate Speech Spawning Violence," Bloomberg News, October 25, 2021, https://www.bnnbloomberg.ca/ facebook-privately-worried-about-hate-speech-spawning-violence-1.1671386; and Barbara Sprunt, "The History behind 'When the Looting Starts, the Shooting Starts,'" National Public Radio, May 29, 2020, https://www.npr.org/2020/05/29/864818368/ the-history-behind-when-the-looting-starts-the-shooting-starts.

22   Kishonna L. Gray, *Black Users in Digital Gaming* (Baton Rouge: Louisiana State University Press, 2020).

23   Gray, *Black Users in Digital Gaming*; and Mayara Araujo Caetano, "They Will Do Anything to Make You React: Deplatforming Racists from the Brazilian Gaming Community," *Gamevironments*, no. 17 (2022), https://journals.suub.uni-bremen.de/ index.php/gamevironments/article/view/198.

24   Anna Anthropy, *Rise of the Videogame Zinesters: How Freaks, Normals, Amateurs, Artists, Dreamers, Drop-outs, Queers, Housewives, and People Like You Are Taking Back an Art Form* (New York: Seven Stories Press, 2012).

25   Abolitionist Teaching Network, "Guide for Racial Justice & Abolitionist Social and Emotional Learning," Abolitionist Teaching Network, August 2020, https:// abolitionistteachingnetwork.org/guide; and Matthew Coopilton, "Critical Game Literacies and Critical Speculative Imagination: A Theoretical and Conceptual Review," *Gamevironments*, no. 17 (2022), https://journals.suub.uni-bremen.de/index. php/gamevironments/article/view/196.

26   *Kai Unearthed*, video game, released February 20, 2021, https://www.kaiunearthed. com; Out of Order Games, *Bloc by Bloc: Uprising*, board game, released March 2022, Out of Order Games, https://outofordergames.com/blocbybloc.

There Will Always Be More of Us: Antifascist Organizing

1   Paul O'Banion, "Autonomous Antifa: From the Autonomen to Post-Antifa in Germany; An Interview with Bender, a German Comrade," It's Going Down, November 20, 2017, https://itsgoingdown.org/autonomous-antifa-germany-interview.

2   O'Banion, "Autonomous Antifa."

3   Peta Steel, *The Battle of Cable Street: They Shall Not Pass; An Account of Working Class Struggles against Fascism* (London: SERTUC, 2017), https://www.tuc.org.uk/ sites/default/files/Cable-Street-book.pdf.

4   Julie Sabatier, "Q&A: PopMob Appeals to 'Everyday Anti-fascists,'" interview with Effie Baum, OPB, August 26, 2019, https://www.opb.org/radio/article/oregon-portland-popmob-anti-fascism-popular-mobilization.

Afterword

1   Those words were published in 2003, but the general notion emerged in our conversations in the weeks immediately after 9/11. See the essay "Above and Below: Them, Them, and Us," in this book.

2   I'm grateful to Matthew Lyons for helping me formulate this point.

3   Unfortunately, the full statement does not appear to be available on the internet as of this writing.

4   "Protest Outside Chicago Area Mosque," CNN, September 13, 2001, http://www.cnn.com/2001/US/09/13/chicago.mosque/index.html. Thank you to my comrades Kieran, Sprite, and Tito for helping refresh my memory of that night. For more information on Islamophobic attacks in the Chicago area after 9/11, see the chapter "Hate Crimes" in the report "Arab and Muslim Civil Rights Issues in the Chicago Metropolitan Area Post-September 11," produced in May 2003 by the Illinois Advisory Committee to the US Commission on Civil Rights, https://www.usccr.gov/files/pubs/sac/il0503/ch2.htm.

Selected Bibliography

The following is a selected list of secondary sources that are cited in this book. We have excluded primary source works, meaning those that are the direct focus of our contributors' analysis or critique, including writings by both far rightists and supporters of the established order. We have also excluded articles that have been cited just to support a factual point. For other sources used, please consult the notes.

Abolitionist Teaching Network. "Guide for Racial Justice & Abolitionist Social and Emotional Learning." Abolitionist Teaching Network, August 2020. https://abolitionistteachingnetwork.org/guide.

Ackelsberg, Martha. *Free Women of Spain: Anarchism and the Struggle for the Emancipation of Women.* Bloomington: Indiana University Press, 1991.

Adugna, Minale. *Women and Warfare in Ethiopia: A Case Study of Their Role during the Campaign of Adwa 1895/96, and the Italo-Ethiopian War, 1935–41.* Gender Issues Research Report Series, no. 13. Addis Ababa, Ethiopia: Organization for Social Science Research in Eastern and Southern Africa, 2001.

Akemi, Romina, and Bree Busk. "Breaking the Waves: Challenging the Liberal Tendency within Anarchism." *Perspectives on Anarchist Theory*, June 29, 2016. https://anarchiststudies.org/breaking-the-waves-challenging-the-liberal-tendency-within-anarchist-feminism-by-romina-akemi-and-bree-busk.

Anti-Fascist Forum, ed. *My Enemy's Enemy: Essays on Globalization, Fascism and the Struggle against Capitalism.* 3rd ed. Montreal: Kersplebedeb Publishing, 2003.

Antiracistantizionist. "Not Quite 'Ordinary Human Beings'—Anti-imperialism and the Anti-humanist Rhetoric of Gilad Atzmon." *Three Way Fight*, March 2012. http://threewayfight.blogspot.com/p/atzmon-critique_09.html.

Batinic, Jelena. "Gender, Revolution, and War: The Mobilization of Women in the Yugoslav Partisan Resistance during World War II." PhD diss., Department of History, Stanford University, 2009.

Beauchamp, Zack. "Incel, the Misogynist Ideology That Inspired the Deadly Toronto Attack, Explained." *Vox*, April 25, 2018. https://www.vox.com/world/2018/4/25/17277496/incel-toronto-attack-alek-minassian.

Benjamin, Ruha. *Race after Technology: Abolitionist Tools for the New Jim Code.* Hoboken, NJ: John Wiley & Sons, 2019.

Berhe, Aregawi. "Revisiting Resistance in Italian-Occupied Ethiopia: The Patriots' Movement (1936–1941) and the Redefinition of Post-War Ethiopia." In *Rethinking Resistance: Revolt and Violence in African History*, edited by Jon Abbink, Mirjam de Bruijn, and Klaas van Walraven. Boston: Brill, 2003.

Berlet, Chip. *Right Woos Left: Populist Party, LaRouchite, and Other Neo-fascist Overtures to Progressives, and Why They Must Be Rejected*. Cambridge, MA: Political Research Associates, 1994.

Berlet, Chip, and Matthew N. Lyons. *Right-Wing Populism in America*. New York: Guilford Press, 2000.

Berneri, C. "Brief Report on Toledo Anti-NSM Protest." *Three Way Fight*, December 12, 2005. http://threewayfight.blogspot.com/2005/12/this-was-forwarded-to-us.html.

Beyerstein, Lindsay. "Beyond the Hate Frame: An Interview with Kay Whitlock & Michael Bronski." *Public Eye* (Political Research Associates), Summer 2015. https://politicalresearch.org/2015/07/27/beyond-the-hate-frame-an-interview-with-kay-whitlock-michael-bronski.

Black, Johannah May. "When Women Bear the Nation's Honour: Fascism and the Woman-as-Symbol under Trump." *Revolutionary Anamnesis*, February 3, 2017. https://johannahmayblack.com/2017/02/03/when-women-bear-the-nations-honour-fascism-and-the-woman-as-symbol-under-trump.

Black Panther Party. "Call for a United Front against Fascism." In *The U.S. Antifascism Reader*, edited by Bill V. Mullen and Christopher Vials. London: Verso, 2020.

Blee, Kathleen M. "Women in the 1920s' Ku Klux Klan Movement." *Feminist Studies* 17, no. 1 (1991): 57–77.

Bodnar, Clay. "Gay Men and the Alternative Right: An Overview." *Hope Not Hate*, April 11, 2018. https://hopenothate.org.uk/2018/04/11/gay-men-alternative-right-overview.

Bonfiglioli, Chiara. "Women's Political and Social Activism in the Early Cold War Era: The Case of Yugoslavia." *Aspasia* 8 (2014): 1–25.

Bordiga, Amadeo, and Edek Osser. "Against Anti-Fascism: Amadeo Bordiga's Last Interview." *Storia Contemporanea*, no. 3 (1973).

Bowles, Nellie. "Jordan Peterson, Custodian of the Patriarchy." *New York Times*, May 18, 2018. https://www.nytimes.com/2018/05/18/style/jordan-peterson-12-rules-for-life.html.

Bowman, Paul. "Fascism and the Three-Way Fight." *Medium*, February 4, 2022. https://eidgenossen.medium.com/fascism-and-the-three-way-fight-4a05b87a4eec.

Bowstern, Moe, Mic Crenshaw, Alec Dunn, Celina Flores, Julie Perini, and Erin Yanke. *It Did Happen Here: An Antifascist People's History*. Oakland: PM Press, 2023.

Bradshaw, Larry, and Lorrie Beth Slonsky. "Eye Witness Accounts by Two Paramedics in New Orleans: Hurricane Katrina—Our Experiences." *Three Way Fight*, September 6, 2005. http://threewayfight.blogspot.com/2005/09/i-received-following-article-from.html.

Bray, Mark. *Antifa: The Anti-Fascist Handbook*. Brooklyn, NY: Melville House, 2017.

Bromma. *Exodus and Reconstruction: Working-Class Women at the Heart of Globalization*. Montreal: Kersplebedeb Publishing, 2012. http://kersplebedeb.com/posts/exodus.

———. "Notes on XXIst Century Socialism." *Three Way Fight*, August 2, 2007. http://threewayfight.blogspot.com/2007/08/notes-on-xxist-century-socialism.html.

Burley, Shane. "The Fall of the Alt-Right Came from Antifascism." *Salon*, April 15, 2018. https://www.salon.com/2018/04/15/the-fall-of-the-alt-right-came-from-anti-fascism_partner.

———. *Fascism Today: What It Is and How to End It*. Chico, CA: AK Press, 2017.

———, ed. *¡No Pasarán! Antifascist Dispatches from a World in Crisis*. Chico, CA: AK Press, 2022.

Byrd, Jodi A. *The Transit of Empire: Indigenous Critiques of Colonialism*. Minneapolis: University of Minnesota Press, 2011.

Cabral, Amílcar. *Revolution in Guinea: Selected Texts*. New York: Monthly Review Press, 1972.

Caetano, Mayara Araujo. "They Will Do Anything to Make You React: Deplatforming Racists from the Brazilian Gaming Community." *Gamevironments*, no. 17 (2022). https://journals.suub.uni-bremen.de/index.php/gamevironments/article/view/198.

Carroll, Caitlin. "The European Refugee Crisis and the Myth of the Immigrant Rapist." *Europe Now Journal*, July 6, 2017. https://www.printfriendly.com/p/g/wmsRa6.

Carroll, William. *The Making of a Transnational Capitalist Class: Corporate Power in the 21st Century*. London: Zed Books, 2013.

Césaire, Aimé. *Discourse on Colonialism*. New York: Monthly Review Press, 2000.

Chen, Chris. "The Limit Point of Capitalist Equality: Notes toward an Abolitionist Antiracism." *Endnotes*, no. 3 (2013).

Churchill, Ward. *A Little Matter of Genocide: Holocaust and Denial in the Americas, 1492 to the Present*. San Francisco: City Lights Books, 1997.

Clark, J. "Three-Way Fight: Revolutionary Anti-Fascism and Armed Self-Defense." In *Setting Sights: Histories and Reflections on Community Armed Self-Defense*, edited by scott crow. Oakland: PM Press, 2018.

Clay, Shannon, Lady, Kristin Schwartz, and Michael Staudenmaier. *We Go Where They Go: The Story of Anti-Racist Action*. Oakland: PM Press, 2023.

Communist International. *The Programme of the Communist International, Together with the Statutes of the Communist International*. London: Modern Books, 1932.

Cooper, Cloee. "Kevin Barrett: Repackaging Antisemitism." Political Research Associates, October 23, 2017. https://politicalresearch.org/2017/10/23/kevin-barrett-repackaging-antisemitism.

Cooper, Cloee, and Sam Smith. "In the Lead-Up to the Election, Special Forces Train Civilians for Insurgency." Political Research Associates, October 30, 2020. https://politicalresearch.org/2020/10/30/lead-election-special-forces-train-civilians-insurgency.

Cooper, Cloee, and Julia Taliesin. "White Nationalist Groups Turn Up at 2018 Women's Marches." Political Research Associates, February 2, 2018. https://politicalresearch.org/2018/02/02/white-nationalist-groups-turn-up-at-2018-womens-marches.

Coopilton, Matthew. "Critical Game Literacies and Critical Speculative Imagination: A Theoretical and Conceptual Review." *Gamevironments*, no. 17 (2022). https://journals.suub.uni-bremen.de/index.php/gamevironments/article/view/196.

Coordinating Committee of Bring the Ruckus. "A Three-Cornered Fight: Tasks of American Revolutionaries in the Twenty-First Century." Bring the Ruckus, December 1, 2003. Available at https://theanarchistlibrary.org/library/coordinating-committee-of-bring-the-ruckus-a-three-cornered-fight.

Cope, Zak. *Divided World, Divided Class: Global Political Economy and the Stratification of Labour under Capitalism*. Montreal: Kersplebedeb Publishing, 2015.

Cornelius, Rebel Jay C., and Insurgente s.c. Rocinante. "Three-Way Fight: Armed Resistance and Militant Anti-Fascism." Anarkismo.net, November 3, 2006. https://web.archive.org/web/20170314114047/http://www.anarkismo.net/newswire.php?story_id=4091.

Coulthard, Glen Sean. *Red Skin, White Masks: Rejecting the Colonial Politics of Recognition*. Minneapolis: University of Minnesota Press, 2014.

Crabapple, Molly. "Hidden Fighters: Remembering America's Black Antifascist Vanguard." *Baffler*, no. 35 (June 2017). https://thebaffler.com/salvos/hidden-fighters-crabapple.

CrimethInc. "CrimethInc. West Coast Tour: December 2019," CrimethInc., November 19, 2019. https://crimethinc.com/2019/11/19/crimethinc-west-coast-tour-december-2019-from-democracy-to-freedom-the-new-upheavals.

Dauvé, Gilles. "Notes on Trotsky, Pannekoek, Bordiga." Theory and Practice, 1973. Available at https://libcom.org/article/notes-trotsky-pannekoek-bordiga-gilles-dauve.

Davis, Angela. *Women, Race & Class*. New York: Random House, 1983.

Derbent, T. *The German Communist Resistance, 1933–1945*. Paris: Foreign Languages Press, 2021.

Dhondt, Geert, Joel Olson, et al. "Debates on Fascism." Bring the Ruckus, October 10, 2008. Available at https://theanarchistlibrary.org/library/ruckus-collective-debates-on-fascism.

Diamond, Sara. *Roads to Dominion: Right-Wing Movements and Political Power in the United States*. New York: Guilford Press, 1995.

———. *Spiritual Warfare: The Politics of the Christian Right*. Boston: South End Press, 1989.

DiBranco, Alex. "Mobilizing Misogyny." Political Research Associates, March 8, 2017. https://politicalresearch.org/2017/03/08/mobilizing-misogyny.

Dimitrov, Georgi. "The Fascist Offensive and the Tasks of the Communist International in the Fight for the Unity of the Working Class against Fascism." In *The Fascist Offensive & Unity of the Working Class*, 1–79. Paris: Foreign Languages Press, 2020.

———. *The Fascist Offensive & Unity of the Working Class*. Paris: Foreign Languages Press, 2020.

Du Bois, W.E.B. *Black Reconstruction in America: An Essay toward a History of the Part Which Black Folk Played in the Attempt to Reconstruct Democracy in America, 1860–1880*. Edited by Henry Louis Gates Jr. Oxford, UK: Oxford University Press, 2007.

Editorial Committee. "Building Everyday Anti-fascism." *Upping the Anti*, no. 19 (February 2, 2017). http://uppingtheanti.org/journal/article/19-building-everyday-anti-fascism.

El-Amine, Rami. "Anti-Arab Racism, Islam, and the Left." *MR Online*, September 3, 2006. https://mronline.org/2006/09/03/anti-arab-racism-islam-and-the-left.

Espinoza, Leslie G., and Angela P. Harris. "Embracing the Tar-Baby: LatCrit Theory and the Sticky Mess of Race." In *Critical Race Theory: The Cutting Edge*, edited by Richard Delgado and Jean Stefancic. 2nd ed. Philadelphia: Temple University Press, 2000.

Evans, Robert. "How the Insurgent and MAGA Right Are Being Welded Together on the Streets of Washington D.C." *Bellingcat*, January 5, 2021. https://www.bellingcat.com/news/americas/2021/01/05/how-the-insurgent-and-maga-right-are-being-welded-together-on-the-streets-of-washington-d-c.

Farbod, Faramarz. "Why Liberal Anti-fascism Upholds the Status Quo." *Common Dreams*, January 24, 2021. https://www.commondreams.org/views/2021/01/24/why-liberal-anti-fascism-upholds-status-quo.

Faye, Shon. "We're Here, We're Queer, We're Racists." Zed Books, February 15, 2017, archived at https://web.archive.org/web/20210516031659/https://www.zedbooks.net/blog/posts/were-here-were-queer-were-racists.

Featherstone, David. "Black Internationalism, Subaltern Cosmopolitanism, and the Spatial Politics of Antifascism." *Annals of the Association of American Geographers* 103, no. 6 (2013): 1406–20.

Fekete, Liz. "Anti-fascism or Anti-extremism?" *Race & Class* 55, no. 4 (2014): 29–39.

Ferguson, Thomas. "From 'Normalcy' to New Deal: Industrial Structure, Party Competition, and American Public Policy in the Great Depression." In *Golden Rule: The Investment Theory of Party Competition and the Logic of Money-Driven Political Systems*, 113–72. Chicago: University of Chicago Press, 1995.

———. *Golden Rule: The Investment Theory of Party Competition and the Logic of Money-Driven Political Systems*. Chicago: University of Chicago Press, 1995.

Ferguson, Thomas, Paul Jorgensen, and Jie Chen. "Industrial Structure and Party Competition in an Age of Hunger Games: Donald Trump and the 2016 Presidential Election." Working Paper No. 66. Institute for New Economic Thinking, January 2018. https://www.ineteconomics.org/research/research-papers/industrial-structure-and-party-competition-in-an-age-of-hunger-games.

———. "Party Competition and Industrial Structure in the 2012 Elections: Who's Really Driving the Taxi to the Dark Side?" *International Journal of Political Economy* 42, no. 2 (Summer 2013): 3–41. https://modernmoneynetwork.org/sites/default/files/biblio/ferguson_jorgensen_chen_intl_journal_of_pol_econ_2013.pdf.

Ferguson, Thomas, and Joel Rogers. *Right Turn: The Decline of the Democrats and the Future of American Politics.* New York: Hill and Wang, 1986.

Flores, Celina, Mic Crenshaw, Erin Yanke, et al. *It Did Happen Here.* Independently produced podcast, 2020.

Francis. "'¡Que se Vayan Todos': Venezuela's Anarchists and the Three-Way Fight." *Three Way Fight*, July 28, 2005. http://threewayfight.blogspot.com/2005/07/que-se-vayan-todos-venezuelas.html.

Futrelle, David. "'Gina Tingles' and the Elders of Zion: Do Alt-Rightists Hate Women as Much as They Hate Jews? *We Hunted the Mammoth*, June 14, 2017. https://www.wehuntedthemammoth.com/2017/06/14/gina-tingles-and-the-elders-of-zion-do-alt-rightists-hate-women-as-much-as-they-hate-jews.

Gais, Hannah. "The Alt-Right Doesn't Know What to Do with White Women." *New Republic*, October 17, 2017. https://newrepublic.com/article/145325/alt-right-doesnt-know-white-women.

Gandesha, Samir. "Posthuman Fascism." *Los Angeles Review of Books*, August 22, 2020.

Gardiner, Steven, and Tarso Luís Ramos. "Capitol Offenses: January 6 2021 & the Ongoing Insurrection." Political Research Associates, January 12, 2022. https://politicalresearch.org/2022/01/12/capitol-offenses-january-6th-2021-ongoing-insurrection.

Gellman, Barton. "The Election That Could Break America." *Atlantic*, November 2020. https://www.theatlantic.com/magazine/archive/2020/11/what-if-trump-refuses-concede/616424.

Gelman, Emmaia. "The Anti-Defamation League Is Not What It Seems." *Boston Review*, May 23, 2019. https://www.bostonreview.net/articles/emmaia-gelman-anti-defamation-league.

Gilmore, Ruth Wilson. *Golden Gulag: Prisons, Surplus, Crisis, and Opposition in Globalizing California.* Berkeley: University of California Press, 2007.

Giroux, Henry. "Neoliberal Fascism and the Echoes of History." Truth Dig, August 2, 2018. https://www.truthdig.com/articles/neoliberal-fascism-and-the-echoes-of-history.

———. "Pedagogical Terrorism and Hope in the Age of Fascist Politics." *CounterPunch*, May 10, 2019. https://www.counterpunch.org/2019/05/10/pedagogical-terrorism-and-hope-in-the-age-of-fascist-politics.

Gittlitz, A.M. "Middle-Class War: A Visit to Staten Island's Autonomous Zone." *Hard Crackers*, December 20, 2020. https://hardcrackers.com/middle-class-war.

Gordon, Lewis R. *Bad Faith and Antiblack Racism.* Atlantic Highlands, NJ: Humanities Press, 1995.

Gray, Kishonna L. *Black Users in Digital Gaming.* Baton Rouge: Louisiana State University Press, 2020.

Griffin, Roger, and Matthew Feldman. *Fascism: Critical Concepts in Political Science.* London: Routledge, 2004.

Hamerquist, Don. "Barack, Badiou, and Bilal al Hasan." *Three Way Fight*, January 24, 2010. http://threewayfight.blogspot.com/2010/01/barack-badiou-and-bilal-al-hasan.html.

———. *A Brilliant Red Thread: Revolutionary Writings from Don Hamerquist.* Edited by Luis Brennan. Montreal: Kersplebedeb Publishing, 2023.

———. "Capitalism in Crisis?" *Three Way Fight*, September 25, 2008. http://threewayfight.blogspot.com/2008/09/capitalism-in-crisis.html.

———. "Fascism & Anti-fascism." In *Confronting Fascism: Discussion Documents for a Militant Movement,* by Don Hamerquist et al. 2nd ed. Montreal: Kersplebedeb Publishing, 2017.

———. "Islamic Radicalism and the Left." *Three Way Fight*, August 9, 2006. http://threewayfight.blogspot.com/2006/08/on-islamic-radicalism-and-left.html.

———. "New Stuff from an Old Guy—Part 1." *Three Way Fight,* October 23. 2018. http://threewayfight.blogspot.com/2018/10/new-stuff-from-old-guy-part-1.html.

———. "New Stuff from an Old Guy—Part 2." *Three Way Fight,* October 28. 2018. http://threewayfight.blogspot.com/2018/10/new-stuff-from-old-guy-part-2.html.

———. "New Stuff from an Old Guy—Part 3." *Three Way Fight,* November 12, 2018. http://threewayfight.blogspot.com/2018/11/new-stuff-from-old-guy-part-3.html.

———. "Responding to Stan Goff's 'Debating a NeoCon.'" *Three Way Fight,* December 15, 2004. http://threewayfight.blogspot.com/2004/12/responding-to-stan-goffs-debating.html.

———. "Thinking and Acting in Real Time and a Real World." *Three Way Fight,* January 27, 2009. http://threewayfight.blogspot.com/2009/01/thinking-and-acting-in-real-time-and.html.

Hamerquist, Don, et al. *Confronting Fascism: Discussion Documents for a Militant Movement.* 2nd ed. Montreal: Kersplebedeb Publishing, 2017.

Hanhardt, Christine. *Safe Space: Gay Neighborhood History and the Politics of Violence.* Durham, NC: Duke University Press, 2013.

Hari, Johann. "The Strange, Strange Story of the Gay Fascists." *Huffington Post,* October 21, 2008. Updated May 25, 2011. https://www.huffpost.com/entry/the-strange-strange-story_b_136697.

Harris, Cheryl. "Whiteness as Property." *Harvard Law Review* 106, no. 8 (June 1993).

Hartman, Saidiya V. *Scenes of Subjection: Terror, Slavery, and Self-Making in Nineteenth-Century America.* New York: Oxford University Press, 1997.

Haslett, Tobi. "Magic Actions: Looking Back on the George Floyd Rebellion." *n + 1,* no. 40 (Summer 2021). https://www.nplusonemag.com/issue-40/politics/magic-actions-2.

Hawthorne, Nate. "State and Capital." LibCom.org, January 7, 2014. https://libcom.org/article/state-and-capital.

Hendrick, Élise. "CounterPunch or Sucker Punch?" *Meldungen aus dem Exil,* July 19, 2015. https://meldungen-aus-dem-exil.noblogs.org/post/2015/07/19/counterpunch-or-suckerpunch.

"International Militant Anti-fascist Network Launch Statement." *Anti-Fascist Forum,* no. 3 (1998): 42–44. Available at https://issuu.com/randalljaykay/docs/antifaforum1998number3124.

"Interview from *Beating Fascism: Anarchist Anti-fascism in Theory and Practice,*" *Three Way Fight,* October 26, 2005. http://threewayfight.blogspot.com/2005/10/interview-from-beating-fascism.html. Originally published as "Anti-fascism Now, Kate Sharpley Library, Class War and 'Three Way Fight.'" In *Beating Fascism: Anarchist Anti-fascism in Theory and Practice,* edited by Anna Key. London: Kate Sharpley Library, 2005.

It's Going Down. "Auburn, AL: Students Chase Off Richard Spencer and Matthew Heimbach's Alt-Right Trolls." It's Going Down, April 19, 2017. https://itsgoingdown.org/auburn-al-students-chase-off-richard-spencer-matthew-heimbachs-alt-right-trolls.

———. "How Trump Is Consolidating His Forces to Hold On to Power." It's Going Down, August 17, 2020. https://itsgoingdown.org/message-in-a-molotov-election-trump.

———. "The Rich Kids of Fascism: Why the Alt-Right Didn't Start with Trump, and Won't End with Him Either." It's Going Down, December 16, 2016. https://itsgoingdown.org/rich-kids-fascism-alt-right-didnt-start-trump-wont-end-either.

———. "This Is America #133: Salem Antifascists Speak-out; Discussion on COVID Deaths, Social Media & Civil War." Podcast. It's Going Down, December 22, 2020. https://itsgoingdown.org/this-is-america-133-salem-antifascists-speak-out-discussion-on-covid-deaths-social-media-civil-war.

Jackson, Rob. "There Is No Such Thing as Revolutionary Inheritance." Louise Michel Library Project, February 12, 2019. https://louisemichellibraryproject.wordpress.com/2019/02/12/there-is-no-such-thing-as-revolutionary-inheritance.

Jaffe, Sarah. "The Long History of Antifa." Interview with Mark Bray. *Progressive*, September 13, 2017. https://progressive.org/latest/the-long-history-of-antifa-jaffe-170913.

Jegroo, Ashoka. "Fighting Cops and the Klan: The History and Future of Black Antifascism." *Truthout*, February 21, 2017. https://truthout.org/articles/fighting-cops-and-the-klan-the-history-and-future-of-black-antifascism.

Jews for Racial & Economic Justice. *Understanding Antisemitism: An Offering to Our Movement*. Pamphlet. Jews for Racial & Economic Justice, November 15, 2017. https://www.jfrej.org/news/2017/11/understanding-antisemitism-an-offering-to-our-movement.

Juárez, Nicolás. "To Kill an Indian to Save a (Hu)Man: Native Life through the Lens of Genocide." *Wreck Park*, no. 1 (2014).

Keskinen, Suvi. "The 'Crisis' of White Hegemony, Neonationalist Femininities and Antiracist Feminism." *Women's Studies International Forum*, 68 (2018): 157–63.

Kirchick, James. "A Thing for Men in Uniforms." *New York Review of Books*, May 14, 2018. https://www.nybooks.com/online/2018/05/14/a-thing-for-men-in-uniforms.

Koulouris, Theodore. "Online Misogyny and the Alternative Right: Debating the Undebatable." *Feminist Media Studies* 18, no. 4 (2018).

Kouvelakis, Stathis. "The French Insurgency." *New Left Review*, nos. 116/117, March–June 2019. https://newleftreview.org/issues/II116/articles/stathis-kouvelakis-the-french-insurgency.

Kropotkin, Peter. *The Conquest of Bread and Other Writings*. Cambridge: Cambridge University Press, 1995.

Lafontaine, Miriam. "The IWW Is Making Labour Anti-fascist Again: How Worker's Unions Are Involved in the Fight against Fascism." *Link*, April 3, 2018. https://thelinknewspaper.ca/article/the-iww-is-making-labour-anti-fascist-again.

Langer, Elinor. *A Hundred Little Hitlers: The Death of a Black Man, the Trial of a White Racist, and the Rise of the Neo-Nazi Movement in America*. New York: Macmillan, 2003.

Laruelle, Marlene. "Aleksandr Dugin: A Russian Version of the European Radical Right?" Kennan Institute Occasional Paper no. 294. Washington, DC: Woodrow Wilson International Center for Scholars, 2006.

Laura. "Liberal Attack on Choice." *Love and Rage* 6, no. 4 (August/September 1995): 3.

Lawrence, Ken. "The Ku Klux Klan and Fascism." *Urgent Tasks* 14 (Fall/Winter 1982), 12. Reprinted in *The U.S. Anti-fascism Reader*, edited by Bill V. Mullen and Christopher Vials. London: Verso, 2020.

Lee, Butch. *The Military Strategy of Women and Children*. Montreal: Kersplebedeb Publishing, 2003.

Lee, Butch, and Red Rover. *Night-Vision: Illuminating War & Class on the Neo-colonial Terrain*. 2nd ed. Montreal: Kersplebedeb Publishing, 2017.

Lees, Matt. "What Gamergate Should Have Taught Us about the 'Alt-Right.'" *Guardian*, December 1, 2016. https://www.theguardian.com/technology/2016/dec/01/gamergate-alt-right-hate-trump.

Lennard, Natasha. "Far-Right Violence Is Going to Be a Threat with or without Trump's Calls to Action." *Intercept*, January 5, 2021. https://theintercept.com/2021/01/05/trump-rally-far-right-violence.

Lenz, Ryan, and Mark Potok. "War in the West: The Bundy Ranch Standoff and the American Radical Right." Southern Poverty Law Center, July 10, 2014. https://www.splcenter.org/20140709/war-west-bundy-ranch-standoff-and-american-radical-right.

Leon, Abram. *The Jewish Question: A Marxist Interpretation*. Mexico City: Ediciones Pioneras, 1950. Available at https://www.marxists.org/subject/jewish/leon/index.htm.

Lines, Lisa. *Milicianas: Women in Combat in the Spanish Civil War*. Lanham, MD: Lexington Books, 2015.

Lorber, Ben. "A Constellation of Threats: Far Rightists Respond to the Black-Led Uprising."

Three Way Fight, July 19, 2020. http://threewayfight.blogspot.com/2020/07/a-constellation-of-threats-far.html.

——. "Understanding Alt-Right Antisemitism." *Doikayt*, March 24, 2017. https://doikayt.com/2017/03/24/understanding-alt-right-antisemitism (site discontinued).

Loroff, Nicole. "Gender and Sexuality in Nazi Germany." *Constellations* 3, no. 1 (2011): 49–61.

Luxemburg, Rosa. *The Accumulation of Capital*. London: Routledge, 2003.

Lynn, Denise. "Fascism and the Family: American Communist Women's Anti-fascism during the Ethiopian Invasion and Spanish Civil War." *American Communist History* 15, no. 2 (2016).

Lyons, Matthew N. "AlternativeRight.com: Paleoconservatism for the 21st Century," *Three Way Fight*, September 10, 2010. http://threewayfight.blogspot.com/2010/09/alternativerightcom-paleoconservatism.html.

——. "The Alt-Right Hates Women as Much as It Hates People of Colour." *Guardian*, May 2, 2017. https://www.theguardian.com/commentisfree/2017/may/02/alt-right-hates-women-non-white-trump-christian-right-abortion.

——. "Alt-right: More Misogynistic than Many Neonazis." *Three Way Fight*, December 3, 2016. http://threewayfight.blogspot.com/2016/12/alt-right-more-misogynistic-than-many.html.

——. "An Alt Right Update." Political Research Associates, August 7, 2017. https://politicalresearch.org/2017/08/07/an-alt-right-update.

——. "Ammon Bundy, the Refugee Caravan, and Patriot Movement Race Politics." *Three Way Fight*, December 20, 2018. http://threewayfight.blogspot.com/2018/12/ammon-bundy-refugee-caravan-and-patriot.html.

——. "Calling Them 'Alt-Right' Helps Us Fight Them." *Three Way Fight*, November 22, 2016. http://threewayfight.blogspot.com/2016/11/calling-them-alt-right-helps-us-fight.html.

——. "Caution Doesn't Make Us Safe: A Review of PRA's Report on the MAGA Movement," *Three Way Fight*, February 17, 2022. http://threewayfight.blogspot.com/2022/02/caution-doesnt-make-us-safe-review-of.html.

——. "Cooptation as Ruling Class Strategy." *Three Way Fight*, June 23, 2020. http://threewayfight.blogspot.com/2020/06/cooptation-as-ruling-class-strategy.html.

——. "Ctrl-Alt-Delete: The Origins and Ideology of the Alternative Right." Political Research Associates, January 20, 2017. https://politicalresearch.org/2017/01/20/ctrl-alt-delete-report-on-the-alternative-right. Also published in *Ctrl-Alt-Delete: An Antifascist Report on the Alternative Right*. Montreal: Kersplebedeb Publishing, 2017.

——. "Defending My Enemy's Enemy." *Three Way Fight*, August 3, 2006. http://threewayfight.blogspot.com/2006/08/defending-my-enemys-enemy.html.

——. "Defending the Three Way Fight Perspective" (letter). *Upping the Anti*, no. 6 (May 2008): 14–17.

——. "Far Rightists Divided on Coronavirus and Trump." *Three Way Fight*, March 19, 2020. http://threewayfight.blogspot.com/2020/03/far-rightists-divided-on-coronavirus.html.

——. "Far Rightists Divided over Hugo Chávez." *Three Way Fight*, March 24, 2013. http://threewayfight.blogspot.com/2013/03/far-rightists-divided-over-hugo-chavez.html.

——. "Feds + Corporate America versus the Occupy Movement." *Three Way Fight*, January 1, 2013. http://threewayfight.blogspot.com/2013/01/fbi-versus-occupy-movement.html.

——. "Frazier Glenn Miller, Nazi Violence, and the State." *Three Way Fight*, May 8, 2014. https://threewayfight.blogspot.com/2014/05/frazier-glenn-miller-nazi-violence-and.html.

——. "Further Thoughts on Hezbollah." *Three Way Fight*, August 26, 2006. http://threewayfight.blogspot.com/2006/08/further-thoughts-on-hezbollah.html.

————. "Hindu Nationalism: An Annotated Bibliography of Online Resources." *Three Way Fight*, June 3, 2008. http://threewayfight.blogspot.com/2008/06/hindu-nationalism-annotated.html.

————. *Insurgent Supremacists: The U.S. Far Right's Challenge to State and Empire*. Oakland: PM Press, and Montreal: Kersplebedeb Publishing, 2018.

————. "Jack Donovan on Men: A Masculine Tribalism for the Far Right." *Three Way Fight*, November 23, 2015. http://threewayfight.blogspot.com/2015/11/jack-donovan-on-men-masculine-tribalism.html.

————. "Liberal Counterinsurgency versus the Paramilitary Right." *Three Way Fight*, November 27, 2012. https://threewayfight.blogspot.com/2012/11/liberal-counterinsurgency-versus.html.

————. "Liberalism's Limits: A Review of Burghart and Zeskind's *Tea Party Nationalism*." *Three Way Fight*, May 30, 2011. http://threewayfight.blogspot.com/2011/05/liberalisms-limits-review-of-burghart.html.

————. "Major Report on Red-Brown Alliances from New Anarchist Website." *Three Way Fight*, February 4, 2018. http://threewayfight.blogspot.com/2018/02/major-report-on-red-brown-alliances.html.

————. "Making America Worse." *Three Way Fight*, July 16, 2016. http://threewayfight.blogspot.com/2016/07/making-america-worse.html.

————. "No Longer a Gendarme for the West: Simon Pirani on Russia's Invasion of Ukraine." *Three Way Fight*, June 11, 2022. http://threewayfight.blogspot.com/2022/06/no-longer-gendarme-for-west-simon.html.

————. "Notes on Women and Right-Wing Movements." Pts. 1 and 2. *Three Way Fight*, September 27, 2005, and October 1, 2005. http://threewayfight.blogspot.com/2005/09/notes-on-women-and-right-w_112787003380492443.html and http://threewayfight.blogspot.com/2005/10/notes-on-women-and-right-wing.html.

————. "Not Just a Smear Tactic." Review of *The Past Didn't Go Anywhere* by April Rosenblum. *Upping the Anti*, no. 5, November 19, 2009. https://uppingtheanti.org/journal/article/05-not-just-a-smear-tactic.

————. "Oath Keepers, Ferguson, and the Patriot Movement's Conflicted Race Politics." *Three Way Fight*, August 28, 2015. http://threewayfight.blogspot.com/2015/08/oath-keepers-ferguson-and-patriot.html.

————. "Occupy Movement: Anticapitalism versus Populism." *Three Way Fight*, December 6, 2011. http://threewayfight.blogspot.com/2011/12/occupy-movement-anti-capitalism-versus.html.

————. "'Racial Dissidents Have Lost the Ability to Organize Openly': Alt-Rightists on Trump, ICE, and What Is to Be Done." *Insurgent Notes*, August 4, 2018. http://insurgentnotes.com/2018/08/racial-dissidents-have-lost-the-ability-to-organize-openly-alt-rightists-on-trump-ice-and-what-is-to-be-done.

————. "Rape, the State, and the Far Right in India." *Three Way Fight*, February 10, 2013. http://threewayfight.blogspot.com/2013/02/rape-state-and-far-right-in-india.html.

————. "Resisting Trump's Coup." *Three Way Fight*, September 27, 2020. http://threewayfight.blogspot.com/2020/09/resisting-trumps-coup.html.

————. "Review of Robyn Marasco's 'Reconsidering the Sexual Politics of Fascism.'" *Three Way Fight*, July 14, 2021. http://threewayfight.blogspot.com/2021/07/review-of-robyn-marascos-reconsidering.html.

————. "Rightists Woo the Occupy Wall Street Movement." *Three Way Fight*, November 8, 2011. http://threewayfight.blogspot.com/2011/11/rightists-woo-occupy-wall-street.html.

————. "Right-Wing Anti-imperialists Are Not Promoting Feudalism: A Reply to Michael Karadjis." *Three Way Fight*, October 10, 2006. http://threewayfight.blogspot.com/2006/10/right-wing-anti-imperialists-are-not.html.

————. "Rising Above the Herd: Keith Preston's Authoritarian Anti-statism." *New*

Politics, April 29, 2011. https://newpol.org/rising-above-herd-keith-prestons-authoritarian-anti-statism.

———. "Some Thoughts on Fascism and the Current Moment." *Three Way Fight*, July 7, 2019. http://threewayfight.blogspot.com/2019/07/some-thoughts-on-fascism-and-current.html.

———. "Strategies to Defend Abortion Access: Three Essays." *Three Way Fight*, July 19, 2022. http://threewayfight.blogspot.com/2022/07/strategies-to-defend-abortion-access.html.

———. "Trump: 'Anti-political' or Right Wing?" *Three Way Fight*, March 15, 2016. http://threewayfight.blogspot.com/2016/03/trump-anti-political-or-right-wing.html.

———. "Trump's Impact: A Fascist Upsurge Is Just One of the Dangers." *Three Way Fight*, December 22, 2015. http://threewayfight.blogspot.com/2015/12/trumps-impact-fascist-upsurge-is-just.html.

———. "Two Ways of Looking at Fascism." *Socialism and Democracy* 22, no. 2 (2008). Republished in *Insurgent Supremacists: The U.S. Far Right's Challenge to State and Empire*. Oakland: PM Press, and Montreal: Kersplebedeb Publishing, 2018.

———. "Ukraine's Upheaval: Between Fascists, Neoliberals, and Kremlin Tools." *Three Way Fight*, February 28, 2014. http://threewayfight.blogspot.com/2014/02/ukraines-upheaval-between-fascists.html.

———. "U.S. Fascists Debate the Conflict in Ukraine." *Three Way Fight*, March 12, 2014. http://threewayfight.blogspot.com/2014/03/us-fascists-debate-conflict-in-ukraine.html.

———. "Who Are Ukraine's Fascists?" *Three Way Fight*, March 4, 2014. http://threewayfight.blogspot.com/2014/03/who-are-ukraines-fascists.html.

Lyons, Matthew N., and Bromma. "Islamic Fundamentalism and the Three-Way Fight: An Exchange." *Three Way Fight*, October 14, 2007. http://threewayfight.blogspot.com/2007/10/islamic-fundamentalism-and-three-way.html.

Marhoefer, Laurie. "Queer Fascism and the End of Gay History." *Notches*, June 19, 2018. https://notchesblog.com/2018/06/19/queer-fascism-and-the-end-of-gay-history.

Marx, Karl. *Capital, Volume 1*. New York: Vintage, 1977.

Mathias, Christopher. "White Vigilantes Have Always Had a Friend in Police." *HuffPost*, August 28, 2020. https://www.huffpost.com/entry/white-vigilantes-kenosha_n_5f4822bcc5b6cf66b2b5103e.

Max. "Hizbullah Victorious Again." *Ideas for Action*, August 16, 2006. http://ideasforaction.blogspot.com/2006/08/hizbullah-victorious-again-to-get.html.

Messersmith-Glavin, Paul. "Interview with Shane Burley." Institute for Anarchist Studies, October 28, 2022. https://www.anarchistagency.com/critical-voices/paul-messersmith-glavin-interview-with-shane-burley-editor-of-no-pasaran-antifascist-dispatches-from-a-world-in-crisis.

Michael, George. "David Lane and the Fourteen Words." *Politics, Religion & Ideology* 10, no. 1 (2011): 43–61.

Minkowitz, Donna. "Hiding in Plain Sight: An American Renaissance of White Nationalism." Political Research Associates, October 26, 2017. https://politicalresearch.org/2017/10/26/hiding-in-plain-sight-an-american-renaissance-of-white-nationalism.

———. "How the Alt-Right Is Using Sex and Camp to Attract Gay Men to Fascism." *Slate*, June 5, 2017. https://slate.com/human-interest/2017/06/how-alt-right-leaders-jack-donovan-and-james-omeara-attract-gay-men-to-the-movement.html.

Moore, Hilary, and James Tracy. *No Fascist USA! The John Brown Anti-Klan Committee and Lessons for Today's Movements*. San Francisco: City Lights, 2020.

MPD150. *Enough Is Enough: A 150 Year Performance Review of the Minneapolis Police Department*. Expanded ed. Minneapolis: MPD150, 2020. https://www.mpd150.com/wp-content/uploads/reports/report_2_compressed.pdf.

Nagel, Joane. "Ethnicity and Sexuality." *Annual Review of Sociology* 26 (2000).

Nagle, Angela. *Kill All Normies: Online Culture Wars from 4chan and Tumblr to Trump and the Alt-Right*. Alresford, UK: Zero Books, 2017.

Nash, Mary. *Defying Male Civilization: Women in the Spanish Civil War*. Denver: Arden Press, 1995.

O'Banion, Paul. "Autonomous Antifa: From the Autonomen to Post-Antifa in Germany; An Interview with Bender, a German Comrade." It's Going Down, November 20, 2017. https://itsgoingdown.org/autonomous-antifa-germany-interview.

Paddock, Richard C. "New Details of Extensive ADL Spy Operation Emerge: Inquiry: Transcripts Reveal Nearly 40 Years of Espionage by a Man Who Infiltrated Political Groups." *Los Angeles Times*, April 13, 1993. https://www.latimes.com/archives/la-xpm-1993-04-13-mn-22383-story.html.

Pearson, Stephen. "'Enter the Amerikaner Free State': The Alt Right and Settler Colonialism." *Journal of Labor and Society* (forthcoming).

———. "'The Last Bastion of Colonialism': Appalachian Settler Colonialism and Self-Indigenization." *American Indian Culture and Research Journal* 37, no. 2 (2013): 165–84.

Postone, Moishe. "Anti-Semitism and National Socialism." In *Germans and Jews since the Holocaust*, edited by Anson Rabinbach and Jack Zipes. New York: Holmes and Meier, 1986. Available at https://libcom.org/article/anti-semitism-and-national-socialism-moishe-postone.

Price, Wayne. "A History of North American Anarchist Group Love & Rage." *Northeastern Anarchist*, no. 3 (Fall 2001). Available at https://theanarchistlibrary.org/library/wayne-price-a-history-of-north-american-anarchist-group-love-rage.

Ranney, David. "Comments on 'Capitalism in Crisis?'" *Three Way Fight*, October 2, 2008. http://threewayfight.blogspot.com/2008/10/dave-ranney-comments-on-capitalism-in.html.

———. *New World Disorder: The Decline of U.S. Power*. Oakland: PM Press, 2014.

Research & Destroy. "The Landing: Fascists without Fascism." Research & Destroy, February 20, 2017. https://researchanddestroy.wordpress.com/2017/02/20/the-landing-fascists-without-fascism.

Richet, Isabelle. "Women and Antifascism: Historiographical and Methodological Approaches." In *Rethinking Antifascism: History, Memory and Politics, 1922 to Present*, edited by Hugo García et al., 152–66. New York: Berghahn Books, 2016.

Ridgeway, James. *Blood in the Face: White Nationalism from the Birth of a Nation to the Age of Trump*. Chicago: Haymarket Books, 2021. Original ed., New York: Thunder's Mouth Press, 1990.

Romano, Aja. "How the Alt-Right's Sexism Lures Men into White Supremacy." *Vox*, April 26, 2018. https://www.vox.com/culture/2016/12/14/13576192/alt-right-sexism-recruitment.

Rose City Antifa. "The Wolves of Vinland: A Fascist Countercultural 'Tribe' in the Pacific Northwest." Rose City Antifa, November 7, 2016. https://rosecityantifa.org/articles/the-wolves-of-vinland-a-fascist-countercultural-tribe-in-the-pacific-northwest.

Rosenblum, April. *The Past Didn't Go Anywhere: Making Resistance to Antisemitism Part of All of Our Movements*. Self-published, 2007. https://www.aprilrosenblum.com/_files/ugd/4dc342_10d68441b6c44ee0a12909a242074ca6.pdf.

Ross, Alexander Reid. *Against the Fascist Creep*. Chico, CA: AK Press, 2017.

rowan. "The Alt-Creeps: A Review of *Against the Fascist Creep* and *Ctrl-Alt-Delete*." Perspectives on Anarchist Theory, no. 30 (2018/2019).

RX. "Cursory Thoughts on Armies, Insurrection, and the Sixth." *Three Way Fight*, August 4, 2005. http://threewayfight.blogspot.com/2005/08/cursory-thoughts-on-armies.html.

———. "Revolt in Oaxaca." *Three Way Fight*, October 31, 2006. http://threewayfight.blogspot.com/2006/10/revolt-in-oaxaca.html.

Sabatier, Julie. "Q&A: PopMob Appeals to 'Everyday Anti-fascists.'" Interview with Effie Baum. OPB, August 26, 2019. https://www.opb.org/radio/article/oregon-portland-popmob-anti-fascism-popular-mobilization.

Sakai, J. *Settlers: The Mythology of the White Proletariat from Mayflower to Modern.* 4th ed. Montreal: Kersplebedeb Publishing, and Oakland: PM Press, 2014.

———. "The Shock of Recognition: Looking at Hamerquist's Fascism & Anti-fascism." In *Confronting Fascism: Discussion Documents for a Militant Movement*, by Don Hamerquist et al. Montreal: Kersplebedeb Publishing, 2017.

Saxton, Alexander. *The Indispensable Enemy: Labor and the Anti-Chinese Movement in California.* Berkeley: University of California Press, 1971.

Sen, Basav. "The Terrifying Global Implications of Modi's Re-election." *CounterPunch*, May 27, 2019. https://www.counterpunch.org/2019/05/27/the-terrifying-global-implications-of-modis-re-election.

———. "Why the Trump/Modi Relationship Is So Dangerous." *CounterPunch*, March 9, 2020. https://www.counterpunch.org/2020/03/09/why-the-trump-modi-relationship-is-so-dangerous.

Shanahan, Jarrod. "The Big Takeover." *Hard Crackers*, January 7, 2021. https://hardcrackers.com/the-big-takeover.

Shanahan, Jarrod, and Zhandarka Kurti. *States of Incarceration: Rebellion, Reform, and America's Punishment System.* London: Reaktion/Field Notes Books, 2022.

Shaw, Devin Zane. "Between System-Loyal Vigilantism and System-Oppositional Violence." *Three Way Fight*, October 25, 2020. http://threewayfight.blogspot.com/2020/10/between-system-loyal-vigilantism-and.html.

———. "On Toscano's Critique of 'Racial Fascism.'" *Three Way Fight*, December 30, 2020. http://threewayfight.blogspot.com/2020/12/on-toscanos-critique-of-racial-fascism.html.

———. *Philosophy of Antifascism: Punching Nazis and Fighting White Supremacy.* London: Rowman & Littlefield, 2020.

Shekhovtsov, Anton. "Aleksandr Dugin's Neo-Eurasianism: The New Right *à la Russe*." *Religion Compass* 3, no. 4 (2009): 697–716.

Simpson, Audra. "The State Is a Man: Theresa Spence, Loretta Saunders and the Gender of Settler Sovereignty." *Theory & Event* 19, no. 4 (2016).

Smith, Andrea. *Conquest: Sexual Violence and American Indian Genocide.* Durham, NC: Duke University Press, 2005.

Smith, Jack. "The Women of the 'Alt-Right' Are Speaking Out against Misogyny. They'd Prefer Absolute Patriarchy." *Mic*, December 8, 2017. https://www.mic.com/articles/186675/the-women-of-the-alt-right-are-speaking-out-against-misogyny-theyd-prefer-absolute-patriarchy.

Sonabend, Daniel. *We Fight Fascists: The 43 Group and Their Forgotten Battle for Post-war Britain.* London: Verso, 2019.

Sparrow, Jeff. "From Misery to Misogyny: Incels and the Far Right." *Overland*, April 27. 2018. https://overland.org.au/2018/04/from-misery-to-misogyny-incels-and-the-far-right.

Srivastava, Neelam. "Anti-colonialism and the Italian Left: Resistances to the Fascist Invasion of Ethiopia." *interventions* 8, no. 3 (2006).

Staudenmaier, Michael. *Truth and Revolution: A History of the Sojourner Truth Organization, 1969–1986.* Oakland: AK Press, 2012.

Staudenmaier, Michael, and Anne Carlson. "Of Chavistas and Anarquistas: Brief Sketch of a Visit to Venezuela." Anarkismo.net, July 3, 2005. https://www.anarkismo.net/newswire.php?story_id=839&region=southamerica&results_offset=20.

Staudenmaier, Michael, and Rami El-Amine. "The Three Way Fight Debate: Challenges for the Left." *Upping the Anti*, no. 5 (October 2007): 115–42.

Steel, Peta. *The Battle of Cable Street: They Shall Not Pass; An Account of Working Class*

Struggles against Fascism. London: SERTUC, 2017. https://www.tuc.org.uk/sites/default/files/Cable-Street-book.pdf.

Strobl, Ingrid. *Partisanas: Women in the Armed Resistance to Fascism and German Occupation (1936–1945)*. Oakland: AK Press, 2008.

Sunshine, Spencer. "The Left Must Root Out Antisemitism in Its Ranks." *Forward*, June 1, 2017. https://forward.com/opinion/373577/leftists-must-root-out-anti-semitism-in-its-ranks.

———. "Three Pillars of the Alt Right: White Nationalism, Antisemitism, and Misogyny." Political Research Associates, December 4, 2017. https://politicalresearch.org/2017/12/04/three-pillars-of-the-alt-right-white-nationalism-antisemitism-and-misogyny.

Sunshine, Spencer, et al. *Up in Arms: A Guide to Oregon's Patriot Movement*. Scappoose, OR: Rural Organizing Project, and Somerville, MA: Political Research Associates, 2016. https://rop.org/resources/up-in-arms-pdf-2.

Tabachnick, Rachel. "The New Christian Zionism and the Jews: A Love/Hate Relationship." *Public Eye* (Political Research Associates), Winter 2009/Spring 2010. https://politicalresearch.org/2010/01/18/the-new-christian-zionism-and-the-jews-a-lovehate-relationship.

Taibbi, Matt. "We're in a Permanent Coup." *TK News by Matt Taibbi*, October 11, 2019. https://taibbi.substack.com/p/were-in-a-permanent-coup.

Tait, Amelia. "Spitting out the Red Pill: Former Misogynists Reveal How They Were Radicalized Online." *New Statesman*, February 28, 2017. https://www.newstatesman.com/long-reads/2017/02/reddit-the-red-pill-interview-how-misogyny-spreads-online.

Thompson, Edward. "Notes on Exterminism, the Last Stage of Civilization." *New Left Review*, June 1, 1980. https://newleftreview.org/I/121/edward-thompson-notes-on-exterminism-the-last-stage-of-civilization.

Three Way Fight. "About Three Way Fight." *Three Way Fight*, July 15, 2013. Updated November 12, 2017. http://threewayfight.blogspot.com/p/about.html.

———. "Antifascist Resources on Ukraine." *Three Way Fight*, March 2, 2022. Updated April 3, 2022. http://threewayfight.blogspot.com/2022/03/antifascist-resources-on-ukraine.html.

———. "Multiracial Far Right: A Conversation with Daryle Lamont Jenkins and Cloee Cooper." *Three Way Fight*, September 14, 2019. http://threewayfight.blogspot.com/2019/09/multiracial-far-right-conversation-with.html.

———. "Understanding A22 PDX: Discussion and Analysis for the Antifascist Movement." *Three Way Fight*, August 29, 2021. http://threewayfight.blogspot.com/2021/08/understanding-a22-pdx-discussion-and.html.

Tijoux, Ana Maria. "We Can't Think of a Feminism, an Anti-patriarchy, without Anti-capitalism." Committee on U.S.–Latin American Relations, March 8, 2017. https://cuslar.org/2017/03/10/ana-tijoux-we-cant-think-of-a-feminism-an-anti-patriarchy-without-anti-capitalism.

Toscano, Alberto. "The Long Shadow of Racial Fascism." *Boston Review*, October 28, 2020.

Traverso, Enzo. *The New Faces of Fascism: Populism and the Far Right*. London: Verso, 2019.

Trotsky, Leon. *Fascism: What It Is and How to Fight It*. New York: Pathfinder Press, 1996.

———. "What Is Fascism: Extracts from a Letter to a Comrade." *Militant* 5, no. 3 (1932).

Tuck, Eve, and Wayne K. Yang. "Decolonization Is Not a Metaphor." *Decolonization: Indigeneity, Education and Society* 1, no. 1 (2012): 1–40.

The Unquiet Dead: Anarchism, Fascism, and Mythology. Self-published, 2017.

Veracini, Lorenzo. *Settler Colonialism: A Theoretical Overview*. London: Palgrave Macmillan, 2014.

Wacquant, Loïc. "Class, Race & Hyperincarceration in Revanchist America." *Daedalus* 139, no. 3 (2010): 74–90.

————. "Deadly Symbiosis: When Ghetto and Prison Meet and Mesh." *Punishment &* *Society* 3, no. 1 (2001): 95–133.

Wang, Jackie. "Against Innocence: Race, Gender, and the Politics of Safety." *LIES: A* *Journal of Materialist Feminism* 1 (2012).

Ward, Eric K. "Skin in the Game: How Antisemitism Animates White Nationalism." *Public Eye* (Political Research Associates), Summer 2017. https://politicalresearch. org/2017/06/29/skin-in-the-game-how-antisemitism-animates-white-nationalism.

Whitlock, Kay. "We Need to Dream a Bolder Dream: The Politics of Fear and Queer Struggles for Safe Communities." *Scholar and Feminist Online*, no. 10.1–10.2 (Fall 2011–Spring 2012). https://sfonline.barnard.edu/we-need-to-dream-a-bolder-dream-the-politics-of-fear-and-queer-struggles-for-safe-communities.

Wilderson, Frank B. *Red, White & Black: Cinema and the Structure of U.S. Antagonisms.* Durham, NC: Duke University Press, 2010.

Williams, Dana M. "Black Panther Radical Factionalization and the Development of Black Anarchism." *Journal of Black Studies* 46, no. 7 (2015): 678–703.

Williams, Kristian. "Comment on Foucault and the Iranian Revolution: The Philosopher and the Ayatollah; 'A Perplexing Affinity.'" *Three Way Fight*, February 28, 2020. http:// threewayfight.blogspot.com/2020/02/comment-on-foucault-and-iranian.html.

————. "Intelligence Report on 'Extremism' Equates Anarchists with Right-Wing Militias." *Truthout*, April 7, 2021. https://truthout.org/articles/ intelligence-report-on-extremism-equates-anarchists-with-right-wing-militias.

————. *Our Enemies in Blue: Police and Power in America.* 3rd ed. Oakland: AK Press, 2015.

Williams, Robert F. *Negroes with Guns.* Detroit: Wayne State University Press, 1998.

Williams, Zoe. "'Raw Hatred': Why the 'Incel' Movement Targets and Terrorises Women." *Guardian*, April 25, 2018. https://www.theguardian.com/world/2018/apr/25/ raw-hatred-why-incel-movement-targets-terrorises-women.

Wilson, Jason. "What Do Incels, Fascists and Terrorists Have in Common? Violent Misogyny." *Guardian*, May 4, 2018. https://www.theguardian.com/commentisfree/2018/may/04/ what-do-incels-fascists-and-terrorists-have-in-common-violent-misogyny.

Wolfe, Patrick. "Settler Colonialism and the Elimination of the Native." *Journal of* *Genocide Research* 8, no. 4 (2006): 387–409.

————. *Traces of History: Elementary Structures of Race.* London: Verso, 2016.

Zeskind, Leonard. *Blood and Politics: The History of the White Nationalist Movement* *from the Margins to the Mainstream.* New York: Farrar, Straus and Giroux, 2009.

Zia, Helen. "White Power Women." *Washington Post*, April 7, 1991. https://www. washingtonpost.com/archive/opinions/1991/04/07/white-power-women/ a30050ed-cf61-46e2-a11f-3b2df977ea08.

About the Contributors

Xtn Alexander. Since first becoming a part of the revolutionary and anarchist youth movements of the late 1980s, Xtn has spent the better part of his time on earth participating in anticop, antiracist, anti-imperialist, and antifascist organizing and action. He works in emergency and trauma medicine. He's an avid supporter of music, art, and radical (sub)cultures and has been involved with *Three Way Fight* since its founding in 2004.

Arturo Castillon is a writer and substitute teacher living in Philadelphia. With Shemon Salam, he is the coauthor of *The Revolutionary Meaning of the George Floyd Uprising* (Daraja Press, 2021) and has published work in *The George Floyd Uprising* (PM Press, 2023) as well as in *Black Quantum Futurism: Space-Time Collapse II* (The AfroFuturist Affair/ House of Future Sciences Books, 2020).

Roberto Santiago de Roock has engaged in anarchist and abolitionist activism for the last twenty-five years, focusing on youth organizing and learning spaces. He is currently a researcher and educator at the University of California, Santa Cruz, where he uses this lens to prepare future educators and critically examine the role of technology in perpetuating oppression while cultivating alternate radical imaginaries.

Don Hamerquist grew up in a logging family near Clallam Bay on Washington's Olympic Peninsula. Don was a "red diaper" baby. His father was a logger and was publicly known as a militant trade unionist and communist. His mother was also an activist and known communist. After high school, Don went to college in Oregon for a few years before getting married, starting a family, and going to work as a truck driver in Portland. He joined the Communist Party in 1958 and quit/ was expelled ten years later. Don moved to Chicago, where he worked in a wide range of factory jobs as a member of the Sojourner Truth Organization until it folded in the early 1980s. After that, Don operated a marginal left printing venture in Chicago with his wife, Janeen Porter. In 2001, Don retired and moved back to Clallam Bay. He lives with Janeen in the house he was raised in—but now with electricity and a phone.

Kdog is a pen name for a veteran of Anti-Racist Action and several revolutionary anarchist organizing projects in the US Midwest.

Kieran is a longtime antifascist anarchist and union militant in occupied Mni Sota Makoce, aka Minnesota.

Tammy Kovich is a longtime anarchist based in Hamilton, Ontario. She loves dogs, hates patriarchy, and strives to be someone who puts her politics into practice on a daily basis. Her research interests include women's participation in riots, revolts, and revolutions; gender and anarchism; and contemporary feminist struggle.

Zhandarka Kurti is an educator and activist. She is the coauthor of *States of Incarceration: Rebellion, Reform, and America's Punishment System* (Field Notes/Reaktion, 2022); an editor of *Treason to Whiteness Is Loyalty to Humanity* (Verso, 2022), a Noel Ignatiev reader; and an editor of the publication *Hard Crackers: Chronicles of Everyday Life*.

Joel D. Lovos has been an educator for six years and, more recently, began engaging in research on video games and learning. This research is motivated by a desire to push for video games as tools for liberation, organization, and creation.

Matthew N. Lyons is the author of *Insurgent Supremacists: The U.S. Far Right's Challenge to State and Empire* (PM Press and Kersplebedeb Publishing, 2018) and coauthor with Chip Berlet of *Right-Wing*

Populism in America (Guilford Press, 2000). He has been a contributor to *Three Way Fight* since 2005, and his writings have also appeared in a number of other leftist and mainstream publications. Matthew is cotrustee of the Lorraine Hansberry Literary Trust, which stewards the literary legacy of the late playwright and activist Lorraine Hansberry.

M. has been involved in abolitionist organizing, education, design, and writing for about fifteen years and is one of the cofounders of the Abolitionist Gaming Network.

Paul O'Banion is an anarchist organizer who has been involved in social movements since the 1980s. He was a member of the Love and Rage Revolutionary Anarchist Federation and of a Minneapolis political collective that worked closely with Anti-Racist Action and other anarchist, Native, and left groups in the 1990s. He has been involved in struggles for abortion rights and women's freedom, for queer liberation, and against war and capitalist ecological destruction. For over the last twenty years, he has organized in the Pacific Northwest, mobilizing people against the US war in Iraq and Afghanistan, doing workplace organizing, and being involved in Occupy Portland. He helped found PopMob (Popular Mobilization) to turn out greater, more diverse numbers of people in opposition to neofascist groups like Patriot Prayer and the Proud Boys. He continues to organize, write, love, and work. Follow him on X (formerly Twitter): @Diggers1616.

Janeen Porter recently retired from a rewarding job in corrections education. She spends her time, in no particular order, fighting the cumulative impact of numerous previous vices, desperately wanting to be on the front line against the ongoing murders by cops, being outraged at environmental homicides throughout the world, fighting the fucked-up health care system, and trying to figure out where her generation went wrong and righting it.

Rowland Keshena Robinson (he/him/his) is an assistant professor in the Department of Political Science at the University of Waterloo in Ontario. A member of the Menominee Nation of Wisconsin and an immigrant from Bermuda, he has lived and worked on the lands of the

Menominee's close kin the Anishinaabeg, as well as the Rotinonshón:ni, in what is now known as southern Ontario since 2005. Rowland maintains long-standing writing and research interests on topics such as settler colonialism, Indigenous critical theory, ideology, narrative and mythology, Marxism and poststructuralism, postmodernity, world-systems analysis, decolonization and decoloniality, race, and law and sovereignty, as well as fascism and antifascism.

rowan lives in Portland, Oregon. She has participated in left-wing politics and social movements since the late 1990s and has complicated feelings about it. Her current practice largely consists of trying to be a PTA mom and teaching her eight-year-old daughter to hate the police.

Shemon Salam is an anti-state communist. With Arturo Castillon, he is the coauthor of *The Revolutionary Meaning of the George Floyd Uprising* (Daraja Press, 2021), is featured in *The George Floyd Uprising* (PM Press, 2023), and has also published work with *Mute Magazine* and *Ill Will*.

B. Sandor is a teacher who lives in Boston.

Jarrod Shanahan is an activist-scholar and assistant professor of criminal justice at Governors State University in University Park, Illinois. He is the author of *Captives: How Rikers Island Took New York City Hostage* (Verso, 2022); coauthor with Zhandarka Kurti of *States of Incarceration: Rebellion, Reform, and America's Punishment System* (Field Notes/Reaktion, 2022); an editor of *Treason to Whiteness Is Loyalty to Humanity* (Verso, 2022), a Noel Ignatiev reader; and an editor of the journal *Hard Crackers: Chronicles of Everyday Life*.

Devin Zane Shaw is the author of *Philosophy of Antifascism: Punching Nazis and Fighting White Supremacy* (Rowman & Littlefield, 2020) and *The Politics of the Blockade* (Kersplebedeb Publishing, 2020), which are works that explore antifascist methodologies in philosophy, the application of the three way fight in solidarity actions for Indigenous resurgence movements, and a philosophical defense of practices of emancipatory community self-defense. He is a coauthor of the multiauthor collaboration *On Necrocapitalism: A Plague Journal*

(Kersplebedeb Publishing, 2021), which chronicles the relationship between COVID-19, capital, and social movements during the period from April 2020 to May 2021. He is coeditor of the book series Living Existentialism, published by Rowman & Littlefield. Although his regular job is to teach philosophy at a community college in so-called British Columbia, he is currently serving as the negotiator for his faculty union.

Michael Staudenmaier is a veteran of many antifascist, anti-imperialist, and anarchist projects over the past three decades. He is coauthor of *We Go Where They Go: The Story of Anti-Racist Action* (PM Press, 2023) and author of *Truth and Revolution: A History of the Sojourner Truth Organization, 1969–1986* (AK Press, 2012). He lives and works in Chicago and northeast Indiana.

Suzy Subways coordinates the SLAM Herstory Project, an oral history of the Student Liberation Action Movement. A member of SLAM! and Love and Rage in the 1990s, she is currently an editor of *Prison Health News*, an anarchist member of Philly Socialists, and a sometimes fiction writer.

Xloi is a journalist based in Oakland.

Index

Page numbers in *italic* refer to illustrations. "Passim" (literally "scattered") indicates intermittent discussion of a topic over a cluster of pages.

ABOUT PM PRESS

PM Press is an independent, radical publisher of critically necessary books for our tumultuous times. Our aim is to deliver bold political ideas and vital stories to all walks of life and arm the dreamers to demand the impossible. Founded in 2007 by a small group of people with decades of publishing, media, and organizing experience, we have sold millions of copies of our books, most often one at a time, face to face. We're old enough to know what we're doing and young enough to know what's at stake. Join us to create a better world.

PM Press
PO Box 23912
Oakland, CA 94623
www.pmpress.org

PM Press in Europe
europe@pmpress.org
www.pmpress.org.uk

FRIENDS OF PM PRESS

These are indisputably momentous times—the financial system is melting down globally and the Empire is stumbling. Now more than ever there is a vital need for radical ideas.

In the many years since its founding—and on a mere shoestring—PM Press has risen to the formidable challenge of publishing and distributing knowledge and entertainment for the struggles ahead. With hundreds of releases to date, we have published an impressive and stimulating array of literature, art, music, politics, and culture. Using every available medium, we've succeeded in connecting those hungry for ideas and information to those putting them into practice.

Friends of PM allows you to directly help impact, amplify, and revitalize the discourse and actions of radical writers, filmmakers, and artists. It provides us with a stable foundation from which we can build upon our early successes and provides a much-needed subsidy for the materials that can't necessarily pay their own way. You can help make that happen—and receive every new title automatically delivered to your door once a month—by joining as a Friend of PM Press. And, we'll throw in a free T-shirt when you sign up.

Here are your options:

- **$30 a month** Get all books and pamphlets plus a 50% discount on all webstore purchases

- **$40 a month** Get all PM Press releases (including CDs and DVDs) plus a 50% discount on all webstore purchases

- **$100 a month** Superstar—Everything plus PM merchandise, free downloads, and a 50% discount on all webstore purchases

For those who can't afford $30 or more a month, we have **Sustainer Rates** at $15, $10, and $5. Sustainers get a free PM Press T-shirt and a 50% discount on all purchases from our website.

Your Visa or Mastercard will be billed once a month, until you tell us to stop. Or until our efforts succeed in bringing the revolution around. Or the financial meltdown of Capital makes plastic redundant. Whichever comes first.

Insurgent Supremacists: The U.S. Far Right's Challenge to State and Empire

Matthew N. Lyons

ISBN: 978-162-963-511-8
$24.95   384 pages

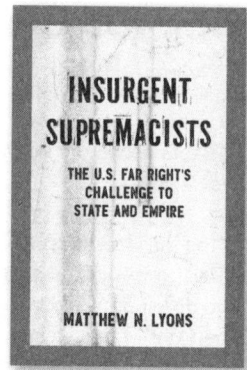

INSURGENT SUPREMACISTS

THE U.S. FAR RIGHT'S
CHALLENGE TO
STATE AND EMPIRE

MATTHEW N. LYONS

A major study of movements that strive to overthrow the U.S. government, that often claim to be anti-imperialist and sometimes even anti-capitalist yet also consciously promote inequality, hierarchy, and domination, generally along explicitly racist, sexist, and homophobic lines. Revolutionaries of the far right: insurgent supremacists.

In this book, Matthew N. Lyons takes readers on a tour of neo-nazis and Christian theocrats, by way of the patriot movement, the LaRouchites, and the alt-right. Supplementing this, thematic sections explore specific dimensions of far-right politics, regarding gender, decentralism, and anti-imperialism.

Intervening directly in debates within left and antifascist movements, Lyons examines both the widespread use and abuse of the term "fascism," and the relationship between federal security forces and the paramilitary right. His final chapter offers a preliminary analysis of the Trump presidential administration's relationship with far-right politics and the organized far right's shifting responses to it.

Both for its analysis and as a guide to our opponents, *Insurgent Supremacists* promises to be a powerful tool in organizing to resist the forces at the cutting edge of reaction today.

"Drawing on deep expertise and years of experience tracking the shifting constellations of the insurrectionist right, Matthew Lyons guides readers through the history, ideology, and agendas of these seemingly obscure but increasingly powerful political forces in America. If you want to understand them, you need to read this book."
—Mark Rupert, author of *Ideologies of Globalization: Contending Visions of a New World Order*

"A brilliant exploration of the U.S. far right today and its many different strains. In wonderfully clearheaded, deeply researched prose, Matthew N. Lyons provides a cogent and innovative analysis of far-right movements, using historical examination and his own contemporary reporting to expose surprising truths about the far right's base, motivations, and ambivalent relationship to capitalism. A vital resource for anyone who wants to fight the alt-right and other 'insurgent supremacists' in our midst."
—Donna Minkowitz, author of *Ferocious Romance: What My Encounters with the Right Taught Me about Sex, God, and Fury*

We Go Where They Go: The Story of Anti-Racist Action

Shannon Clay, Lady, Kristin Schwartz, and Michael Staudenmaier with a Foreword by Gord Hill

ISBN: 978-1-62963-972-7 (paperback)
      978-1-62963-977-2 (hardcover)
$24.95/$59.95   320 pages

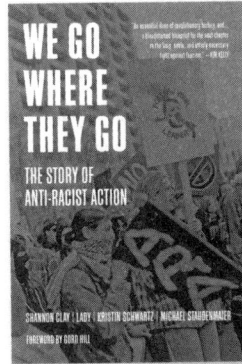

What does it mean to risk all for your beliefs? How do you fight an enemy in your midst? *We Go Where They Go* recounts the thrilling story of a massive forgotten youth movement that set the stage for today's antifascist organizing in North America. When skinheads and punks in the late 1980s found their communities invaded by white supremacists and neo-nazis, they fought back. Influenced by anarchism, feminism, Black liberation, and Indigenous sovereignty, they created Anti-Racist Action. At ARA's height in the 1990s, thousands of dedicated activists in hundreds of chapters joined the fights—political and sometimes physical—against nazis, the Ku Klux Klan, anti-abortion fundamentalists, and racist police. Before media pundits, cynical politicians, and your uncle discovered "antifa," Anti-Racist Action was bringing it to the streets.

Based on extensive interviews with dozens of ARA participants, *We Go Where They Go* tells ARA's story from within, giving voice to those who risked their safety in their own defense and in solidarity with others. In reproducing the posters, zines, propaganda, and photos of the movement itself, this essential work of radical history illustrates how cultural scenes can become powerful forces for change. Here at last is the story of an organic yet highly organized movement, exploring both its triumphs and failures, and offering valuable lessons for today's generation of activists and rabble-rousers. *We Go Where They Go* is a page-turning history of grassroots anti-racism. More than just inspiration, it's a roadmap.

"I was a big supporter and it was an honor to work with the Anti-Racist Action movement. Their unapologetic and uncompromising opposition to racism and fascism in the streets, in the government, and in the mosh pit continues to be inspiring to this day."
—Tom Morello

"Antifa became a household word with Trump attempting and failing to designate it a domestic terrorist group, but Antifa's roots date back to the late 1980s when little attention was being paid to violent fascist groups that were flourishing under Reaganism, and Anti-Racist Action (ARA) was singular and effective in its brilliant offensive. This book tells the story of ARA in breathtaking prose accompanied by stunning photographs and images."
—Roxanne Dunbar-Ortiz, author of *Loaded: A Disarming History of the Second Amendment*

The George Floyd Uprising

Edited by Vortex Group

ISBN: 978-1-62963-966-6
$22.95   288 pages

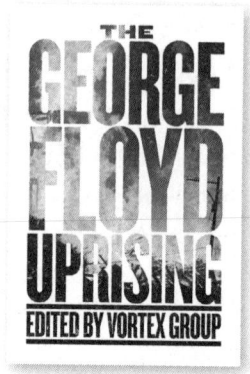

In the summer of 2020, America experienced one of the biggest uprisings in half a century. Waves of enraged citizens took to the streets in Minneapolis to decry the murder of George Floyd at the hands of the police. Battles broke out night after night, with a pandemic-weary populace fighting the police and eventually burning down the Third Precinct. The revolt soon spread to cities large and small across the country, where protesters set police cars on fire, looted luxury shopping districts, and forced the president into hiding in a bunker beneath the White House. As the initial crest receded, localized rebellions continued to erupt throughout the summer and into the fall in Atlanta, Chicago, Kenosha, Louisville, Philadelphia, and elsewhere.

Written during the riots, *The George Floyd Uprising* is a compendium of the most radical writing to come out of that long, hot summer. These incendiary dispatches—from those on the front lines of the struggle—examines the revolt and the obstacles it confronted. It paints a picture of abolition in practice, discusses how the presence of weapons in the uprising and the threat of armed struggle play out in an American context, and shows how the state responds to and pacifies rebellions. *The George Floyd Uprising* poses new social, tactical, and strategic plans for those actively seeking to expand and intensify revolts of the future. This practical, inspiring collection is essential reading for all those hard at work toppling the state and creating a new revolutionary tradition.

"*Exemplary reflections from today's frontline warriors that will disconcert liberals but inspire young people who want to live the struggle in the revolutionary tradition of Robert F. Williams, the Watts 65 rebels, and Deacons for Defense and Justice.*"
—Mike Davis, author of *Planet of Slums* and *Old Gods, New Enigmas*

"*This anthology resists police and vigilante murders. It is not an easy read. We will not all agree on its analyses or advocacy. Yet, its integrity, clarity, vulnerability, love and rage are clear. As a librarian who archives liberators and liberation movements, I recognize essential reading as a reflection of ourselves and our fears. With resolution, this text resonates with narratives of mini-Atticas. The 1971 prison rebellion and murderous repression by government and officialdom reveal the crises that spark radical movements and increasing calls for self-defense. This volume offers our cracked mirrors as an opportunity to scrutinize missteps and possibilities, and hopefully choose wisely even in our sacrifices.*"
—Joy James, author of *Resisting State Violence: Radicalism, Gender, and Race in U.S. Culture*